Introducing
Reason™ 4

Introducing Reason™ 4

CLIFF TRUESDELL

WILEY PUBLISHING, INC.

Acquisitions Editor: Mariann Barsolo
Development Editor: Pete Gaughan
Technical Editor: Scott Hirsch
Production Editor: Elizabeth Ginns Britten
Copy Editor: Liz Welch
Production Manager: Tim Tate
Vice President and Executive Group Publisher: Richard Swadley
Vice President and Executive Publisher: Joseph B. Wikert
Vice President and Publisher: Neil Edde
Media Associate Project Manager: Laura Atkinson
Media Associate Producer: Angie Denny
Media Quality Assurance: Josh Frank
Book Designer: Maureen Forys
Compositors: Chris Gillespie and Kate Kaminski, Happenstance Type-O-Rama
Proofreader: C.M. Jones
Indexer: Nancy Guenther
Cover Designer: Ryan Sneed
Cover Image: iStockphoto

Dear Reader,

Thank you for choosing *Introducing Reason 4*. This book is part of a family of premium quality Sybex books, all written by outstanding authors who combine practical experience with a gift for teaching.

Sybex was founded in 1976. More than thirty years later, we're still committed to producing consistently exceptional books. With each of our titles we're working hard to set a new standard for the industry. From the paper we print on, to the authors we work with, our goal is to bring you the best books available.

I hope you see all that reflected in these pages. I'd be very interested to hear your comments and get your feedback on how we're doing. Feel free to let me know what you think about this or any other Sybex book by sending me an email at `nedde@wiley.com`, or if you think you've found a technical error in this book, please visit `http://sybex.custhelp.com`. Customer feedback is critical to our efforts at Sybex.

Best regards,

Neil Edde
Vice President and Publisher
Sybex, an Imprint of Wiley

Acknowledgements

I'd like to thank Matt Wagner, Mariann Barsolo, Jim Compton, Scott Hirsch, Liz Britten, and Liz Welch for all of their insight, help, and hard work in making this book a reality. I'd also like to thank Dina Butler at M-Audio, Vince Bedford at Guitar Center San Francisco, Thel Rountree at HowAudio.com and Kent Carter at BeatHive.com, my amazing and always supportive family, Marilyn, Charlie, Daniel, Clifford, Rose and Sam, my great friends, Nate Perry and Scott Tusa at Take Root, Ignacio Orellana-Garcia, Michael Scanlan, Chris Albon, Aaron Haines, Colin Douglas, Jen Satzger, Robert Stratton and Jeff Gentry.

Special thanks to everyone on the Noise Board (Hi Rachael!) for much needed comic relief.

About The Author

Cliff Truesdell is a recording engineer and musician at Take Root recording studio in San Francisco and the author of *Mastering Digital Audio Production: The Professional Music Workflow with Mac OS X* (Sybex, 2007). Cliff's credits as a musician, composer and producer include original music for television shows, independent movies and video games. His recent work includes the video course *Ableton Live: Fundamentals* for HowAudio (www.howaudio.com).

Cliff's digital audio blog and podcast "Making Music with OS X" can be found on iTunes and at www.mmwosx.blogspot.com.

Contact: cliff@clifftruesdell.com

CONTENTS AT A GLANCE

Contents

Introduction

Welcome to Introducing Reason 4. Whether you already have experience with digital music creation or are completely new to it, you are probably aware that the possibilities available today for creating music in the digital environment are truly staggering. Over the last decade as computers have gotten faster and available storage space has increased, the many software companies creating digital audio programs have kept pace, upping the ante with new features, instruments, effects, and available options with every new release.

Along with the virtually unlimited opportunities now available for professional musicians and recording engineers, the average home computer has more than enough resources to run many of today's most powerful digital audio programs, including Reason. These advances have put the ability to build powerful digital audio-based home studios well within the reach of students, hobbyists, professionals, and amateur musicians alike.

From the beginning, Propellerhead's Reason program has represented a new way of working with digital audio and thinking about digital music creation. Their revolutionary idea of presenting the user with an entirely self-contained rack of virtual instruments, effects, and routing devices places all of the tools needed for recording, editing, sequencing, saving and exporting at the user's disposal in a single interface. And, as you'll learn in these pages, not only can Reason be used on its own, but the ability to combine Reason with other digital audio programs through the ReWire protocol has made the program an indispensable tool in many studios that use other programs as their primary digital audio workstation.

Today's digital audio programs continue to grow and expand both in feature sets and complexity. With its unique combination of multiple instrument and effect devices, flexible routing, and MIDI control functionality, Reason in particular offers literally limitless possibilities for creating and sequencing digital audio. Above all, what this book aims to do is to give you the tools and information you need to create your own workflow and to best harness Reason 4's resources to make your own original music.

What You Will Learn from This Book

In this book you'll learn everything you need to know to create music with Reason 4. Starting with necessary information about system requirements and acquiring external hardware for your specific needs, you'll learn how to install and configure the program. You'll then find detailed instructions and examples that show you how to use all of the program's included instruments, effects, and routing devices. You'll also learn how to combine all of the various elements contained within the Reason program, ultimately culminating in important lessons on arranging, mixing, and exporting complete songs in the book's final chapter.

Along the way you'll also learn some very important information about digital audio, synthesizers and various synthesis techniques, digital sampling, working with MIDI, and signal processing. Much of what you learn in this book about these and other subjects will be useful to you not only in Reason 4, but also in any recording environment, whether digital or analog.

Who Should Read This Book

This book is designed for the new or intermediate Reason user who wants to gain in-depth knowledge of the program's features and functionality, as well as for the experienced user who wants to increase their knowledge, improve their Reason workflow, and access features and functionality they may not already be familiar with. Whatever your current skill level, with Reason or with other digital audio programs, the lessons and exercises in this book will guide you toward an increased understanding of both the Reason program and digital audio in general.

How to Use This Book

Beginning-level Reason users should read *Introducing Reason 4* in a linear fashion from Chapter 1 on. This is the best way to approach the text. Though each chapter is focused on specific elements of the Reason environment, information is included in each chapter that will be relevant to working with other aspects of the program. However, if you are interested only in learning about specific instruments, devices, or features, once you have read Chapters 1 and 2 you can move ahead to chapters covering topics that interest you, returning to previous chapters for reference and information as needed.

Intermediate and advanced Reason users who would like to learn about a specific instrument, device, effect or some of the new features found in Reason 4 should feel free to consult those chapters specifically. (Features introduced in Reason 4 are marked with a symbol in the margin like the one shown here.)

Introducing Reason 4 takes a tutorial, learn-by-doing approach in which virtually all major features and techniques are demonstrated by hands-on exercises. Both new and experienced users should plan to study this book with Reason and possibly a MIDI hardware device up and running. Experienced users who intend to use this book for learning about specific features may plan to skip Chapter 2, but be sure to see the section there called "Setting Preferences for the Rest of This Book"; it covers important information about setting up Reason's preferences for working with the exercises found in Chapters 3 through 10.

How This Book Is Organized

Chapter 1, "Getting Started," covers the basic information you need to get started with Reason 4, including hardware considerations, installing, and configuring Reason.

Chapter 2, "Working in Reason," covers basic information about Reason's interface, instruments, and effects including basic operation techniques, terms, and concepts.

Chapter 3, "The Dr. Rex Loop Player," looks at using the Dr. Rex device to play and edit loops along with working with REX loops in the Reason sequencer.

Chapter 4, "The Redrum Drum Computer," is a comprehensive look at Reason's drum sampler device. Topics include creating and editing drum kits and recording and sequencing complete drum tracks.

Chapter 5, "Reason's Synthesizers," covers the basics of digital synthesis along with the details and functionality contained within all three of Reason's synthesizer devices: the SubTractor Analog Synthesizer, the Malström Graintable Synthesizer, and the Thor Polysonic Synthesizer.

Chapter 6, "Reason's Samplers," includes information about the basics of digital sampling along with in-depth looks at both of Reason's included sampler devices, the NN-19 and the newer, more advanced NN-XT.

Chapter 7, "Reason's Effects," cover's each of Reason's many included signal processing effects and their individual uses, including the uses and features of Reason's advanced patch loading effects.

Chapter 8, "Other Devices and Features," looks at the Reason devices and features that don't fit neatly in to the instruments or effects categories, including the Matrix Pattern Sequencer, BV512 Vocoder and the new RPG-8 Monophonic Arpeggiator.

Chapter 9, "The Combinator," is a detailed look at Reason's Combinator device, which allows you to create and save Reason instruments and effects in simple or complex configurations you can recall whenever needed.

Chapter 10, "Arranging, Mixing, and Exporting," covers all of the important information you'll need to finish your Reason projects, including an in-depth look at Reason 4's new sequencer functionality and using Reason in conjunction with other digital audio programs via ReWire.

What's on the CD

The CD included with this book contains files to be used in conjunction with many of the book's tutorials. This includes samples, loops and patches for Reason's instruments and other devices as well as complete Reason songs that demonstrate the results of specific exercises.

The CD also features an exclusive Reason ReFill featuring REX loops from www.BeatHive.com.

CHAPTER 1

Getting Started

Before you begin creating music with Reason 4, you'll need to install and register the program. You'll also need to decide what kind of peripheral gear you'll want to use with Reason. In this chapter we'll cover your options for your Reason studio, including your computer and external hardware such as MIDI keyboards, and control surfaces. We're also going to cover some basic digital audio information.

Topics include:

- **About Reason**

- **What You Need to Create Music with Reason**

- **Reason Terminology**

- **Installing Reason**

- **Setting Reason's Preferences**

- **Reason Support Resources**

- **Content for Reason**

- **A First Look at Reason**

About Reason

Reason is a completely self-contained virtual recording studio, containing all of the instruments, effects, and sequencing functionality you need to create music in any genre. Reason's synthesizers, samplers, and signal processing devices give the user access to an unlimited supply of sounds and sound-shaping possibilities, as well as endless possible routing options, all available within the Reason environment.

The first release of Reason, version 1.0, appeared in 2000 and was an immediate hit with digital audio music producers around the world. Reason's creators, Propellerhead Software, were already known for ReCycle, their loop-editing software, and for the ReBirth RB-338 virtual instrument, which was based on the Roland TB-303 Bass Synthesizer and the Roland TR-808 and TR-909 drum machines (see the sidebar "ReCycle and ReBirth").

The idea behind the Reason software was simple and original: an entirely self-contained "virtual rack" of instruments and effects, mimicking the kinds of setups you might find in a typical hardware-based recording studio, combined with a virtual sequencer for arranging and editing complete performances and songs. Not only does the program effectively replicate an incredible range of hardware devices, but it does so at a fraction of the cost. A hardware-based studio with all of Reason's devices would cost much more than the program alone, even after factoring in the cost of a computer and a MIDI keyboard to work with Reason.

Reason version 1 introduced the Redrum Drum Computer, the Dr. Rex Loop Player, the SubTractor Analog Synthesizer, and the NN-19 Digital Sampler instruments, along with many audio effects; the Mixer 14:2 mixing console; and the Reason sequencer. Each successive release of Reason has expanded the program's functionality while retaining all of the included instrumentation and effects from previous versions.

In 2002 Reason version 2.0 introduced the Malström Graintable Synthesizer and the NN-XT Advanced Sampler. In 2003 Reason version 2.5 introduced the Scream 4 Distortion and the RV7000 Advanced Reverb along with the Unison and Spider routing devices that allow users to combine and split signals from multiple instruments and effects. Reason 3, released in 2005, added the MClass Mastering suite and the Combinator device, which can be used to combine and save multiple instruments and effects in recallable configurations. Reason 3 also introduced new Browser functionality for accessing, organizing, and loading samples, loops, and patches for Reason's devices.

The current version, Reason 4, was released in October 2007 and includes a complete redesign of the Reason sequencer and the addition of a new instrument, the Thor Polysonic Synthesizer. Reason 4 also includes two other new devices: the RPG-8 Arpeggiator, for creating arpeggiated performances with Reason's instruments, and the ReGroove mixer, for adding dynamic and rhythmic variations to Reason tracks.

RECYCLE AND REBIRTH

The ReCycle program "slices" audio loops into sections and then exports them in the REX format so that they can be played back at varying tempos, edited and altered, or even entirely rearranged to create new performances. You'll be learning more about ReCycle and the REX format in Chapter 3, "The Dr. Rex Loop Player."

ReBirth was officially discontinued in 2005 but Propellerhead has made the program available as a free download for both Mac OS 9 and Windows operating systems (Windows 98, NT, ME, and XP). You can find out more about the ReBirth RB-338 at www.rebirthmuseum.com.

What Reason Can Do

Reason 4 is a complete set of virtual music creation tools. Unlike other DAW (digital audio workstation) programs that make use of various plug-in formats to use virtual instruments and effects, every instrument, effect, and routing device used by Reason is contained within the Reason program and interface. These elements are combined with Reason's powerful sequencer, enabling the user to create, edit, arrange, and export entire songs from start to finish entirely within the Reason program.

Something else that sets Reason apart from other virtual instrument and DAW programs is the ability to route Reason's various devices in unique and interesting ways. Reason's instruments and effects can be connected, layered, and used to control and affect each other in endless and often surprising combinations.

Reason contains its own built-in mixing consoles and multiple ways to record, program, edit, automate, and sequence performances. Reason also does an excellent job of maximizing your computer's resources to allow you to create complicated, complex, intricate pieces of music.

As any quick look at the Propellerhead Software website will show you, Reason lends itself particularly well to electronic and dance music genres, and has become the program of choice for many hip-hop and urban music producers. Reason is also the go-to program for many people who work with and create loops or compose music for video games, television shows, commercials, and movies. Reason's versatility makes it an invaluable tool in any digital studio. Working and experimenting with any one of Reason's instruments can lead to hours and even days of creative possibilities. Combining any two or more elements in Reason increases the creative possibilities exponentially.

Another unique feature of Reason is the way that the program lends itself to collaborative use with other DAW software. It's no coincidence that ReWire, the protocol that allows Reason to be used in conjunction with other DAW programs, has become an industry standard and an important piece of functionality of every major DAW program.

REWIRE

ReWire is a protocol that allows two DAW programs to communicate with each other. Originally created by Propellerhead Software and the Steinberg music software company to allow the ReBirth RB-338 and Cubase programs to work together, ReWire has become a standard feature of most DAW programs as well as many virtual instruments. By utilizing the ReWire protocol, you can route an entire stereo mix or individual tracks from Reason to another DAW program. Many producers take advantage of ReWire to create songs in Reason, and then use another DAW program for final mixes. The specifics of using ReWire will be covered in detail in Chapter 10.

What Reason Can't Do

There are a few things that Reason doesn't do:

- You can't record audio directly into the program.
- You can't use Reason to control external MIDI devices.
- Reason does not support Steinberg's VST (Virtual Studio Technology), Audio Units, or any other kind of third-party plug-in effect or plug-in virtual instrument.

However, all of these functions can be found in most other DAW programs (Live, Logic, ProTools, Digital Performer, etc.), and through the use of ReWire you can combine Reason with any of these programs and access these kinds of functionality.

Reason Is 100 Percent Digital

Reason is an entirely digital program, meaning that everything that takes place in Reason happens within your computer or in conjunction with a connected MIDI device that is sending digital information to the program. However, many elements of Reason are specifically designed to mimic analog functionality. One example of this is the SubTractor Analog Synth, which isn't analog at all but contains functionality, signal-routing, and sonic abilities that are based on popular analog synthesizers. Another example is Reason's audio routing functionality, which uses virtual cables and virtual jacks to connect instruments and effects to each other and to Reason's mixers.

Buying Reason

You can buy Reason directly from the Propellerhead website at www.propellerheads.se. The program is also available from your local music retailer and many online music retailers. Reason can sometimes be found as part of a bundle, with an included MIDI controller or other incentives. Prices can vary depending on where you purchase Reason, so it's worth checking around for the best deal possible.

If you haven't yet purchased Reason, you may be considering a local Internet bulletin board, eBay, or another online auction site. If you are planning to purchase Reason from one of these resale sources, make sure you are dealing with a reputable seller. More often than not, a deal that looks too good to be true will turn out to be a copied DVD or pirated version of the program.

Upgrading from a Previous Version

Reason users who already own any previous version of the program can buy an upgrade to Reason 4 at a reduced cost. The upgrade is available from the Propellerhead website and from your local or online music retailer. The upgrade disc contains exactly the same content as the full-version disc. The Reason 4 upgrade disc does not come with a serial number, but includes an upgrade code. Once you've installed the Reason 4 upgrade, go to the Propellerhead website and sign in to your account. There you'll be able to enter the upgrade code to receive your new serial number by e-mail.

Academic Versions

Academic versions of every release of the Reason program are made available for students and anyone affiliated with an academic institution. Academic versions of Reason are full-featured in every way, and registered users have access to the same content on the Propellerhead website. The difference between the Academic version and the full version is that users of the Academic version are not eligible for upgrades. For example, if you purchased an Academic version of Reason 3, you are not eligible to buy the discounted upgrade to Reason 4.

Technically you must prove affiliation with an academic institution to buy Academic versions of any software, but some sellers will (illegally) overlook this requirement. If you see a boxed version of Reason offered anywhere at a large discount, you'll want to make sure you are not purchasing an Academic version of the software.

Reason Adapted

Along with the full version of Reason, there's also a "light" version available called Reason Adapted. Reason Adapted is bundled with ReCycle, all versions of ProTools LE, as well as many other hardware and software digital audio products.

Reason Adapted is a good way to become familiar with the Reason interface and grasp how the program works. Different versions will have different levels of functionality, but generally, Reason Adapted will be limited to a set number of instruments and won't support any content other than the included sound bank.

Anyone who has received a copy of Reason Adapted can upgrade to the full version of Reason at a significant discount. Go to the Propellerhead website and click the PropShop link at the top of the page, then look for the Reason Adapted Upgrade link. This book assumes you are working with the full version of Reason.

The Reason 4 Demo

A demo version of Reason 4 is available on the Propellerheads website. You can download the Reason 4 demo by clicking the Download link at the top of the page. The demo version comes with a limited number of sounds and quits after 20 minutes.

Transferring Licenses

If you would like to buy or sell a used copy of Reason, licenses can be transferred from one owner to the next. This includes access to tech support, applications, free content, upgrade discounts, and more on the Propellerhead website. To transfer a license both the buyer and seller must have user accounts at www.propellerheads.se. The seller needs to know the buyer's Propellerhead account username. To transfer a license, click the My Account link at the top of the Propellerhead website home page, click the My Registered Products link, and follow the instructions to transfer a single license or multiple licenses.

What You Need to Create Music with Reason

To make music with Reason 4, your studio setup could be as simple as a laptop and a set of headphones or as complex as a dedicated CPU, a hardware audio interface, multiple MIDI controllers, a hardware mixing board, a digital audio workstation program to "ReWire" Reason into, and expensive studio monitors. Most Reason users create music in studios that fall somewhere in the middle of these two extremes.

Many of the decisions you make regarding your gear will be dependent on a number of factors. These include the kind of music you're making, the environment you are working in, and of course, your budget. The following are some ideas, some mandatory and some not, for setting up your Reason studio.

Your Computer

Along with the program itself and the included files, you will, of course, need a computer to create music with Reason. Reason 4 can be run on both the Microsoft Windows and Mac OS X operating systems. Aside from some minor differences in the File menu (which we'll get to later in this chapter), Reason looks and works exactly the same on both operating systems. The following are the minimum system requirements for using Reason 4.

Windows:

Windows XP SP2 or Vista

Processor: Intel P4/AMD Athlon XP or better

Memory: 512MB of RAM minimum, 1GB recommended

Screen resolution: 1024x768

2GB of free hard disk space

DVD reader

16-bit Windows-compatible audio card, preferably with DirectX or ASIO drivers

Mac OS:

Mac OS X 10.4

Processor: G4 1GHz and up or Intel Mac

Memory: 512MB of RAM minimum, 1GB recommended

Screen resolution: 1024×768

2GB of free hard disk space

DVD reader

These represent the absolute minimum system requirements needed to run the Reason program. Having a faster computer with more RAM and more free hard drive space will mean having much more power and flexibility at your disposal when working with Reason. While the minimum system requirements for installing and running Reason 4 suggest at least 2GB of free space, both Windows and Mac OS X operating systems will run better with a minimum of 10GB of unused hard drive space and at least 1GB of installed RAM.

These benefits will include access to higher numbers of tracks (also known as track count) and to more of Reason's instruments effects in your sessions, along with the ability to use higher-quality sample files to create better-sounding music.

Whenever possible, having a computer specifically dedicated to Reason and/or any other audio applications is preferable. In many cases, this won't be possible, but there are things you can do to keep any computer in optimum shape.

On Windows systems it's a good idea have antivirus and anti-spyware programs installed as well as perform regular maintenance routines, such as defragmenting your hard drive. Windows Vista has a number of system diagnostic and maintenance tools available in the Control Panel.

On Macs you can keep your computer healthy by regularly using free programs such as OnyX (www.titanium.free.fr) or TinkerTool (www.bresink.com) to clean and maintain your system.

Sound Cards and Audio Interfaces

Sound cards and audio interfaces are used to both record audio into and send audio out of your computer. All Apple computers come with standard built-in audio functionality that can be used to work with Reason. Many are capable of recording.

Almost all Windows operating system computers come with a built-in sound card that can be used for Reason, and many have some recording input capability as well. Since you won't be recording directly into Reason, having a separate hardware audio interface is optional, though the program will certainly work with just about any Mac- or Windows-compatible audio interface currently available.

If you plan to record your own audio tracks in another DAW program while using Reason via ReWire, or you plan on recording original content for Reason (such as creating original loops or samples to load into Reason's devices), you could record into your computer's built-in audio input or included sound card. However, you will almost always be better off with a separate hardware audio interface, which will offer better audio connections and sound quality.

Figure 1.1 shows Avid's popular M-Audio MobilePre USB audio interface.

Figure 1.1

The M-Audio MobilePre USB audio interface

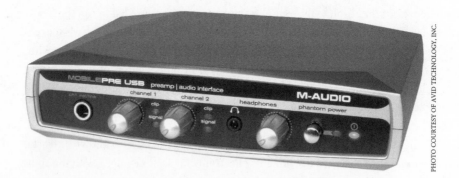

PHOTO COURTESY OF AVID TECHNOLOGY, INC.

A hardware audio interface can be as simple and inexpensive as a USB audio device with one or two inputs, or a more complex FireWire interface with multiple inputs such as those made by PreSonus (www.presonus.com), M-Audio (www.m-audio.com), or any number of digital audio hardware manufacturers.

When looking at the many options available, you'll want to take a few things into account, such as how many audio inputs and outputs will you need and what sample rates and bit depths the device capable of using to record and play back audio (see the sidebar "Sample Rate and Bit Depth").

You can research more information about digital audio hardware interfaces by checking out review sites such as Harmony Central (www.harmony-central.com) or audioMIDI (www.audiomidi.com), or digital audio websites such as Tweakheadz Lab (www.tweakheadz.com).

Many audio magazines have websites with reviews and articles along with forums dedicated to audio recording in general and, often, digital audio in particular. Some of these are:

Sound on Sound, www.soundonsound.co.uk

Electronic Musician, www.emusician.com

Tape Op, www.tapeop.com

Virtual Instruments, www.virtualinstrumentsmag.com

Music Tech, www.musictechmag.co.uk

> Another option, discussed at the end of this section, is to buy a device that combines audio
> and MIDI recording functionality.

If you already own and use an audio interface, configuring your already connected
device is covered in the "Setting Reason's Preferences" section of this chapter.

MIDI Hardware

A MIDI keyboard is essential to getting the most out of Reason. While it's possible to create
music entirely within the program's interface, adding a MIDI keyboard to your workflow
will greatly enhance your ability to create music with Reason, even if you have no previous
keyboard experience.

As we'll see later in this book, built into the Reason program are a great number of
editable parameters, many of which can be controlled externally, thereby adding an
incredible range of possibilities to your creative arsenal.

There are many options for working with various MIDI devices, including hardware
MIDI interfaces, MIDI keyboards, and other kinds of controllers and control surfaces.

WHAT IS MIDI?

MIDI, which stands for Musical Instrument Digital Interface, was first introduced in 1983 as a
way for multiple synthesizers to communicate with each other. As digital and computer audio
has developed, MIDI has been incorporated in some way into just about every digital audio
workstation program available. In Reason's case MIDI information is used to record and create performances, both within the program and by using an external MIDI keyboard or other
controller device. MIDI information can also be used to control many of Reason's parameters
externally.

In the early days of digital recording, the process of installing and using MIDI devices with
digital audio software could be quite daunting, especially to non-technophiles. MIDI also
came to be associated in many people's minds with tinny-sounding files used to play audio
on their computers and sterile-sounding performances created with early MIDI technology.
Advances made in recent years have made uses of MIDI technology both user-friendly and
highly flexible.

continued

WHAT IS MIDI? *(continued)*

You can use Reason and its included MIDI functionality extensively with little or no under-standing of how it actually works. However, the more you know and understand about MIDI, the more access you'll have to the functionality of your MIDI keyboard or interface as well as MIDI functionality within Reason. In Chapter 2's "Reason and MIDI" section, you'll learn more about how Reason uses MIDI.

MIDI Interfaces

Depending on your studio setup you may already have a MIDI interface. If you don't already have one, you may or may not need to purchase one in order to use a MIDI device with Reason. Many of today's MIDI keyboards and controllers can plug directly into your computer's USB ports. In fact, many are even USB-powered. However, if your MIDI keyboard or controller does not have USB connectivity, then you will need to have a MIDI interface.

MIDI interfaces range from very simple and inexpensive models such as the E-MU Xmidi 2x2 from E-MU Systems (www.emu.com), shown in Figure 1.2, to more expensive devices with multiple outputs and other features, such as the ability to synchronize multiple MIDI devices, digital audio programs, and hardware.

Having a MIDI hardware interface is a good idea if you are planning to use multiple MIDI devices in your sessions or you need to synchronize Reason with software that's running on other computers.

Instructions for installing and configuring specific MIDI hardware interfaces will be included with the device. If you are using a MIDI hardware interface, make sure that its drivers are current and up to date by going to the manufacturer's website.

Figure 1.2

The E-MU XMIDI 2x2

PHOTO COURTESY OF E-MU SYSTEMS.

KEEPING YOUR DRIVERS CURRENT

Most audio and MIDI devices will require that you install drivers in order for your computer to communicate with the device correctly.

Your audio interface, MIDI keyboard, or control surface will come with a CD or DVD containing the necessary drivers. It's very important that you make sure your drivers are the most up-to-date available for your operating system. It's possible that minor or major operating system updates can take place between the time your hardware device is packaged and shipped and when you buy it. This can make the packaged drivers that come with your hardware obsolete.

You can find specific information about operating system compatibility on the device's packaging and also often on a "read me" file contained on the CD or DVD with the device's drivers. This will usually include a link for downloading any driver updates.

If you install an update or a new operating system, you may have to download and install new drivers in order for your audio and MIDI hardware to work correctly.

If you are unsure about the currently installed drivers for your hardware interfaces, go directly to the manufacturer's website and download the compatible drivers for your operating system.

MIDI Controllers

The term *MIDI controller* can refer to both hardware and software components, but in the context of this chapter it refers specifically to hardware devices used to transmit MIDI data to Reason.

MIDI KEYBOARD CONTROLLERS

A MIDI keyboard will be your single most important external tool for creating music with Reason. Your MIDI keyboard can be used to play Reason's synthesizer and sampler instruments to create melodies, bass lines, and drum tracks. MIDI notes played on your MIDI keyboard will be recorded onto tracks in Reason's sequencer, where they can be edited, manipulated, and arranged to create individual tracks and entire performances.

Many MIDI keyboards can also be used to control Reason's playback functionality, including launch loops and sequences, and even to access some editing and mixing functionality.

The simplest MIDI keyboards start at around $50 and go up from there. For working with Reason, it's a good idea to consider getting at least a mid-price range ($100 to 300) MIDI keyboard that contains extra functionality such as Pitch Bend and Mod wheels and other knobs and sliders. This extra functionality can be used in conjunction with various parameters to control Reason's functionality remotely.

Examples of this type of MIDI keyboard include the Novation ReMOTE SL and the M-Audio Axiom 49, shown in Figure 1.3.

Many companies manufacture a wide range of MIDI keyboards, including Roland's Edirol product line (www.edirol.com), Novation (www.novationmusic.com), M-Audio (www.m-audio.com), and Korg (www.korg.com).

Figure 1.3

The M-Audio Axiom 49 MIDI controller

Photo courtesy of Avid Technology, Inc.

MIDI CONTROL SURFACES

The term *MIDI controller* can be used to describe a MIDI keyboard, but there are various other kinds of MIDI controllers as well. A MIDI controller can also be a hardware set of sliders, knobs, and/or pads that can be used to mix, trigger samples and loops, or externally control Reason's instruments and effects. These kinds of MIDI devices are known as *control surfaces*.

Some popular control surfaces for working with Reason include the Evolution UC-33e (www.m-audio.com), The M-Audio Trigger Finger (www.m-audio.com) (Figure 1.4), the Frontier Tranzport (www.frontierdesign.com), the WaveIdea Bitstream (www.waveidea.com), and the Novation Remote Zero SL (www.novationmusic.com).

Figure 1.4

The Trigger Finger control surface

PHOTO COURTESY OF AVID TECHNOLOGY, INC.

All of the resources suggested earlier for researching audio interfaces will be useful in finding out more about MIDI keyboards and control surfaces as well.

MORE ON MIDI
For specific information about how Reason works with MIDI, see the "Reason and MIDI" section of Chapter 2.

COMBINED AUDIO AND MIDI INTERFACES

Buying an interface that combines audio and MIDI functionality is a great solution if you are looking for a way to simplify your digital music studio setup. Most companies that make audio and MIDI interfaces have products that combine both features in a single unit.

Reason Terminology

The following are some terms and concepts used throughout this book, relating to both digital audio in general and the Reason program in particular:

Reason Rack The Reason rack is the shell or core of the Reason interface. An empty rack contains the Reason Hardware Device, used to send audio from the program to your computer's audio outputs or your attached audio interface; the Reason sequencer, used for arranging and editing your tracks; and the Transport panel, where you'll find Reason's playback functionality and much more.

Reason Device A Reason device is any of the various components that can be added to the Reason rack to create songs. This includes all of the program's instruments and effects as well the routing, pattern sequencing, and arpeggiator components.

Reason's Instruments Reason's instruments are any Reason devices that can create sound. This includes the program's synthesizers, samplers, and the Dr. Rex Loop Player. Reason's instruments will be covered generally in Chapter 2 and in greater detail in Chapters 3–6.

Reason Effects Reason's effects are signal-processing components used to alter and enhance the sounds created by Reason's instruments. This includes the program's half-rack effects, which include reverb, delay, and various other standard audio effects. Reason also features two effects capable of loading and saving patches: the RV7000 Advanced Reverb and the Scream 4 Sound Destruction Unit. The MClass Mastering effects were added in Reason 2.5 to give Reason users better options for mastering their final mixes.

Reason's effects are discussed in general in Chapter 2 and covered in detail in Chapter 7.

The Reason Sequencer A sequencer is a hardware or software device that is used to "sequence," or arrange, a performance or multiple performances. In digital audio, a sequencer can refer to a digital audio workstation program, or as in Reason's case, a component within such a program. The sequencer is found in the bottom part of the Reason rack and can be used to create and edit performances as well as arrange them.

ReFills ReFills are Propellerhead's compressed format for organizing and distributing content for Reason's devices. Reason comes with two ReFills: the Reason Factory Sound Bank, which contains content for all of Reason's devices, and the Orkester ReFill, which contains content specifically for Reason's samplers. You'll find more information about ReFills, including resources for finding commercial, free, and demo content from Propellerhead and many third-party sources, later in this chapter.

Patches Patch files contain specific information that is used to save and recall settings on Reason's instruments and effects. This information tells the device which settings to use and, if appropriate, which samples to load and where they are located. You can create your own patch files either from scratch or by altering existing patches such as those found on the Reason Factory Sound Bank.

REX Files REX files are loops in the .rx2 format, created in the ReCycle program. REX files are generally used with the Dr. Rex Player but can also be used in Reason's sampler devices.

Automation Automation is the ability to record the movement of Reason's knobs, buttons, sliders, and faders. Reason allows automation of many available features, including many obscure or unexpected parameters.

Installing Reason

Installation of the Reason program is fairly simple. Unlike previous versions of Reason, which came on multiple CDs, Reason 4 comes on a single DVD containing the Reason program itself along with the Reason Factory Sound Bank and the Orkester Sound Bank ReFills.

> If you are upgrading from a previous version of Reason, you should uninstall or delete the existing version before installing Reason 4.

Installation Instructions

Follow these instructions to install Reason on your computer. If you have a previous version of Reason installed, you'll need to delete the program first. On a Mac you can just drag the Reason folder to the Trash. On Windows you'll need to run the uninstaller located in your Reason folder:

1. Insert the Reason DVD into your computer DVD reader.

2. On a Mac, copy the Reason folder to your Applications folder. On Windows double-click the Install Reason icon.

3. Locate the Reason program icon on your hard drive or Start menu and double-click it to start the program.

4. Click the Agree button to agree to the terms and conditions of the Licensing Agreement.

5 If necessary, reinsert the Reason 4 DVD in to your DVD reader. Reason will copy the Reason Factory Sound Bank and Orkester ReFills to your Reason folder.

6. Enter your username, organization, and license number in the Enter License Number dialog.

7. Click OK.

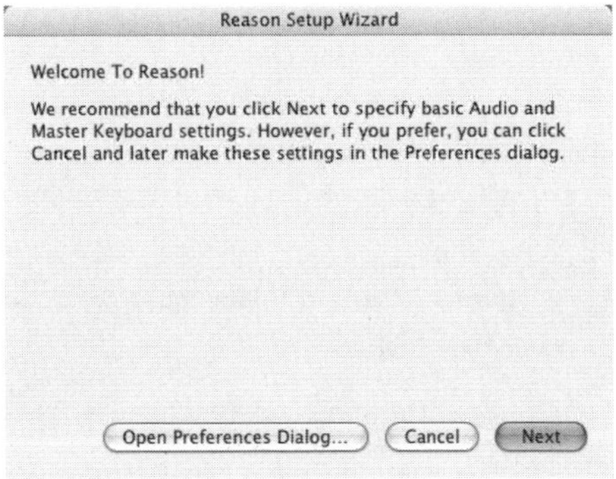

Once you've finished the installation process, the Reason Setup Wizard will appear (Figure 1.5).

Figure 1.5

The Reason Setup Wizard

You can use the setup wizard to quickly go through the process of choosing your audio output preferences and setting up your Master Keyboard (the MIDI device you'll use to play Reason's instruments). If you know which audio output you want to use and if you are able to assign your connected MIDI keyboard as your Master Keyboard, then the setup wizard may do everything you need to get Reason configured and ready to use.

For more advanced setup options, click the Open Preferences Dialog button at any time during the setup wizard process, or cancel the Wizard and open Reason's Preferences from the menu bar. On Windows choose File → Preferences; on Mac OS X choose Reason → Preferences.

For further instructions and details about Reason's Preferences, see the next section, "Setting Reason's Preferences."

Once you've finished or cancelled the setup wizard, if you have an active Internet connection you can click the Register Now button to go to www.propellerheads.se and register your copy of Reason 4. You can also register at any time by choosing Contacts → Register Reason Now.

REGISTERING REASON

Creating an account at www.propellerheads.se and registering Reason 4 will give you access to free ReFills containing lots of great sounds, to Propellerheads Reason forums, to tech support, and to free utilities such as ReLoad (for creating ReFills from AKAI format sample discs) and the ReFill Packer (for creating your own ReFills).

Registering Reason also means that if you decide to sell the program you can transfer the license quickly and easily. You'll also be able to order a replacement disc for your Reason 4 DVD for a small fee should it get lost, stolen, or damaged.

Setting Reason's Preferences

If you've already cancelled or gone through the setup wizard and want to change any of your Reason settings, you can do so at any time by accessing Reason's Preferences. Again, on Windows you do this by selecting File → Preferences; on Mac OS X you can get to Reason's Preferences by choosing Reason → Preferences.

ONE-MINUTE PREFERENCES

Even if you cancelled the setup wizard, you can still go through the process of setting up Reason's preferences very quickly. Once you know for sure that all of your MIDI and audio connections are in place, follow these instructions for a fast setup of the Reason program and your MIDI devices:

1. Open Reason's Preferences from the Edit menu (Windows) or the Reason menu (Mac).

2. Select Audio Preferences from the Preferences drop-down menu at the top of the window and choose your preferred audio output device from the Audio Output drop-down menu.

3. Select Keyboards and Control Surfaces and click the Auto-Detect Surfaces button.

4. If your MIDI device or devices appear on the Attached Surfaces list, you may see a pop-up window with specific instructions pertaining to your devices. Follow any instructions as necessary and click OK.

   If your connected MIDI device or devices do not appear, see the "Keyboards and Control Surfaces" section later in this chapter for further instructions.

5. If you only have one MIDI device connected, Reason will make this your Master Keyboard. If you have more than one MIDI device connected, select the device you intend to use as your main MIDI keyboard in the Attached Surfaces list and click the Make Master Keyboard button.

6. Close Reason's Preferences.

General Preferences

When you open Reason's Preferences, the first window, shown in Figure 1.6, will display Reason's General Preferences.

You can choose between Reason's four different preference windows—General, Audio, Keyboards and Control Surfaces, and Advanced—by clicking the drop-down menu at the top of the Preferences window.

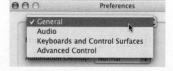

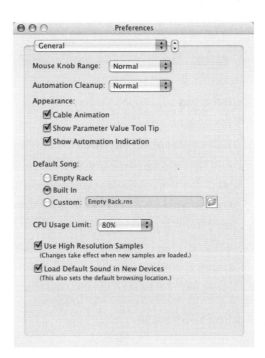

Figure 1.6

Reason's General Preferences

Mouse Knob Range This setting controls how much precision you'll have when adjusting Reason's parameter knobs and sliders. The Normal setting allows you to adjust most of Reason's parameters in increments of 2. If you find that you need access to more precise settings, you can open Reason's Preferences and change this setting at any time. The difference between Precise and Very Precise will not be apparent on most parameter knobs.

Automation Cleanup The Automation Cleanup setting determines how Reason works with and displays track and device automation. We'll come back to this setting in the "Advanced Automation" section of Chapter 10.

Cable Animation Reason displays the routing between its virtual instruments using the visual metaphor of a physical device's back panel, with cables and input plugs. To view and work with Reason's routing, press the Tab key on your computer's keyboard. With Cable Animation selected the cables will move slightly when first viewed or when later moved or re-routed. Disabling Cable Animation saves a miniscule amount of processor resources and is entirely a matter of personal preference.

Show Parameter Value Tool Tip With this setting selected, every time you move your mouse over any knob, display, button, or adjustable parameter, a tool tip displays information, including the object's name and the parameter's current numeric value, if applicable.

Show Automation Indication With this box selected, whenever a knob, slider, or other Reason parameter is automated you'll see a green outline around the parameter.

Default Song The Default Song setting determines which song will be loaded whenever you start the Reason program or create a new Reason song.

> **Empty Rack** This setting will create an empty Reason rack when you create a new song.

> **Built-in** This setting will automatically load the default Reason demo song when you start the program. Each new session you create will use the included mixer and Mastering template, covered in Chapter 2.

> **Custom** This setting lets you specify a template song, either from the included templates or your own custom-made template.

Leave this selection as Built-in for now. Later in this chapter we'll look at the default demo song along with Reason's other included demo songs. In Chapter 2 you'll select a template song for working with the exercises in this book.

Audio Preferences

Once you've set General Preferences, select Reason's Audio Preferences, shown in Figure 1.7.

Figure 1.7

Reason's Audio Preferences

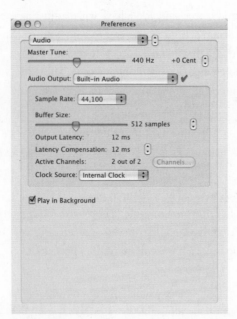

Master Tuning With this slider you can adjust the overall tuning for your all of your Reason songs up or down as much as one semitone. This would be useful if, for example, you wanted to emulate the tuning of baroque instruments, where A = 435 Hz.

Audio Output Select your preferred playback device from the Audio Output menu.

Windows users may have any of the following options to choose from: ASIO, DirectX, or MME drivers. If your sound card or hardware audio interface uses ASIO drivers, then this should be your first choice, since ASIO drivers will give you the best available performance. If ASIO is not an option, choose DirectX. You should select MME only if it is your only available option. MME drivers are part of the Windows operating system and should be used only as a last resort.

Mac users can choose either Built-in Audio or any connected hardware audio interface that appears on the list.

Sample Rate The Sample Rate setting can be used to choose between different available sample rates. Which options are visible depends entirely on your chosen audio output device. If your device supports higher sample rates, you can choose one from the list. If you are unsure of which sample rate to choose, select 44,100. For more information on sample rates, see the "Sample Rate and Bit Depth" sidebar in this section.

Buffer Size The Buffer Size setting determines the amount of *latency* you'll experience when working with Reason and your selected audio output device. Latency is the difference in time between when you play a key on your MIDI keyboard to trigger a Reason instrument and when you hear it through your speakers or headphones. The buffer size will be set automatically, but you can raise or lower it with the Buffer Size slider.

If you are hearing a significant delay, you can try lowering the buffer size. If you are experiencing glitches and dropouts when playing back or recording into Reason, you can try raising the buffer size. Unless you are experiencing noticeable delays or other problems in your Reason audio, this setting should be left alone. Sometimes your latency settings will involve a bit of a trade-off. You may have to put up with a bit of latency to get the most consistent audio playback.

Output Latency This shows you the amount of latency time in milliseconds. Reason sets this automatically in relation to the buffer size.

Latency Compensation This setting compensates for latency and is automatically set to match the output latency time. Latency Compensation can be adjusted manually by using the up and down arrows if you are attempting to synchronize Reason with a master program that doesn't support ReWire. Otherwise, it's best left at its default setting to match the output latency settings.

Active Channels If your audio output device supports multiple outputs, the Channels button for this setting will be activated. Click the Channels button to open a dialog (Figure 1.8) that will allow you to specify which outputs are active for your audio output device.

You can take advantage of this option if you are planning to route Reason's output to an external hardware mixer.

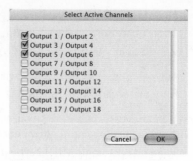

Figure 1.8

The Select Active Channels dialog

SAMPLE RATE AND BIT DEPTH

Two terms that you'll see a lot a lot in this book and in just about anything you read related to digital audio are *sample rate* and *bit depth*. These terms refer specifically to two elements that determine the quality of digitally recorded and digitally created sound.

To simplify a complicated subject, in digital audio *sample rate* refers to the number of times an analog audio signal is "sampled" or captured in one second by the analog-to-digital converter. The standard sample rate for CDs and many digital audio applications is 44,100 kHz. This means that every second of audio contains 44,100 individual samples. If you cut that in half to 22,050 kHz, you'll have half the number of samples, and therefore a less accurate representation of a recorded signal or a lower-quality digitally created sound. Most high-quality DAW programs currently available are capable of recording and creating audio at up to 96,000 kHz. As the technology improves, even higher sample rates are becoming more common.

Bit depth refers to the dynamic range of sound that is actually recorded. Sounds recorded or created at higher bit rates contain a greater range of high and low frequencies. Currently the most commonly used bit depth for digital audio recording is 24 bits, though lower and higher bit rates can be used. Eventually most audio is exported or converted to 16 bits for CD duplication.

As you'll see in the Sample Rate section of Reason's Audio Preferences, the sample rate and bit depths you can use with Reason depends on your computer's built-in audio system or your sound card or audio interface. Available sample rates vary from system to system, the most common being 44,100 kHz, 48,000 kHz, and 96,000 kHz.

You'll work with these concepts when setting up Reason's preferences, working with Reason's samplers, and exporting loops and entire songs. Outside of Reason you'll see these terms used when working with other DAW programs, "ripping" audio from CDs, creating MP3 and AAC files, and elsewhere. If you are unsure of which settings to use in any given exporting situation, the most common bit depth and sample rate settings are 16/44,100.

Keyboards and Control Surfaces

The Keyboards and Control Surfaces preferences window is shown in Figure 1.9.

If you have a MIDI device or multiple MIDI devices that you want to use with Reason, make sure they are connected and powered on; then click the Auto-Detect Surfaces button. Reason will then scan your computer looking for any attached MIDI devices that it recognizes. Reason has built-in settings for many, though not all, popular MIDI devices, including both keyboards and other controller devices.

To set up a single MIDI keyboard or control surface, follow these instructions:

1. Make sure your MIDI keyboard is attached and powered on and that all of the devices drivers are installed and current.

2. Click the Auto-Detect Surfaces button. If Reason recognizes your device, it appears in the Attached Surfaces window.

3. Follow any specific instructions that appear relating to your specific MIDI device.

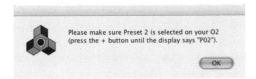

4. Make sure that the Use With Reason box is checked and that the device is recognized as your Master Keyboard.

5. Select Standard under Master Keyboard Input to make your keyboard available as the default input device for any selected track.

In Step 2, if Reason does not recognize your MIDI keyboard or control surface, you'll see the message "No keyboards or control surfaces were auto-detected." You can add your MIDI keyboard manually by following these steps:

1. Click the Add button.

2. Choose your manufacturer and model from the drop-down menus. If either your manufacturer or model does not appear, select <OTHER> for either category.

3. For some keyboards and control surfaces, Reason will have specific instructions that will need to be followed in order to use your device with Reason. These instructions will be clearly visible in the Add Surface window (Figure 1.10).

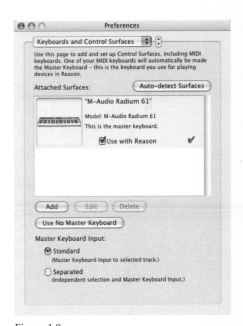

Figure 1.9

Reason's Keyboards and Control Surfaces preferences

Figure 1.10

The M-Audio Radium 61 is one of the devices that require specific instructions for use with Reason.

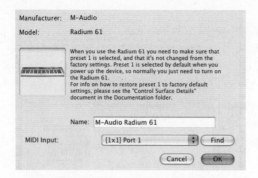

4. Select the correct MIDI input from the MIDI Input drop-down menu. You can also set this up automatically by clicking the Find button and pressing any key on your connected MIDI device.

Adding Multiple MIDI Devices

Depending on whether Reason automatically recognizes one or more of your devices, you can follow either or both of the previous tutorials to set up multiple devices.

Once your multiple devices have been added to the Attached Surfaces list, you'll want to specify a specific device as the Master Keyboard. You do this by selecting the device in the Attached Surfaces list and clicking the Make Master Keyboard button (Figure 1.11).

Figure 1.11

Select one of the multiple devices to use as the Master Keyboard.

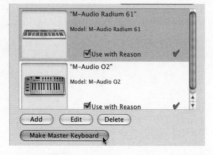

Once you've set up Reason to work with a specific MIDI device or control surface, you'll want to make sure it's always plugged in and powered on before you start Reason. If not, you'll see an error message letting you know that Reason was unable to properly set up Control Surfaces.

Advanced Control

Reason's Advanced Control preferences
(Figure 1.12) can be used to configure multiple MIDI devices to control Reason.

   To make a MIDI input available for
Advanced Control, select it from the Bus A,
B, C, or D drop-down menus. This option
will be covered in more detail in Chapter 10.

MIDI Clock Sync

Some uses for MIDI Clock include synchronizing Reason with other programs or with
other instances of Reason running on different computers. Reason can only work as a
MIDI Clock Slave, meaning it can receive
but not send MIDI Clock information.
Choose your Master MIDI input from the
MIDI Clock Sync list.

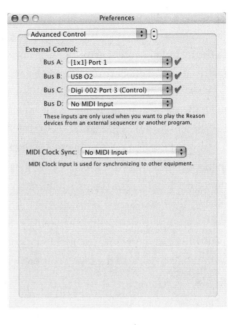

Figure 1.12

**Reason's Advanced
Control preferences**

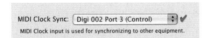

Chapter 2 contains specific settings for Reason's preferences that you'll need to change for
working with the exercises in this book.

Reason Support Resources

Reason comes with extensive documentation, including an operation manual and a "Getting Started Guide," both in PDF format. They can be found in the Reason\Documentation\
English folder.

   Propellerhead's website, www.propellerheads.se, has an online support database where
you can find solutions to frequently encountered problems and the answers to frequently
asked questions. You access the online support database by clicking the Support link at the
top of the Propellerheads home page.

   If you are unable to find the answers you're looking for in the support database, you
can e-mail Propellerheads Tech Support by choosing Reason from the Support e-mail
addresses drop-down menu at the bottom of the Support page.

Content for Reason

ReFills are collections of files in a compressed self-contained format. The ReFill (.rfl) format is similar to a .zip file, except that it doesn't need to be opened in order to gain access to the included content. Most Reason content is found in ReFills, though all of Reason's instrument and effect patches can exist outside of the ReFill format.

Vast numbers of ReFills are available, containing synthesizer patches, drum kits for the Redrum Drum Computer, loops for the Dr. Rex Loop Player, and every imaginable instrument for Reason's Samplers.

Some of the highest-quality ReFills are made and sold by Propellerhead themselves, including Reason Drum Kits 2.0, Essential Pianos, and the Abbey Road Keyboards collection. Registered Reason users also have access to many high-quality free and demo ReFills directly from www.propellerheads.se.

Aside from the Propellerhead website, many commercial, demo, and free ReFills are available from many sources, including your local or online music instrument and software retailer. A few of the many companies that create content for Reason are:

www.loopmasters.com

www.sonicreality.com

www.lapjockey.com

Some ReFills will focus on a specific Reason instrument such as a Reason synth or sampler. Other ReFills might contain patches and files for multiple Reason devices, including synth patches, sample patches, individual samples, REX files, and patches for Reason's Advanced Effects. ReFills can also contain MIDI files and complete Reason song files, which are sometimes included to provide examples of possible uses for a ReFill's included patches and files.

> Refills are by far the most common format for Reason content, but all of Reason's patch formats can exist outside of the ReFill format.

File Formats

Each Reason device that is capable of loading and playing patches has its own unique file format. Each file format is represented by its own icon and file extension. Figure 1.13 shows the icon and file extensions for Reason's synthesizer instruments.

Figure 1.13

Reason's synthesizer patch formats

Reason's sampler instruments, which include the Redrum Drum Computer covered in Chapter 3 and the NN-19 Digital Sampler and NN-XT Advanced Sampler covered in Chapter 6, can also load and play back individual samples and loops in the AIFF, Wave, and SoundFont formats. The individual slices that make up REX files can also be used as individual samples with Reason's sampler devices.

More information about content for specific devices can be found in the chapters pertaining to those devices throughout this book.

Saving and Exporting Songs

Reason is capable of exporting finished songs or sections of songs in both the AIFF and Wave formats. Simply choose File → Export Song As Audio File or File → Export Loop As Audio File.

Reason songs can also be saved as either Reason Song Files (.rns) or Reason Published Song Files (.rps).

The Reason Song File format is for works in progress and can be opened and edited at any time. You can save your current session as an .rps file at any time by choosing File → Save or File → Save As.

The Reason Published Song format is for sharing finished songs with other Reason users. This option can be are accessed by choosing File → Publish Song.

Both of these options will be covered in more detail in Chapters 2 and 10.

BACKING UP REASON FILES

Having a way to back up your work is important in any digital audio recording studio. The best method is to have a second external hard drive to copy all of your Reason related files to. This should include your ReFills and samples as well as your Reason song files, both finished and in progress.

If you don't have an external hard drive, another option would be to regularly back up your work by burning CDs or DVDs.

A First Look at Reason

At this point, you're probably eager to get started using Reason, so in the last section of this chapter we'll do just that. Locate the Reason program on your hard drive or use the desktop shortcut or Dock icon to launch the program. If you've left this Preference setting alone, by default Reason will start by loading the demo song. If you already have Reason open, quit the program and relaunch it to see the default Reason song.

Figure 1.14 shows Reason demo song.

Figure 1.14

The Reason default demo song

The scroll bars on the left side of the rack and at the bottom of the sequencer can be used to view any currently unseen elements of the current Reason song.

Reason's default demo song makes use of much of the program's functionality, including various instruments, effects, and devices. At the top of the Reason rack you'll see the Reason Hardware Device, where the output of the Reason program is sent to your computer's audio output.

> If your computer is experiencing problems such as glitches or audio dropouts when playing back the default song, that probably means your system doesn't have enough processing power for complex Reason songs. You can still learn and use the Reason program, but you'll need to upgrade your computer and/or install more RAM to get the most out Reason.

Directly under the Hardware Device is the Mastering Combi, a Combinator patch with presets for mastering your Reason songs. Below the Mastering Combi is the song's Mixer 14:2, a mixing board device that you'll find in just about every Reason session. Below the Mixer 14:2 you'll see the instruments, effects, and other Reason devices that make up this Reason song.

You can collapse and expand the individual interface for any of Reason's devices using the show/hide button on the left side of each device.

Finally, at the bottom of the rack you'll find the Reason sequencer, where the MIDI performances that trigger and control Reason's devices are arranged, along with any automation the song contains. At the very bottom of the rack is the Transport panel with Reason's stop, start, and other playback buttons, along with other functionality related to recording and sequencing Reason songs. All of these features will be covered in Chapter 2 and expanded on in detail throughout this book.

Other Demo Songs

Along with the default demo song, Reason comes with a folder of demo songs. These will be located in your Reason folder, the same folder that contains the Reason program. Reason's demo songs are great way to see some of the things that are possible with Reason.

Locate the folder Reason\Demo Songs on your hard drive and double-click any song to open it. When you open any of the demo songs, you'll see a splash screen containing an image. Click the Show Info button to see the song's details or click OK to go directly to the song.

These songs are all in the Reason Published Song format (.rps). You can experiment with these songs by adjusting parameters and moving various elements around, but the RPS format will not allow you to save any changes you make or export the audio.

Summary

The purpose of this introductory chapter has been to give you a clear idea of what you can use Reason 4 to do and how to make the program work for your specific workflow.

After a brief history of Propellerhead Software, You learned about some of the hardware audio devices Reason can be used with. In particular, you learned the importance of having an external MIDI keyboard to create performances with Reason's instruments and the option of using multiple MIDI devices to control various aspects of the Reason program. This was followed by definitions of important, frequently used digital audio and Reason 4 terminology, which you'll be seeing throughout this book. With this information you're now able to make decisions about what kind of setup best suits your needs.

Next you learned how to quickly install and configure Reason, with an in-depth description of all of Reason's Preferences that you can refer to later as you become more familiar with the program's more complex functionality and options. You then learned about content for Reason's device, including individual patches and the ReFill format, as well as some sources of that content, including the Propellerhead website third-party content providers. All of this knowledge will be useful to you as you progress through this book, as well as later on when you explore more advanced uses of Reason.

Finally, you got your hands on the Reason program itself by loading and playing some of the demo songs that are included with the program. After reading this chapter you now have a solid foundation and clear ideas about the tools and concepts you need to begin creating music with Reason 4.

Working in Reason

In this chapter you'll get an overview of the entire Reason program, including all of the components that make up a Reason song. You'll be introduced to all the elements that make up the Reason interface, as well as creating and working with Reason's instruments and effects. Once you have a basic understanding of each of Reason's components, you'll learn how to play and record performances in Reason. You'll also work with Reason's default preferences, first creating settings to be used in this chapter's exercises and then at the end resetting them as needed for the remaining chapters.

Topics in this chapter include:

- Setting Preferences for This Chapter
- The Reason Interface
- Reason's Devices
- The Tool Window
- The Reason Browser
- Reason and MIDI
- The Transport Panel
- The Sequencer: Basics
- Creating and Recording Performances
- The Matrix Pattern Sequencer: Basics
- Routing Options in Reason
- Saving Reason Songs
- Setting Preferences for the Rest of This Book

Setting Preferences for This Chapter

In Chapter 1 you got a look at Reason's preferences. You need to make some simple changes and double-check some Preferences settings to make sure that the instructions and exercises in this chapter work correctly.

> At the end of this chapter, you'll set different preferences that will be needed for the exercises in the following chapters.

Open Reason's Preferences by selecting Edit → Preferences → Reason → Preferences. In the General Preferences window, choose Empty Rack as the Default Song.

In the same General Preferences window, make sure that Load Default Sounds In New Devices is selected.

With these Preferences settings in place, every new Reason song you create will start with a completely empty Reason rack and every new Reason instrument you create will have a preloaded patch or loop file and be ready to play.

Next, select Keyboards and Control Surfaces Preferences. Make sure you have at least one MIDI keyboard controller connected and that it has been designated as the Master Keyboard. If you need further instructions on doing this, you can find them in Chapter 1.

Under Master Keyboard Input, make sure Standard is selected.

These settings will ensure that you can follow along easily with all of this chapter's exercises. You can now close Reason's Preferences and proceed with the rest of this chapter.

The Reason Interface

All of the work you do in Reason will take place entirely within the three components that make up the program: the Reason rack, the Reason sequencer, and a new component added in Reason 4, the Tool window. The rack and the sequencer are connected by default, but can be separated so that you can have a better view of each component and access more workspace. The Tool window, which features device creation and performance editing functionality, is a floating dialog that appears to the right of the rack and sequencer.

The Reason Rack

The Reason rack is the framework that contains the instruments and other devices you'll use to create your Reason songs. The sequencer, attached to the bottom of the rack, is where you'll arrange and edit your performances. Create a new Reason song with an empty rack by choosing File → New. Figure 2.1 shows an empty Reason rack with the attached sequencer.

The Reason rack is the shell of the program. An empty Reason rack won't have any instruments or effects, but it will contain the Reason Hardware Device at the top, the attached Reason sequencer, and at the bottom the Transport panel containing Reason's play and record functionality.

Floating to the right of the Reason rack you'll see Reason 4's new Tool window, shown in Figure 2.2.

> If the Tool window is not currently visible or you'd like to close it, you can press the F8 key on your computer's keyboard to show or hide it. You can also choose Window ≻ Show Tool Window or Window ? Hide Tool Window.

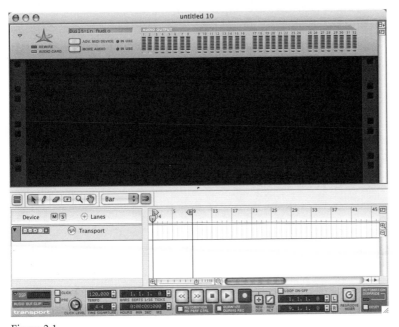

Figure 2.1

An empty Reason rack with the attached sequencer

Figure 2.2

Reason 4's new Tool window

We'll take a look at each of these components in detail in this chapter.

You can resize the entire rack vertically by clicking and dragging on the bottom right corner, but there is no way to resize the rack horizontally.

When the Reason sequencer is attached to the rack, you can resize it vertically by clicking and dragging the line at the top of the sequencer that separates it from the rest of the rack. Move your cursor to the line that separates the sequencer from the empty space on the rack. Your cursor will change to a double-sided arrow when it is at the correct point for resizing the sequencer.

In the upper-right corner of the Reason rack are two small buttons. The bottom button can be used to show and hide the sequencer when it's attached to the rack. The top button can be used to detach the sequencer from the rack.

Detaching the Sequencer

Detaching the sequencer is a great way to access more room to work in both the rack and the sequencer. Detaching the sequencer can be very useful when you are making a final mix-down, especially for Reason songs with a lot of tracks. If your computer and video card support it, one option is have two monitors connected so that you can view the rack in one and the sequencer in the other.

Besides using the buttons shown earlier, you can also detach the sequencer from the rack by choosing Window → Detach Sequencer Window. The detached sequencer can be resized both vertically and horizontally.

Both the rack and the detached sequencer will have a Transport panel. Any change that's made on either component's Transport panel will be reflected in the other.

With the rack and sequencer detached, you can use the keyboard shortcut Ctrl/⌘+1 to bring the rack to the front and Ctrl/⌘+2 to bring the sequencer to the front. You can toggle between the detached sequencer and the rack using the keyboard shortcut Ctrl/⌘+~.

> With the sequencer connected to the rack, the Ctrl/⌘+2 keyboard shortcut can be used to toggle between the default view with both components visible and having the sequencer area take up the entire rack.

Reattach the sequencer at any time by minimizing the sequencer window; just choose Window → Attach Sequencer or click the Reattach Sequencer button in the upper-right corner of the sequencer.

Reason's Devices

Reason devices include all of the program's instruments, effects, mixers, and routing components. To see all the devices Reason includes, check the Devices tab on the Tool window (Figure 2.2). Make sure the Instruments, Effects, and More boxes are all checked, and then use the scroll bar on the right side of the Tool window to view all of Reason's included devices.

Each device is unique in its uses and functionality, and the following chapters explore them in depth. This section presents the features that are shared by all of Reason's devices, including how devices are created and named.

Creating Devices

Creating a device means adding an instance of it to the rack so you can use it in the Reason song you're creating. The methods of doing that are quite simple, but they illustrate an important point about Reason for new users: Reason is a highly flexible program and you'll often find that there are multiple ways to accomplish the same tasks. These options allow Reason users to create their own workflow. Reason's various menu options for creating devices are just one example of this kind of flexibility. The following are Reason's options for adding any of the program's devices to the rack.

Figure 2.3

Creating a device with the Tool window

Using the Tool Window

In the Tool window's Devices tab you can select any Reason device and either double-click it or click the Create button, as shown in Figure 2.3, to add an instance of that device to the rack.

Using the Menu Bar

The menu bar is the row of drop-down menus for basic operations available at the top of your screen. Reason's menu bar contains a Create menu that can be used to create any of Reason's devices. Figure 2.4 shows the Create menu.

Select any device from this list to add it to the Reason rack.

Using the Context Menus

Context menu is the familiar term for the type of menu that appears when you right-click (Windows or Mac OS X) or Ctrl-click (Mac OS X only) at a particular location in a software interface. The options offered depend on where in the interface you click, as the software designers anticipate what you probably want to do there. Reason has a number of context menus. For example, clicking on a knob or slider on any device or clicking on different areas of the sequencer will bring up various context menus

Figure 2.4

The menu bar's Create menu

that let you do things like edit or delete parameter automation or work with specific sequencer functionality. Two of the context menus include options to create Reason devices.

> Windows users and Mac OS X users with a two-button mouse can right-click to access much of Reason's functionality. Mac OS X users with a single-button mouse can Ctrl-click to access the same features.

THE EMPTY RACK CONTEXT MENU

Figure 2.5

The context menu for an empty rack

The context menu that's called up by right-clicking/Ctrl-clicking an empty rack looks almost exactly like the Create menu found on the menu bar. This makes sense because when the rack is empty, the first thing you probably want to do is create a device of some kind. Figure 2.5 shows the empty rack context menu.

Paste Devices and Tracks
Create Instrument...
Create Effect...

Combinator

Mixer 14:2
Line Mixer 6:2

SubTractor Analog Synthesizer
Thor Polysonic Synthesizer
Malström Graintable Synthesizer
NN19 Digital Sampler

You may need to use your mouse to scroll through the empty rack context menu to locate the device you'd like to create. The only difference between the Create menu and the empty rack context menu is that the context menu includes the option Paste Devices and Tracks. This option can be used when copying and duplicating Reason's devices while keeping any loaded patches or altered settings in place.

> You can also access the Paste Devices and Tracks functionality from the Edit menu.

THE DEVICE CONTEXT MENU

If you click on an empty area (not on a knob, slider, or other parameter) of an existing Reason device, you'll see an entirely different context menu. This menu contains relevant editing functionality for the selected device. You'll also see a Create option on this context menu, which will take you to a submenu that you use to create Reason devices. Figure 2.6 shows the context menu that appears when you right-click/Ctrl-click on Reason's Dr. Rex Loop Player instrument. This option will allow you to quickly create and route instruments and effects devices at any place in the rack.

Naming Devices

All of Reason's devices are given a default name, based on the name of the device and the order in which they are created. For example, if you add two SubTractor synthesizers to a rack, the first will be automatically named "SubTractor 1" and the second will be named "SubTractor 2." Usually you'll want to name a device to identify its function in

your composition, such as "Bass Synth." You can rename any device at any time by clicking the default name that Reason has assigned and typing a new name. This name change will also be reflected on the device's channel strip on the session's mixer and also on the device's track in the sequencer.

Other Device Tasks

All of Reason's devices also have a small triangle in the upper-left corner that is used to maximize or minimize the instrument in the rack. If you have any devices in your rack that don't require any editing on the interface, you can minimize them to make room. Alt/Option-clicking any single device will minimize all of the current devices in a rack.

Figure 2.6

The Dr. Rex Loop Player's device context menu

All of Reason's devices can be added or deleted to any Reason session at any time. You add or create devices via the Tool window, Create menu, or context menus, as shown in the previous section.

To delete a device, select it in the rack and use the keyboard shortcut Ctrl/⌘+Delete.

The Hardware Device

The Hardware Device, shown in Figure 2.7, will always appear at the top of the Reason rack. It's the only Reason device in the rack that can't be deleted or moved.

The Hardware Device is, of course, not really hardware. It's a software approximation of an audio interface. The Hardware Device sends the output of the Reason program to whichever Audio Output hardware device you selected in Reason's Audio Preferences, as described in Chapter 1. The Hardware Device is Reason's connection to the outside world. As you'll see in Chapter 10's section on ReWire, Reason is capable of routing audio to up to 64 individual outputs or 32 stereo pairs. This can be used in conjunction with your audio interface or with ReWire. We'll look at advanced output routing with the Hardware Device and ReWire in Chapter 10.

Figure 2.7

The Reason Hardware Device

When you create an empty rack, only the first 32 outputs of the Hardware Device will be visible. View the rest of the Hardware Device's available outputs by clicking the More Audio button on the device's interface.

Press the Tab key on your computer's keyboard to view the back panel of the Hardware Device. Figure 2.8 shows the back panel of the Hardware Device with all 64 outputs visible.

Figure 2.8
The back panel of the Reason Hardware Device

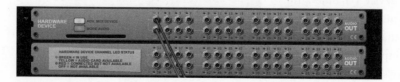

The Advanced MIDI Device

The Advanced MIDI Device is connected to the Hardware Device but hidden by default. You can access the Advanced MIDI Device by clicking the Show MIDI External Control Panel button on the Hardware Device.

Figure 2.9 shows the Advanced MIDI Device. If you have set up multiple MIDI controllers in Reason's Advanced MIDI Preferences window, then you can use the Advanced MIDI Device to assign them to specific devices.

The Mixer

The Mixer 14:2, shown in Figure 2.10, will be the nerve center of your Reason songs.

Figure 2.9
The Advanced MIDI Device

Figure 2.10
The Reason Mixer 14:2 device

You can add a Mixer 14:2 to any Reason song by choosing Create → Mixer 14:2, by right-clicking/Ctrl-clicking in the empty rack area and choosing Mixer 14:2 from the context menu, or by double-clicking Mixer 14:2 in the Devices tab of the Tool window.

Reason's Mixer 14:2 is designed to work like a software version of a hardware mixer and contains much of the same functionality you'd find on any recording studio's mixing board. Starting each new Reason song by adding a Mixer 14:2 is standard operating procedure for most Reason users.

The mixer is made up of 14 individual channel strips, each capable of receiving either mono or stereo input from any Reason instrument or effect. On the right side of the mixer you see the device's Auxiliary (Aux) Return knobs. These knobs are part of the mixer's send and return functionality, used to add effects to individual tracks. You'll learn more about sends and returns in the section "The Effects" later in this chapter. On the bottom left of the mixer is the Master Level fader, which controls the mixer's overall volume output.

> The Mixer 14:2 is one of two mixers available in Reason. The other, the Line Mixer 6:2, is more useful for submixes and Combinator patches. Unless it's specifically stated otherwise, any reference to the mixer refers to a Mixer 14:2.

Channel Strips

Each of the mixer's 14 channel strips contains volume level, panning, solo, mute, and EQ (equalization) functionality, along with four Aux Send knobs for adding effects. Figure 2.11 shows a single channel strip.

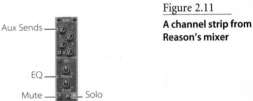

Figure 2.11

A channel strip from Reason's mixer

Level Fader At the bottom of each channel strip is the channel's Level fader. This controls the overall volume for any audio produced by an instrument or effect that's been routed to that channel. All of Reason's instruments have built-in volume level functionality, but this is the parameter you should generally use to control the overall volume of any single track. Level faders on each channel have a range of 0 (silent) to 127 (loudest) and start at a default setting of 100. After you've made any adjustments, you can return any fader to its default level by Alt/Option-clicking it.

Panning The Panning knob is used to set where each track will be placed in the stereo field. Turning the knob all the way to the left will output to the left speaker; turning to the right will output to the right speaker. The Panning knobs have range of –64 hard left) to 63 (hard right). The default setting of 0 sends the signal equally to your left and right speakers. You can return any Panning knob to its default value at any time by Alt/Option-clicking it.

Mute Clicking the Mute button will silence the selected track. Multiple tracks can be muted at once by clicking their individual Mute buttons.

Solo Clicking the Solo button will silence the audio from any other tracks. Multiple tracks can be soloed at once by clicking their individual Solo buttons.

EQ Just above the volume fader, each channel features basic EQ (equalization) functionality. Using the channel strip EQ knobs, you can boost or cut treble or bass frequencies. In order for the EQ to work, you must activate it by clicking the Channel EQ On/Off button at the top left of each EQ section.

Aux Sends At the top of each channel strip are the Aux Sends, which are used to add effects using the mixer's send and return functionality.

Sends and returns are common features on hardware mixing consoles. They allow you to use a single instance of a plug-in instead of multiple instances, which can save processor resources. You can also use the send and return functionality to achieve uniform results by using the same effect on multiple instruments. See the section "The Effects" later in this chapter for more specific details and instructions on using the mixer's sends and returns.

The Mixer's Routing Features

When you add a Mixer 14:2 to an empty rack, its output is automatically sent to Outputs 1 and 2 on the Hardware Device, as shown in Figure 2.12.

Figure 2.12

Reason's default routing

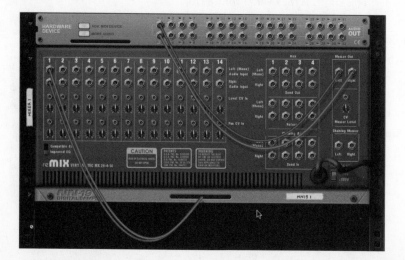

When you add any new Reason instrument to a song, its output will be automatically routed to the first available mixer channel. All of Reason's stereo instruments will automatically be routed to both the left and right inputs of the first available channel (also shown in Figure 2.12).

> Reason's only mono instrument, the SubTractor Analog Synth, will be routed to the Left (mono) audio input only.

You can view Reason's automatic routing functionality for yourself by following these steps:

1. Choose File → New to create a new Reason song.
2. Create a Mixer 14:2 from the Create menu, a context menu, or the Tool window.
3. Create an NN-19 Digital Sampler instrument using any of your device creation options.
4. Press the Tab key on your computer's keyboard to view the automatic routing that Reason has created.

You've now had a look at some of Reason's basic default routing functionality. Later in this chapter you'll learn about some of your options for changing device routing in Reason.

AUX SEND AND RETURN

You can select any device in the Reason rack just by clicking on it. The currently selected device will have a colored outline around it. Selecting the mixer and adding any of Reason's effect devices to your Reason song will automatically route the effect to Reason's send and return functionality. Up to four effects can be added at to any Mixer 14:2. This process is covered in the section "The Effects" later in this chapter.

CHAINING MASTER

If you need more than 14 tracks for your Reason songs, you can create multiple mixers. When you create a mixer, select it in the rack, and then create a second mixer, Reason will create automatic Chaining Master routing, sending the output of the second mixer to the first (Figure 2.13).

CHAINING AUX

By creating a mixer, selecting it in the rack, and then creating a second mixer, Reason will also create automatic Chaining Aux routing so that you'll have access to any send effects already connected to the first mixer (Figure 2.14).

Figure 2.13

Chaining Master routing sends the output of your second mixer to the first.

Figure 2.14

Chaining Aux routing gives you access to Send effects.

COMPATIBLE AND IMPROVED EQ

The mixer's EQ functionality was improved in Reason 2.5. For older songs created in Reason version 1 or 2, you can access the original EQ by selecting the Compatible setting.

CV INPUTS

The Mixer 14:2 also features CV (control voltage) inputs. This feature allows you to use any Reason devices with CV output functionality to control panning and level settings on the mixer. You'll learn more about CV later in this chapter.

A Quick Look at Working with the Mixer

Here's an exercise that uses the topics covered so far to try out some of the features of the mixer:

1. Create a new Reason song (File → New).

2. Create a Mixer 14:2.

3. Create a Dr. Rex Loop Player.

4. Because of the Preferences settings you chose at the beginning of this chapter, the Dr. Rex Loop Player has been created with a preloaded loop file. Click the Preview Loop button at the top of the Dr. Rex to hear the currently loaded loop.

5. With the loop playing, adjust the volume and panning on the Dr. Rex's mixer channel (Channel 1). Turn on the EQ section and raise and lower the bass and treble settings to hear how the mixer can be used to work with the sound created by a Reason instrument.

> Use the Tab key on your computer's keyboard to view the back of the rack and see all of the default routing that's been created, connecting the Dr. Rex and the mixer.

You've now seen some of the basic functionality of Reason's Mixer 14:2 device.

Reason's Instruments

Reason's included instruments each contain an incredible range of options for creating sounds and performances. All of Reason's instruments are easy to use in basic ways, yet also have virtually unlimited possibilities built in. The synthesizer and sampler devices in particular offer both simple operation and complex functionality. We'll be covering each instrument in detail in Chapters 3–6. Reason's instruments are:

The SubTractor Analog Synthesizer One of the original Reason instruments included in version 1, the SubTractor Analog Synthesizer (Figure 2.15) is the most basic of Reason's synthesizer instruments but still contains an awesome array of sound-sculpting options. Based on a combination of analog synthesis techniques, the SubTractor has many features that you'll find on Reason's other synthesizer and sampler instruments, making it an excellent learning tool for digital audio concepts in general and Reason in particular. The Sub-Tractor is frequently used to create bass lines and synthetic drum sounds as well as bell and organ-like tones. You'll learn more about the SubTractor Analog Synthesizer, and all of Reason's synths, in Chapter 5.

Figure 2.15

The SubTractor Analog Synthesizer

The Malström Graintable Synthesizer The Malström (Figure 2.16) is a unique instrument that's based on "graintable" synthesis, a term and concept invented by Propellerhead Software specifically for this device. Combining aspects of granular and wavetable synthesis, the Malström comes with a collection of built-in sounds (the wavetable aspect) that have been chopped into tiny sections (the granular aspect). These built-in sounds can be accessed and manipulated in an endless variety of ways, making the Malström an incredibly versatile device. The Malström also features audio inputs and can be used to process the output of other Reason instruments, making it useful as an effects devices as well.

Figure 2.16

The Malström Graintable Synthesizer

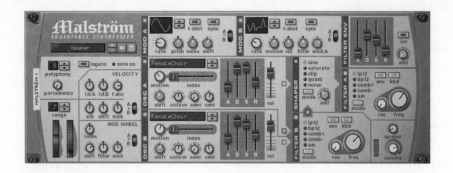

The Thor Polysonic Synthesizer New in Reason 4, the Thor Polysonic Synthesizer (Figure 2.17) takes complexity, possibility, and available options to entirely new levels. Thor comes with a multitude of choices for creating and combining different types of synthesis, including various oscillator and filter types, a dizzying assortment of routing options within the device itself along with its own built-in effects, and a pattern sequencer.

The Dr. Rex Loop Player The Dr. Rex Loop Player (Figure 2.18) loads and plays audio loops in the REX format. REX loops are audio loops that have been converted using Propellerhead's ReCycle program and sliced into individual sections for various kinds of audio manipulation. The Dr. Rex interface can be used to make pitch adjustments or to add synthesis effects to any loop. Used in conjunction with the Reason sequencer, loops can be altered by tempo and completely deconstructed and rearranged to create entirely new performances.

The Rex player is frequently associated with drum loops but can be used to play any kind of looped audio file.

The Dr. Rex Loop Player is the topic of Chapter 3.

Figure 2.17

The Thor Polysonic Synthesizer

Figure 2.18

The Dr. Rex Loop Player

The Redrum Drum Computer Loosely based on hardware drum machines such as the Roland TR-808 and TR-909 models, the Redrum Drum Computer (Figure 2.19) is technically one of Reason's sampler devices rather than a synthesizer. Redrum can load and play pre-created patches (`.drp` files) containing entire drum kits, each sample assigned to a different channel. Combining built-in step programming and pattern sequencing functionality, Redrum can be used to program simple or complex beats and rhythms. As a sampler Redrum can also load and play individual Wave, AIFF, SoundFonts, and the individual slices that make up REX files.

Along with the Matrix Pattern Sequencer, this instrument is also considered one of Reason's pattern devices. Used in conjunction with the Reason sequencer, Redrum can be used to create and arrange entire drum tracks for your Reason songs.

The Redrum Drum Computer is the topic of Chapter 4.

The NN-19 Digital Sampler One of the Reason's original devices, the NN-19 Digital Sampler (Figure 2.20) is based on hardware samplers used in the 1980s and 1990s. The NN-19 contains basic sampler functionality and is used less since the introduction of Reason's more powerful NN-XT Advanced Sampler. Because of its economy with processor resources and relatively straightforward interface, however, the NN-19 is still a very useful device and also makes a great learning tool for anyone just starting out with digital sampling.

Figure 2.19

The Redrum Drum Computer

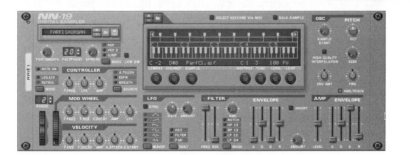

Figure 2.20

The NN-19 Digital Sampler

The NN-XT Advanced Sampler Introduced in Reason 2.0, the NN-XT Advanced Sampler (Figure 2.21) brings complex multilayered sampling functionality to Reason. The NN-XT allows you to play back, edit, and create intricate sample patches, providing realistic instrumentation along with limitless creative possibilities.

The NN-19 Digital Sampler and NN-XT Advanced Sampler are the topics of Chapter 6.

Figure 2.21

The NN-XT Advanced Sampler

Adding Instruments to Reason Songs

Instruments can be added to your Reason songs using any of the methods you've already learned using the Tool window or the Create or context menus.

At the beginning of this chapter, you made sure that you had assigned a Master Keyboard and chosen Standard under the Master Keyboard Input setting. With these settings in place, when you add an instrument to a Reason song a sequencer track is automatically created and the new instrument receives what is known as Master Keyboard Input.

This means that any new instrument you add should be ready to be played using your MIDI keyboard controller.

PLAYING REASON'S INSTRUMENTS

All of Reason's instruments can be played by triggering MIDI notes in any of the following ways:

- By using a MIDI keyboard
- By using the Pencil tool to draw MIDI notes in the instrument's track in the Reason sequencer (covered later in this chapter)
- By using a Matrix Pattern Sequencer (also covered in this chapter)

Reason's synthesizers and samplers are generally played using a MIDI keyboard or Matrix Pattern Sequencer. The Dr. Rex Loop Player and Redrum Drum Computer can also be played using either of these methods (see the "Playing Redrum and the Dr. Rex" sidebar).

Follow these steps to create and play a few of Reason's instruments:

1. Create a new Reason song by selecting File → New or using the keyboard shortcut Ctrl/⌘+N.

2. Add a Mixer 14:2.

3. Add a SubTractor Analog Synthesizer.

4. Play a few notes on the SubTractor using your MIDI keyboard.

5. Now add a Thor Polysonic Synthesizer to your song.

Figure 2.22

The SubTractor and Thor tracks in the sequencer

When you create a Reason instrument, a track is automatically created for that instrument in the sequencer. Figure 2.22 shows the SubTractor track and the Thor track that have been automatically created in the Reason sequencer.

Every time you create a new instrument it will automatically be given Master Keyboard Input, meaning that your MIDI keyboard will automatically be disconnected from the previous instrument and connected to the new instrument. This is indicated by the keyboard that appears on the bottom of the icon on the instrument's track and the outline around the icon.

You can switch Master Keyboard Input at any time just by selecting the track on the sequencer's track list for the device that you want to trigger with your MIDI keyboard. Whichever track is selected is given Master Keyboard Input and can be played by your MIDI keyboard.

PLAYING REDRUM AND THE DR. REX

The Dr. Rex Loop Player can be used by loading a loop and triggering individual slices using a MIDI keyboard or by drawing notes in the instrument's track. The most common way to use the Dr. Rex is load a REX file into the device and then send the file information to the sequencer for editing and arranging. All of these techniques are covered in Chapter 3.

The Redrum Drum Computer can also be used by loading a Redrum Drum Kit patch or individual samples, then triggering the samples with a MIDI keyboard. This is a frequently used method for creating drum and percussion tracks. Just as often, patterns are programmed within Redrum's interface and then sent to the sequencer for arranging or drawn in the sequencer using Reason's Edit mode functionality. All of these options are covered in detail in Chapter 4.

Shared Functionality

All of the Reason devices that use patches to load and save settings have some important shared functionality. This includes all of the Reason instruments (except the Dr. Rex Loop Player—see the sidebar "Browsing and Loading REX Loops") and the RV7000 Advanced Reverb and Scream 4 Distortion effects covered later in this chapter. Figure 2.23 shows the patch display for the NN-XT.

Figure 2.23

The NN-XT's patch display and buttons

Select Previous Patch
Load Patch
Save Patch

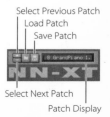

Select Next Patch
Patch Display

Patch Name Display This LED displays the name of the currently loaded patch. The patch display can show up to 16 characters. If the patch's name is too long to fit in the display, only the first 16 characters will be shown. Clicking "Menu" on the patch name display will open a menu that shows all of the patches located in the same folder as the currently loaded patch. At the top of this context menu is the option to open the Patch Browser in order to locate other compatible patches for the device.

Select Previous Patch Click this button to select the previous patch in the current folder.

Select Next Patch Click this button to select the next patch in the current folder.

Browse Patch Clicking the Browse Patch button will open the Reason Browser, which you can use to locate patches for the device.

Save Patch All of the Reason devices that use patch formats include the ability to create patches from scratch or to alter and save patches. Any changes you make to a patch can be saved and recalled at any time. Clicking the Save Patch button will open a Save dialog where you can choose a location or create a new folder to save your new or edited patch.

BROWSING AND LOADING REX LOOPS

The Dr. Rex Loop Player has slightly different browsing and loading functionality than other instruments. Since the Dr. Rex loads and plays loop files in the REX format, instead of patch options it has Loop Display, Select Next Loop, Select Previous Loop, and Browse Loop buttons.

You'll also notice that the Dr. Rex does not have a Save Loop button. However, strategies for saving settings made to Dr. Rex loops within the device are covered in Chapter 3.

 **Browse Sample** Reason's Sampler instruments, the NN-19, the NN-XT, and the Redrum also contain Browse Sample buttons on their interfaces, allowing you to load individual samples. This includes any Wave or AIFF files on your system or from Reason ReFills. Reason Sampler instruments also allow you to load the individual slices that make up REX loops.

 Mod Wheel All of Reason's instruments except the Redrum Drum Computer contain Mod Wheel functionality. Like a slider or knob, the Mod Wheel is a control that moves the value of some parameter up or down; exactly what it controls varies from device to device, and it can be assigned to control a variety of settings and parameters. Any Reason instrument's Mod Wheel can be controlled with your mouse by clicking and dragging up or down. If your connected MIDI keyboard has a Mod Wheel, selecting any device in the track list will enable Mod Wheel control from the device. The NN-XT has a second Mod Wheel for extra functionality.

Pitch Bend All of Reason's instruments except the Redrum Drum Computer contain Pitch Bend Wheel functionality. This is used to raise or lower the pitch of single notes or chords as they are being recorded or played back.

Edit and Context Menus

The options available in the menu bar's Edit menu will change depending on the Reason device that is currently selected. These differences are especially important to note when working with Reason's instruments. You'll work with each instrument's Edit menu functionality throughout the course of this book. Figure 2.24 shows the Edit menu for the Dr. Rex Loop Player.

As you saw earlier in the section "Creating Devices," you can also access the Edit menu options for any Reason device by right/Ctrl-clicking on a blank area of the device to view the device's context menu. Figure 2.25 shows the SubTractor's context menu.

At the top of both the Edit menu and the device context menu you'll see cut, copy, paste, delete, and duplicate options. Each context menu will also contain two submenus. The Go To submenu is used to navigate to different devices in the Reason rack, and the Create menu that you saw earlier in this chapter can be used to create new devices.

The rest of the visible menu choices will vary depending on which device is currently selected in the Reason rack. The SubTractor and Malström both have simple menus with options to copy and paste patches between devices, to initialize the currently selected device (delete any patches or settings), and to open the Browser. The sampler devices have the same options, along with others that specifically pertain to sampler functionality.

The Dr. Rex has very simple Edit and context menus, while Redrum has a number of pattern-related features that you'll also find in the Matrix Pattern Sequencer's Edit and context menu.

Figure 2.24

The Edit menu for the Dr. Rex Loop Player

Figure 2.25

The SubTractor's context menu

The Effects

Reason includes many effects devices, which fall into three categories: the basic effects, the advanced effects, and the MClass effects. Chapter 7 covers all of Reason's effects in detail. In these next sections, we'll explore the basics of each type of effect and some of the ways that effects are commonly used in Reason songs.

The Basic Effects

Reason's standard effects include a number of basic, easy-to-use signal processors that would be found in any digital or analog studio. These include the DDL-1 Digital Delay, shown in Figure 2.26.

Figure 2.26

The DDL-1 Digital Delay

All of these effects can be used either as inserts or sends, though certain effects such as the PH-90 Phaser and the Comp-01 Compressor are more commonly used as inserts on a single device, while effects such as the DDl-1 Digital Delay Line or the RV-7 Digital Reverb are more often used as send effects.

The Advanced Effects

Reason's Advanced effects include the Scream 4 Distortion, shown in Figure 2.27, and the RV7000 Advanced Reverb.

The Scream 4 and the RV7000 are the only two Reason effects that can load and save patches. The Scream 4 has an outstanding range of distortion and compression options, from mild coloration to an array of tweaked-out sounds mimicking digital and analog overdrive, as well as different kinds of distortion and analog tape effects. Patches for the Scream 4 can be found in the folder Reason Factory Sound Bank\Scream 4 Patches.

The RV7000 Advanced Reverb has many advanced reverb settings and features, including delay options. The RV7000's basic settings are accessed from the device's main panel. Further options can be accessed by opening the Remote Programmer by clicking the Show/Hide Programming Panel triangle on the lower left of the RV7000 interface.

Patches for the RV7000 can be found in the folder Reason Factory Sound Bank\RV7000 Patches.

Figure 2.27

The Scream 4 Distortion

The MClass Effects

The MClass effects include the Compressor, Maximizer, EQ, and Stereo Imager (which is shown in Figure 2.28).

These effects were introduced in Reason 2.5 to improve Reason's mastering capabilities. The MClass effects provide the Reason user with the ability to apply all of the tricks and techniques used by professional mastering engineers to balance levels and improve the overall sound quality of their final mixes.

Each of the MClass effects can be used as an insert or a send effect, though they are generally used either as inserts on individual devices or routed between the mixer and the Hardware Device to process an entire mix.

Figure 2.28

The MClass Stereo Imager

Inserts and Sends

Effects can be utilized in Reason sessions in many different ways, including a variety of standard and creative routing options. The two most common ways to use Reason's effects devices are as insert effects and as send effects.

Creating Insert Effects

An insert effect is an effect that "inserted" into the signal flow after one specific instrument. For example, if you have Reason song and you want to add a delay effect to your piano track, you could "insert" the delay effect after the piano instrument. Reason has more default routing functionality for this. Any time you select an instrument in the rack and then create an effect, the following routing is created:

Instrument → Effect → Mixer 14:2

To set up insert effect routing in Reason, follow these steps:

1. Create a new Reason song.

2. Add a Mixer 14:2.

3. Create an NN-19 Digital Sampler. Based on the Preferences settings made at the beginning of this chapter, the NN-19 will be created with its default Farfisa Organ patch loaded. Play a few notes with your MIDI keyboard to hear the instrument's sound before the effect is added.

4. Select the NN-19 in the Reason rack and create a PH-90 Phaser from the Create menu, a context menu, or the Tool window.

5. Use your MIDI keyboard to play a few notes with the effect added.

Figure 2.29

Figure 2.29

Reason's automatically created insert effect routing.

Input from NN-19

Output to mixer

When you created your NN-19, Reason automatically routed it to the Mixer 14:2. When you selected the NN-19 in the rack and created the PH-90, Reason automatically created the new routing shown in Figure 2.29.

You can add more effects to an instrument at any time. This is known as creating an "effects chain." Which device you select before creating any new effect will determine the order of effects:

- If you select the PH-90 and create a new effect, it will be automatically routed after the PH-90.

- If you select the NN-19 and create a second effect, the new effect will be automatically routed before the PH-90.

The last device in the chain will be reflected in the track's name on the mixer. This can be confusing since it names your track "delay 1" or "phaser 1." However, you can change this at any time by clicking the name field on the last device in your chain and typing a new name that will be more meaningful.

The order of effects in an effects chain is very important. In some cases you may not notice the difference, but in other cases switching the order of effects can drastically alter the sound. See Chapter 7 for more details on effects chains.

SHOWING AND HIDING REASON'S CABLING

Reason's animated cables are really fun and give you a great visual representation of Reason's routing. Sometimes when you are working with complex creative routing, the cables can get in the way, even blocking things you'll need to see.

You can hide the cabling by pressing the letter L on your computer's keyboard. With the cables hidden, you can still mouse over any input or output jack to see what it's connected to.

Send Effects

Send effects are routed through the mixer's send and return functionality and can be used on multiple tracks at once. This can be useful in creating uniform effects, such as having one type of delay or reverb used on multiple tracks. In the case of processor-intensive effects such as the RV7000 Advanced Reverb, having one instance of an effect can also save processor resources.

Send to RV7000

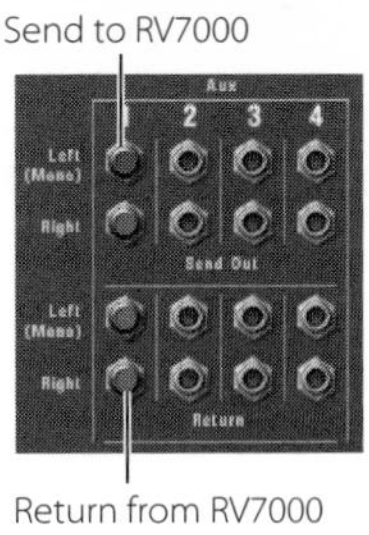

Figure 2.30
Automatic send and return routing

To add a send effect to a Reason song, select the song's Mixer 14:2 and then create an effect using the Create menu, a context menu, or the Tool window.

The effect will automatically be routed through the Mixer's Aux Send and Return section, as shown in Figure 2.30.

Return from RV7000

How Sends and Returns Work

The top eight jacks in the mixer's Aux section (Figure 2.29) are Send outputs. They can send audio from every channel on the mixer out to any connected effects.

The signal is processed (effected) by the effect and then "returned" to the mixer via the bottom row of inputs, the Returns.

The four red Aux Send knobs at the top of each track determine the amount of signal that's sent to any effect. Raising the Aux Send knob sends more signal to the effect, increasing the amount of effect you hear.

The amount of effect that's returned to the mixer can be adjusted by increasing or decreasing the Return level knobs in the top-right corner of the mixer.

Creating Send Effects

In this exercise you'll use a Dr. Rex Loop Player to work with multiple send effects. Follow these steps to create reverb and delay effects routed through the mixer:

1. Create a new Reason song.

2. Add a mixer and a Dr. Rex Loop Player.

3. Click the Preview button to hear the Dr. Rex loop.

4. Click anywhere on the mixer (preferably not on a button) to select it in the rack and create an RV7000 Advanced Reverb.

5. Raise the Send 1 knob to hear the reverb.

6. Select either the RV7000 or the mixer and create a DDl-1 Digital Delay Line.

   If you select the mixer, the DDL-1 will appear on top of the RV7000 in the Reason rack. If you select the RV7000 and create the DDL-1, it will appear below the RV7000. Either way it will be assigned to Aux Send 2.

7. Raise the Aux Send 2 knob to hear the Delay effect.

These effects will now be available to use with any instrument that you add to your Reason song. You can add up to four send effects to any mixer and increase or decrease the amount by adjusting either the Aux Send or Aux Return knobs.

The Tool Window

Another new feature in Reason 4 is the Tool window. The Tool window combines three separate areas of functionality in one easy-to-access interface. Each area is accessed by selecting from the three tabs at the top of the Tool window.

The first view, the Devices tab, is quite simple, allowing you to create new instruments, effects, and devices simply by selecting them and clicking the Create button (Figure 2.31).

Using the checkboxes at the top of the Devices tab, you can decide which Reason devices can be accessed with the Tool window.

The next tab is the Tools view.

Much of the functionality accessed in the Tools view was found in the sequencer in previous versions of Reason, including many of the audio editing and quantization features. Some of this functionality will be covered later in this chapter in the section "The Sequencer: Basics" and in more detail in Chapter 10's "The Sequencer: Advanced" section.

The third view is the Groove tab (Figure 2.32).

These settings are all related to working with the ReGroove mixer to work with and alter the feel and rhythmic style of your Reason drum, percussion, and instrument tracks and will be covered in Chapter 8.

Figure 2.31

Create a device by selecting it in the Devices tab of the Tool window.

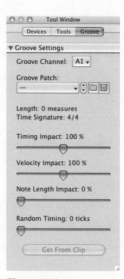

Figure 2.32

The Tool window's Groove tab

The Reason Browser

Reason's Browser is used to load samples, loops, and patches for Reason's instruments and effects, to load MIDI files, and to open Reason songs. It can also be used to organize your Reason-related content for quick access to frequently used complete ReFills and individual instruments and patches.

Figure 2.33 shows the Reason Browser.

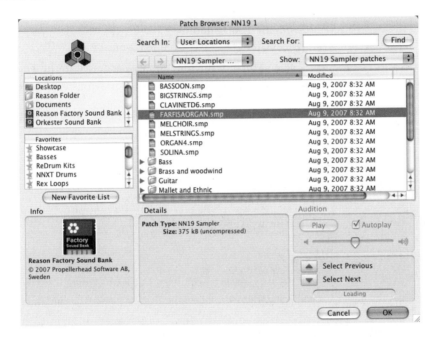

Figure 2.33

The Reason Browser

The Browser will always have the same basic interface but has multiple modes, depending on which file types you are currently using it to locate. The top of the Browser will always display its current mode and any file types that it can currently see and load.

You can close the Browser at any time by clicking the Cancel button on the lower-right corner. Once you've located the patch, sample, loop, song, or other file you want to load, click the Open or OK button on the lower-right corner of the Browser. This will load or open your file and close the Browser.

Sample Browser: NN19 1 (.aif .aiff .wav .wave .sf2 .rcy .rx2 .rex)

The following are the various Browser modes and how they are accessed:

The Patch Browser Clicking the Browse Patch button on any of Reason's patch loading instruments or effects opens the Patch Browser. Only the patches relevant to that instrument will be available (the one exception being the NN-XT, which can load NN-19 patches).

The Sample Browser Clicking the Browse Sample button on any of Reason's sampler instruments opens the Sample Browser. The Sample Browser can recognize and load the widest range of formats of any Reason Browser mode. These include Wave, AIFF, and SoundFont files, as well as the individual slices that make up REX format loops.

The REX File Browser Clicking the Browse Loop button on the Dr. Rex Loop Player opens the REX File Browser, which can recognize, preview, and load loops in the .rcy, .rx2, and .rex formats. The REX File Browser can also be opened by selecting a Dr. Rex Loop Player and choosing Edit → Browse ReCycle → Rex File and by right/Ctrl-clicking on the Dr. Rex interface and choosing Browse ReCycle → Rex File from the context menu.

The MIDI File Browser Selecting File → Import MIDI File will open the MIDI File Browser, which can see and load standard .mid and .midi files.

The Song Browser Choosing File → Open opens the Reason Song Browser. The Reason Song Browser can open the Reason song formats .rns, .rps, and .rsb.

The Browser Interface

The Browser is made up of different sections, all of which work together to help you organize, preview, and load patches, samples, songs, and files. The following describes the various sections of the Browser and how each section works.

The File and Folder List

Most of the right side of the Browser is taken up by the file and folder list. Figure 2.34 shows the folder list you'll see when you select the Reason Factory Sound Bank.

Figure 2.34

The file and folder list

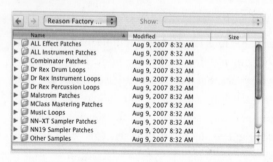

The file and folder list displays the content of any ReFill, folder, or location selected in the Locations list at the top left of the Browser. You can navigate within the file and folder list by double-clicking any folder to open it or by clicking the triangle on the left side of any folder or ReFill to view its contents.

Locations

The Locations list can be used to access frequently used ReFills, locations, and folders.

By default this section will contain your Desktop, the folder containing the Reason program, your My Documents/Documents folder, the Reason Factory Sound Bank, and Orkester Sound Bank ReFills. These items cannot be moved or removed from the Locations list. You can add ReFills, folders, or locations (including an entire hard drive) to the Locations list by dragging directly from the Browser's file and folder list. Any new locations you add will appear below the included default locations. To organize your added locations, you can then select them in the Locations list and drag up or down to reorder them. Remove a location at any time by right/Ctrl-clicking the location and selecting Remove from the context menu that appears.

Selecting a ReFill, folder, or location in the Location window will display its contents in the Browser's main window. Folders contained within ReFills can be added to the locations view but individual patches and files cannot (see the Favorites view).

Favorites

The Favorites section is used to organize your most frequently used files and patches for easy access. You can create as many Favorite lists as you want, each for different instruments, effects, or categories based on any criteria you choose.

Create a new Favorites list by clicking the New Favorites List button. A new list with the default name "New Favorites List" will be created at the bottom of the current list.

Rename your new list by selecting it in the Favorites section and right/Ctrl-clicking and choosing Rename from the context menu.

Only individual files can be added to Favorites lists, not folders and ReFills. Patches, samples, REX loops, even MIDI files and Reason songs can be added to your Favorites lists. Add a file to your new Favorites list by selecting it in the Browser's file and folder window and dragging it onto your list. Select any Favorite list to view its contents in the file and folder window.

Info

This section will display relevant information about any selected ReFill, including the ReFill's name, creator, and any copyright information.

Details

This section will display relevant information about any ReFills, patches, REX files, individual samples, or Reason song files currently selected in the Browser. Information displayed will vary depending on the file format.

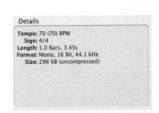

- Depending on the specific Refill, the Details window may display information about the ReFill's content, including specific instruments and effects and, if available, a website URL for the ReFill's creator.

- Selecting a synthesizer patch will display the patch's instrument.
- Selecting an NN-19 or NN-XT sampler patch or Redrum drum kit will display the patch's instrument and the combined file size of all the included samples.
- Selecting a Combinator patch will display a list of all of the included devices.
- Selecting a REX file will display the file's default tempo and time signature, length in bars and seconds, whether the file is stereo or mono, its bit depth and sample rate, and the file's size.
- Selecting a Reason Published Song or Reason Song File can display a variety of information, including the artist, song tempo, length and time signature, as well as other information included by the song's creator.

Audition

On the bottom right is the Audition section. Here you can preview selected REX loops and individual samples using the REX File Browser mode and the Sample Browser mode.

To automatically play any selected REX loop or sample, make sure that the Autoplay option is checked.

With the Autoplay option checked, any loop you select in the REX File Browser and any sample you select in the Sample Browser will begin playing automatically. You can adjust the preview volume using the Autoplay's volume slider. The Audition section also has a single button with stop and play functionality. Stop playback of any sample or loop by clicking the button. After a sample or loop has been stopped or has ended naturally, you can repeat playback by clicking the same button.

Select and Load

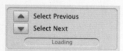

Using the Select Previous and Select Next buttons or your computer keyboard's up and down arrows, you can scroll through any available files. The Loading Indicator will turn red while a patch, loop, or sample is loading. Patches with multiple samples or larger loops and sample files will take longer to load. Once a file is loaded, the Loading Indicator will return to its default gray color.

Searching in the Browser

On the top left of the Browser, you'll see the Browser's search field.

You can use the Browser's search functionality to search for specific files in any location, including your hard drive(s), your ReFills and folders on your Locations list, or the currently selected folder or ReFills in the Browser's main window.

Determine the location of your search by selecting from the Search In drop-down menu. Selecting Local Disks will scan your entire system.

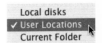

Selecting User Locations will scan all of the folders and ReFills on your Locations list. Selecting Current Folder will search only in the currently displayed folder or folders in the Browser's main window.

Previewing Patches in Real Time

When the Browser is being used to load a Reason instrument patch, it receives Master Keyboard Input. This means that you can also use the Browser to preview synth and sample patches in real time. Just create any synth or sampler instrument and use its Browse Patch button to open the Browser. Navigate to any folder containing patches for your instrument and select any patch to preview it by playing your MIDI keyboard.

CREATING INSTRUMENTS AND EFFECTS WITH THE BROWSER

Another way to open the Browser is by choosing Create → Create Instrument or Create → Create Effect from the File menu or by using the keyboard shortcuts Ctrl/⌘+I (Create Instrument) or Ctrl/⌘+F (Create Effect).

Using the Create Instruments option lets you view every available Reason instrument patch, including Combinator patches. Because the Browser automatically receives Master Keyboard Input, you can select any instrument patch and use your MIDI keyboard to preview it by playing a few notes. Once you have found a patch you like, click the OK button on the lower-right side of the Browser and Reason will create the instrument you've chosen.

Using the Create Effects option lets you browse through all of Reason's effects patches, including any Combinator effects patches, along with the Reason Factory Sound Bank's RV7000 and Scream 4 patches.

Reason and MIDI

In Chapter 1 you learned a bit about what MIDI is and the importance of having at least a basic MIDI keyboard controller when working with Reason. Before you get further into working with Reason, you should have a better understanding of certain terms and concepts related to MIDI and how it's used throughout the Reason program.

Playing Reason's Instruments

The most obvious use of MIDI with Reason is one we've already begun to look at in this chapter: triggering Reason's instrument devices by playing notes on a connected MIDI keyboard.

Every time you play a note on your MIDI keyboard, a MIDI message is sent to Reason. MIDI messages can include a lot of different kinds of information. In this case the information is very simple: which note or notes to play and how hard to play them (see the "MIDI and Velocity" sidebar). All of your instrument performances in Reason are created using MIDI messages. This includes performances that are created by playing instruments, drawn in the sequencer, or triggered using the Matrix Pattern Sequencer.

MIDI AND VELOCITY

The term *velocity* represents how hard a MIDI note will be triggered. Velocities range from 0 (silent) to 127 (maximum). Most MIDI keyboards are velocity sensitive, meaning that pressing a key lightly on your MIDI keyboard will result in a lower velocity; pressing harder will result in a higher velocity. Velocity and volume are closely related, though not exactly the same thing. Higher velocities will generally result in higher volumes, but velocity is more about the force of specific performance. For example, hitting a snare drum with medium force and with maximum force will result in distinctly different sounds, though at similar volume levels.

Velocity is recorded as part of any performance created with your MIDI keyboard and can be edited in the Velocity lane in the Reason sequencer's Edit view.

How MIDI Notes Correspond to Musical Notes

Any MIDI keyboard controller can trigger up to 128 notes. Most have considerably fewer than 128 keys, but many will have the option to shift between octaves, thereby giving you access to the entire range of available notes.

MIDI notes are sometimes referred to by their individual note numbers (0 through 127) and sometimes by the note name and octave (for example, G1 or B7). This can be confusing at first, especially since different music software and hardware MIDI devices will use different octave and numbering systems to indicate specific notes. To keep things simple, let's focus on how Reason implements MIDI note functionality.

Table 2.1 lists all the MIDI note names and numbers as they are implemented in Reason.

In Reason the note Middle C is the equivalent of the MIDI note #60 and is also known as C3. Notice that the range of MIDI notes extends well beyond that of a piano, the basis of standard Western musical notation. In that range, low piano A is MIDI 21 (A–1) and the highest note is B6, or MIDI 107. This means that some MIDI note numbers are available for other uses in Reason.

Other systems used by different software programs and hardware MIDI devices may not include negative values. These systems will have a range of C0 (0) to G10 (127). These programs and hardware devices will consider MIDI note #60 (Middle C) to be C5.

In Chapter 6 you'll see that certain MIDI notes are often associated with specific sounds in a drum kit.

Table 2.1

MIDI Note Numbers and Corresponding Reason Note Names

MIDI NOTE NUMBER	NOTE NAME IN REASON	MIDI NOTE NUMBER	NOTE NAME IN REASON	MIDI NOTE NUMBER	NOTE NAME IN REASON	MIDI NOTE NUMBER	NOTE NAME IN REASON
0	C–2	40	E1	80	G#4	120	C8
1	C#–2	41	F1	81	A4	121	C#8
2	D–2	42	F#1	82	A#4	122	D8
3	D#–2	43	G1	83	B4	123	D#8
4	E–2	44	G#1	84	C5	124	E8
5	F–2	45	A1	85	C#5	125	F8
6	F#–2	46	A#1	86	D5	126	F#8
7	G–2	47	B1	87	D#5	127	G8
8	G#–2	48	C2	88	E5		
9	A–2	49	C#2	89	F5		
10	A#–2	50	D2	90	F#5		
11	B–2	51	D#2	91	G5		
12	C–1	52	E2	92	G#5		
13	C#–1	53	F2	93	A5		
14	D–1	54	F#2	94	A#5		
15	D#–1	55	G2	95	B5		
16	E–1	56	G#2	96	C6		
17	F–1	57	A2	97	C#6		
18	F#–1	58	A#2	98	D6		
19	G–1	59	B2	99	D#6		
20	G#–1	60	C3	100	E6		
21	A–1	61	C#3	101	F6		
22	A#–1	62	D3	102	F#6		
23	B–1	63	D#3	103	G6		
24	C0	64	E3	104	G#6		
25	C#0	65	F3	105	A6		
26	D0	66	F#3	106	A#6		
27	D#0	67	G3	107	B6		
28	E0	68	G#3	108	C7		
29	F0	69	A3	109	C#7		
30	F#0	70	A#3	110	D7		
31	G0	71	B3	111	D#7		
32	G#0	72	C4	112	E7		
33	A0	73	C#4	113	F7		
34	A#0	74	D4	114	F#7		
35	B0	75	D#4	115	G7		
36	C1	76	E4	116	G#7		
37	C#1	77	F4	117	A7		
38	D1	78	F#4	118	A#7		
39	D#1	79	G4	119	B7		

How other DAW programs and devices describe MIDI notes will not be a concern when you are working exclusively in the Reason program. If you are using ReWire to route Reason into another DAW program, check that program's documentation to make sure that it uses the same standard for describing MIDI notes.

OTHER MIDI-CONTROLLED PARAMETERS

Triggering Reason's instruments with a MIDI keyboard is just the tip of the iceberg when it comes to working with MIDI in Reason. MIDI messages (also known as Controller messages) can also be used to control an incredible range of Reason's parameters. To get an idea of just how many of Reason's parameters can be controlled via MIDI, try the following:

1. Create a new Reason song.

2. Add a Mixer 14:2.

3. Add a SubTractor and an RV7000.

4. Select Options → Keyboard Control Edit Mode.

5. Select each device one at a time by clicking anywhere on the devices.

Figure 2.35 shows a single channel strip from a Reason mixer in Keyboard Control Edit Mode.

Any parameter on the currently selected device with a down-facing arrow can be controlled by MIDI data. All of Reason's devices contain some or many parameters that can be mapped to external MIDI controls and adjusted, moved by working with your connected MIDI controller. If your MIDI keyboard is equipped with any knobs or sliders, it's likely that Reason has already assigned specific controls to specific parameters. You can find out which ones are already mapped by selecting Options → Remote Override Edit Mode. A colored circle will represent any parameters that are already assigned to a specific knob, button, or slider on your MIDI controller. Moving your mouse over any already mapped parameter will tell you what the parameter is and what it's already mapped to on your MIDI controller.

Figure 2.35

A channel strip from a Reason mixer in Keyboard Control Edit Mode

Osc Octave - Standard mapped to M-Audio Radium 61 : Knob 13

Every time you select a different instrument in the rack, not only can you play it with your MIDI keyboard, but you may also be able to adjust specific parameters using the automatically assigned knobs and faders. It's also possible to reassign individual parameters to suit your own workflow. You'll learn more about MIDI mapping and override mapping in Chapter 10.

WHY 127? ACTUALLY, IT'S 128

You may have noticed a recurring theme with MIDI information in general and with Reason's knobs and sliders in particular: most of Reason's parameters have a value range of either 0 to 127 (a total of 128) or from −64 to 63 (also a total of 128), with 0 being the center value.

The number 128 occurs frequently in digital technology because of the way digital information is created, stored, and transmitted. In Reason's case, it recurs specifically because of how MIDI devices send and receive information.

You'll see the same thing in many DAW program parameters, and it's a good indication that an external MIDI device can control the specific parameter you are working with.

You can find out more about MIDI information and how it's transmitted in Peter Kirn's excellent *Real World Digital Audio* (Peachpit, 2005).

The Transport Panel

The Transport panel at the bottom of the Reason interface, shown in Figure 2.36, contains Reason's playback controls and various recording options as well as some of Reason's most important features, including click track options, tempo and time signature settings, and looping functionality.

Some of the Transport panel's functionality is used to control where the position locator and the left and right locators, shown along with the end locator in Figure 2.37, are placed in the sequencer.

Any Transport panel settings that can be used to adjust these locators can also be controlled by clicking and dragging these locators with your mouse. The left and right locators (labeled L and R) are used to set the start (left) and end (right) loop points with Reason's looping functionality.

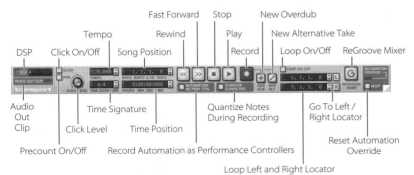

Figure 2.36

The Transport panel

Figure 2.37

The position, left, right, and end locators

The left and right locators are also used when sending data from Reason's devices to the sequencer. You can use keyboard shortcuts to move the left and right locators around in the sequencer. Alt/Option-clicking in the ruler at the top of the sequencer moves the left locator; Ctrl/⌘-clicking moves the right locator. The position locator is used to determine where playback will begin when you click the Transport panel's Play button or press the spacebar.

The end locator (labeled E) is used to determine the end point for files that are being exported to Wave or AIFF format using the File menu. You can adjust any of the locators by clicking them and dragging with your mouse.

The Transport Panel Features

Each parameter on the Transport panel serves a valuable function in Reason. These are the features of the Transport panel, from left to right:

DSP The DSP (Digital Signal Processing) LED lets you know how much of your computer's processor resources are currently being used. If this value gets too high, you may need to remove some instrument or effects devices. If you haven't already, you can also open Reason's General Preferences and raise the CPU Usage Limit setting.

Audio Out Clip The Audio Out Clip LED turns red anytime the volume of your Reason song "clips," or goes over the maximum volume that can be achieved without digitally distorting. If the Audio Out Clip lights up, reduce the overall volume of your session by lowering the Master Level fader on your Mixer 14:2. If you are still hearing unwanted distortion, check the individual volume levels on each track.

Click On/Off The Click On/Of button turns Reason's built-in click track on and off. Reason's click track is a metronome that you can use as a tempo guide when creating instrument performances. The click track's tempo is determined by the session tempo.

Precount On/Off This button turns Reason's Precount functionality on and off. Precount gives you a one-measure count-off that you can use to prepare yourself for recording. The Precount tempo corresponds to the session's tempo. Precount can be used in conjunction with or independently of the click track. The number of beats that you hear is determined by the time signature. In Reason's default 4/4 time signature, you'll hear four beats of Precount; if the session is in 3/4 time, you'll hear three beats; and so on.

Click Level The Click Level knob sets the volume level for Reason's Precount and click track. Use your mouse to raise or lower the Precount and click track volume as needed.

Tempo The Tempo setting is used to set the tempo or speed of a Reason song. Tempos are measured in Beats Per Minute (BPMs) and can be adjusted with an accuracy of up to 1/1000th of a BPM. The default tempo for a new Reason song is 120 BPMs. You can change tempo in one of three ways: by clicking in the Tempo display and dragging up to raise the tempo or down to lower it; by clicking in the Tempo display and using your computer's keyboard to type numeric values; or by using the up and down arrows on the right side of the display to raise or lower the current song's tempo.

New in Reason 4 is the ability to change tempo during a song with automation.

Time Signature Used to set the time signature for the current Reason song. In Reason time signatures can be set from 1/2 to 16/16.

Time signatures can be raised or lowered by clicking and dragging up or down in the numeric display, by clicking in the Time Signature display and typing numeric values, or by selecting a number in the display and using the up and down arrows on the right side of the display to raise or lower the value.

The first number in time signature indicates the number of beats per measure. The second number indicates the type of note that will divide the measure. For example, in 3/4 time (also known as "waltz" time), there are three notes per measure and 1/4 notes divide measures. In 7/8 time, there are seven beats per measure and 1/8 notes divide measures.

Song Position This setting shows the location of the position marker in bars, beats, 1/16 notes, and ticks (a tick equals 1/240 of a 1/16 note). Clicking and dragging up or down in any field in the Song Position display will change that value and move the position locator. Moving the position locator in the sequencer will be reflected in the Song Position display.

Time Position The Time Position display corresponds with the Song Position display, showing the location of the position locator in the sequencer in hours, minutes, seconds, and milliseconds. Typing numeric values in any of the Time Position fields can also move the position locator.

Rewind Clicking the Rewind button will move the song position locator back one bar from its current position. Click and hold the Rewind button with your mouse to move back in repeated one-bar increments.

Fast Forward Clicking the Fast Forward button will move the song position locator forward one bar from its current position. Click and hold the Fast Forward button down with your mouse to move back in one-bar increments.

Stop Click the Stop button to stop playback at any time.

If you have started playback from a point other than the beginning of a song, click the Stop button once to stop playback, a second time to return the position locator to the last starting point, and a third time to send the position locator to the beginning of the song.

Play Click the Play button to begin playback at any time. Playback will begin from wherever the position locator is currently located in the sequencer.

Record Automation As Performance Controllers Reason 4 features new automation functionality that automatically creates lanes and clips for automation data (see the section "The Sequencer: Basics" later in this chapter). Turning on Record Automation As Performance Controllers means that all controller automation is included in your performance, creating a single clip instead of multiple clips.

Quantize Notes During Recording Turn this button on to apply quantization during the recording process. The amount of quantization applied is determined by the Quantize setting in the Tools tab of the Tool window.

New Overdub Clicking the New Overdub button creates a new recording lane. Your original performance will be heard as you record a new performance.

New Alternative Take Clicking New Alternative Take creates a new recording lane and silences your previous take, giving you the chance to make multiple attempts at recording a performance. The New Overdub and New Alternative Take functionality is covered in "The Sequencer: Advanced" section of Chapter 10.

Loop On/Off This button turns Reason's looping playback and recording functionality on and off. With Reason's looping functionality activated, playback will continuously loop within parameters set by the left and right locators. This will only take place if the position locator is currently within the range selected by the left and right locators. If the position locator is moved outside of the range selected by the left and right locators, playback will disregard the looping functionality.

Loop Left and Right Locator These LEDs can be used to set the position of the left and right locators. You can click on any number to select it and drag up and down, type in a numeric value, or use the up and down arrows to move the locators.

Go To Left/Right Locator Click either of these buttons to move the position locator to the left or right locator.

ReGroove Mixer Clicking the ReGroove Mixer button on the Transport panel will launch Reason 4's new ReGroove mixer, which can be used to alter the rhythmic properties of any instrument track. The ReGroove mixer is covered in Chapter 8.

Reset Automation Override Click this button to stop any new automation that's being recorded over existing automation.

KEYBOARD SHORTCUTS FOR THE TRANSPORT PANEL

Many keyboard shortcuts have been added or reassigned in Reason 4. Using keyboard shortcuts with the Transport panel can greatly increase your efficiency when working in Reason.

Spacebar stops and starts playback.

Shift+Enter/Shift+Return once stops playback, a second time returns the position locator to
the last start point, and a third time sends the position locator to the beginning of the song.

Your computer keyboard's numeric keypad contains some especially useful and timesav-
ing functionality:

Enter—Play

0—Stop

1—Go to left locator

2—Go to right locator

3—Create new overdub note lane for the selected track

4—Rewind one bar (hold down the 4 key to rewind multiple bars)

5—Fast-forward one bar (hold down the 5 key to fast-forward multiple bars)

6—Create new alternate take note lane for the selected track

9—Turn the click track on and off

.—Move the position locator to the beginning of the song

/—Turn looping on and off

+—Increase the tempo

-—Lower the tempo

*—Start recording—also stop recording but not playback

Using the Transport Panel

Follow these steps to experiment and familiarize yourself with some of the Transport
panel's basic functionality:

1. Create a new Reason song.

2. Add a Mixer 14:2 and a Dr. Rex Loop Player.

3. Click the To Track button on the Dr. Rex interface.

Clicking the To Track button sends the REX loop data from the Dr. Rex to the sequencer. The left and right locators determine where this data appears in the sequencer.

4. Click the Loop On/Off button to turn Looping on.

5. Click the Play button or press your computer keyboard's spacebar to begin playback.

Spend some time working with the Transport panel and its associated keyboard shortcuts (see the "Keyboard Shortcuts for the Transport Panel" sidebar); it's a good exercise for speeding up your Reason workflow.

The Sequencer: Basics

The sequencer has received a radical overhaul in Reason 4. In fact, both newcomers and experienced Reason users may encounter a bit of a learning curve when starting to work in the sequencer.

At its most basic, the sequencer is where you'll create arrangements for your Reason songs, but the sequencer is much more versatile than that. It can also be used to create and edit instrument performances and create and edit an incredible range of instrument and effect automation.

One of the most confusing aspects of the Reason sequencer is that its views and features change depending on what kind of a device you are dealing with, which aspect of a track you are working on, and which tool is currently selected. The sequencer also has two distinct view modes: the Arrange mode and the Edit mode.

Arrange View

Figure 2.38 shows the sequencer in its default Arrange mode.

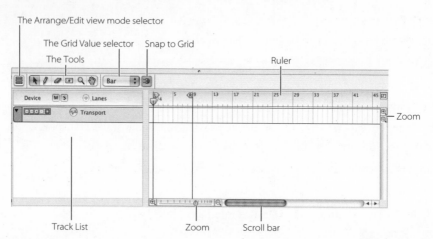

Figure 2.38

The Reason sequencer in Arrange mode

The Arrange view is the default view for Reason's sequencer. In the Arrange view you'll do most of your recording (though it's possible to record in Edit view) and all of your arranging.

The top left of the sequencer contains the Arrange/Edit view mode button for switching between view modes. Next to that are the five tools you'll use to navigate and work in the sequencer. Next to the tools you'll see Reason's Snap To Grid drop-down menu and On/Off button.

Directly below the tools you'll find the track list containing all of the device tracks that make up the current Reason song.

On the right side of the sequencer is the Detach Sequencer button.

The scroll bars at the bottom and right side of the sequencer can be used to navigate in the sequencer.

Click the Zoom buttons on the bottom and right sides of the sequencer to zoom in and out of the Arrange view. Dragging the Zoom slider at the bottom left of the sequencer window to the right will zoom in. Drag the slider to the left to zoom out.

Edit View

The Edit view is used for editing performances and automation, but it's also used for creating performances from scratch. What the Edit view looks like varies depending on the kind of track that's being edited. Figure 2.39 shows the Edit view for an NN-XT Advanced Sampler track.

By default, the Edit view contains an Overview lane that can be used to move and arrange clips, a Note lane that can be used to create and edit MIDI performances, and a Velocity lane that can be used to edit MIDI note velocity settings. As you'll see in Chapter 10, Automation lanes and Pattern lanes can also be created and edited in the Edit view.

You can switch between the Edit and Arrange modes by using the keyboard shortcut Shift+Tab.

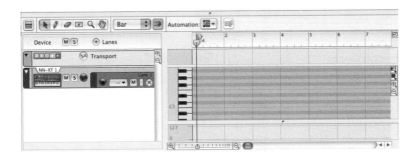

Figure 2.39

The Edit view for an NN-XT advanced Sampler track

Sequencer Terminology

The following are some terms and concepts you should become familiar with for working in the Reason sequencer:

Clips In previous versions of Reason, users had the option to create groups of notes. Reason 4 makes use of the concept of clips. Every MIDI performance, whether recorded from a keyboard or created in the sequencer, is automatically part of a clip (Figure 2.40).

Clips can be split, joined, selected, and moved around the sequencer individually or in groups. They can also be individually named and assigned any of a range of colors. Clips can also be created on one track and copied or moved to another.

Events Any data included in a clip is considered an event. This can include MIDI notes or automation envelopes.

Tracks Each instrument in Reason is automatically assigned a track when it's created. Reason's effect devices are not automatically assigned a track but a track can be created for them if you want to create effect automation.

Lanes In the Arrange view each track will be created with a single lane. However, multiple lanes can be added at any time, allowing for alternative takes and performances made up of MIDI note events on multiple lanes. Lanes can also be added for automation, and Reason's pattern devices can have pattern arrangement lanes. Figure 2.41 shows a Reason instrument track with multiple lanes.

There are differences between lanes in the Arrange view and lanes in the Edit view. By default, the Edit view for any Reason instrument will contain three lanes: the Overview, onenote lane in the center, and the Velocity lane. When a track has multiple lanes, the Edit view's note lane will display the MIDI performance of the note lane that is selected in the track list.

Figure 2.40

Multiple clips in the sequencer's Arrange view

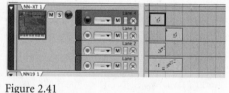

Figure 2.41

Multiple lanes on a single track in the Arrange view

Understanding Tracks, Lanes, and Clips

When you're working with instruments and other devices in the Reason sequencer, it's important to understand the difference between tracks and lanes. Multiple recording lanes are a new addition to the Reason 4 sequencer.

When you create an instrument, it will automatically be assigned to a single track in the track list. But within that track it is possible to have multiple lanes. Each lane can contain its own MIDI performance. You can create as many lanes as you want for any track and even simultaneously trigger the same device with performances on multiple lanes. You can also mute or delete lanes containing unwanted performances. Multiple lanes can also be selected and combined, creating a single lane from multiple takes.

Every new recording or performance you create, whether you create a new lane or not, exists as a clip. Clips can be moved between lanes or even between tracks. When you combine multiple lanes, any overlapping events will be merged as a single clip.

Lanes open up many possibilities in Reason 4, including creating layered performances, recording complex parts and combining them, and creating drum tracks by recording one piece of a drum kit at a time.

The Sequencer Interface

In the following sections, we'll look at the sequencer's basic components, including the tools and the track list.

The Toolbar

The features found on the Toolbar are used to access the Reason sequencer's music creation, editing and arranging functionality.

View Mode Selector The View Mode selector is used to switch between the Arrange and the Edit view.

The Selection Tool In both the Arrange and Edit views, the Selection tool is used to select and move clips. When you have selected a clip, you can use the Selection tool to resize the clip by clicking and dragging the arrows on either side of the clip. You can select this tool in the sequencer with your mouse or by pressing Q.

The Pencil Tool The Pencil tool is used to draw information on tracks and lanes in the sequencer. In the Arrange view, this includes drawing clips and automation envelope information.

In the Edit view, the Pencil tool is used to draw clips and also to draw notes in the selected note lane and velocity information in the Velocity lane, and can also be used to create and edit automation.

Selecting the Pencil tool also makes the Select Time Signature and Select Pattern buttons visible at the top of the sequencer. These options can be used with Reason's pattern devices to create and sequence arrangements. You can select this tool in the sequencer with your mouse or by pressing W.

The Erase Tool The Erase tool is used to erase clips, notes, and automation information in both the Arrange and Edit views. You can select this tool in the sequencer with your mouse or by pressing E.

The Razor Tool The Razor tool is used to cut clips at selected points. The Razor tool works in the Arrangement view and in the Overview lane of the Edit view. You can select this tool in the sequencer with your mouse or by pressing R.

The Magnify Tool This tool is used to zoom in or out of either sequencer view. Click any clip, track, or lane to zoom in. Alt/Option-click to zoom out. You can also click and drag across multiple clips, lanes, and tracks to zoom in or out. You can select this tool in the sequencer with your mouse or by pressing T.

The Hand Tool Select this tool to navigate around either sequencer view without zooming in or out. This tool is particularly useful in the Edit view's note lane. You can select this tool in the sequencer with your mouse or by pressing Y.

Grid Selector Used in conjunction with the Snap To Grid button, this drop-down menu sets the increments for a number of functions within the sequencer.

Snap To Grid Button This button turns on the sequencer's Snap To Grid functionality. With Snap To Grid enabled, any clip editing or note editing or creation you perform will snap to the sequencer's grid according to the value selected in the Grid Value drop-down. Any locator positions adjustments you make will also conform to the Grid based on the Grid Value selected. This will have many applications as you progress through this book, including synchronizing clips and notes.

Track Parameter Automation Selecting a track on the track list and clicking this button shows you a list of the available parameters that can be automated. Choosing a parameter from the list will create an automation lane on the selected track.

Create Pattern Lane Active only when one of Reason's pattern devices is selected in the track list, this button creates a pattern lane. The Pencil tool can then be used in conjunction with the Select Pattern drop-down menu to create pattern arrangements.

Clip Position and Clip Length These are only visible when a clip is selected. The Clip Position and Clip Length indicators display information about any selected clip's location and length. They can also be used to move and resize clips.

The Track List

The track list contains a separate track for each Reason instrument in the current song. The Transport panel is also given a track, which is always visible at the top of the track list.

Some Reason devices, such as the RPG-8 and the Matrix Pattern Sequencer, will also automatically be assigned a track in the track list, while other devices such as Reason's effects will not have tracks created automatically. This keeps your track list from becoming unnecessarily cluttered with tracks that may not actually be needed. If it turns out that you need to create a track for an effects device, that option is available.

Tracks can be created manually for Reason's effects if you intend to automate them.

A REASON INSTRUMENT TRACK

Each instrument track will have the same basic functionality. Figure 2.42 shows two instrument tracks in the track list.

Figure 2.42

Two instrument tracks in the track list

Tracks can be moved up or down in the track list by clicking and dragging on the track handle on the far left of each track. Rearranging tracks does not have any effect on the routing or device order in the rack.

You can minimize a single track by clicking the track handle arrow in the top-left corner of each track. You can minimize all of the tracks in the track list by Alt/Option-clicking any track handle arrow.

Each instrument track has these components:

Mute Silences the selected track so you can focus on other tracks as you're creating a song. Multiple tracks can be muted at any time by clicking each track's mute button. Unmute multiple tracks at once by clicking the All Mute Off button at the top of the track list.

Solo Clicking any track's Solo button plays the track alone, muting all other tracks. Multiple tracks can be soloed at once by clicking each track's solo button. Clicking the All Solo Off button at the top of the track list will deselect the solo button on all currently soloed tracks.

Record Enable Parameter Automation Turn this button on to enable automation recording. Automation recording allows you to record any movement of knobs, faders, and sliders. See the "Automation" section later in this chapter.

Record Enable Click this button to prepare the selected track to receive MIDI note information for recording performances played on your attached MIDI keyboard.

Select Groove This drop-down menu is where you will choose the settings for working with the ReGroove mixer, covered in Chapter 8.

Mute Note Lane Click this button to mute the output of any MIDI notes on the currently selected note lane.

Note Lane Activity This meter lets you know if there's any MIDI note activity on the lane. A muted lane will not show any note lane activity.

Delete Note Lane This button can be used to delete any note lane. Be careful with this one because you can easily delete the wrong performance. If you do delete a lane by mistake, you can use the Ctrl/⌘+Z Undo keyboard shortcut to get it back.

Creating and Recording Performances

Your options for creating and arranging music have changed drastically in Reason 4's new sequencer, and much of that has specifically to do with how Reason works with tracks. Where previous versions of Reason gave you the option to group notes, Reason 4 automatically creates groups of notes, called clips, out of any recorded performance. In these next few exercises, you'll learn the basics of recording and creating MIDI performances in the Reason sequencer.

Recording a Performance

In this exercise you'll combine some of the things you've learned in this chapter to record a Reason instrument being played using your MIDI keyboard. Follow these steps to record a Reason instrument performance:

1. Create a new Reason song.

2. Add a Mixer 14:2.

3. Add an NN-XT Advanced Sampler and play a few notes on your MIDI keyboard to make sure it's receiving MIDI input.

4. Turn on the Click and Precount buttons on the Transport panel.

5. Click the Record button on the Transport panel.

6. After the four-beat count-off, begin playing notes on your MIDI keyboard.

7. When you've finished playing, stop recording by clicking the Stop button on the

Transport panel or by pressing the spacebar on your computer's keyboard.

You'll now see your newly created clip in the sequencer, probably very similar to the clip shown in Figure 2.43.

At this point you have a number of options, including editing your clip in the Arrange or Edit view. More details on clip editing can be found in Chapter 10.

Figure 2.43

A recorded clip in the sequencer

Creating New Note Lanes

If you would like to add more notes to your performance or you'd like to try a completely new take, you can do either by creating a new note lane within your track. You have two options for creating note lanes: creating an overdub lane will allow you to add new notes to a performance, while creating a new alternative take lane will mute the previous performance. You can un-mute the previous performance later by turning off that lane's mute button.

To create a new note lane, select your track in the track list and click either the New Overdub or New Alternative Take button on the Transport panel. You can also select a track in the track list and type the number **3** on your numeric keypad to create a new overdub lane or the number **6** to create a new alternative take.

> Selecting a track on the track list and clicking the New Note Lane button at the top of the track list will create a new overdub track.

You can create as many overdubs and alternative takes as you want for any track. You can delete a note lane at any time by clicking any lane's Delete Note Lane button. You can also combine the MIDI events on multiple lanes by right/Ctrl-clicking any track in the track list that contains multiple lanes and choosing Merge Note Lanes On Tracks from the context menu (Figure 2.44).

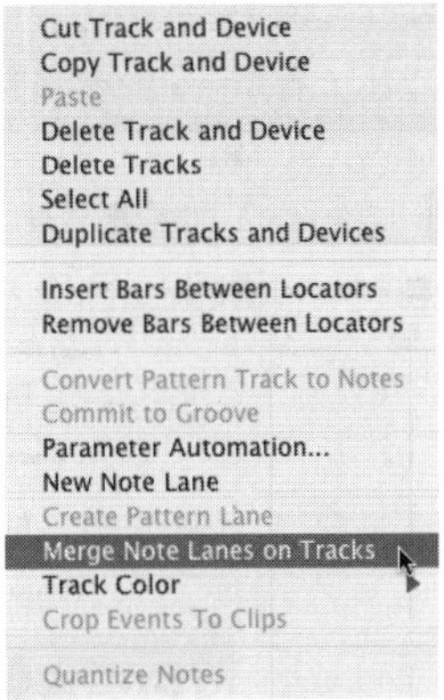

Figure 2.44
Merging note lanes

Recording with Quantization

Reason's Quantize During Recording functionality, found on the Transport panel, can be very useful for creating better sounding performances by automatically fixing any timing imperfections as you record.

This exercise uses the Tool window and the sequencer together and is a good example of how these two components interact.

1. Create a new Reason song and make sure the Tool window is visible (use the keyboard shortcut F8 to show and hide the Tool window).

2. Create a Mixer 14:2 and an NN-XT Advanced Sampler.

3. Choose the Tools tab in the Tool window.

4. Open the Quantization view.

5. Set the quantization value to 1/4 (Figure 2.45).

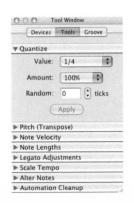

Figure 2.45
Setting a quantization value

6. Click the Quantize During Recording button on the Transport panel.

7. Enable the Click Track and Precount.

8. Click the Record button or press the * key on your computer keyboard number pad to begin the count-off and recording.

9. Play some notes and chords on your MIDI keyboard.

10. Once you've recorded a performance, stop playback and recording.

Once you've created your recording, double-click the newly created clip to view the individual notes that you've recorded in the sequencer's Edit view. You may have to use the scroll bars or the Hand tool to view the notes in the Edit view note lane. You'll notice that all of the start point of all of the notes that you played have been automatically lined up at 1/4 note divisions in your clip.

This is a drastic use of quantization. The settings you choose for this feature should depend on the type of performance you are creating. For more intricate performances, you might choose a quantization setting of 1/16 or higher. You can experiment with different values for different types of performances to become comfortable with this feature. It's important to note here that when you create a performance with Record Quantization enabled you are stuck with the performance as quantized. There's no way to access the performance as played, so be sure to choose the correct quantization settings before you begin recording.

WHAT IS QUANTIZATION?

Quantization in Reason 4 is used to take a performance or sequence of MIDI notes and adjust them according to settings that you choose. Generally quantization is used to "fix" imperfect timing in a performance. The most obvious use of this feature is to adjust timing mistakes by aligning notes to a set Grid Value.

Because slight imperfections in the way humans play any instrument can be the key to creating realistic performances, Reason takes this into consideration when it comes to working with program's quantization functionality. You'll learn more applications for this functionality in Chapter 10.

Quantization can be applied during the recording process or after using the Quantization tab in the Tool window.

Creating Performances in the Sequencer

Another option for creating performances in Reason is to draw notes in the sequencer's Edit view. This method can be used to create performances with any Reason instrument but is especially useful for creating drum performances with the Redrum Drum Computer or with a drum kit in one of Reason's sampler devices. Follow these steps to create a drum performance in the Reason sequencer:

1. Create a new Reason song.

2. Add a Mixer 14:2 and a Redrum Drum Computer.

3. Set the Grid Value drop-down menu to ⅛ and enable Snap To Grid.

4. With the Redrum track selected in the track list, click the Switch To Edit Mode button on the sequencer.

You now have access to the track-editing options for the Redrum track. The note lane in the center of the Edit view can be used to draw MIDI notes and create your performance.

You can preview the various available sounds in the Redrum's preloaded kit by moving your mouse over the left side of the Note lane. When the cursor turns into a speaker icon, you can click your mouse to preview the sample.

This feature is available in the Edit view note lane for every Reason instrument track.

5. Select the Pencil tool and draw a clip. Once a clip has been created, you can then use the Pencil tool to draw MIDI notes inside the clip.

6. Use the Pencil tool to draw notes in the Edit view's note lane.

7. Click the Play button on the Transport panel to hear your newly created performance.

Automation

Automation is the process of recording the movements of various knobs, sliders, and other parameters. With automation you can make changes to parameter settings throughout the course of a song. The adjustments you make are saved as clips and given a lane on the device's track in the sequencer. Some uses for automation include turning tracks on and off, adjusting track volume and panning settings, and bringing effects in and out of a mix.

Automation is another feature that's implemented very differently in Reason 4 than in previous versions. Though previous versions of Reason had extensive options for creating automation, they were often confusing to work with. Reason 4 makes the process of creating and editing automation much simpler and easier. Just as Reason 4 uses clips and lanes for MIDI recording, it also introduced clips and lanes for automation recording.

Automating Instruments

The following exercise will get you started using Reason 4's automation functionality. Follow these steps to automate parameters on any Reason instrument:

1. Create a new Reason song.

2. Create a Mixer 14:2 and add any Reason instrument.

3. Click the Record button on the Transport panel.

4. With Reason recording, click and drag to adjust a few parameter knobs and sliders on your Reason instrument.

Figure 2.46

Automation clips in the sequencer

With Reason in record mode, every time you adjust any parameter that can be automated a new automation lane is created, along with a clip containing the automation data. Figure 2.46 shows automation clips in the sequencer.

5. Stop recording and return the position locator to the beginning of the song.

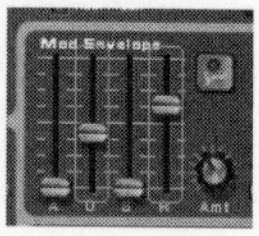

Any parameters that are automated will now be outlined in green in the Instrument's interface.

> You can disable parameter automation for any Reason instrument by turning off the Record Enable Parameter Automation button on the instrument's track.

Automating Effects

Many of the parameters on Reason's effects can be automated as well. In order to automate an effect, you'll need to create a sequencer track for it first. This is done by selecting the effect in the rack and choosing Edit → Create Track For (selected effect) or by right/Ctrl-clicking the device and choosing Create Track For (selected effect) from the context menu.

Once a track has been created for your Reason effect, the automation process is exactly the same as with Reason's instruments.

Editing Automation

Once automation has been created, it can easily be edited, though using the sequencer's editing functionality may take some getting used to. To edit your automation, follow these steps:

1. Choose the sequencer's Selection tool and double-click the automation clip that you want to edit. This will open the clip for editing. You can also use to the Selection tool at any time to resize the clip by clicking and dragging the arrows at either end of the clip.

2. Use the sequencer Zoom functionality to zoom in on the clip if necessary.

3. Select the Pencil tool and use it to draw your changes directly on the automation clip.

When you are done editing the automation clip, use the Selection tool to click any other lane in the sequencer to close the clip and return to the normal sequencer view.

There's More…

You'll be working with Reason's sequencer as it pertains to specific devices throughout this book and then learning the sequencer in depth in Chapter 10's "The Sequencer: Advanced" section.

The Matrix Pattern Sequencer: Basics

One of the devices that you will be working with throughout this book is the Matrix Pattern Sequencer. The Matrix is one of two pattern devices in Reason (the other is the Redrum Drum Computer). Reason's pattern devices have their own built-in sequencing options. This means that you can create multiple patterns within the pattern device interface and arrange them however you want using Reason's automation functionality.

The Matrix Pattern Sequencer works by sending CV (control voltage) messages to Reason's devices. CV can be used to trigger notes and to control many of the parameters found on Reason's instrument and effects devices. The Matrix has a lot of possible uses within Reason. In this introduction you'll learn the basics of using the Matrix to trigger a Reason instrument.

WHAT IS CV?

CV stands for control voltage. Before the invention of MIDI, CV devices were used to send electrical signals to an analog synthesizer to trigger notes. The Matrix Pattern Sequencer and other Reason devices use a digital approximation of CV. Traditionally, CV information was very limited and only used for simple tasks such as triggering a single note and choosing its pitch. Reason implements a more complex virtual version of CV that can be used to control many parameters on Reason devices.

With the Matrix you can send signals to your effects and instruments using all three of the kinds of CV messages available in Reason:

Gate CV is used to trigger notes much like a MIDI keyboard, though it does not contain pitch information.

Note CV controls the pitch of notes triggered by Gate CV.

Curve CV is independent of Note and Gate CV and is most often used to control filter and panning, though it can be used to control pitch.

More detailed information on CV and its many uses in Reason can be found in the "Matrix Pattern Sequencer: Advanced" section of Chapter 8.

The Matrix Interface

Figure 2.47 shows the Matrix Pattern Sequencer's interface.

Figure 2.47
**The Matrix Pattern
sequencer**

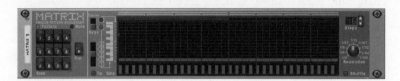

Banks and Patterns The Matrix is capable of storing up to 36 individual user-created patterns. Each of the four banks at the bottom is capable of storing up to eight patterns. Patterns are created by selecting a bank and a pattern, then using your mouse to program Note CV and Gate CV in the Note and Gate Value sections of the Matrix. The default pattern is Bank A, Pattern 1.

You can also switch to Curve Edit mode (described in a moment) and create multiple patterns using Curve CV.

Pattern Enable With Pattern Enable selected, the Matrix will send CV information to the connected device. This option is enabled by default whenever you create a Matrix Pattern Sequencer.

The Run Button Starting and stopping playback with the Transport panel will automatically stop and start the Matrix. By clicking the Run button you can turn the Matrix on and off independently of the sequencer.

Mode Selector: Curve and Key Modes When the default Key Edit mode is selected, you can use the Matrix interface to program notes in the Note Value section. In Curve Mode, you can program Curve CV in the Curve Value section.

The Octave Selector The Matrix interface has a one-octave range for programming notes. With the Matrix in Key Edit mode, you can use the octave selector switch to access notes in a five-octave range.

Steps By default, the Matrix is created with a 16-step pattern. Use the arrows on the right or click and drag up or down on the LED to adjust the pattern from 1 to 32 steps in length.

Resolution The Matrix default tempo plays one note for every 1/16 note. This works pretty well at the default Reason song tempo of 120 BPM. If you want to create patterns at a faster or slower tempo, you can adjust the Resolution knob.

Shuffle The Shuffle button is used in conjunction with the Global Shuffle Amount knob on the ReGroove mixer. See the "ReGroove Mixer" section in Chapter 8 for more details.

Creating a Synth Sequence with the Matrix

The Matrix Pattern Sequencer can be used with any Reason instrument but is particularly useful with Reason's synthesizers. Follow these steps to create a synthesizer melody with the Matrix:

Figure 2.48

The Matrix Pattern Sequencer's default routing

1. Create a new Reason song.

2. Add a mixer 14:2 and a SubTractor.

3. With the SubTractor selected, create a Matrix Pattern Sequencer.

When you create the Matrix with a device selected, Reason will create automatic routing, connecting the Note and Gate CV outputs of the Matrix to the Note and Gate CV inputs of the SubTractor (see the "What Is CV?" sidebar). Figure 2.48 shows the Matrix's default CV routing. CV connections are made with yellow or light green cables.

Click the Run key on the Matrix interface to begin playback. Clicking either the Start or Record button on the Transport panel will also start the Matrix.

4. Use your mouse to create different notes in the Note Value section.

5. Use the Octave selector to choose note in higher or lower octaves.

Experiment with the different Resolution values using the Resolution knob.

You'll learn more about creating and arranging performances with the Matrix Pattern Sequencer in the "Matrix Pattern Sequencer: Advanced" section in Chapter 8.

Routing Options in Reason

All of Reason's devices contain highly flexible routing options. As you've already seen in this chapter, most Reason devices will be created with routing automatically in place. However, at no time is any Reason device locked into any routing configuration.

Reason's audio and CV routing options can be used to open up unlimited creative possibilities. In fact, it would be impossible to cover all of the possible routing configurations contained within the Reason program.

You've seen that clicking the Tab key or selecting Options → Toggle Front/Rear allows you to view the connections between your Reason devices. You can adjust the audio and CV routing for any Reason device simply by clicking and dragging its input or output jack.

If a connection between the two devices or parameters is possible, Reason will allow you to create it, though not every connection will produce a result. You can also create new routing by right/Ctrl-clicking any audio or CV input or output to view a context menu that shows you every available connection (Figure 2.49).

If connections are possible, Reason will allow them to happen. If a connection is not possible, Reason will not allow it. For example, any audio output can be connected to any audio input. If you try to connect an audio input to another audio input, Reason will not make the connection.

Hold down the Shift key when creating any device to bypass Reason's automatic routing functionality and create an unconnected device.

Saving Reason Songs

Reason also has two different formats for saving songs: the Reason Song File (.rns)format and the Reason Published Song (.rps) format. Each of these formats has different uses, though Reason users frequently share songs in both formats.

Songs saved in either .rns or .rps format that were created in earlier versions of Reason can be opened in Reason 4, but songs created in Reason 4 cannot be opened in earlier versions of Reason.

Saving a Reason Song File

The Reason Song File format saves all of your instrument, patch, and arrangement information in a recallable file with the extension .rns. This is the format that you will choose when saving works-in-progress or even finished Reason songs that you may want to open later. By saving your session as a Reason Song File, you have complete access to your song, including all of Reason's options for editing, resaving, and exporting.

Other Reason users can also share, open, edit, and save Reason songs that have been saved in the .rns format, provided that they have access to any third-party ReFills or outside samples or REX files used to create the song.

Save any Reason song as a Reason Song File by choosing File → Save or File → Save As, selecting a location in the Save dialog, and clicking the Save button.

Creating a Published Song File

The Reason Published Song file format (`.rps`) is used for sharing Reason songs that are complete. Many Reason users use this format to share songs with other Reason users. For example, the Demo songs included with Reason that you saw in Chapter 1 were all saved in the Reason Published Song format. Songs in this format can be edited and altered, but you won't be able to save any changes you make. When an `.rps` song is opened, it can be exported as a Wave or AIFF file, but once any changes have been made exporting is disabled.

Create an `.rps` song by choosing File → Publish Song. Select a location for your song in the Save dialog and click the Save button.

More Saving Options

If a Reason song uses content from a ReFill other than the Factory Sound Bank or Orkester, then that ReFill must be present on the system of the Reason user who wants to open the song file. If any ReFills used in a song are not present, the song may load but with samples or patches missing.

If your Reason song contains content such as samples or REX files that come from a source other than a Reason ReFill, these files must either be present on the system attempting to open the song or self-contained within the Reason song.

You'll find more information on these subjects and other options for saving and exporting Reason songs in Chapter 10.

Setting Preferences for the Rest of This Book

At the beginning of this chapter you set Reason's Preferences to better learn the basics of the Reason interface, including the sequencer and Reason's devices. For the exercises in the rest of this book, you'll need to change your Preferences settings again to quickly access a Reason template that already contains a Mixer 14:2 and the MClass Mastering Combi. You'll also want to create all of your new Reason instruments without preloaded patches to better learn the functionality of each device.

To set Reason's preferences for the remaining chapters in this book:

1. Open Reason's Preferences.

2. In the Default Song area, choose Custom.

3. Click the folder icon to open the Reason Browser.

4. Select the Reason Folder in the Locations list and use the Browser's Main window to open the Template Documents folder.

5. Select the `Mixer and Mastering.rns` template file and click the Open button at the bottom of the Browser. The Mixer and Mastering template is now your default Reason song.

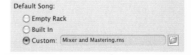

With the Mixer and Mastering template as your default Reason song, every new session you create will contain the MClass Mastering Combi and a Mixer 14:2 already in place. Next, make sure that the Load Default Sound In New Devices box is deselected.

☐ Load Default Sound in New Devices
(This also sets the default browsing location.)

This ensures that every new Reason devices is created in its default state, without any preloaded patches or setting.

Summary

In this chapter you learned all of the basic information you need to start creating music with Reason 4, beginning with the program's interface and some basic navigation and information. You then learned about creating devices, including Reason's instruments and effects, along with the similar functionality found in each of Reason's instruments.

Each component of the Reason program was covered in detail, giving you both a basic understanding of each feature along with indications of the possibilities inherent in each component and device. You also learned how Reason uses MIDI information. Combining this with details about the Reason sequencer and how tracks, lanes, and clip functionality are used, you developed enough knowledge to begin recording and creating your own performances in Reason.

Everything that you've learned so far has set the groundwork for you to learn each aspect of the Reason program in detail. All of the information covered in this chapter is also related to the most important concept of all: Reason's flexibility and the infinite creative possibilities that the program contains.

CHAPTER 3

The Dr. Rex Loop Player

In this chapter we'll take our first in-depth look at a Reason instrument: The Dr. Rex Loop Player. The Dr. Rex is used to play back, alter, edit, and sequence loop files. The most common types of loops used in the Dr. Rex are drums and percussion, but the Dr. Rex is not limited to working with any specific type of looped performance. Synthesizers, guitars, and bass lines are all frequently found in Reason ReFills and other REX file collections. Any kind of instrumental performance or sound that can be recorded can be converted to a REX format loop for use in Reason. The versatility of the Dr. Rex means that you can quickly get started creating entire tracks and Reason songs with this one device.

Topics in this chapter include:

- **Dr. Rex Basics**

- **Basic Editing Features**

- **The Envelopes, Filter, and LFO**

- **Dr. Rex and the Reason Sequencer**

- **Dr. Rex and MIDI Devices**

- **Automating the Dr. Rex**

- **Effects and the Dr. Rex**

- **Creating a Filter Sweep with Automation**

- **Using the LFO to Create Filter Effects**

- **Using the LFO to Create Panning Effects**

- **Using the Mod Wheel as a Wah-Wah**

Dr. Rex Basics

The Dr. Rex Loop Player loads and plays back REX format files. REX files are audio loops that have been converted to the .rx2 format using Propellerhead Software's ReCycle program (see the sidebar "Creating REX Loops with ReCycle"). When an audio loop is converted to a REX file (usually from Wave or AIFF format), the file is cut into sections known as "slices." Once a file has been sliced, exported to REX format, and loaded into a Dr. Rex Loop Player, you can make universal changes to the entire file, or you can make changes to individual slices.

This approach is very different from the pitch shifting and time stretching performed by other looping programs such as Sony's ACID, Ableton Live, and Apple's GarageBand. Pitch-shifting and time-stretching programs change the entire loop at once, while the Dr. Rex .rx2 format performs similar functionality by altering one slice at a time. Slices generally consist of one musical note, drum hit, or a single chord, though ReCycle can be used to create slices that consist of larger sections of an audio file.

This kind of precise control over individual slices is especially useful when working with drum loops and percussion files, though any instrument performance or recorded sound can be converted to the REX format. However, there are some audio files that will not work well as REX loops. These include evolving synth pads and soundscapes, quickly played performances with lots of rushed notes, or loops with heavy reverb and delay where notes or chords are blurred together. The best REX loops will contain clearly defined notes, chords, and rhythms.

The REX format first appeared in 1994. Since then there have been some improvements to the format. The most current (and common) REX files created in ReCycle 2.0 or higher can be either mono or stereo and will have the file extension .rx2. Files created in previous versions of ReCycle are mono only, but can also be loaded and played in the Dr. Rex. These include Windows-only REX format files with the extension .rcy and Mac-only files with the extension .rex.

CREATING REX LOOPS WITH RECYCLE

ReCycle is a program also created by Propellerhead that is used to convert Wave or AIFF loops into the REX format files. Here are some reasons you might consider buying a copy of ReCycle:

- If you'd like to have access to your Wave format and Apple Loops format loop collections in Reason. Some loop collections and libraries are already available in REX format, but many are not.

- If you are creating your own loops in Reason or in other DAW programs that you'd like to load and use in Reason songs.

- If you are creating your own loops and samples from vinyl records, CDs, or MP3 files that you'd like to loop and use in Reason.

Along with the ability to export loops in the REX format, the current version, ReCycle 2.1, has some other useful functionality. You can quickly export all of the individual slices that make up a REX file for use in any digital sampler, and you can edit existing REX loops in many ways. ReCycle also comes with the "light" version of Reason, called Reason Adapted, as well as the ReLoad application for converting AKAI S1000 and S3000 sample discs to ReCycle-ready formats.

If you'd like to learn more about ReCycle you can download a demo version from www.propellerheads.se and try it out. I also cover the process of using ReCycle to create REX loops in my book *Mastering Digital Audio Production: The Professional Music Workflow with Mac OS X* (Wiley, 2007).

ReFills and Other Rex Content

The Reason Factory Sound Bank comes with three separate folders containing .rx2 format drum loops, percussion loops, and musical instrument loops.

Unlike many of the other file types used in Reason devices, REX files are not unique to the Dr. Rex and the Reason program. Pro Tools, Logic, Cubase, Digital Performer, and other digital audio workstation programs can open, play back, and sometimes convert and export REX files to Wave and AIFF format (though only ReCycle can convert files *to* the REX format). As a result, unlike other Reason file formats, REX files are often found outside of ReFills. In fact, it's common for commercially available loop libraries to be found in Apple Loops, Wave, and REX formats.

Even though REX files are often found as part of loop collections, there are many ReFills available containing REX format loops and files. If you are not planning to create your own REX files with the ReCycle, you will almost certainly want to increase your REX collection with third-party ReFills or loop collections. Some excellent commercial collections with high-quality REX files are available from:

Zero-G: www.zero-g.co.uk

Nine Volt Audio: www.ninevoltaudio.com

PowerFX: www.powerfx.com

Loopmasters: www.loopmasters.com

PROSONIC Studios: www.prosonic-studios.com

These sites and many others usually offer free samples of a number of REX loops that can give you an idea of their products' quality and whether they are stylistically compatible with your music. Google searches for "REX files" or "REX loops" will turn up a wealth of commercial, free, and demo REX loops and ReFills. In addition, this book's CD features REX content from www.BeatHive.com.

The Dr. Rex Interface

The Dr. Rex has the most straightforward interface of all of Reason's instruments, but it still has many features and a great range of included options for working with and editing REX loops. Figure 3.1 shows the Dr. Rex interface.

Figure 3.1

The Dr. Rex interface

Browse and Select Loop Buttons   Waveform Display   Filter and Filter Envelope

Pitch Bend and Mod Wheels   Slice-Editing Knobs   LFO   Amplitude Envelope

In the center of the interface is the Waveform Display. This window shows the currently loaded REX file, including the individual slices that make up the loop. At the top of the Waveform Display you'll see the default tempo for any loop that is currently loaded into the Dr. Rex.

The knobs and buttons along the top and bottom of the Loop Display contain the parameters used to perform most of the basic work and editing functions used to manipulate REX files.

On the top left of the Dr. Rex interface are the Browse Loop, Select Next Loop, and Select Previous Loop buttons, as well as the LED display that shows the name of any currently loaded loop.

You'll notice that unlike Reason's other instruments the Dr. Rex does not have a Save button. This is because the Dr. Rex does not load and play patches. Technically this means that you can't save any changes or edits you make to a REX file as you would with a sampler or synthesizer patch or a Redrum drum kit. However, there are some ways to work around this limitation, which will be covered later in this chapter.

Also on the left side of the interface are the Pitch Bend and Mod Wheel functionality found on most Reason instruments.

The right side of the interface contains the Filter, Filter Envelope, LFO, and Amp Envelope sections. These are common parameters found on most synthesizer and sampler devices. Each of these will be covered in this chapter, specifically as they relate to the Dr. Rex. These parameters are also covered in greater detail in Chapter 5.

There's one important feature that's easy to miss on the Dr. Rex: the Master volume level for the Dr. Rex is located on the bottom-right side of the instrument just below the word "Amp" in Amp Envelope.

Audio Settings

Located just below the Browse and Select buttons are three parameters related to the audio output of the Dr. Rex.

POLYPHONY

The Polyphony setting is a feature found on most Reason instruments. This setting determines how many notes a device can simultaneously play at once.

With REX files it's unlikely that you'll need to play more than two or three slices at one time. Since the default setting for the Dr. Rex is six notes, unless you have the need to use more notes at once you can leave this setting alone. Even if you never expect to play more than three notes at once, there's no need to lower the number, because having unused extra notes has no effect on your processor resources.

HIGH QUALITY INTERPOLATION

Next to the Polyphony Display is the High Quality Interpolation button. When High Quality Interpolation is activated, Reason will use a more complicated algorithm to interpret and play back the currently loaded loop. This can result in better sound quality for any Dr. Rex loop, but more often than not the effect of turning on High Quality Interpolation will not be noticeable.

If you have a Reason song with many devices and effects or you are working on an older computer and would like to save processor resources, you can leave this setting alone. If you have the power available, you may want to experiment with this setting for individual loops and see if you can notice a difference in sound quality.

LOW BANDWIDTH

Located just to the right of the High Quality Interpolation button, the Low Bandwidth On/Off button can be used to eliminate some of the high frequencies in a REX loop. This can have a noticeable effect on certain REX files and be unnoticeable on others.

Turning the Low Bandwidth on can free up some of your computer's processor resources, if this is an issue. Otherwise it's best left alone, since eliminating the high frequencies from some loops can cause them to sound less clear and distinct in your Reason songs.

Routing

Use the Tab key on your computer's keyboard to view the back panel of the Dr. Rex. Figure 3.2 shows the default routing that is created when you add a new Dr. Rex Loop Player to a Reason song.

The Dr. Rex is a stereo instrument. The left and right outputs of the Dr. Rex are automatically routed to the left and right inputs of the first available channel on your Reason song's Mixer 14:2.

Figure 3.2

**The back panel of
the Dr. Rex**

Figure 3.2

**The back panel of
the Dr. Rex**

As you can see, the back panel of the Dr. Rex also contains some interesting routing features, including Gate and Modulation inputs and outputs. We'll be utilizing this routing functionality in conjunction with other Reason devices in upcoming chapters.

Previewing and Playing Loops

There are two ways to preview loops that you want to load into the Dr. Rex: either at their original tempo, or at the current session tempo.

All of this chapter's exercises require that you set Reason's Preferences according to the instructions at the end of Chapter 2.

To preview loops at their original tempo, follow these steps:

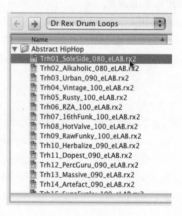

1. Create a new Reason song and add a Dr. Rex.

2. Click the Browse Loop button to open the Reason Browser.

3. Use the Browser to navigate to the folder `Reason Factory Sound Bank\Dr Rex Drum Loops\Abstract HipHop`.

4. Make sure the Browser's Autoplay function is turned on, and then click any `.rx2` file to preview the loop.

Details

Tempo: 90 (90) BPM
  Sign: 4/4
Length: 4.0 Bars, 10.7s
Format: Stereo, 16 Bit, 44.1 kHz
  Size: 1.8 MB (uncompressed)

You can also open the Browser at any time using the keyboard shortcut Ctrl/⌘+B.

At the bottom of the Browser window you'll see some important information about the currently playing REX loop, including the loop's default tempo, time signature, length, format, and file size.

Once you have located a loop that you wish to use in your session, click the OK button on the lower-right corner of the Browser to load it. If you'd like to use the loop at its original tempo, you'll have to change the tempo of your Reason song to match the loop.

The Preview Button

Hearing a loop at its original tempo can be useful, especially when you are using a Dr. Rex loop as the starting point for creating a song or track. On the other hand, if you are planning on adding a Dr. Rex drum or musical loop to a song that's already in progress, hearing a loop at its default tempo can make it difficult to get a feel for whether it will work with your current song.

If you have a Reason song already in progress and you want to hear how a specific REX loop might or might not fit, you'll want to preview the loop at your Reason song's current tempo. To do this, start playback of your song, and then click the Preview button on the Dr. Rex interface before you click the Browse Loop button.

By clicking the Preview button before opening the Browser, you preview your REX loops at the Reason song's current tempo, syncing up perfectly with your song. Again, once you've located a REX loop that you'd like to use, click OK in the Reason Browser to load it.

Once a REX file is loaded, you can use the Preview button to stop and start playback of the Dr. Rex at any time.

Switching Loops

Select Previous Loop and Select Next Loop can be used to scroll through other loops in the same directory.

> As discussed in Chapter 2, you can also use the Browser's up and down arrows to change loops in real time.

The LED display next to the Select button shows the name of the currently loaded REX file. Clicking the LED will show you a list of the available REX files in the current directory as well as another option for opening the Browser.

After a loop has been loaded into the Dr. Rex, you can open the Browser at any time and select a new, different loop to replace it.

Basic Editing Features

The Waveform Display and the knobs immediately above and below it, shown in Figure 3.3, can be used to edit and alter REX files in some very exciting ways.

Using just these parameters, you can make minor or drastic adjustments to REX files, possibly even creating a completely new-sounding performance just by working with these settings.

Figure 3.3

The Waveform Display

Transposing Loops

There are multiple ways to use the Dr. Rex to transpose an entire loop at once. Follow these steps:

1. Create a new Dr. Rex and load any loop from one of the Reason Factory Sound Bank\Dr Rex Drum Loops folders.

2. Click the Preview button to hear the loop.

3. With the loop playing, use your mouse to click any note on the keyboard at the bottom of the Waveform Display.

This method can be a great way to quickly change the tone of a drum track. Even though the loop's tempo doesn't actually change, the higher pitch can give the illusion of speed, while the lower pitch can give the illusion of a slower, lazy feel.

This can be useful in working between various genres as well. Raising the pitch of drum loop can result in a familiar Glitch or IDM style sound. Lowering the pitch can immediately conjure up Downtempo, Dubstep, or Trip-Hop sounds.

You can make greater or smaller adjustments to the pitch of a loop by using the knobs in the Oscillator Pitch section above the right side of the Waveform Display.

Since transposition is especially useful when working with instrument loops, we'll use an instrumental REX file for this example:

1. Create a new Dr. Rex and load any loop from one of the Reason Factory Sound Bank\Dr Rex Instrument Loop\Guitar Loops folders.

2. Click the Preview button to hear the loop.

3. With the loop playing, adjust the Octave knob.

The Octave knob can be used to alter the loop's pitch up to four octaves higher or lower than the original pitch.

Use the Oscillator Fine Tune knob in the center to make smaller pitch adjustments. This can come in handy if your instrumental REX file is slightly out of tune with your session.

The Oscillator Envelope knob works in conjunction with the Filter Envelope and is covered later in this chapter.

Working with Slices

One of the great things about the REX format in general and the Dr. Rex Loop Player in particular is the ability to micro-edit REX loops. When you load a REX loop into the Dr. Rex, what you're seeing in the center of the Waveform Display are the actual slices that make up the currently loaded loop. Each slice can be adjusted by pitch, panning position, volume level, and decay time.

Selecting Slices

There are three ways to select the individual slices that make up a REX loop:

Use Your Mouse You can select individual slices by clicking on them in the Waveform Display using your mouse.

Use the Select Slice Knob The Select Slice knob selects individual slices so that they can be adjusted with the following four knobs. The number in the Waveform Display just above the Select Slice knob corresponds to the selected slice.

Use Select Slice Via MIDI Button Turning on the Select Slice Via MIDI button lets you use your MIDI keyboard to choose a slice for editing. Reason will map the slices automatically to corresponding MIDI notes on your MIDI keyboard, starting at the note C1.

PREVIEW AND SELECT

You can preview individual slices by using your mouse to Alt/Option-click any selected slice in the Waveform Display. If you have the Select Slice Via MIDI button activated, Alt/Option-clicking will both preview *and* select the slice.

Editing Slices

Figure 3.4 shows the four knobs that can be used to adjust the parameters of each individual slice.

Figure 3.4
The slice editing knobs

Set Slice Pitch This knob sets the pitch for the currently selected slice and can be used to raise or lower the selected slice by up to 50 semitones. The number in the Waveform Display just above the Set Slice Pitch knob represents the value in semitones that pitch has been shifted.

Set Slice Pan The Set Slice Pan knob is used to set the panning position for the currently selected slices. The number in the Waveform Display just above the Set Slice Pan knob represents the panning value. The default setting, 0, is center, –64 is hard left, and 63 is hard right.

Set Slice Level The Set Slice Level can be used to adjust the volume for each slice. The default value is 100. The volume can be raised to 127 or lowered to 0. You can silence any slice in a REX loop by selecting it and lowering its level to 0.

Set Slice Decay The Set Slice Decay controls the decay time for any selected slice. Drastically lowering the Decay setting of a slice can create a clipped sound. You may also want to lower the Decay setting to control the decay of a long slice in a loop that's been slowed down.

With just these parameters, we can unlock a huge amount of the Dr. Rex Loop Player's power. Take some time to load a few of the included Reason Factory Sound Bank REX loops and see what you can do by adjusting individual slices. Follow these steps to start editing the slices of a REX drum loop:

1. Create a new Dr. Rex and load any drum loop from the Reason Factory Sound Bank.

2. Activate the Select Slice Via MIDI button.

3. Alt/Option-click any slice to both select *and* preview it.

4. Use the Set Slice Pitch and Set Slice Pan to raise the pitch and adjust the panning of the selected slice.

5. Alt/Option-click the slice to hear the difference.

6. Make changes to multiple slices, and then click the Preview button to hear how the loop sounds.

To get an idea of how the Set Slice Decay works, select any slice and lower the decay drastically to create a quick cutoff.

To get a feel for how these parameters can be used to alter melodic loops, use these same steps on any instrument loop REX file. As you are working with melodic loops, you may find that by adjusting the pitch for a single slice or two you can make a REX loop fit in with an existing melody on another Reason instrument track. This can come in handy when you want to add a melodic REX loop to an existing song and find that it's very close but not a perfect fit. You can also create entirely new melodies by making adjustments to multiple slices.

The Envelopes, Filter, and LFO

On the right side of the Dr. Rex interface, you'll see four separate sections: the Filter, the Filter Envelope, the LFO, and the Amplitude Envelope.

These are all common features on both hardware and software synthesizers and samplers. Filters, envelopes, and LFOs are discussed in greater detail in Chapter 5. In this section we're going to cover these parameters specifically as they relate to the Dr. Rex.

Amplitude Envelope

The Amplitude Envelope section on the lower-right side of the Dr. Rex interface contains common ADSR (attack, decay, sustain, and release) settings found on many hardware and software synthesizer and sampler instruments.

The Amplitude Section parameters affect each slice individually, meaning that the settings start over again for each slice, not the entire loop. Because the slices that make up a REX file tend to go by very quickly, you may not often hear the effect of the Amplitude Envelope, though it will sometimes be more noticeable on slower REX files with longer individual slices.

By default the Amplitude Envelope Decay setting is all the way up to 127. You can quickly get an idea of how these settings can affect each slice by loading any drum loop, clicking the Preview button, and gradually lowering the Decay setting. The effect is similar to using the Waveform Display to select each slice and lower its decay setting to create short, clipped sounds.

The Filter

Filters are used to do exactly what the name implies: change sounds by filtering out frequencies. The Filter can be turned on and off by clicking the button on the top left of the Filter section.

The Filter has five modes. You'll also find the same or similar options on the Filter sections of each of Reason's synth and sampler instruments:

Notch The Notch mode removes midrange frequencies.

High Pass 12 Cuts low frequencies, allowing only high frequencies through.

Band Pass 12 Cuts both high and low frequencies, leaving midrange.

Low Pass 12 Cuts high frequencies, allowing only low frequencies through.

Low Pass 24 A second Low Pass Filter. Also cuts high frequencies, allowing only low frequencies through.

You can switch between filter types by selecting them with your mouse or by using the Mode button on the bottom right of the Filter section.

Frequency The Frequency slider determines the frequencies that will be cut.

Resonance The Resonance or Res slider can be used to increase or decrease the range of frequencies that are cut.

With the Filter turned on and any mode selected, the Frequency slider can be used to set the general range of cut frequencies, while the Resonance slider controls the characteristic of the filter shape for the selected frequency range. Raising the Res slider widens the range of selected frequencies; lowering the slider creates a narrower selection.

The Filter can be automated on its own to create filter sweep effects and can also be linked to the LFO section just below it. Both of these strategies are explored in examples later in this chapter.

Filter Envelope

Just to the right of the Filter is the Filter Envelope. Like the Amplitude Envelope, the Filter Envelope also contains the common ADSR parameters, only this time they control the shape of the filter, not the overall volume of each slice.

The obvious use of Filter Envelope is to affect the Filter section. Less obvious is that the Filter Envelope can also be used to affect the pitch of your loop in conjunction with the Envelope Amount knob.

To get an idea of how the Filter Envelope can be used to control the Filter, load any instrument loop from the `Reason Factory Sound Bank\Dr. Rex Instrument Loops\Guitar Loops` folder. Then follow these steps:

1. Click the Preview button to begin play back of the loop.

2. Make sure the Filter On/Off LED is set to On.

3. Select the Low Pass 12 (LP12) mode.

4. Adjust the Frequency (Freq) and Resonance (Res) knobs to 64.

5. Adjust the Filter Envelope Amount slider to 64.

Using these settings as your starting point, try experimenting with the different sliders, beginning with the Attack setting. Raising and lowering the Filter Amount Envelope will determine how much of an effect the Filter Envelope has on the Filter. You can also adjust the Filter's Frequency and Resolution as well as choosing from the different Filter modes to create different effects.

With the Filter section turned off, you can use Filter Envelope to create pitch-bending effects with the Oscillator Envelope Amount knob.

Create a new Dr. Rex and load another Guitar loop. Lowering the Oscillator Envelope amount knob will result in a rising pitch, while raising the knob will result in a descending pitch. Again, try experimenting with the different settings, starting with the Attack slider.

The LFO

The LFO (Low Frequency Oscillator) is another feature of most virtual synths and samplers. LFOs are waveforms that are used to alter or affect another waveform or sound. In this case, any one of the six waveforms on the left side of the LFO can be used to create changes to the Oscillator (pitch), the Filter, or the Panning.

At the top of the LFO section you'll see the Sync button. It's a good idea to turn this on when using the LFO. The Sync button will synchronize the effects of the LFO with the current session tempo.

The available waveforms on the Dr. Rex are a Triangle, Inverted Sawtooth, Sawtooth, Square, and two "random" waveforms. Each waveform will have a noticeably different effect on your loop when selected.

You can choose among waveforms by clicking on them directly in the interface or by using the LFO1Wave button on the bottom left of the LFO Section.

Figure 3.5

**The Pitch Bend and
Mod Wheel section**

The LFO can only be used on one parameter at a time. Choose among the Oscillator, Filter, and Panning options by clicking the LFO Destination button at the bottom right of the LFO section.

Two examples later in this chapter show you some possible applications of the LFO within the Dr. Rex.

Pitch Bend and Mod Wheel

The Dr. Rex also contains Pitch Bend and Mod Wheel functionality, shown in Figure 3.5, that is similar to the same features on Reason's synths and Sampler instruments.

The Pitch Bend wheel can be adjusted either with your mouse or with a connected MIDI keyboard or other MIDI controller. You can use the Pitch Bend wheel to raise or lower the pitch of any REX loop up to 24 semitones in either direction.

The available range of the Pitch Wheel is set in the Range display just above the Pitch Bend and Mod Wheels.

Next to the Pitch Bend and Mod Wheels are six knobs. The top row of three knobs can be used in conjunction with the Mod Wheel to create Filter effects, and the bottom row can be used to create Velocity effects. See the examples later toward the end of this chapter for a detailed exercise in which you'll use the Mod Wheel in conjunction with the Filter settings.

The Velocity Section

The bottom row of knobs just below the Mod Wheel parameters are for creating velocity-related effects.

Using these parameters, you can change the sound of any REX slice in relation to the velocity used to trigger the slice. When you use the Copy REX Loop to Track functionality, slices are sent to the sequencer with a uniform velocity of 64. To use the Velocity parameters, you either have to change the Velocity value in the Velocity lane or use your MIDI keyboard to trigger samples with harder or softer velocity. See the section "Adjusting Velocity" later in this chapter for more information on using these parameters.

Dr. Rex and the Reason Sequencer

Using the Reason sequencer, we can access an entirely new range of options for working with REX loops. This includes including adjusting timing, rearranging slices to create new performances, utilizing the sequencer's velocity track for greater dynamic effects, and more.

Copy to Track

You'll do all the work of arranging, sequencing, and editing your Dr. Rex tracks in the Reason sequencer. To get the MIDI information from Dr. Rex into the sequencer, you'll use the Dr. Rex's Copy to Track functionality. Follow these steps to send a REX loop to a sequencer track:

1. Use the left and right locators to select the start and end point of the REX loop data. (See Chapter 2 if you need a refresher on these tools.)

2. Make sure the Dr. Rex is selected in the Reason sequencer's track list, and then click the Send MIDI To Sequencer Track button, located just above the Waveform Display in the Dr. Rex interface.

You can also send the MIDI data to the sequencer by choosing Edit → Copy Rex Loop To Track from Reason's menu bar (Figure 3.6) or by right/Ctrl-clicking on any empty area on the Dr. Rex interface.

If your Reason song contains more than one device, you'll want to make sure that you've selected the correct Dr. Rex track in the sequencer before you click the To Track button. If you have a different track selected in the sequencer, Reason will send your MIDI information to the wrong track.

In some cases, sending patterns from the Dr. Rex and other Reason devices to the "wrong" track can create interesting results. This is a method that's definitely worth experimenting with once you are familiar with Reason's instruments and the sequencer.

The REX loop will be copied to your sequencer track as a complete clip or as a series of clips, as shown in Figure 3.7.

Reason will always copy at least one entire REX loop to a sequencer track. If the loop is two measures long and you use the left and right locators to select only one measure of a track, Reason will still create a clip containing the entire two-measure loop.

> If you've altered a REX file using any of the slice-editing features found on the Dr. Rex interface that we covered earlier in this chapter, those individual edits will still be heard. Even though you've sent the individual slices to the sequencer, they are still being played back through the Dr. Rex.

Figure 3.6

A REX loop in the Reason sequencer

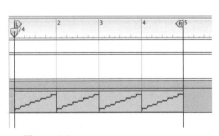

Figure 3.7

A REX loop in the sequencer's Arrange window

Clicking the Send MIDI To Track button or selecting Edit → Copy Rex Loop To Track a second time will create a new pattern lane in the Dr. Rex sequencer track with new copies of your clip or multiple clips.

NEW LOOPS FROM EXISTING LOOPS

One way to quickly create new patterns and loops is to load a loop into a Dr. Rex, send it to a sequencer track, and then use the Select Next Loop, Select Previous Loop, or Browse Loop buttons to load a new REX file in to the Dr. Rex. The result of this is that the pattern you created with the first loop will then be used to trigger the slices of the second loop.

One way to make this process especially interesting is to try it with two extremely different loops. For example, try sending a drum loop to a sequencer track and using the pattern to trigger an instrument loop, or vice versa.

Editing and Arranging Clips

Once your REX files have been copied to a sequencer track, you can make decisions about where in your Reason song you'd like the loop to play back and for how long. Since your REX loop has been copied to the sequencer as a clip or multiple clips, it's a simple matter to select any clip with your mouse and move it to a new location.

One option is to copy and paste a REX clip or multiple clips to create your arrangement. First, copy a clip or clips by selecting one or more clips in the sequencer track and using the keyboard shortcut Ctrl/CM+C or by choosing File → Edit → Copy. Use your mouse to move the playhead to a new location in the sequencer, and then use the keyboard shortcut Ctrl/⌘+V to paste a duplicate of the REX loop or loops to a new location.

You can also use the Alt/Option-drag copying methods to duplicate a selected clip or clips.

Chopping Clips

One way to come up with new tracks from existing REX loops is to chop them at strategic points, and then rearrange the MIDI data to create new rhythms. You can also use this method to create a loop from only one section of a longer REX loop. Follow these steps to rearrange a REX loop in the sequencer:

1. Create a new Dr. Rex and send the loop to the sequencer.

2. Make sure that Snap To Grid is turned on and and choose a Grid value of ¼ From the Grid value drop down menu. With these settings selected, all of your edits will take place at clearly defined points on the Dr. Rex's sequencer track.

3. If necessary, zoom in on the clip using the Magnify tool.

4. Select the Razor tool and slice the loop into multiple sections.

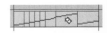

5. Use the Selection tool to rearrange the new sections, or Alt/Option-drag or copy and paste a specific selection to create an entire loop from one section.

You can create a new clip by selecting the rearranged sections and choosing File → Edit → Join Clips or right/Ctrl-clicking and choosing Join Clips from the context menu.

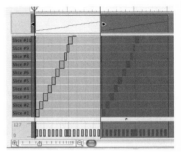

Rearranging Rex Slices to Create New Loops

So far we've been looking at the editing options that are available in the Reason sequencer's Arrange mode. By switching from the Arrange mode to the Edit mode, we can access even more functionality.

Switch to Edit mode by double-clicking any clip in the sequencer or by clicking the Switch To Edit mode button at the top left of the sequencer window. If you double-click a clip to open Edit mode, you can immediately select and edit individual notes. If you use the Switch To Edit mode button, you can select a specific clip for editing by double-clicking it in the Overview lane. Figure 3.8 shows a REX loop in the sequencer's Edit mode view.

Figure 3.8

A REX loop in Edit mode view

What you are seeing here is all of the individual slices that make up this REX loop, arranged chronologically. The large lane in the center is called the REX lane. On the left side of the REX lane, each slice is represented, starting from Slice #1. Clicking on any slice name on the left side of the REX lane will preview the slice, as shown here:

Using the sequencer's tools, which were covered in Chapter 2, you can move, erase, and draw new slices, creating minor variations or entirely new performances.

Once you've altered a clip, you can either use the Overview lane or return to Arrange mode to edit, resize, or slice the new clip.

SNAP TO GRID AND LOOP MODE

Working with REX loops in the Edit mode offers a good opportunity to take advantage of Reason's Snap to Grid and Loop Playback functionality. By activating Snap To Grid and setting the value to ⅛ or ⅟₁₆, any slices you move or create will automatically be in time with your Reason song.

By activating Reason's Loop mode and using the left and right locators to create a one-, two-, or four-measure loop, you can then begin playback (click Play on the Transport panel) and actually create changes and edits in real time with the sequencer's tools.

Adjusting Velocity

Figure 3.9

The Velocity lane for a REX file

When you send your MIDI slice data to a sequencer track, the velocity for each slice is set to 64 by default. This is the exact middle of the available dynamic range, the highest being 127 and the lowest being 0. The Dr. Rex's Velocity lane always appears at the bottom of the sequencer window when you switch to Edit mode view. Figure 3.9 shows the default Velocity lane for a typical REX file.

This default setting can work very well for drum loops, especially since many REX loops are created from live drum performances. In these cases, the dynamics of the performance are actually contained within the performance in the loop. However, if you decide that you do want to increase the dynamic range of a REX loop, you can use the Pencil tool to draw changes to velocity in the Velocity lane.

You can also use the Tools tab of the Tool window to create random changes to velocity, as you'll see later in this chapter.

Once you have created variation in velocity you can use the Velocity parameter knobs on the Dr. Rex interface to create more variation in the tone and level of your individual REX slices. Make sure the Dr. Rex's Filter section is turned on; then adjust the Filter Envelope and Filter Decay settings to vary the tone of your REX slices based on different velocities.  Raise the Amplitude Velocity Amount knob (try a setting of 40 or higher) to have higher and lower velocities increase and decrease the volume of your REX slices.

Dr. Rex and the Tool Window

Reason 4's new Tool window contains functionality that works very well with your Dr. Rex sequencer tracks. Following are some ideas you can use to take advantage of options in the Tool window to change, edit, and rearrange your REX loops. The following suggestions will work in both Edit and Arrange modes. However, you'll get a better view of what's actually happening to the individual slices of your REX loops by working in the Edit mode view.

Quantize

The Tool window's Quantize functionality (in the Tools tab) can be used to create variations on your existing Rex Loops. Follow these steps to work with the Tool window's Quantize functionality:

1. Create a new Dr. Rex, then load any drum loop.

2. Send the loop to the Dr. Rex track in the sequencer.

3. Select the loop or multiple instances of the loop in the sequencer.

4. Click the Tools tab of the Tool window and open the Quantize setting.

Most REX drum loops will be in standard 4/4 time signatures. You can use the Quantize setting to quickly create a triplet feel by selecting the 1/8-note triplet setting (1/8T) and clicking the Apply button (Figure 3.10).

You can create other variations to beats by experimenting with the Value, Amount, and Random settings. It's easy to quickly make a beat unrecognizable, and not always in a good way. Experiment with applying different settings, using the Edit/Undo functionality to return to the original unedited loop if you've achieved any unwanted results.

Figure 3.10

Quantize functionality in the Tool window

Pitch (Transpose)

This is different from the transposing we did earlier in the Dr. Rex interface. In the Tool window you can transpose the MIDI notes in the sequencer, which isn't particularly useful with REX loops, since shifting the notes of a REX loop up or down will mean the highest or lowest notes won't trigger any REX slices. However, the Pitch Randomize functionality can be used to create unexpected beats and melodies from REX slices.

1. Select any REX loop in the sequencer.

2. Select the Randomize button (Figure 3.11).

3. Set the Low note to C1.

4. Set the High note to C2 (you can go higher for REX loops with more slices).

5. Click the Apply button.

As with any of Reason's randomization features, you might not come up with something useful on the first try. You can always create a brand-new pattern by clicking the Apply button again.

You may also come up with something that's close to being useful but not exactly. Random patterns can be a good starting point for new ideas and can often be helped with a small amount of editing.

Figure 3.11

Pitch (Transpose) functionality in the Tool window

> Try creating a random pattern and then applying one of the Quantization options from the previous section.

Alter Notes

The Alter Notes function is similar to Randomization, but gives you more control over how much the loop is changed. For example, selecting a clip in the sequencer and setting Alter Notes to 20%, as shown in Figure 3.12, will change one out of every five notes in the selected clip.

This can be a good way to come up with minor variations to REX loops. A good way to take advantage of this functionality is to create multiple copies of a REX loop and then alter each one using a low percentage value. You can then choose among variations to create an arrangement.

Figure 3.12

Setting Alter Notes to 20% will alter one out of every five notes in the clip.

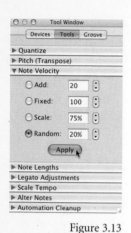

Figure 3.13

Note velocity functionality in the Tool window

Note Velocity

One way to add more dynamics to a REX loop is to use the Note Velocity section of the Tools window (Figure 3.13).

This is similar to using the method described earlier in this chapter of using the Draw tool to create dynamic variations. In this case you'll use the Note Velocity view to create random variations to the velocity of each individual slice.

1. Select a clip in the sequencer.

2. Select Random in the Note Velocity view.

3. Set the desired percentage.

4. Click the Apply button.

Applying a small amount of Note Velocity variation can be an effective way to create a more realistic, humanized feel in drum or percussion loops that sound too rigid.

Scale Tempo

The Scale Tempo setting is great for working with REX loops that have disparate tempos. For example, you may have a Reason song with a session tempo of 70 BPM and a REX loop that sounds great for your song at its default tempo of 140. Unfortunately when you load the loop into your Dr. Rex Loop Player, Reason slows the beat down to half speed, playing it back at 70 BPM. Here's where the Scale Tempo function can help out:

1. Create a new Dr. Rex and load any REX loop.

2. Send the Loop to the Dr. Rex sequencer track.

3. Select the clip in the sequencer.

4. Click the Double button in the Scale Tempo section (Figure 3.14).

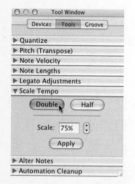

Figure 3.14

Scale Tempo functionality in the Tool window

Along with doubling the speed of your loop, this process will also cut the loop's length in half, so you'll have to do some copying and pasting to fill out your track.

You can also use the Scale Tempo function to perform the opposite effect, cutting the tempo of a loop in half and doubling its length.

Another option is to use the Scale setting to adjust the loop by a percentage. You should be careful with this, though, because more often than not the results of adjusting by percentage will be a loop that is out of time with your Reason song.

DR. REX AND THE REGROOVE

The ReGroove can be used to quickly add slight variations or a completely new feel to your Dr. Rex loops in the sequencer. You can find out more about the ReGroove in Chapter 8. There are also some quick strategies for using the ReGroove covered in Chapter 4 that can be applied to your REX loops as well.

Dr. Rex and MIDI Devices

You can also use a MIDI keyboard and other MIDI controller devices to play the individual slices of a REX loop. By combining this method with the sequencer's MIDI recording functionality, you can trigger individual slices in real time and create a new loop from a live performance. This is especially useful for creating new tracks from drum and percussion loops, but it can also be used to create new instrument performances or work with any kind of REX loop.

As you saw earlier in this chapter when using the Select Slice Via MIDI button on the Dr. Rex interface, the first slice of any Rex loop will correspond to the note C1 on your MIDI keyboard. C1 will trigger the second slice, D1 will trigger the third, and so on.

1. Create a new Dr. Rex and load any drum loop from the Reason Factory Sound Bank.

2. Turn on Reason's click track and Precount. You may also want to lower the tempo of your Reason song to make it easier to play along with the click track.

3. Make sure you've selected the Dr. Rex track in the sequencer and that the track is armed to receive MIDI information.

4. Click the Record button in the Transport panel.

5. Use your MIDI keyboard to play the individual slices of the REX file to create a new drum loop.

You can now go into the Reason sequencer's Edit mode view and fix any imperfections in your performance manually, or by using the Quantize functionality in the Tool window with the techniques covered earlier in this chapter and in Chapter 2.

While this method's obvious application is to create new drum performances out of drum loops, it can also be used to create new melodic performances from instrument loops. In fact, because the REX loop of an instrument performance will be out of sequence (compared to playing a normal sample mapped out across a keyboard), you will often find yourself coming up with unexpected melodies and patterns when triggering REX slices with your MIDI keyboard.

More MIDI Tricks

Reason and the Dr. Rex also utilize some unexpected MIDI functionality that makes it possible to use your MIDI keyboard to transpose and trigger entire REX loops. This can be useful for both live performance and sequencing:

- Playing any MIDI note between D-1 and C0 will transpose the loop's pitch up between 1 and 12 semitones.

- Playing any MIDI note between B-2 and C-3 will transpose the loop's pitch down between 1 and 12 semitones.

- The MIDI note C-1 will return the loop to its original pitch.
- MIDI note D0 will play the entire loop.

You can combine aspects of this functionality in interesting ways. For example, you could transpose a loop down using any of the B–2 through C–3 keys, then trigger the loop by playing D0. Or you could transpose a loop up, then use the MIDI note C1 and higher to play individual slices.

Automating the Dr. Rex

Throughout this book we'll be looking at automation as a creative technique. Something I'll be mentioning repeatedly is the fact that just about all of the knobs, sliders, and faders on every Reason device can be adjusted and automated. The Dr. Rex has many obvious parameters that can be automated and some unexpected ones as well.

Creating Automation in the Dr. Rex Interface

The best way to get a look at the parameters of any device that can be automated is to take a look at the device's interface in Remote Override Edit mode, shown in Figure 3.15. To do this, select make the Dr. Rex is selected in the Reason rack and choose Options → Remote Override Edit Mode.

The specific colors may be different on your computer, but as shown in Figure 3.15 the parameters that have a yellow knob indicate that they have been automatically mapped to corresponding knobs and sliders on a connected MIDI interface. The parameters with a blue arrow indicate that they are capable of being controlled by an external MIDI device, but are not currently assigned to any specific button, pad, knob, or slider on the connected MIDI interface.

Most, but not all, of the parameters indicated with the blue arrows can be automated. In the case of the Dr. Rex, the exceptions are the Select Next Patch and Select Previous Patch buttons, the Polyphony and Range settings, the High Quality Interpolation button, and the Low Bandwidth button.

Figure 3.15

The Override Edit mode for the Dr. Rex

Knobs indicate assigned parameters

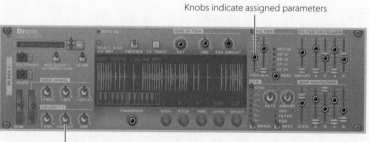

Arrows indicate unassigned parameters

You'll find more specific information on MIDI automation and mapping in the sections on automation and mapping in Chapter 10.

Now that you've had a look at the parameters on the Dr. Rex that can be automated, select Options → Remote Override Edit Mode again to return to Reason's normal operation mode.

Although it's possible to create automation in the Dr. Rex interface while playing a loop using the Preview button, you'll achieve better results by sending the REX loop to the sequencer first.

Follow these steps to try out automation in Dr. Rex:

1. Create a new Dr. Rex and load any loop.

2. Use the left and right locators to set up a four-measure loop in Reason's sequencer.

3. Turn on Reason's looping functionality by clicking the Loop On/Off LED on the Transport panel.

4. Use the Send MIDI Sequence To Track button in the Dr. Rex interface to send the REX file to the Dr. Rex track in the sequencer.

5. Make sure your Dr. Rex track is selected in the sequencer's track list and the Record Enable Parameter Automation button is turned on to receive automation information.

6. Click the Record button on the Transport panel.

7. With the loop playing back, adjust various knobs, sliders, and buttons on the Dr. Rex interface.

For every automated parameter that you adjust, Reason will create a new Automation lane in the Dr. Rex's sequencer track. As the loop reaches the end of the four-measure cycle and returns to the beginning, you'll also see the familiar green outline around any parameter that is now automated.

CREATING AUTOMATION IN THE SEQUENCER

Just like Reason's other devices, all of the parameters that can be automated in the Dr. Rex interface can be automated by using the Reason sequencer alone. Creating and editing automation in the sequencer is somewhat more complicated than creating it in an instruments interface. This process is covered in detail in the "The Sequencer: Advanced" section of Chapter 10.

Effects and the Dr. Rex

Like all of Reason's instruments, the Dr. Rex can be used in conjunction with all of Reason effects devices, either as Insert or Send effects. Different effects will be appropriate for different situations, depending on the kind of loop you are using the Dr. Rex to load, play, and sequence. The following are a few of the more frequent uses of Reason's effects with the Dr. Rex:

Compression Many Dr. Rex loops can benefit greatly from compression, which can be used to limit the dynamic range of a performance, raising the volume of quiet sounds and lowering the volume of louder sounds. Drum loops in particular can be enhanced by the use of compression. Reason's Comp-01 Compressor/Limiter and the MClass Compressor are both excellent options for adding life to drum loop and helping it to stand out in a mix. These effects are best added as Inserts rather than Sends.

The MClass Maximizer If you find that your Dr. Rex loops are too quiet or are getting lost in your mix, you can use the MClass Maximizer to quickly boost the volume and presence of a drum track or other loop. Add the MClass Maximizer as an Insert effect.

Reverb Along with compression, reverb is one of the most commonly used effects with drum tracks. In many cases, reverb will be applied to a specific piece of a drum kit—for example, a snare drum or a kick drum. However, reverb can also be applied to an entire drum loop to add a small amount of "live room" sound or to create noticeable cavern, hall, or echo effects. Reason's RV-7 Digital Reverb and RV7000 Advanced Reverb are best used in conjunction with the Dr. Rex as a Send effect.

The Scream 4 The Scream 4 Distortion can be used to good effect either as an Insert or a Send. The Scream makes an excellent choice for quickly adding a small or large amount of distortion or more drastic compression-style effects.

These are just a few of your options for using effects with the Dr. Rex. Chapter 7 has much more detail about each of Reason's included effects devices.

The rest of the chapter looks at some creative examples that you can try with the Dr. Rex Loop Player.

> Make sure you've followed the instructions in Chapter 2 for setting Reason's Preferences before you begin the exercises in this chapter.

Creating a Filter Sweep with Automation

To get an idea of exactly how the Filter Section works, we'll try one of its most frequent uses: to create a filter sweep. The filter sweep is a familiar effect in electronic music, frequently used on the kinds of drum and synth tracks that you'll create with REX loops.

Use the information covered earlier in "The Filter" section of this chapter to follow these steps and create a filter sweep:

1. Create a new Dr. Rex and load any REX loop from the Reason Factory Sound Bank\ Dr. Rex Drum loops folder.

2. Create a four-measure loop in the sequencer.

3. Send the REX loop to the Dr. Rex sequencer track.

4. Select the Filter Mode LP12.

5. Set the Filter Resonance to 40.

6. Set the Filter Frequency around 50.

7. Make sure your Dr. Rex track header is selected in the sequencer and the Record Enable Parameter Automation button is turned on to receive automation information.

8. Click the Record button on the Transport panel.

9. With the loop playing, raise and lower the Filter Frequency value to create a filter sweep.

Reason will automatically create an automation clip, visible in the Automation lane. This can be very useful in creating arrangements. For example, suppose you have created a filter sweep but you want to use it on just a section, not on your complete track. In this case, you can copy or move the automation clip to the desired section of your arrangement.

Using the LFO to Create Filter Effects

In the previous example, we created a filter sweep effect by automating the Filter Frequency slider. Using the information covered earlier in the LFO section of this chapter, follow these steps to use the LFO to generate a similar effect:

1. Create a new Dr. Rex and load any loop.

2. In the Filter section, lower the Filter Frequency slider to 75 and make sure the default low pass filter LP12 setting is selected.

3. Turn on the LFO Sync Enable button.

4. Select the Triangle Waveform.

5. Set the Rate knob to 8/4.

6. Set the Amount knob to 64 (or higher for a more dramatic effect).

7. Click the Preview button to begin playback of the loop.

The Triangle waveform will create a standard sweeping effect. Try each of the other five waveforms to hear the differences in how each can be used to create filter effects. You can create more variations on the filter effects by adjusting the Rate and Amount knobs as well.

Using the LFO to Create Panning Effects

Using the LFO to control the panning of a loop is a fun, quick, and easy way to create a noticeable effect:

1. Create a new Dr. Rex and load any REX loop.
2. Turn on the LFO Sync Enable button.
3. Use the Waveform button to select the Square Wave.
4. Click the Destination button and select Pan.
5. Raise the Amount knob significantly (at least 100).
6. Set the Rate knob to 2/4.
7. Click the Preview button.
8. Adjust the Rate knob to hear a faster or slower panning effect.

Once again, you can create different types of effects by using the Waveform button to select a different waveform and by adjusting the Amount and Rate knobs.

Using the Mod Wheel as a Wah-Wah

The Mod Wheel can be used to control both Filter and Velocity parameters. In this example, we'll focus on the filter aspects and create a familiar guitar effect using one of Reason's included guitar REX files:

1. Create a new Reason song with a tempo of 85 BPM.
2. Create a new Dr. Rex and load the file Reason Factory Sound Bank\Dr. Rex Instrument Loops\ElGt_Faith_Cm_085.rx2.
3. Adjust the Filter Frequency knob to 37 and the Filter Resonance knob to 37.

4. Click the Preview button to start playback of the loop.
5. Use the Mod Wheel on your MIDI controller to adjust the frequency. If you have a MIDI controller without a Mod Wheel or don't have a MIDI controller at all, you can use your mouse to click and drag the Mod Wheel on the DRLP interface. Dragging up and down slowly will create a filter sweep effect; dragging up and down quickly will create a wah-wah effect.

You can make this effect a permanent part of your Reason song by sending the REX loop to a sequencer track and recording the adjustments to the Mod Wheel with Reason's automation functionality.

Using Multiple Dr. Rex Loop Players

One very cool thing about the Dr. Rex is that you can use multiple instances of the instrument to quickly create complete songs. Since the Dr. Rex can load and play back any kind of instrument loop it's easy to add drum, bass, percussion, and melody loops to a Reason song and build a backing track or complete arrangement in a matter of minutes.

1. Create a new Reason song and add three or more Dr. Rex Loop Players. You'll use the Preview button to try out multiple REX files at once before sending the REX files to individual sequencer tracks.

2. Load a REX file into one Dr. Rex at a time. Once you've decided on a specific REX file for a track, name the Dr. Rex accordingly (drum, guitar, synth, etc.).

3. Use the transpose and slice editing functionality within the Dr. Rex interface to make any necessary changes. For example, you can turn a guitar or synth loop into a bass loop by transposing the loop one or more octaves down, or change a drum or instrument loop with transposition, slice editing, or Filter effects.

4. Use the Copy to Track functionality to send the REX loops to individual sequencer tracks, and then perform additional edits and create your arrangement.

Another instance where multiple Dr. Rex Loop Players will come in handy is creating a complete drum track, since only one REX loop can be loaded at a time. While it's possible to create a complete drum track containing multiple performances by rearranging a single REX loop, you're often better able to create a more dynamic performance with multiple loops on more than one Dr. Rex.

The included CD has an example file of a Reason song created entirely with Dr. Rex Loop Players in the folder Examples\Chapter 3\MultiRex.rns.

Summary

In this chapter you learned how to use the Dr. Rex Loop Player to create rhythmic and instrumental tracks and performances for your Reason songs, using elements of the device's interface both alone and in conjunction with the Reason sequencer to edit and arrange REX format loops.

For context, you learned some of the history of REX format loops and the ReCycle Program, as well as where to locate content for use with the Dr. Rex Loop Player. You then learned the basics of operating the Dr. Rex, beginning with an overview of the interface, then moving on to Slice editing functions and the Filter, Envelope, and LFO sections, all of which can be used independently or together to make subtle or drastic changes to existing percussion and melodic REX loops. Using the elements of the Dr. Rex interface, you can now create your own original performances by editing existing REX format loop files.

Next, you learned about the process of using the Dr. Rex with Reason's sequencer, including strategies for altering and editing sections of REX loops, micro-editing by rearranging individual slices and using the Tool window in conjunction with a Dr. Rex sequencer track. Also covered were using the Dr. Rex with MIDI, some basic automation tips, and some suggestions for audio effects, followed by a set of examples designed to further familiarize you with some of the many features of the Dr. Rex.

All of these lessons can be combined to create individual tracks and even entire Reason songs using this versatile Reason device.

CHAPTER 4

The Redrum Drum Computer

Most of your Reason songs will contain some kind of drum or percussion track. While the Dr. Rex Loop Player is great for quickly creating backing tracks using preexisting loops, the Redrum Drum Computer will be your go-to instrument for creating original rhythmic patterns and then sequencing them into entire performances. The Redrum is one of Reason's sampler instruments, but unlike its other sampler instruments (the NN-19 Digital Sampler and NN-XT Advanced Sampler, both discussed in Chapter 6), the Redrum's features and functions have been created specifically to optimize it for use with drum- and percussion-related samples. Redrum's sampler functionality allows you to load samples in different audio formats from many different sources, and then edit them to create your own original kits. You can also load, play, edit, and sequence loops, sound effects, and other kinds of audio files.

Topics in this chapter include:

- **Redrum Basics**

- **Working with Patterns**

- **Creating Arrangements**

- **Advanced Pattern Programming**

- **Creating and Saving Kits**

- **Automating the Redrum**

- **Using Effects with the Redrum**

- **Redrum and the ReGroove Mixer**

- **Creating and Exporting Loops**

- **Creative Routing with the Redrum**

- **Working with Samples and Loops**

Redrum Basics

The Redrum is a sampler with the ability to load 10 different samples at once, combined with a built-in step sequencer designed to play back each sample at specific times. The instrument's pattern sequencing functionality allows you to create and arrange multiple performances, either within the instrument's interface or in conjunction with the Reason sequencer. This makes the Redrum the perfect tool for quickly creating rhythmic backing tracks, and it's especially versatile for creating tracks that mimic hardware drum machines such as the Roland 808 and 909 models, on which the instrument's interface is loosely based.

You can add the Redrum to any Reason song by selecting Create → Redrum Drum Computer, by clicking the Redrum icon in the Tools pop-up window, or by right-clicking (Windows) or Ctrl-clicking (Mac) in any blank space in the Reason rack.

Using existing Redrum kits is very easy. The Reason Factory Sound Bank comes with 18 folders containing collections of drum kits in various styles and genres. Many third-party ReFills are available that you can use to further expand your collection of kits. One of the Redrum's most exciting features is the instrument's ability to load and trigger samples in multiple formats from any location on your hard drive, including ReFill content, your own original samples, or third-party loop and sample libraries and discs.

The Redrum can load and play stereo and mono audio files in the AIFF (.aif), Wave (.wav) and SoundFont (.sf2) formats, and can also load and play the individual slices that make up any REX format file.

Each sample is assigned its own individual channel strip with a variety of options for editing the samples. New kits can either be created from scratch or by replacing one or more samples in existing kits. Any edits that are made within a kit can be saved as part of the kit.

In previous versions of Reason, one of the biggest challenges faced by Redrum users was creating realistic, human-sounding performances. As we'll see in this chapter, Reason 4's addition of the ReGroove Mixer makes this process much easier.

Redrum is also considered one of Reason's pattern devices, along with the Matrix Pattern Sequencer (introduced in Chapter 2 and discussed further in Chapter 10). Many of the same arrangement techniques covered in this chapter can also be used with the Matrix Pattern Sequencer.

The Redrum Interface

The Redrum interface, shown in Figure 4.1, is divided into three main sections. Along the top are the 10 individual channel strips, while most of the bottom of the Redrum interface is taken up by the step sequencing and pattern programming area. In the lower left of the interface is the Patch Select area. The Master Level for the Redrum is located at the top left.

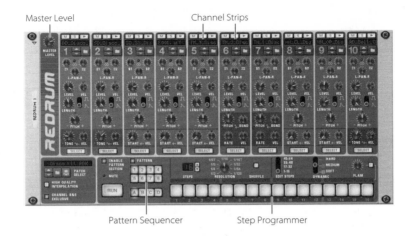

Master Level   Channel Strips

Pattern Sequencer   Step Programmer

Figure 4.1

**The Redrum
interface**

As with all of Reason's instruments, the Browse Patch button is used to open the Reason
Browser and locate any patches the instrument is capable of loading. For the Redrum
you'll be working with Redrum kits that use the file extension .drp. It's important to note
that the samples that make up a kit are not actually contained within the .drp files. As with
most sampler file formats, the patch file merely contains "pointers," which let the program
know where the individual sample files that make up the kit are stored.

Basic Routing

To get a look at the Redrum's default routing, create a new Reason song and add a
Redrum Drum Computer, then use the Tab key to view the back of the Redrum instrument, shown in Figure 4.2.

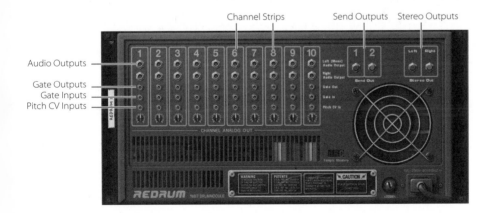

Channel Strips   Send Outputs   Stereo Outputs

Audio Outputs

Gate Outputs
Gate Inputs
Pitch CV Inputs

Figure 4.2

**The back panel
of the Redrum**

As you can see, when you add a Redrum to a Reason song, the program creates a standard routing configuration, sending the left and right outputs to the left and right inputs of the first open track on the song's Mixer 14:2.

Reason also automatically creates Effects Send routing, which we'll look at in more detail later in this chapter.

Effects Send routing is connected by default for only one Redrum instrument per Reason song. If you add multiple instances of a Redrum to a Reason song, you'll have to configure the Effects Sends manually for each new Redrum. Each individual channel has the ability to be routed as a mono signal, using the left (mono) audio output or in stereo, using both the left (mono) and right audio outputs. When you connect the left (mono) output to the left (Mono) input of a stereo device, Reason will automatically attach both cables to create stereo routing. The Redrum's back panel also includes Gate CV In, Gate CV Out, and Pitch CV In routing options, all of which we will be using in this chapter.

Working with Patterns

Creating patterns out of prerecorded drum samples is the most common use for the Redrum Drum Computer. Reason comes with an excellent supply of ready-made drum kits, and Redrum's interface contains some great functionality, designed to help you create interesting patterns with variation and dynamics. In the following examples, we'll begin the process of creating beats with the Redrum by loading kits, creating some basic drum patterns, and working with Redrum's programming features.

Loading a Kit

In the Patch Select section you'll see the Select, Browse, and Save buttons found on most Reason instruments. Follow these steps to load a Redrum drum kit:

1. Click the Browse Patch button to open the Reason Browser.

2. Use the Browser to navigate to the folder Reason Factory Sound Bank\Redrum Drum Kits. Here you'll see a selection of folders, shown in Figure 4.3, that contain drum kits for various styles and genres.

3. Open the folder Rock Kits and select the kit Groovemasters Rock Kit 1.drp.

4. Click the OK button at the bottom of the Browser.

I've suggested using this particular kit because it contains some standard drum sounds, which make it easy to describe some of the Redrum's important basic functionality. Once you have a rudimentary understanding of creating patterns, you should go back and check out some of the Reason Factory Sound Bank's more interesting drum kits.

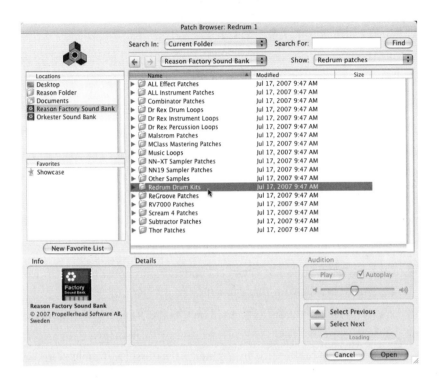

Once you've selected and loaded a drum kit, you can use the Select Next Patch and Select Previous Patch buttons to load other kits in the same folder. You can also quickly change kits by clicking on the LCD just above the Patch Select buttons and choosing from the displayed list of all of the Redrum kits in the current directory.

Creating Drum Patterns

The process of programming a basic beat is fairly simple, but the ins and outs of creating interesting, complex rhythmic patterns can be difficult. Having some background in drumming or percussion is helpful, but even if you have no experience at all with live drumming or creating beats and patterns with samplers or drum machines, it's easy to get started working with Redrum. If your programming skills need work, don't worry—I'll be covering lots of tips and suggestions for creating drum patterns and sequences throughout this chapter.

Programming a Simple Beat

Let's start things off by creating a straightforward drum pattern using the Groovemasters Rock Kit 1. Once a drum kit is loaded, the process of programming a beat takes place in the Step Programmer, shown in Figure 4.4. Each button is a step, essentially one beat in a 16-beat pattern.

Figure 4.4
The Redrum Step Programmer

To access the Step Programmer, at the bottom of each channel strip on the Redrum you'll see a Select button.

Clicking the Select button of a specific channel strip allows you to use the Step Programmer to program a pattern with that channel strip's currently loaded sample. Clicking once on an empty step in the Step Programmer step will trigger a sample. Clicking a second time will delete the step. If you want to create a beat in real time, you can click the Run button to start playback and hear how your beats sound as they are being created. Here's how to create a simple kick/snare/hihat pattern:

1. Click the Select button on Channel 1 and use your mouse to click once on Steps 1, 7, and 9. This will create your kick drum pattern.

2. Click the Select button on Channel 2 and use your mouse to click once on steps 5 and 13. This will create your snare pattern.

3. For the hihat, click the Select button on Channel 8 and use your mouse to click once on Steps 1, 5, 9 and 13.

Figure 4.5 shows (a) the kick drum pattern, (b) the snare drum pattern, and (c) the hihat pattern.

Figure 4.5

The three individual patterns defined in this example

(a) Channel 1, the kick drum

(b) Channel 2, the snare drum b

(c) Channel 8, the hihat

4. Click the Run button to play your drum pattern.

REAL-TIME PROGRAMMING

One of the great things about the way Redrum works is that you can use it to create your beats in real time. This means you can create your rhythm patterns "live," while playing back your already existing musical tracks. For a quick look at this method, open the Examples\Chapter 4\ Songs\BuildAlong.rns file on the accompanying CD. Just start playback of the song and then use your mouse to program a beat along with the included looping musical track.

If you make a mistake when programming a pattern, you can use the standard Undo and Redo keyboard shortcuts: Ctrl/⌘+Z to undo and Ctrl/⌘+Y to redo.

If you're not happy with a pattern you've created, you can delete it and start over again at any time by using the keyboard shortcut Ctrl/⌘+X to cut the pattern. You can also choose Edit → Clear Pattern from the menu bar.

The Programming Features

Just above the Step Programmer are a number of parameters that you can use to make your drum patterns and rhythmic sequences more interesting. These include options for adjusting the length and speed of your patterns and for adding dynamic range to your performance.

Pattern Length

By default, when you create a new Redrum you're given an empty 16-step pattern to work with. Using the up or down arrows on the Pattern Length selector, you can increase or decrease the number of steps in your drum pattern. This can be used in multiple ways, including creating longer or shorter drum patterns and working in odd time signatures.

CREATING LONGER PATTERNS

Creating patterns longer than 16 beats is easy to do with the Redrum, but working with longer patterns can take some getting used to. You can create patterns with up to 64 steps at a time, but since the pattern sequencer only has only 16 viewable steps, some of the time you'll be working with steps you can't see. The easiest way to get an idea of how this works is to program a pattern in the default 16-step mode, and then click the up arrow to raise the number of steps to 32. Click the Run button to play the 32-step pattern. You can see that the first 16 steps of the pattern are visible.

In order to view and edit the second 16 steps, you'll need to use the Edit Steps switch to select Steps 17–32.

CREATING SHORTER PATTERNS

Creating shorter patterns is easier. Just lower the number of steps in your pattern. For an easy example, try creating an eight- or four-step pattern.

WORKING IN DIFFERENT TIME SIGNATURES

The Pattern Length selector makes it easy to work in different time signatures. For example, to work in 7/8 time you would use the Edit Steps selector to lower the number of steps to 7 and then change the time signature on the Transport panel.

Sometimes working in different time signatures will require a bit of basic math. For instance, continuing with the example of working in 7/8 time, you could also choose 14 steps, 21 steps, or 28 steps to create your patterns. How comfortable you are working in odd time signatures will often depend on how much experience you have with drums, percussion, and programming. If you are new to these concepts, it's a good idea to get as comfortable as possible working in the default 4/4 mode, and then branch out as you learn more.

Resolution

By adjusting the Resolution knob, you can quickly increase or decrease the tempo of your Redrum pattern.

Adjusting the resolution from the default 1/16 setting to the 1/8 setting cuts the beat's tempo in half (1/2 time). Choosing 1/8T or 1/16T lets you program a triplet feel, and raising the resolution from 1/16 to 1/32 doubles the tempo (double-time). This flexibility can be useful for programming beats, making it possible to create a rhythm at a slower tempo and then adjust the resolution to play back at the correct speed. You'll find this useful for creating fast rhythms for jungle-style beats and working in other high-tempo genres.

> When you increase the number of steps or change the resolution setting, you are only working with the currently selected pattern. This will be important to be aware of later in this chapter when you are sequencing multiple patterns to create an arrangement.

Adding Dynamics

The Redrum has a simple built-in feature that you can use to quickly add dynamics to your drum sequences. This is the Dynamic selector located just above the Step Programmer on the left of the interface.

There are several ways to work with the Dynamic selector. The default setting for Redrum's dynamics is Medium. This means that every step you create in the Redrum will be created with a velocity of 80.

One way to work is to create your patterns with medium dynamics, and then select the Hard setting and go through your session clicking any hits that require more force. You can then do the same with the Soft setting, clicking any steps that require less velocity. Clicking any step a second time will delete it.

> Later in this chapter we'll be using the sequencer to adjust the dynamics of our Redrum beats, giving you much more control over the dynamics of your loops and patterns.

You can create an entire pattern with Hard or Soft velocity steps by adjusting the Dynamic selector before you create your pattern. You can also Alt/Option-click any step to create Soft velocity step or Shift-click to create a Hard velocity step.

Flam

Named after a rudimentary drum technique, the Flam button can be used to create the sound of a drummer hitting a drum twice, quickly.

   This can be used to add an element of realism to a drum beat and can also be used to create drum rolls. Here's how to create a drum roll with the Flam button:

1. Create a new Redrum.

2. Turn on the Flam button and adjust the Flam amount knob to 127.

3. Click the Select button to select any channel containing a Snare drum.

4. Click and drag your mouse across the entire Step Programmer to create a flammed snare on every step. You can tell whether the flam is on for any specific step by the light that's just above the step.

5. Click the Run button to start playback.

   Try adding dynamics to the roll by using the Dynamic selector to add Hard and Soft hits to the pattern. Try adjusting the Flam amount for slightly different results. Use a setting in the 105–109 range for an even sound.

Shuffle

Turning on the Shuffle button causes the Redrum to respond to the Global Groove Amount setting in the ReGroove Mixer.

   The Global Groove settings can be used to quickly adjust the rhythmic feel of any or all of the tracks in a Reason song. This feature is covered in more detail in "The ReGroove Mixer" section in Chapter 8. You can try out this feature by following these steps:

1. Make sure that the Flam button is turned off from the previous exercise and create a 16-step Redrum pattern with a hihat on each step. The easiest way to do this is to click on the first step and then hold your mouse down and drag all the way across the Step Programmer.

2. Click the Run button to start playback.

3. Click the ReGroove Mixer button on the Transport panel.

4. Slowly raise the Global Shuffle Amount knob on the bottom left of the ReGroove Mixer.

   This is a quick way to add groove or a "swing" feel to your Redrum beats. As we'll see later, the ReGroove mixer contains much better functionality for achieving the same kind of results, but with more control and variation options.

Creating Arrangements

Now that we have an overview of the Redrum's features and basic drum programming, the real fun starts as we get into creating multiple patterns and variations to use as complete rhythm tracks for your songs.

Banks

Patterns

Figure 4.6

The Pattern Select and Bank Select buttons

Just to the right of the Step Programmer are the four Bank Select and eight Pattern Select buttons, seen in Figure 4.6.

Select any bank by clicking A, B, C, or D. Once a bank is selected, you can then select a pattern from 1 to 8. When you create a new Redrum, Bank A Pattern 1 is selected by default. Using the four banks and eight patterns, you can create up to 32 different patterns to use in any one song. When you want to create a new beat, just choose an empty pattern and create a new rhythm in the Step Programmer.

Creating and Playing Back Multiple Patterns

The first thing you'll need to create an arrangement is multiple drum patterns to arrange. Don't worry about creating the perfect beat right now; you're just going to use a few simple patterns to get a feel for how the pattern sequencing functionality works. Follow these steps to quickly create and play back multiple patterns:

1. Create a new Reason song and add a Redrum Drum Computer; then load any Redrum kit from the Reason Factory Sound Bank.

2. Make sure pattern Bank A - Pattern 1 is selected.

3. Create a simple drum pattern.

Now we're going to copy the pattern you've created on Bank A Pattern 1 to the empty Bank A Pattern 2.

4. Make sure that Redrum is selected and use the keyboard shortcut Ctrl/⌘+C to copy the pattern on Bank A Pattern 1.

5. Select Bank A Pattern 2 and use the keyboard shortcut Ctrl/⌘+V to paste the pattern there.

> You can also use Reason's menu bar to copy and paste patterns by choosing Edit → Copy Pattern and Edit → Paste Pattern. If you have a two-button mouse, you can right-click and select Copy Pattern and then Paste Pattern from the context menu.

6. Use the Step Programmer to create some variation, adding or taking away snare or hihat hits.

7. Use Steps 4 through 6 to copy, paste, and create a third variation on Bank A Pattern 3.

To hear your patterns as a sequence, click the Run button and use your mouse to switch between Patterns A1, A2, and A3 as the Redrum plays.

Recording a Sequencing Pattern

In order to sequence our patterns, we're going to have to use (surprise!) the Reason sequencer. The easiest way to create a sequence of Redrum patterns is to record automation of the Bank Select and Pattern Select buttons in real time. You're going to use the three patterns you created on Bank A in the previous exercise to create your first sequence. As you become more adept at the process, you can try working with more patterns across more banks. Don't worry about sequencing a perfect performance; as you'll see, it's easy to edit an existing sequence and make any needed changes after the recording.

1. Select the Redrum track in the sequencer's track list, as shown in Figure 4.7, and then make sure the track's Record Enable button is on so that the track is armed and ready to receive MIDI information.

2. Select Bank A and Pattern 1.

3. Click the Record button on the Transport panel to begin recording.

4. Switch between beats by using your mouse to switch between patterns and create your sequence.

As soon as you select the second pattern in your sequence, Reason will create a new Pattern lane in the sequencer window, shown in Figure 4.8. On the Pattern lane you'll see your sequence as a series of clips. The clips represent automation that's been recorded into the sequencer. Also, as a result of automation being created, the next time you begin playback of the Reason song you'll see the green outline around the Bank Select and Pattern Select buttons that indicates automation.

The process of creating pattern sequences in real time may be a little awkward at first. A big part of the process is learning exactly when to trigger the next pattern. This involves anticipating the upcoming change and selecting the next pattern a little ahead of the beat. You'll find that with practice, you'll soon develop your own rhythmic flow.

Figure 4.7

The Redrum track header in the sequencer

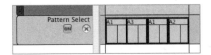

Figure 4.8

The pattern track in the sequencer

Editing a Pattern Sequence in the Sequencer

Even after you've been working with this method of recording sequences for a long time, you'll often find the need to edit your sequences, either to fix mistakes or just to

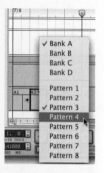

try out new arrangement ideas. Here's how to rearrange your drum sequence in the sequencer:

1. In the sequencer, select any clip in the Redrum's pattern track to highlight it.

2. Click and drag at the top of the selected pattern to move it to a new location in the pattern track.

3. Click the left or right arrows to extend or shorten the pattern.

4. You can create copies of clips by selecting them with your mouse and Alt/Option-dragging.

Another way to alter your clip arrangement is to select and zoom in on any clip, and then click the upside-down arrow near the clip's top-left corner. This opens a pop-up menu (see Figure 4.9), allowing you choose a pattern from any bank and replace the pattern for the selected clip.

> When you're creating patterns for sequencing, it's a good idea to always leave at least one pattern blank for intros and for sections of the song where the drums drop out. You may also want to create patterns containing solo hihat, kick drum, or other isolated instruments for count-offs, breakdowns, and other sections of your arrangement.

Advanced Pattern Programming

If you are new to drum programming or your drum programming abilities can use some improving, Reason has some built-in functionality that can help. Along with some of the techniques you'll be learning in the following sections, one of the best ways to learn about working with the Redrum is to check out how other Reason users work with the instrument. Just go to www.propellerheads.se and click on the Songs link from the menu at the top of the page. Not every Reason song will use a Redrum, so you may have to download a few to find what you're looking for.

Along with the suggestions in this chapter, when it comes to honing your pattern-making skills there's no substitute for trial and error along with lots of experimentation with different sounds and rhythms. Luckily, working with Reason and the Redrum makes this process easy and fun.

Editing Drum Patterns in the Sequencer

Using the Copy to Track functionality of the Redrum opens up an entirely new world of programming and editing possibilities for your drum patterns. Using this method, you can create patterns in the Redrum Step Programmer and then send the MIDI notes to the sequencer for editing and rearranging. You'll also have access to many other features, such as the ReGroove mixer, which we'll cover in this chapter, and other sequencer functionality. Follow these steps to create a drum pattern in the Redrum and edit it in the sequencer:

1. Create a new Redrum, load any Redrum kit, and then create a pattern using the Step Programmer.

2. In the sequencer, we'll get ready to create a four-measure clip by setting the timeline's left locator to the beginning of Bar 1 and the right locator to the end of Bar 4.

3. Choose Edit → Copy Pattern To Track or right/Ctrl-click any empty area on the Redrum and choose Copy Pattern from the context menu. You'll now see that a clip has been created containing your drum pattern on Lane 1 in the Redrum track in the sequencer, shown in Figure 4.10.

Before you click Play on the Transport panel to play the pattern back, it's important to turn off the Enable Pattern Section Playback button on the Redrum.

If you don't do this, Reason will trigger both the MIDI notes in the sequencer and the steps in the Step Programmer, causing a flanged, unclear sound.

This is an easy step to miss and a very common mistake.

4. Double-click the new clip in the sequencer to open the Pattern and Velocity lanes, shown in Figure 4.11.

5. In the Pattern lane, use the Pencil tool to add more notes and the Selection tool to move existing notes around.

6. In the Velocity lane you can use the Pencil tool to raise and lower the velocity of each step in the drum pattern.

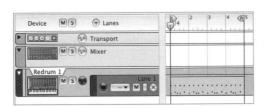

Figure 4.10
The new Redrum clip

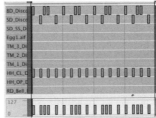

Figure 4.11
The Pattern and Velocity lanes

Creating a Pattern from Scratch

You can also use similar techniques to create a drum track from scratch in the sequencer. Just create a new Redrum, then click the Edit Mode button on the top left of the sequencer to view the instrument's Pattern and Velocity lanes.

Use the Pencil tool to create a clip by clicking and dragging in the Pattern lane and then use the Pencil and Selection tools to create and edit your drum patterns.

This is just the tip of the iceberg when it comes to editing performances in the sequencer, and you'll learn much more about this subject in the "The Sequencer: Advanced" section of Chapter 10.

Recording a Pattern in the Sequencer with MIDI

Another way to create drum and percussion tracks is to use your MIDI keyboard or other controller device to play the samples of a Redrum drum kit. Any Redrum kit can be triggered by playing the 10 notes on your MIDI keyboard that start at C1 (MIDI note 36). If you need more information on MIDI and connecting your MIDI devices, see Chapter 1.

Here's an easy method for using a MIDI controller to play and record a drum pattern in the sequencer:

1. Create a new Reason song with a Redrum Drum Computer.

2. Load any kit from the Reason Factory Sound Bank.

3. Make sure your MIDI controller is connected and powered on, if necessary. Try out your MIDI controller by using the notes C1–A1 to trigger the samples in currently loaded Redrum kit.

4. Turn on Reason's click track and adjust the Click Level volume knob as needed. (See Chapter 2 if you need a refresher.)

5. Click on the Pre button to activate Reason's Precount functionality for a four-beat count-in.

6. Check the Loop On/Off button on the Transport panel to make sure Reason's looping functionality is turned off.

7. Click the Record button in the Transport panel, wait for the count-off, and begin recording.

This is a very efficient method to use if you're confident in your real-time playing skills. If you are just starting out with this kind of recording, give yourself some time to practice and improve your playing skills. This method is a good way to create drum tracks with the built-in dynamics and imperfections that come from a "live" performance.

Editing and Arranging Recorded Patterns

Once you have recorded a pattern, you can edit it using the same editing techniques covered earlier in this chapter. You can also create arrangements of multiple recordings by using the Play locator to begin recording at different places in the sequencer timeline and then using the Selector tool to resize and move different clips.

If you are adept at playing rhythmic performances on a MIDI keyboard, this method can be a great way to create your drum tracks. However, if you don't have too much experience or rhythmic ability, this process will often involve overdubbing, quantization, and taking advantage of features of the sequencer. These and more are covered in the "The Sequencer: Advanced" section of Chapter 10.

Using the Randomize Features

The Redrum includes some interesting randomization functionality that can be quite useful for quickly creating interesting and unusual patterns. By utilizing some of the skills we've covered earlier in this chapter, you can also use the randomization feature as the starting point for more straightforward patterns. Let's take a step-by-step look at the basics of this interesting feature:

1. Create a new session with a Mixer 14:2 and a Redrum or choose Edit → Init Patch to clear the currently loaded instrument.

2. Use the Browse Patch button to open the Browser and load any Redrum drum kit.

3. Click any empty area on the Redrum interface to make sure the instrument is selected and highlighted.

4. Choose Edit → Randomize Pattern or access Randomize Pattern by right/Ctrl-clicking to view the context menu.

5. Click the Run button or start playback in the Transport panel to hear the newly created pattern.

What Reason has done here is create a rhythmic pattern by randomly placing notes in the step sequencer. It's randomly selected dynamics for the pattern as well. Since it's completely random, the pattern will sometimes seem like a noisy mess. Quite often, however, Reason will create a pattern that is usable or close to usable.

You can quickly make minor (or major) adjustments to a random Redrum pattern and turn it into a usable performance. Here are some suggestions for using the randomize functionality as a starting point for creating drum patterns:

- Use the keyboard shortcut Ctrl/⌘+J to shift the pattern one step to the left and use Ctrl/⌘+K to shift to the pattern one step to the right.

- With the pattern playing back, use the Mute (M) and Solo (S) buttons at the top of each channel strip to hear which samples and patterns sound good. For example, try soloing the kick and snare, then adding the hihat or a percussion sample. If a particular sample sounds loud and out-of place, use the Mute button to turn it off.

- Use your mouse to eliminate those notes that don't work in the Step Programmer, or to create additional steps to add to the rhythm.

- Use the Dynamic selector to raise or lower the velocity of any hits that need to be harder or softer.

- Work specifically with the kick drum and snare drum samples to make sure that they are being triggered at "standard" points within the sequence: for example, kick drum on beats 1 and 9 and snare on 5 and 13.

Along with Randomize Pattern, there's also a Randomize Drum option. This works in exactly the same way but randomizes only the currently selected channel. To use this feature, click the Select button at the bottom of any channel strip and choose Edit → Randomize Drum from the menu bar.

Altering a Pattern

Similar to the Randomize features are the Alter features, also found on the Edit menu. Choosing Edit → Alter Pattern or using the keyboard shortcut Ctrl/⌘+T will create a new pattern from the existing steps currently programmed in the Redrum. So if you have four kick drum hits and two snare hits, choosing Alter Pattern will create a new pattern with the same number of kicks and snares, assigned to different steps in the Step Programmer. You can also use the Alter feature on a single, selected channel by choosing Edit → Alter Drum.

Channel 8&9 Exclusive

Activating the Channel 8&9 Exclusive button means that any sample played on Channel 9 will silence any sample played on Channel 8.

When a sample on Channel 8 is played after a sample on Channel 9, Channel 9's output (the decay part of a sample) will be also be silenced. This may sound a bit confusing, but it's useful for creating open/closed hihat rhythms, and as a result you will often find closed hihat samples on Channel 8 of Redrum kits and open hihat samples on Channel 9. Here's how to use Channel 8&9 Exclusive functionality on a hihat rhythm:

1. Create a Redrum and load the Groovemasters Kit1.drp.

2. Click the Select button on Channel 8 and then click and drag your mouse across each step in the Step Programmer.

3. Click the Run button to start playback.

4. Click the Select button on Channel 9, then add two or three steps of open hihat anywhere in the Step Programmer.

5. Turn the Channel 8&9 Exclusive button on and off to hear the difference.

Matching a Dr. Rex Loop

Another way to work on your drum programming skills is to create a drum track with a Dr. Rex Loop Player and then try to re-create it with the Redrum. Along with honing your programming skills, this method can also be useful for beefing up an existing beat or coming up with new variations on a rhythmic that you like.

The process is very simple. Just create a new Reason song with a Dr. Rex and a Redrum. Locate a REX beat that you like and use the Copy to Track function to send it to the sequencer.

Select and load any Redrum Drum Kit; then with the Dr. Rex loop playing, try matching the beat in real time. Start with either the kick drum or the snare drum, and then move on to the cymbals and percussion. You may find that it's impossible to truly mimic certain beats, especially complicated rhythms with a lot of groove, variation, and performance dynamics. But even if you are unable to make a "perfect" re-creation, this kind of experiment will often lead you to creating interesting patterns of your own, as well as give you insight into the kinds of elements that make up a good beat.

Creating and Saving Kits

Redrum can easily be used to create your own custom kits from Wave or AIFF samples, SoundFonts (.sf2 format), or the individual slices that make up a REX file, or any combination of the three. You can create your kits from scratch or mix and match samples from existing kits, ReFills, and your own samples. Redrum's editing and saving functionality also makes it easy to edit and save an existing kit with major or minor changes, such as variations of level, velocity, pitch, panning, and other settings.

Editing the Samples

Within the Redrum interface are a number of parameters, specifically chosen to work with drum and percussion samples. These parameters can be used to great effect with other types of samples as well. All of Redrum's sample editing functionality is found in the instrument's individual channel strips.

Common Channel Strip Parameters

Each channel strip shares some basic functionality. Figure 4.12 shows the common parameters found on each of the Redrum's channels. The best way to try out the various parameters is to create a new Redrum, load any kit, create some patterns, then make adjustments to each parameter in real time.

Mute Use the Mute button to silence playback of any channel.

Solo Use the Solo button to hear any selected channel by itself. Multiple channels can be muted or soloed at once.

Trigger Use the Trigger button to preview the sample that's currently loaded.

Sample Display The Sample Display shows the name of the current sample. Clicking the display's LCD will open a list of all the sample files residing in the same directory.

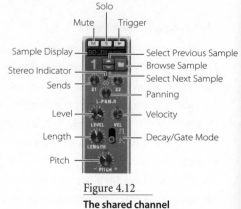

Figure 4.12

The shared channel strip parameters

Just below the Sample Display, the next three buttons function similarly to the Browse Patch functionality:

Select Previous Sample Selects the previous sample in the current directory

Select Next Sample Selects the next sample in the current directory

Browse Sample Opens the Reason Browser, letting you search for any sample files that the Redrum can load

The rest of the parameters are all specifically related to how the file is heard, routed, altered, and played back by Redrum:

The Sends Labeled S1 and S2, when a Redrum is created two effects sends are automatically routed to the mixer. For more on this see, the "Using Effects with the Redrum" section later in this chapter.

Stereo Indicator If a stereo sample is currently loaded into a channel, this LCD lights up.

Panning Allows you to adjust the left or right panning of the sample. This is especially useful in creating realistic sounding drum kits.

Level and Velocity These two knobs control the overall output of each individual channel.

Length The Length knob controls the amount of time a selected sample will be played. Reducing the length can be useful when dealing with a sample that's too long. It can also result in a shorter, unnaturally clipped sound, especially when the channel is in Gate mode.

Decay/Gate Mode Decay mode allows a sample to die out naturally; Gate mode causes the sample to be cut short. Each channel on the Redrum is set by default to Decay mode.

Pitch The Pitch control can be used to raise or lower the pitch of a sample. This can have a dramatic effect.

Using just these basic parameters, you can come up with lots of different effects and find a number of interesting ways to work with the sounds contained in your Redrum kits.

As you can see, there are some other parameters on individual channels that I haven't covered here. We'll look at these individual channel strip parameters next.

Individual Channel Strip Parameters

There are also individual controls assigned to various channels. These are designed to work with specific types of drum samples and are found on the channels most commonly associated with those types. Channels 1 and 2 will often be kick drum and snare drum, Channels 6 and 7 will often be Toms, and Channels 8 and 9 will often be closed and open hihats, respectively. On Channel 10 you'll often find a Crash or Ride cymbal.

Start and Velocity Channels 3, 4, 5, 8, and 9 have Start and Velocity knobs.

The Start knob controls the point within the sample where playback will begin when the sample is triggered. This tool can be used to diminish a sample's harsh attack or to cut out unnecessary silence at the beginning of a sample. The Velocity To Sample Start knob can be used to determine by velocity when the sample begins playback.

Tone and Velocity Controls Channels 1, 2, and 10 have Tone and Velocity knobs.

Used by itself the Tone knob is a basic EQ. Lowering the knob results in a lower (more bass frequencies) tone. Raising the knob results in a higher (more treble frequencies) tone. Using it in conjunction with the Velocity knob, however, things get a bit more interesting. By adjusting the tone and volume knobs in opposite directions, you can create more realistic drum performances by raising the tone automatically, in conjunction with the velocity of a performance.

To get an idea of how this works, create a snare drum pattern with a soft, medium, and hard snare drum. Then adjust the Tone knob all the way to the left and the Velocity all the way to the right. Use the Dynamic selector to program Hard, Soft, and Medium hits on the selected channel to hear the difference these adjustments make.

Bend, Rate, and Velocity Controls Channels 6 and 7 have Pitch, Bend, Rate, and Velocity controls.

These controls can be used in conjunction with the Dynamic selector, your MIDI keyboard, or the Velocity lane in the Reason sequencer to create changes in how the channel's currently loaded sample is played based on the velocity of the note used to trigger it. To get an idea of how these parameters work, load the Groovemasters Rock Kit 1.drp from the Reason Factory Sound Bank. Select Channel 6 and program drum hits using the Dynamic selector to choose Hard and Soft velocities. Raise the Pitch and Bend knobs; then lower the Velocity setting. Try adjusting the Rate for faster or slower changes to the sound.

Editing Existing Kits

One way to quickly create your own Redrum drum kits is to use an existing kit and make some changes. Many Reason users find that the Redrum kits that are included in the Reason Factory Sound Bank and other ReFills are quite good, but can benefit from slight adjustments or from switching out one or two samples with better sounds. For example, you can quickly switch out kick drums in most patches by clicking the Select Next Sample and Select Previous Sample buttons on Channel 1and trying out other kick drum samples that reside in the current sample's folder. If you are not happy with any of those sounds, click the Browse Sample button and navigate to an entirely new folder of samples.

You can take this a step further by creating a drum pattern and switching out sample types as well. For example, create a beat with a good hihat pattern, then replace the hihat with a snare drum, a noise effect, a musical note, or any other sample.

Switching Out Samples

Combining your favorite samples from different Redrum kits is easy and can be used to create new and interesting kits. Follow these steps to create and save a custom kit from the samples included on the Reason Factory Sound Bank:

1. Create a new Redrum and load any drum kit from the Reason Factory Sound Bank\ Redrum Kits folder.

   At the top of each Redrum channel are the Browse Sample button and the Select Next Sample and Select Previous Sample arrows. Just above the Browse and Select Sample buttons you'll see the LCD displaying the name of the current sample loaded into the channel.

2. Click on Channel 1's LCD to view a list of the samples that reside in the same folder as the sample that's currently loaded on Channel 1 (Figure 4.13).

3. Select any of the files on the list to replace the current sample.

Figure 4.13
Click on a channel's LCD to view samples in the same folder as the channel's current sample.

For even more samples to choose from, follow these steps:

1. Click Channel 1's Browse Sample button to view the current folder where this channel's drum sample is located.

2. Use the Browser's navigation drop-down menu to go up a level, where you'll see that this folder is one of many containing drum samples that make up the included Reason Redrum kits (Figure 4.14).

Figure 4.14

Navigating up one folder level gives you access to even more samples.

3. Open any folder and you'll see more individual samples. Using the Browser, any one of these samples can be loaded into any channel on the Redrum.

4. Make sure that the Browser's Autoplay functionality is on, then select any individual sample to preview it. When you find a sample you like, click the OK button to load it into Channel 1, replacing the original sample.

After switching out a few samples and creating your own kit, click the Save Patch button, then choose a name and location for your new kit.

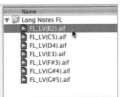

Creating New Kits from Scratch

In the previous example you saw how you could take any ReFill sample and switch it with another to create a new kit. When creating your own kits, you can actually draw from any number of resources to create a single kit, including sample CDs, ReFills, loop libraries, or any collection of Redrum-compatible sound files. Follow these steps to create a brand-new Redrum drum kit from a variety of sources, file types, and locations:

1. Create a new Reason song and add a Redrum.

2. Next, use Channel 1's Browse Sample button to open the Browser.

3. Navigate to the folder `Reason Factory Sound Bank\Other Samples\FX - Vox`. Any of these `.aif` samples can be loaded into any channel of the Redrum.

4. Use Channel 2's Browse Sample button to navigate to open the Browser. Select the `Orkester Sound Bank\Percussion` instrument category folder. Select any instrument and open one of its subdirectories. What you're seeing in this folder are some of the individual `.aif` samples that make up the Orkester's NN-19 and NN-XT sampler patches. Once again, any of these can be loaded into the Redrum and used on any channel.

Using the Browse Sample button, you can load content from the included Reason Factory Sound Bank, Orkester Sound Bank, and just about any Refill. This includes the individual samples that make up Redrum kits, as well as the samples that make up patches for the NN-19 and NN-XT samplers, and the slices that make up REX files. In other words, excluding patches for Reason's synthesizers, almost all of the content you'll find on just about any ReFill can, in some way, be used in the Redrum.

Moving on, you are not at all limited to ReFill content for your Redrum kits. Let's take a couple more samples from a totally different source to add to your kit:

5. Use Channel 3's Browse Sample button to open the Browser and locate the folder containing the example files for this chapter. Locate the folder `Examples\Chapter 4\ Samples` and select any file.

6. Click Channel 4's Browse Sample button and use the Browser to locate the folder `Examples\Chapter 4\Rex Loops`.

7. Double-click any Rex loop to view its individual slices; then select any slice and click OK to load it as a sample.

8. Click the Save Patch button and choose a name and location for your new Redrum drum kit.

Keeping It All Together

If you are going to be creating Redrum kits from various sources, it's a good idea to get organized early on. Let's say you create a kit from a combination of samples from different sources. If you move any of these original source files, the next time you try to load your kit with Redrum's Browse Patch button or open a Reason song that uses that uses your kit, Reason will present you with the Search dialog. The process of scanning your entire hard drive for a missing file or files can take quite a while. And if you've moved the sample off your hard drive altogether, you may not be able to locate it at all.

If possible, you may want to create a folder specifically for samples that you plan to use in Redrum kits and then keep that folder in a set location. Name your folder **Redrum Samples** or **Reason Samples** and keep it together with your other Reason-related files and folders.

RULES AND REGULATIONS

You may have noticed that among various Redrum kits there are no set rules to what kinds of drum samples should be loaded into specific channel strips. In general, you'll find that many Redrum kits contain some kind of kick drum sample in Channel 1, but from there things can go in any direction. Sometimes a second, alternative kick will found on Channel 2—often it will be a snare drum sample, but it's just as possible to find a percussion or sound effect there as well.

This can be both good and bad when it comes to working with multiple kits. The good part is that when you create a beat with one kit and then use the Browse Patch functionality to load another kit, you can sometimes come up with interesting results.

When creating your own original kits, you may want to create certain rules for yourself—for example, Channel 1 for kick drum sounds, Channels 2 and 3 for snare sounds, and Channels 4 and 5 for toms or other percussion. Channels 8 and 9 are often used for closed hihat and open hihat, respectively, in order to take advantage of the Redrum's "8&9 exclusive" functionality.

Playing REX Slices

As we saw briefly in the previous example, along with Wave, AIFF, and SoundFont files, the Redrum also has the ability to load and play back the individual slices that make up REX format files. This includes the current `.rx2` format as well as the older Rex formats, `.rcy` and `.rx1`.

REX slices can make particularly good drum samples because they are often taken directly from well-recorded human drum performances.

Here's how to use one of Reason's included REX files to create a Redrum kit:

1. Create a new session with a Redrum drum computer.

2. Use Channel's 1's Browse Sample button to open the Browser.

3. Use the Browser to navigate to `Reason Factory Sound Bank\DRRexLoops\Abstract Hip Hop`.

4. You can treat the individual REX files just like folders containing samples. To view the individual slices that make up a REX file, you can either click the triangle next to the file name to view the file's contents or double-click the file to open it and see the available slices (Figure 4.15).

5. For your kick drum, select the first slice of the loop, `Trh01_Soleside_80_eLab.rx2 [0]`, and click OK to load it into Channel 1 of the Redrum.

6. Click the Browse Sample button on Channel 2 and the Browser will automatically take you to the same directory. For your snare drum, select `Trh01_Soleside_80 _eLab.rx2 [2]`.

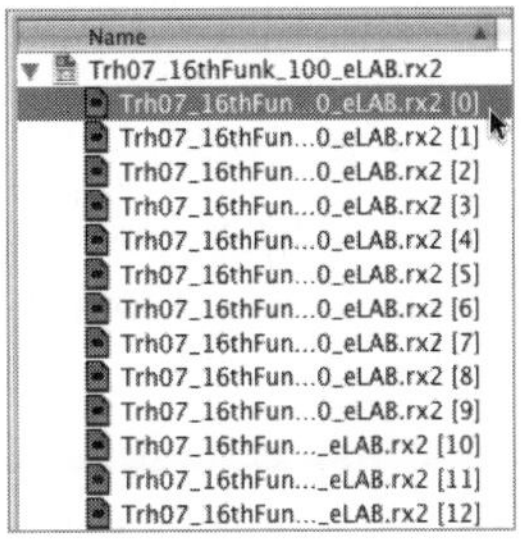

Figure 4.15

Viewing the individual slices that make up a REX file

From here you can click each channel's Browse Sample button, use the Browser to preview the sound of each slice, and load whichever samples you'd like to use to create your kit.

Try this method with a non-percussion loop. Along with being a nice way to quickly create Redrum drum kits from a drum loop, this method can also be used to create unexpected melodic performances. Try using these same steps to load the slices from a REX file of an instrument loop, then sequencing the slices to create an entirely new performance. Take it even further by editing the slices with the Channel Strip parameters or adding effects.

A DIFFERENT VIEW

The exercise on loading and playing REX slices in the Redrum is a great example of how different instruments will "see" files differently in the Reason Browser. The Redrum sees each .rx2 loop file as a folder containing individual .rx2 drum hits. If you were using the Browser to preview and load this file into a Dr. Rex Loop Player, you'd only have the option of loading it as a complete file—Reason wouldn't even show you the slices. On the other hand, if you wanted to load this same file into an NN-19 or an NN-XT sampler, you might see either option, depending on whether you were using those instruments' Browse Patch or Browse Sample buttons.

Automating the Redrum

Earlier we looked at creating a sequence by selecting different patterns and recording our selection in real time to create and save a drum sequence. You may have noticed that once this recording was done, we were able to see a green outline around the Pattern buttons. This is the indicator of automation.

In Reason, when it comes to creating automation there aren't a lot of limits to what you can and can't do. With the Redrum you can automate all of the knobs on each channel strip. To get an idea of what this means for your creative possibilities, try loading a Redrum kit, setting up a four-measure loop, and clicking the Record button on the Transport panel.

Follow these steps to automate a hihat sample's pitch and panning parameters:

1. Create a new Redrum and load any kit that contains a hihat sample.

2. Click the Select button on the channel strip containing the hihat sample.

3. Click and drag across the Step Programmer to trigger the hihat on each step.

4. Use the left and right locators in the Reason sequencer timeline to create a four-measure loop. Turn Reason's looping functionality on.

5. Click the Record button in the Transport panel to begin recording.

6. Adjust the Pan knob and the Pitch knob.

This also creates two new tracks in the sequencer that we can also copy and paste along with our track data. We'll look at copying and pasting as well as drawing automation in more detail in Chapter 10.

Creating Your Own Redrum Samples

One of the best ways to get really creative with Redrum is to create your own drum, percussion, or other sound samples. You can use these original sounds to build your own individual kits, or just add them to the collections of sounds that you choose from when building new kits. There are an infinite number of possibilities here, from the more obvious, such as taking individual drum or percussion sounds from a CD, record or MP3, to the more esoteric. When you think about it, pretty much any sound that you can hear can be recorded and with a bit of audio editing can be saved as a Wave or AIFF file.

Chapter 6 contains information on creating your own samples from a variety of sources.

Using Effects with the Redrum

Using Reason's built-in effects is a great way to make your beats and sample patterns more interesting. Effects can be used to work with standard recording and mixing techniques that are often used to help tracks stand out in a mix, such as using reverb and compression. Along with these standard techniques, Reason's effects and routing capabilities make much more possible. In the next few examples, I'll cover some frequently used techniques and also give you some direction toward accessing some more creative options for working with the Redrum.

As you saw in Chapter 2, you can add effects in Reason songs either as inserts or sends. You can add up to four send effects to a Reason song by selecting the Mixer 14:2 and using the Create menu or the Tools window.

The Redrum has some unique functionality in this regard—you can access the first two send effects on the Mixer 14:2 on any Redrum channel by using the S1 and S2 knobs at the top of each channel strip.

Using Send and Insert Effects

Open the Reason Song file Examples\Chapter 4\Songs\RedrumSends.rns to see a typical Reason song with an RV7000 and a DDL-1 Delay used as send effects. Try adjusting the S1 and S2 knobs on each channel to increase or decrease the amount of each effect being applied to the channel. Using this method you can access effects for individual channels. For example, you can use this to add reverb to a snare drum, or delay to a hihat while leaving your other channels "dry."

By using insert effects with Redrum, you can quickly add an effect to an entire drum pattern or sequence. You can add insert effects by selecting your Redrum in the Reason rack and choosing an effect from the Create menu or the Tools window. This will automatically route the output of your Redrum to the input of the new effect. You can create a chain of insert effects by selecting the last effect and creating a new one.

The output of your insert effects will be automatically routed to the Mixer 14:2. The track's name on the Mixer 14:2 will change to reflect the name of the last effect in your chain. Figure 4.16 shows the automatically created insert effects routing with a Redrum and an RV7000 Advanced Reverb.

Figure 4.16
**Redrum's insert
effects routing**

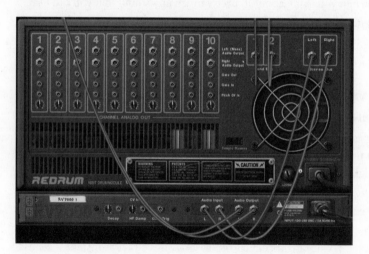

Adding Reverb

Adding reverb to digitally created drum tracks is one of the most commonly used techniques for adding ambience or mimicking the sound of a live recording.

In live or studio recording sessions, reverb can often be achieved by using room microphones, which pick up the sound of the concert hall or the recording studio. Even in these cases, reverb will often be added in the mixing process, using either hardware or software effects units to create an even more realistic sound.

Since digital music creation in general and virtual drum instruments in particular do not involve actual recording, we're faced with an entirely different challenge. Many virtual drum kits, including some of Reason's Redrum kits, contain samples that have reverb added. For an example of this, check out the Rim_DubHead.WAV on Channel 10 in Dub Kit 01.

More often than not, however, kits will be created with a minimum of reverb, so that users can add as much or as little as they think the track, song, or session needs.

Both of Reason's included reverb effects, the RV-7 Digital Reverb and the RV700 Advanced Reverb, can be used to add reverb to Redrum tracks as either insert or send effects. The RV-7 is simple and easy to use, and it also takes up significantly less of your processor's resources than the RV7000.

The RV7000, however, has much more going on, including a whole range of editable parameters that can be used for greater control over your reverb effects. The RV7000 can also to create echo effects, "backwards" effects, and more. Both the RV-7 and the RV7000 are covered in Chapter 7.

Adding Compression

Compressing the dynamic range of a performance is an important part of any mix and we'll be looking at it in more detail in both Chapter 7 and Chapter 10.

One of the most common uses of compression is on drum tracks. With a digital drum machine like Redrum, you'll have the opposite problem that's faced by engineers recording live drums. With a live drummer the goal is often to tame or control the dynamics of performance by using compression to achieve a consistent volume level in a recording. With a digital performance, we're often looking in the opposite direction—trying to add elements that mimic the imperfections of a human performance.

At the same time, other uses of compression include bringing out the harmonic overtones of a specific instrument and "pumping" an instrument (or drum set) up in the mix. This is definitely a concept that will have varied amounts of usefulness depending on a number of factors, including the specific drum samples you are using and the range of dynamics you've created with programming or with the ReGroove mixer.

Most important, as with any audio effect or mixing concept, you'll want to take the specific song or project you are working on into consideration, judging for yourself what sounds best in the final mix. Here are some ways to use Reason's compression effects to improve your Redrum tracks:

Use the Comp-01 You can add the Comp-01 as an insert effect with high Ratio, low Threshold, high Attack, and low Release settings to quickly "pump" your track. Try experimenting with various settings for subtle or obvious changes to your drum tracks.

Use the MClass Compressor The MClass compressor is a more advanced compression effect than the Comp-01. For a thicker drum sound, try increasing the Input Gain setting and raising the Compression Ratio, then adjusting the Threshold, Attack, and Release settings.

Use the MClass Maximizer The MClass Maximizer is Limiter, which is essentially a powerful compressor, geared toward making a specific track or an entire mix sound louder.

Use the MClass Combi If you are using the built-in template, the MClass Mastering Suite Combi will be automatically added to your Reason songs between the Mixer 14:2 and the Hardware Device. You can also use the MClass Mastering Suite Combi as an insert effect to quickly beef up the sound of your drums.

More Effects Ideas

The following ideas are just a few of the available options for using Reason's effects with the Redrum. Try experimenting with combinations of effects as inserts, sends, or both to come up with your own sounds and mix ideas. Chapter 7 and Chapter 8 both have more information and ideas for using effects and for creative routing possibilities.

Using Delay

Adding a delay as an insert effect and delaying your entire drum mix can lead to a big messy sound, but using a delay as a send effect on the main mixer and then bringing it into your drum mixes has endless uses. This can be great when automated for occasional effect or used to create new rhythmic patterns when applied to a snare, hihat, or any one or more samples in your kit.

Quick and Dirty Tricks with the Scream 4 Distortion

One way to quickly create drums that stand out is to add a Scream 4 Distortion unit as an insert or send effect. This can be used as a compressor for a subtle effect or boost, or it can be used to create a range of different types of distortion. The various presets that come with the Scream 4 are a good starting point. To instantly create a lo-fi drum sound, try some of the patches in the Drum Processing folder or add some analog-style warmth with the patches in the Warm Saturation folder. The Instrument tweaks and Fidelity FX folders contain patches that can be used to make your drum tracks nearly unrecognizable.

You can add distortion, warmth, or other effects as send effects to individual drums and samples or to an entire Redrum performance.

Flange and Phase

Adding a flange or phase effect can be very interesting with drums. This especially useful for breakdowns and any sections where your drums are soloed. You can also try adding a Phase or Flange as a send effect and using it on your hihat, percussion, or snare channels for some interesting results.

Once again you have the option to bring Reason's automation functionality into the mix here. Remember that for send effects you can automate the two sends on each Redrum channel and the overall mix send on the mixer's Aux Send 1 knob. The various parameters on your insert effects can be automated as well.

Redrum and the ReGroove Mixer

Reason 4's new ReGroove mixer can add an amazing new element to your Redrum patterns and sequences. As you've seen, the Redrum has lots of great features and in past versions or Reason it's always been possible (if a bit complicated) to adjust, humanize, and add an element of groove to your Redrum tracks. The ReGroove mixer and the new sequencer functionality take this kind of functionality to a whole new level.

The ReGroove is covered in detail in its own section in Chapter 8, but since it's especially useful with the Redrum, it's a good idea to cover the basics of using these two devices here.

The first element in this process is sending your Redrum pattern to a sequencer track, since the ReGroove mixer only works in conjunction with recorded data on sequencer tracks. Here's how to get started using the ReGroove on your Redrum tracks:

1. Create a new Reason song with a Redrum.

2. Load the kit `Reason Factory Sound Bank\Redrum Drum Kits\Groovemasters Kit1.drp`.

3. Program a beat using the default settings. Any kind of kick/snare rhythm will work, but in order to really experience the ReGroove, program the hihat on every step.

4. In the sequencer, use the left and right locators to create a four-measure loop.

5. Select the Redrum in the rack and choose Edit → Copy Pattern To Track. You've now created a new clip containing the MIDI notes that make up your beat. Make sure you turn off the Pattern Enable Section button on the Redrum interface to avoid triggering the performance in Redrum and the sequencer simultaneously.

6. Click the ReGroove Mixer button on the Transport panel to make the device visible.

7. On the Redrum track header in the sequencer, click the Select Groove drop-down menu and choose A1.

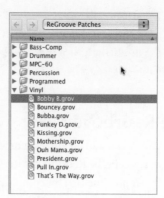

Figure 4.17

**Click the Browse
Groove Patch
button.**

8. Channel A1 on the ReGroove is the first channel, on the left side of the device. Click the Browse Groove Patch (the folder icon) on Channel A1 to open the Reason Browser. Locate the folder Reason Factory Sound Bank\ReGroove Patches\Vinyl and select the patch Bobby B.grov and click OK to load it (Figure 4.17).

Click the spacebar to begin playback and you'll hear the effect that the current Groove Patch is having on the beat. You can use the on/off LCD at the top of the ReGroove Channel A1 for a before-and-after comparison. Use the Select Next Patch and Select Previous Patch buttons to try out different grooves.

If you are happy with a specific Groove Patch, you can apply it permanently to any clip by selecting Commit To Groove from the Select Groove drop-down menu.

The workflow that you use to work with the ReGroove and your Redrum tracks is entirely up to you. One possibility is to create a complete drum sequence or a set of patterns in the Redrum, send them to your sequencer track, then experiment with different settings with the ReGroove mixer. Another option would be to create multiple clips and use Reason's looping functionality to preview and commit different grooves to different clips.

All of these options and more are covered in the ReGroove section of Chapter 8.

In the rest of the chapter you'll apply the basics you've learned to some Redrum projects.

Make sure you've followed the instructions in Chapter 2 for setting Reason's Preferences before you begin the examples in this chapter.

Creating and Exporting Loops

The Redrum is a fantastic tool for creating original drum loops. Using the Redrum's pattern programming along with Reason's looping and exporting functionality, you can quickly establish a workflow that can be used to easily create loops for use in Sony's Acid, Apple's GarageBand, Ableton Live, and other loop-based DAW programs. Using the ReCycle program covered in Chapter 3, you can also create loops for reuse in your Reason songs in the Dr. Rex Loop Player. Here's how to quickly create and export a drum loop with the Redrum:

1. Create a new Reason song with a Redrum.

2. Load any Redrum drum kit.

3. Program a drum rhythm.

4. Use the left and right locators in the sequencer to create a two-, four-, or eight-measure loop.

5. Select File → Export Loop As Audio File from Reason's menu bar.

In the first dialog that appears, choose a name and location for the new loop. You'll also have the option to choose between AIFF and Wave formats. Generally speaking, if you are working on a Mac you'll want to choose AIFF format and on Windows, the Wave format. However, either format is fine and both are essentially interchangeable.

Next you'll have the option for choosing the sample rate and bit depth. If you are familiar with these options and know that you'll be working with your loops in higher sample/bit sessions, you can choose the appropriate settings here. For maximum compatibility with other programs, or if you are not sure which settings to choose, go with the default Sample Rate setting of 44,100 Hz and a Bit Depth value of 16. More information on sample rates and bit depths can be found in the "Sampler Basics" section in Chapter 6.

Some important things to take into consideration when creating loops for exporting:

• Make sure that any delay or reverb effects don't go over the end of the loop. If delay or reverb effects are cut off too quickly at the end of a loop, it will sound unnatural as the loop starts again from the beginning.

• Check the output level on the ReMix's Master Track. If your signal is too loud, adjust the volume on the Redrum or on the Redrum's track in the Mixer 14:2.

Creative Routing with the Redrum

Along with the standard mono and stereo output options, the back of the Redrum also has Gate Out, Gate In, and Pitch CV In. Each of these represents an entire range of creative uses, including the ability to use the Redrum to play and affect other devices and the ability to connect other Reason devices to the Redrum in strange and unexpected ways.

Creating Individual Outputs

One way to take advantage of the Redrum's routing options is to send the instrument's outputs to individual tracks in a new Mixer 14:2. This is sometimes known as creating a "submix," and gives you the advantage of having even more control over levels, panning, and effects. Having control over all of your drum tracks in a Mixer 14:2 and being able to work with levels using faders instead of knobs also allows you a much better visual representation of what's going on with each track. Follow these steps to create your own submix configuration with a Redrum and a Mixer 14:2:

1. Create a new Reason song.

2. We want to create our own routing for these devices so we're going to add Mixer 14:2 and a Redrum to our session as unconnected devices. To do this, hold down the Shift key and choose Create → Mixer 14:2.

3. Next, hold down the Shift key and add a Redrum.

4. Rename the song's default Mixer 14:2 **Main Mix**.

5. Rename the second Mixer 14:2 **Drum Mix**.

6. Use the Tab key to view the routing of the Reason rack.

Now we're going to use Reason's flexible routing features to assign each of our drum tracks to its own Mixer 14:2 track.

1. Click and drag the Left (Mono) Audio Output for Channel 1 on the Redrum to the Left (Mono) Audio Input of the Drum Mix Mixer 14:2. This will automatically create stereo routing for the channel, giving you access to the left/right panning features of a stereo track.

2. Using the same method, connect outputs 2–10 on the Redrum to inputs 2–10 on the Drum Mix.

3. Now connect the Master Outs of the Drum Mix device to Track 1 on the Main Mix device.

At this point you can load any Redrum drum kit and program a beat. To test out your new mixing options, create a pattern using multiple channels and use the Drum Mix mixer to adjust panning and volume for each Redrum channel.

If you'd like to route send effects to your submix, select the Drum Mix Mixer 14:2 and add any effect. You'll have to manually connect the Send Outs 1 and 2 from the Redrum to the Left (mono) Chaining Aux inputs on the Drum Mix Mixer 14:2.

Figure 4.18 shows the complete routing from the Redrum to the Drum Mix mixer.

Once you've completed all of the necessary routing, use the Tab key to flip the rack back around to the front view so you can work with the individual channels on the Drum Mix mixer.

Figure 4.18

The routing from the Redrum to the Drum Mix Mixer 14:2

COMBINATE IT

You'll be learning much more later on in this book about Reason's Combinator device, but for right now the Redrum submix you've just set up is a great chance to save your routing as a recallable combinator for quick and easy access to any Reason song. Just use your mouse to select the Drum Mix mixer, the Redrum, and any send effects you've created, then choose Edit → Combine. Click the Save Patch button on the Combinator interface to save your new Combinator patch. You can find an example of a submix Combinator patch on the accompanying CD in the folder Examples\Chapter 4\Patches\DrumSub.cmb.

Controlling Redrum with the Matrix

The Redrum's Gate In and Pitch CV In can be used along with Matrix Pattern Sequencer to come up with some unique sounds and patterns. Follow these steps to use Reason's two pattern devices to create some interesting and unusual sounds and patterns:

1. Create a new Reason song and add a Redrum.

2. Hold down the Shift key and create an unconnected Matrix Pattern Sequencer.

3. Use the Tab key to view the routing options on the back of the Reason rack. Route the Gate CV from the Matrix to the Gate In on Redrum's Channel 1.

4. Route the Curve CV output on the Matrix to the Pitch CV In of Channel 1, as shown in Figure 4.19.

5. Use the Tab key to view the front of the rack.

6. Switch the Matrix into Curve Edit mode and use your mouse to draw some variations in the Curve Edit display.

Figure 4.19

Gate CV and Note CV routing from the Matrix to the Redrum

Click Channel 1's Browse Sample button and load any sample. At this point you've got virtually unlimited options. Any sample, Wave or AIFF loop or REX slice, can be loaded and used for this experiment. Some will, of course, work much better than others. I recommend starting with some of the samples contained in the folder `Reason Factory Sound Bank\Redrum Drum Kits\xclusive drums-sorted`.

To get an idea of some of the possibilities here, select the Matrix and create a random pattern by using the keyboard shortcut Ctrl/⌘+R or by choosing Edit → Randomize Pattern.

7. Click the Play button on the Transport panel to begin playback of the pattern.

What's happening here is that the Gate CV output of the Matrix Pattern Sequencer is being used to trigger whatever sample you've loaded into Channel 1, while the Curve CV is being used to alter the pitch of the sample.

Here you can work with the techniques covered earlier in the "The Matrix Pattern Sequencer: Basics" section of Chapter 2. For more control over the pattern's rhythm, you can draw your own patterns by working with the Gate velocity values at the bottom of the Matrix interface.

Try this technique out on a wide range of samples, including sound effects and loops.

As always, with the Matrix there are more possibilities for routing, triggering, and altering playback. Take some time to try out each possible connection and programming option. For example, try routing Note CV instead of Curve CV to the Pitch CV input on the Redrum.

Another option for using a similar technique is to create multiple Matrix Pattern Sequencers and routing the Gate CV from each one to trigger different samples.

Using One Redrum to Trigger Another

The Redrum's Gate Out functionality can be used to trigger other devices, including another Redrum. Here's a quick way to set up a triplet feel by using one Redrum's Gate Out to trigger a second Redrum. Follow these steps to use one Redrum to trigger another:

1. Create a new Reason song and add a Redrum. Name it **MainDrum**.

2. Load the `Groovemansters Rock Kit 1.drp` kit from the `Reason Factory Sound Bank\Redrum Drum Kits` folder.

3. Hold down the Shift key to add a second, unconnected Redrum to your Reason song. Name the unconnected Redrum **Trigger**.

4. Create a simple kick/snare pattern on the first Redrum. I suggest starting with a kick on the 1 and 9, snare on the 5 and 13. Once you have a basic understanding of how this routing works, you can experiment with more interesting rhythms.

5. Use the Tab key to view the routing. On the Trigger Redrum, connect the Gate Out of Channel 1 to the Gate In of Channel 8 on the first Redrum.

6. Change the Steps value to 12 and the Resolution to 1/8T on the Trigger Redrum.

7. Use the Dynamic selector to create Hard velocity hits on steps on 1, 4, 7, and 10 on the Trigger Redrum's Channel 1.

You can take this method further by taking advantage of the Channel 8&9 Exclusive functionality. Create a second routing from the Trigger Redrum's Channel 9 to the Main-Drum Redrum's Channel 9, then trigger the open hihat on one or more steps.

Working with Samples and Loops

The Redrum was created to work very well with the kind of short, quick samples that are generally associated with drums and percussion. But it's important to remember that it is a sampler device and therefore you're not at all limited to using any specific type of sample. In fact, the Redrum is useful for triggering and sequencing longer samples and even loops.

Triggering Individual Samples

Something that I've mentioned a few times in this chapter is that you are not limited to using the Redrum to play drum samples and kits. The Redrum is a nice, easy-to-use device for loading and triggering individual samples of any kind.

The process is simple—in fact, it's considerably easier than using one of Reason's more complex samplers to achieve the same result. Here's how to use the Redrum to trigger and sequence samples:

1. Create a Reason song with any kind of content. One possibility is to use a couple of Dr. Rex Loop Players to set up a simple drum and melody loop. The important thing is that you have some kind of rhythmic background to trigger your samples over.

2. Create a new Redrum and use the Browse Sample button on Channel 1 to open the Browser. Navigate to the folder `Reason Factory Sound Bank\Other Samples\FX-Vox` and load the sample `BadSinging_eLab.aif`.

3. Click the Browse Sample button on Channel 2 and load a second sample.

4. Click the first step on the Step Programmer to trigger the sample when you start playback.

5. Click the Play button on the Transport panel to begin playback of your session.

You can now use Channel Strip 1's editing features to work with your sample. For example, you'll often find when triggering samples that they are more than one measure long. You'll notice that this is the case with the `BadSinging_eLab.aif` sample. As a result, the sample is being retriggered before it ends. You can fix this by shortening the sample using the Length knob. You may also want to switch the Decay/Gate mode to Gate to stop the sample short instead of having it fade out.

Working with the Pitch knob is also a great way to create unusual sound effects from samples. Try loading a spoken word loop or sample, then automating the Pitch knob.

You can load up to ten different samples and use the Bank and Pattern buttons to record automation, triggering them at any time during the course of your Reason songs. Of course, you aren't limited to using ReFill content for your samples. You can find spoken word, sound effects, and all kinds of loops from a variety of sources.

Summary

In this chapter, you learned about one of Reason's most-useful instruments for creating drum and percussion tracks, the Redrum Drum Computer. Since rhythmic tracks are an important component in just about every genre of music, it's very likely that the Redrum will be an important feature in many, if not most of your Reason projects.

You first learned the basic features and uses of the Redrum's interface, followed by instructions on how to program simple patterns to use as backing tracks for your Reason songs. You then learned how to use those patterns as the basis of a simple arrangement by combining the Redrum's banks and patterns with Reason's automation and sequencer functionality. You also learned how to greatly expand your library of Redrum drum kits by using samples from multiple sources and editing those samples within the Redrum interface.

Many of the ideas and concepts in this chapter have been geared specifically toward utilizing the Redrum to create backing rhythm and percussion tracks. Much of the work involved in honing these kinds of skills can be developed through trial and error. With the topics covered in this chapter you are well on the way to creating interesting and dynamic drum, percussion, and sample arrangements for your Reason songs and projects.

Reason's Synthesizers

Reason's synthesizers feature some of the program's most intricate and in-depth sound-shaping options. Because many of Reason's instruments and effects contain features that are specifically related to synthesis, understanding some of the basic concepts behind how synthesizers create and alter sound is one of the keys to getting the most out of Reason. One benefit of learning the ins and outs of Reason synth devices is a better understanding of all the Reason instruments and many of the effects. This chapter covers Reason's three synthesizer instruments: the SubTractor Analog (or Polyphonic) Synthesizer, the Malström Graintable Synthesizer, and the Thor Polysonic Synthesizer. In addition to those instruments, Reason's NN-XT and NN-19 samplers both offer "synth parameters," which provide functionality commonly associated with synthesizers to alter sampled sounds. The Dr. Rex Loop Player also provides synth parameters. The synthesizer concepts covered in this chapter will inform your use of those devices as well.

Reason's synthesizers make excellent learning tools for gaining a better working knowledge of Reason and of digital audio in general. What you'll learn in this chapter is how various synthesizer elements and parameters interact to create and alter sounds. This information will help you to control sound in Reason, including creating your own sounds and patches with all of Reason's devices.

Topics in this chapter include:

- **Synthesizer Basics**

- **Synthesizer Components**

- **The SubTractor Analog Synthesizer**

- **The Malström Graintable Synthesizer**

- **The Thor Polysonic Synthesizer**

Synthesizer Basics

In this section you'll learn about some of the basic components that are found on all of Reason's synthesizers. Many of these parameters and concepts will also be useful when working with the NN-19 and NN-XT samplers and the Dr. Rex Loop Player.

To better understand how Reason's synthesizers work, let's start off by looking at the various synthesis techniques they use.

Types of Synthesis Used in Reason

All of Reason's synths are based on combinations of different types of synthesis. Even the SubTractor, nominally based on one type of synthesis (subtractive—hence the name), contains features directly drawn from other synthesis types. The Malström utilizes its own unique combination of two synthesis types (granular and wavetable), while the Thor Polysonic Synthesizer contains virtual representations of six different synthesis types just as its starting point for creating patches. The following are some basic definitions and explanations of popular synthesis techniques, all of which are used in Reason's synths.

Subtractive Synthesis

In *subtractive* synthesis an oscillator creates a sound (a waveform) and then a filter is used to reduce (subtract) frequencies from the waveform to tailor a specific sound. The Sub-Tractor takes its name from this kind of synthesis, though as you'll see later in this chapter it's just one element in the SubTractor's makeup. Both the Malström and Thor synthesizers also contain filter sections that can be used to shape the sound of your patches by removing frequencies, as do the NN-19, NN-XT, and Dr. Rex instruments. Some examples of hardware synthesizers that use Subtractive synthesis are the early Moog synthesizers, the Sequential Circuits Prophet 5, and the Yamaha CS-80. While subtractive synthesis may be associated with the thick, futuristic sounds produced by early synthesizers utilized in the late 1960s and '70s by artists such as Emerson, Lake, and Palmer, Parliament-Funkadelic, and Devo, elements of subtractive synthesis are included in many of today's hardware and software synthesizers.

FM Synthesis

In *frequency modulation* synthesis, a sound created by one oscillator (the *carrier*) is modulated or altered by another (the *modulator*). Most FM synthesizers feature multiple oscillators, known as *operators*. The SubTractor includes FM synthesis capabilities in that its second oscillator can be used to affect the first oscillator. The Thor also contains an FM Pair oscillator option. FM synthesis is often associated with Yamaha's DX7 synthesizer, an FM synth that was very popular throughout the 1980s and '90s with such artists as Kraftwerk, Depeche Mode, The Cure, and Nine Inch Nails.

Phase Offset Modulation

Phase offset modulation uses a duplicate of a waveform, slightly offset from the original, causing variations in sound that can range from thinning out a synth patch to creating thick overtones. The two waveforms are either multiplied or subtracted, creating a new version of the produced sound. The SubTractor can create phase offset modulation within each of its oscillators, and Thor contains a Phase Modulation oscillator option, which works in a similar way.

Wavetable Synthesis

In *wavetable* synthesis, sampled sounds are used as the starting point for creating a patch. This can be any sound at all, often a recorded instrument. The samples can then be accessed, often at the same time. By starting playback at different points within the samples, you create different sounds.

The Malström is based on a combination of wavetable synthesis and granular synthesis, and Thor includes a Wavetable oscillator option. It should be noted that only the sampled sounds included with both of these instruments can be used to create patches. There's no option for adding new sampled sounds in either device.

Wavetable synthesis is often associated with evolving sounds, synth pads. and ambient textures. Popular hardware wavetable synthesizers have included the Waldorf PPG Wave 2 and the Korg WaveStation, whose users include Jan Hammer and the band Genesis. The startup sound that is used to this day on all Apple computers was created on a Korg WaveStation.

Granular Synthesis

In *granular* synthesis, sounds created from a variety of possible sources are split into extremely small increments known as grains. These grains are then altered and played back in different order to produce different sounds. This method can be used to create a wide variety of sounds, though in many cases splitting samples into tiny increments and playing them back predictably results in a grainy, distorted sound.

The Malström's Graintable synthesis uses this concept as one of its starting points, splitting the synth's included wavetables into individual grains that can be adjusted and altered. Though it is most commonly found in the digital realm, some hardware synths like the Roland V-Synth also make use of granular synthesis.

Synthesizer Components

All synthesizers, both hardware and virtual, contain some or all of the components covered in this section. Each of Reason's synthesizers has all of these components in one form or another.

Reason's synthesizers, like most virtual and hardware synths, all share some basic components and similar routing functionality. In Reason's SubTractor and Thor devices, the sound of any patch starts with the oscillator section and goes to the filter section, and then to the amplitude envelope generator. The sound of your patches can then be further altered with various possible modulation envelopes and with LFOs (low frequency oscillators). With the Malström you'll see that the order of signal flow is slightly different, but the components are all there and the results are similar.

Oscillators

Oscillators are a synthesizer's sound generators; they create the basic waveforms that the other synthesizer components will modify. In Reason's synthesizers the sound of a patch will always begin with either a single oscillator or with multiple oscillators. The Oscillator sections found on all of Reason's synths all contain multiple sounds to choose from as the starting point for creating patches.

> The Oscillator and Oscillator Pitch sections found on the NN-19 Digital Sampler and the Dr. Rex Loop Player don't actually generate any sound or waveforms, so they are not true oscillators. However, they do contain pitch controls similar to those found in the Oscillator sections of Reason's synths.

There are four basic waveform types that are found on most of Reason's oscillators. These waveforms are also found, along with others, in the LFO sections of all of Reason's instrument devices, except the Redrum.

Basic Waveforms

As sound generators, the waveforms each have a distinctive tone. The range of sounds among basic waveforms can be attributed to differences in overtones among different wave types (see the individual descriptions that follow).

Though some waveforms may be associated with certain types of sounds, there are no rules as to what kind of waveforms you should start with when creating your patches. You can hear what each of these waveforms sounds like in its "raw" form by creating a SubTractor and using the Oscillator 1 section's Waveform Display to scroll through the first four waveforms.

 Saw The Saw (or Sawtooth) waveform contains both odd and even harmonics and has a bright, grainy sound. The Saw wave is a good starting point for creating cutting lead lines but makes a useful starting point for creating any kind of patch.

 Square The Square waveform contains only odd harmonics, which creates a hollow sound that is a good starting point for imitating wind instruments, plucked string sounds, and bells.

Triangle Like the Square wave, the Triangle contains only odd harmonics, though in this case with different characteristics that create a smoother sound. Sonically somewhere between the Square and Sine waveforms, the Triangle waveform is a good starting point for flute, bell, or organ tones.

Sine A sine waveform generates a very smooth tone with no overtones and is an excellent starting point for electric piano-like sounds and smooth bass tones.

> The Sine, Square, Triangle, and Saw waveforms are also associated with LFOs, which will be covered shortly. In the LFO context they do not generate sound, but are used to alter existing sounds. Most of the LFO sections of all of Reason's synths will contain these waveforms as well as some other variations.

The Oscillator sections found on all of Reason's synthesizers include these and many other waveform options. Some are variations on these standard waveforms; some are based on entirely different, sampled sounds. The SubTractor features 32 oscillator waveforms, while the Malström features a total of 82 oscillator sounds to choose from. Thor contains 6 oscillator types, each mimicking a specific type of synthesis. Within each of the Thor's oscillators are multiple waveforms to choose from, along with many possible settings and variations.

Synthesizer patches on all of Reason's synths can be created with one, two, or, in the case of Thor, three oscillators generating sound at once.

Envelope Generators

Envelope generators are used to control various elements in a synthesizer patch, changing the patch's volume, filter settings, modulation settings, and more over a period of time.

Envelope generators found on all of Reason's synths include the Amplitude Envelope, used to control various aspects related to the volume and playback of a Reason synth patch; Filter Envelopes, which control how filters open and close; and Modulation Envelopes, which can be assigned to various parameters within Reason's synths. Modulation envelopes are used to modulate or alter any assigned parameter.

Figure 5.1
The Malström's Oscillator Amp Envelope section

Most envelope generators, including the filter and modulation envelopes found on Reason's instruments, contain what are known as ADSR parameters in the form of individual sliders or knobs (see Figure 5.1).

ADSR stands for Attack, Decay, Sustain, and Release. Some envelopes will also contain Delay and Hold functionality.

ADSR (and Delay and Hold)

The following are definitions for each of the parameters found on Reason's envelope generators:

Attack Controls the time it takes from when an event is triggered until it reaches its maximum level.

Decay Controls the time it takes for an event to drop from its peak level to the level it will remain at as long as the note continues.

Sustain Determines the level at which the event will remain after the decay time has elapsed. In the case of an Amplitude envelope, this will be as long as the MIDI key is held down or the MIDI event in the sequencer is still triggering the note.

Release Controls the time it will take an event to fade after it's been released. In an Amplitude envelope using a higher release value will cause a note to continue playing after you've released the note on your MIDI keyboard or after the note event has ended in the sequencer.

Some of Reason's envelope generators also include Delay and Hold parameters:

Delay Most envelope generators work instantaneously. If the envelope generator includes a Delay knob, it can be used to start the envelope's effect after a set period of time.

Hold Hold is sometimes found between the Attack and Decay parameters and is used to set an amount of time that an event will be held at the envelope's peak before it begins decaying.

All of Reason's synthesizers, samplers, and the Dr. Rex Loop Player include amplitude and filter envelopes. All of Reason's synths and the NN-XT include modulation envelopes.

Using an Amplitude Envelope

If you are unfamiliar with ADSR envelopes, the best way to learn about how they work is to start by experimenting with amplitude envelopes. Adjusting the Attack, Decay, Sustain, and Release parameters of an amplitude envelope in real time will give you a clear audio representation of how envelope generators work.

> Make sure you've followed the instructions at the end of Chapter 2 for setting Reason's Preferences before you begin the exercises in this chapter.

In the exercise that follows, you'll use the Amplitude Envelope section of the SubTractor to get a basic idea how envelopes work:

1. Create a new Reason song and add a SubTractor.

2. Play MIDI notes on your MIDI keyboard to hear the default Amplitude Envelope settings.

3. Next, play a few notes while gradually raising the Attack Slider, marked with an "A" in the Amp Envelope section on the right of the SubTractor.

When the Attack is set to 0, any note you play starts immediately. You can hear very clearly that as you raise the Attack time slider, each note you play grows more and more gradually from silence to its peak level. This has some practical applications—for example, creating realistic string sounds or swelling synthesizer pads. If you are playing a sample or synth patch that has a noticeable pop or click at the beginning, try raising the Attack slider to eliminate it.

You'll find explanations and exercises for working with filter and modulation envelopes later in this chapter.

ADJUSTING PARAMETER VALUES

Many of the exercises in this chapter ask you to set exact values with various parameter knobs and sliders. Depending on your Mouse Knob Range Preferences, you may find that you are unable to set the exact values required for an exercise. If this is the case, you can either set the suggested values as close as possible with your current settings or follow these steps to set Reason's Preferences to enable more precise parameter adjustment:

1. Open Reason's Preferences.

2. Choose the General tab.

3. Select Very Precise from the Mouse Knob Range drop-down menu.

4. Close Reason's Preferences.

You can also hold down the Shift key while selecting any parameter to allow greater precision.

The Decay parameter controls how quickly the sound decays from the peak volume level to the Sustain level. Try working with the Decay slider by starting with the following settings:

Attack: 0

Decay: 0

Sustain: 64

Release: 0

While playing and holding single notes on the SubTractor with your MIDI keyboard, raise the Decay parameter for each new note. As you raise the slider, it will take longer for the note to decay from its peak volume to the Sustain level. Experiment with higher and lower Decay and Sustain levels to hear how the two parameters interact.

The Sustain parameter is used to create longer note events. With higher Sustain values, notes can last as long as your MIDI key is held down. The opposite can also be true. Create quick, staccato notes using low Decay and Sustain values.

The Release parameter is easy to understand. To hear it in practice, set an Attack level of 0 and Release level of 0, with Decay and Sustain settings at 64; then play quick notes on the SubTractor with your MIDI keyboard while raising the Release slider. You can use the Release parameter when creating ambient sounds or to mimic a piano's sustain pedal.

Experiment further with each of the Amplitude Envelope settings to better understand how they interact.

Filters

All of Reason's synthesizers use filters to shape sounds by removing, or filtering out, selected frequencies.

Most synthesizers and samplers, both hardware and virtual, will contain some kind of Filter section or multiple sections. Filters are found on all of Reason's synthesizers and samplers, as well as the Dr. Rex Loop Player. Most of Reason's instruments contain similar Filter sections, though some, such as the Malström and Thor synths, contain some variations and extra options.

Filter Types

Figure 5.2

The NN-19's Filter section

Figure 5.2 shows the Filter types available on the NN-19 Digital Sampler, which are typical of those found throughout Reason's instruments.

Here's a brief explanation of each filter type:

Low Pass Low Pass filters are used to reduce the high frequencies within a signal and allow low frequencies to "pass" through. Most Reasons synths and samplers contain two options: the Low Pass 12 (LP12) and Low Pass 24 (LP24). The Low Pass 24 filter is a more drastic filter than the Low Pass 12, which allows more harmonic content to pass through the filter.

High Pass The opposite of a Low Pass filter, a High Pass filter reduces the low frequencies in a signal and allows high frequencies to pass through. You'll find High Pass 12 filters (HP12) in the Filter section of most Reason instruments.

Band Pass A Band Pass filter allows only a selected section of frequencies to pass through, rejecting both the high and low frequencies on either side of the selected frequency range.

Notch Notch filters, also known as "band reject" filters, are the opposite of Band Pass filters. Notch filters remove a selected frequency range, allowing low and high frequencies on either side to pass through.

> If you want to learn more about Reason's Filter sections, Reason's included manual contains visual representations of the Low Pass, High Pass, Band Pass, and Notch filter types.

Some of Reason's Filter sections also feature these kinds of filter envelopes:

Comb A Comb filter applies a very short delay to certain frequencies. This means that the effect of a Comb filter can sound much like a chorus effect and sweeping through the filter with the Frequency parameter can also create sweeping sounds, much like the Flanger and Phaser effects covered in Chapter 7. Both the Malström and Thor feature Comb+ and Comb– filter options. Using the Comb– filter will result in a noticeable cut in the bass frequencies of your patch.

AM AM stands for Amplitude Modulation. The AM filter found on the Malström works like a ring modulator by adding a new waveform and multiplying the output, often resulting in clanging, detuned, metallic sound.

> The Thor Polysonic Synthesizer also contains some unique filter options that you'll learn about later in this chapter.

Working with Filters

Most of Reason's Filter sections contain Frequency and Resonance parameters that are used to make adjustments to the range of frequencies selected or cut by specific filter types. Figures 5.3 shows on the left the Frequency and Resonance sliders found on the SubTractor synth and on the right the same controls on the Malström synth.

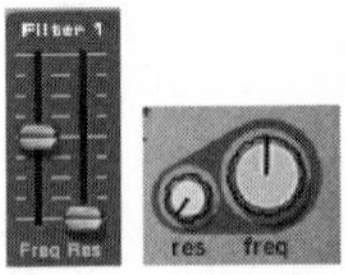

Frequency Within each filter type, you can select a range of specific frequencies with the Frequency slider or knob. With High or Low Pass Filter settings, the Frequency control determines the cutoff point at which certain frequencies are not allowed to pass through the filter. With Notch and Band Pass filters, the Frequency parameter determines the specific frequencies from the incoming signal that will be cut or allowed to pass.

Figure 5.3

The Frequency and Resonance controls in the SubTractor (left) and the Malström (right)

Resonance Choosing a specific filter type selects a specific frequency range. A filter's Resonance slider or knob is used to emphasize specific frequencies within the selected range. With Notch or Band Pass filters, the Resonance parameter works exactly like the "Q" functionality found on Reason's EQ devices (Chapter 7) and can be used to zoom in on specific frequency ranges, defining a wide or narrow band.

When working with High Pass or Low Pass filters, raising the Resonance parameter emphasizes the frequencies around the range selected with the Frequency slider.

Follow these steps to begin working with the Filter 1 section of the SubTractor synthesizer:

1. Create a new SubTractor or initialize the current patch (choose Edit → Initialize Patch or Ctrl/⌘-click the SubTractor and choose Initialize Patch from the context menu).

2. Play a few notes on the MIDI keyboard to hear the sound of the initialized SubTractor.

3. The default filter mode is LP12 (Low Pass 12). While playing notes on your MIDI keyboard, raise and lower the Filter and Resonance sliders to hear how they alter the filter's output.

4. Select each filter type and try the same thing with both the Frequency and Resonance sliders.

You can also create Filter Frequency effects automatically, as described in the following sections on working with Filter Envelope generators and LFOs.

Filter Envelopes

Most of Reason's filters are "hardwired" within each device to a Filter envelope section. These filter envelopes contain the same parameters you saw earlier with amplitude envelopes and act in essentially the same ways. However, in the case of filter envelopes the Attack, Decay, Sustain, and Release parameters work in relation to how a filter is opened and closed.

Even though filter envelopes follow the same kinds of conventions as amplitude envelopes, they may be a little harder to work with at first, because the effects are not always as clearly noticeable. In the following exercise you'll use the SubTractor's Filter Envelope section to begin working with this very useful tool:

Figure 5.4

The SubTractor's Filter Envelope section

1. Create a new SubTractor or initialize the existing one. Play a few notes with your connected MIDI keyboard to hear the initialized patch.

The default setting for an initialized SubTractor patch uses the Low Pass 12 filter. You can leave this setting as it is for now. The parameters you'll be working with are found in the Filter Envelope section just below Filter 1 (Figure 5.4).

The Filter Envelope's ADSR sliders all control the Filter 1 Frequency slider.

2. At the bottom right of the Filter Envelope section is the Amount knob. This knob controls how much effect the Filter Envelope section will have on Filter 1's frequency. Raise the Amount to 127 to hear the maximum effect.

3. Raise the filter envelope's Attack slider to around 80. You can hear clearly that longer Attack times cause the filter to open slowly. In this case, once the filter reaches its peak it drops off very quickly, because the Decay, Sustain, and Release parameters are all set to low values.

4. Set the Attack slider to around 64 and then raise and lower the Decay parameter to hear the effect of the filter decaying quickly and slowly from its peak level.

5. The Sustain parameter determines the range at which the filter stays open after the Decay time has elapsed, as long as the note is being held. With an Attack setting of 64 and a Decay setting of 35, raise and lower the Sustain parameter to hear how it works on the overall sound.

USING THE RELEASE PARAMETER

The Release parameter determines how long the filter envelope will remain open after the note played on your MIDI keyboard has been released.

In order to hear how the filter envelope's Release parameter works, you must use it in conjunction with the amplitude envelope's Release parameter.

1. Set the filter envelope's Attack, Decay, and Sustain values to 64.

2. Raise the amplitude envelope's Release slider to 85.

3. Play notes on your MIDI keyboard, holding them for about one second each as you slowly raise the filter envelope's Release slider from 0 to 90. You can hear the filter staying open longer and longer as your raise the Release slider.

You can find this example as a SubTractor patch on the accompanying CD: `Examples\` `Chapter 5\SubTractor\Filter1.zyp`.

INVERTING THE FILTER

The Filter Envelope section of the SubTractor contains a Filter Envelope Invert button, a parameter found on a number of envelope generators in Reason.

Clicking this button inverts the individual slider settings so that each parameter has the opposite of its current setting. In the case of a filter envelope, the inverted settings close the envelope over time instead of opening it.

Modulation Envelopes

You can see very clearly from the previous exercises how filter envelopes can be used to create evolving synthesizer sounds. These same concepts can also be applied to the modulation envelopes, which are used to control even more parameters on Reason's synths. Figure 5.5 shows the SubTractor's Mod Envelope section.

Figure 5.5

The SubTractor's Mod Envelope section

The modulation envelopes found on the SubTractor and Thor as well as the NN-XT Advanced Sampler work exactly like the amplitude and filter envelopes but can be assigned to various parameters. In this exercise you'll learn how to use the SubTractor's Mod Envelope section to control various parameters:

1. Create a new SubTractor or initialize your currently loaded SubTractor patch.

2. Raise the mod envelope's Amount knob to 64.

3. Play and hold single notes on your MIDI keyboard while raising the Attack slider.

By default the mod envelope is routed to Oscillator 1's pitch control. As you raise the Attack slider, you can hear the envelope taking longer and longer to reach its peak level. The default Decay and Sustain settings result in a quick dropoff back to the original pitch.

4. Raise the Decay slider for a slower decay.

5. Raise the Sustain slider to have the note sustain at a higher pitch.

As you saw earlier with the filter envelope, the Release parameter only works in conjunction with the amplitude envelope's Release slider. With the mod envelope's Release slider at a lower value the envelope closes (stops having an effect on the sound) as soon as you release the notes on your MIDI keyboard. By setting a higher Release value for the mod envelope, you ensure that the envelope stays open even after you stop playing the notes on your MIDI keyboard.

6. Raise the Amplitude Envelope section's Release slider to 64 or higher; then quickly play and release notes or chords on your MIDI keyboard while raising the mod envelope's Release slider to hear the effect change.

In this case, the SubTractor's Mod Envelope section can be used to control the pitch of Oscillator 2, the Mix knob, the FM knob, both oscillators' Phase knobs, and Filter 2's Frequency slider.

> In order for the mod envelope to have any effect on the Osc 2, FM, or Mix parameters, Oscillator 2 must be activated. See the "SubTractor Analog Synthesizer" section of this chapter for more details.

Use the mod envelope's Destination button to switch between and experiment with each of these parameters.

You can find this example as a SubTractor patch on the accompanying CD: `Examples\ Chapter 5\SubTractor\ModEnv.zyp`.

Both the NN-XT Advanced Sampler and the Thor Polysonic Synthesizer Mod Envelope sections can be routed to these same kinds of parameters and more.

> You can also use the SubTractor's Mod Envelope CV output to control even more parameters on the SubTractor and other Reason devices with the mod envelope. See the section "SubTractor Routing Options (CV)" later in this chapter.

LFOs

LFOs are used to shape and control sounds by using an oscillator-generated waveform on traditional synthesizers.

LFOs are found on most of Reason's instrument devices and are generally capable of the same kinds of functionality. The most common routing options are for LFOs to be used on pitch, filter, and panning parameters. However, many Reason LFOs can be routed to any number of parameters, both within a specific LFO section and by using the LFO CV outputs found on the back panels of most Reason instruments. LFOs are also found on some of Reason's effect devices.

The two Reason instruments that don't have LFO sections are the Redrum and the Malström synth. However, the Malström has two Modulator sections that work very much like LFOs, but with more available options. These will be covered in the "Malström Graintable Synthesizer" section of this chapter.

Figure 5.6 shows the Dr. Rex LFO section, which is similar to those found on the NN-19 and NN-XT samplers, the SubTractor, and the Thor synthesizer.

Figure 5.6

The Dr. Rex's LFO section

Destination The *destination* is the parameter being modulated by the LFO. Destination parameters are chosen by clicking an LFO Destination (Dest) button or, in the case of the NN-XT and Malström, by adjusting a Destination parameter knob.

Waveforms In most cases, the shape of the LFO is chosen by clicking a waveform button to select from one of the LFO's available waveforms. All of Reason's LFOs contain some of the standard waveforms covered earlier in this chapter: Sine, Triangle, Saw, and Square. Other waveform choices are also available, depending on the specific device and LFO section.

Sync This parameter is available on many LFO sections and on the Modulator (MOD) sections found on the Malström synth. Activating an LFO's Sync button allows you to synchronize the LFO's effect with the tempo of the current Reason song.

Aside from controlling whatever parameters can be directly assigned within an instrument's interface, LFOs generated by any Reason instrument can also be used to control other Reason devices via the CV outputs found on the back of many Reason devices. With CV, LFOs can be used to control various parameters on all of the program's instruments, effects, and the mixer.

CV connections are discussed throughout this book. Chapters 1 and 8 in particular contain basic and in-depth information on what CV is and how it can be used in Reason.

Working with an LFO

This exercise will give you a basic idea of how an LFO can be used to adjust the parameters on Reason's synthesizers. Follow these steps to use the SubTractor's LFO 1 to create a filter sweep effect:

1. Create a SubTractor Analog synth.

2. Play a note on your MIDI keyboard and hold it down while raising and lowering the Filter 1 Frequency slider.

3. Return the Filter 1 Frequency slider to its default value of 64.

You can Ctrl/⌘-click any parameter to return it to its default value.

Now you're going to perform the same effect, using an LFO to modulate Filter 1's frequency settings.

4. Raise the LFO 1 Amount knob to 64.

5. Select the Filter Frequency (F. Freq) destination by clicking on it or using the Destination button.

6. Play a few notes on your MIDI keyboard. You can now clearly hear the LFO raising and lowering Filter 1's frequency, as though the slider were being adjusted.

7. Adjust the speed of the LFO effect by turning the Rate knob to the left or to the right. With the Sync button turned off, the Rate knob has a value range of 0 to 127.

8. Click the Sync button to synchronize the LFO with the current Reason song's tempo. The Rate knob now has a value range of 16/4 to 1/32.

You can also make further adjustments to the sound with the filter's Frequency and Resonance sliders. Try using the Waveform selector button to switch the different waveforms for different effect. Raise and lower the Rate and Amount knobs for even more variation.

Experiment with LFO 1 by using the Destination button to send the LFO to the various available parameters.

> In order for the LFO to have any effect on the Oscillator 2, FM, or Mix destinations, you'll need to turn on Oscillator 2.

You can find this example as a SubTractor patch on the accompanying CD: Examples\ Chapter 5\SubTractor\FilterSweep.zyp.

Using an LFO to Control Panning

As mentioned earlier, Reason's synth parameters can be used via CV to control a number of things in Reason. This exercise in controlling panning shows just one of the many ways you can use CV routing for control in Reason.

1. Create a new Reason song.

2. Create a SubTractor.

3. Use the Tab key to flip to the back of the Reason rack.

4. Route LFO 1 CV out to the mixer's Channel 1's panning input (Figure 5.7).

Figure 5.7

CV routing between the SubTractor and the Mixer 14:2

5. Play notes on your MIDI keyboard to hear the panning effect.

6. Turn on the LFO 1 Sync button to synchronize the panning effect to the current Reason song. You can also make further adjustments to the Rate and waveform shape within the LFO 1 section.

In this case the LFO 1 Amount knob has no control over the amount of the effect. When sending LFO CV out of a Reason device, you adjust the amount of effect using the CV input value knob on the controlled device. In this case it's the Channel 1 Pan CV knob.

You can find this example as a Reason song file on the accompanying CD: Examples\Chapter 5\Songs\CVPanning.rns.

The SubTractor Analog Synthesizer

As you've already seen in this chapter, Reason's SubTractor Analog Synthesizer is a complex device with a lot of available patch creation and sound-generating options. Many of the elements that make up the SubTractor have been taken from or inspired by different types of synthesis. How these elements can be combined within a single patch is what gives the SubTractor its ability to create such a wide range of sounds. Figure 5.8 shows the SubTractor interface.

Figure 5.8

The SubTractor Analog Synthesizer

Loading, Playing, and Saving Patches

Reason comes with a large collection of SubTractor patches, which can be found in the folder Reason Factory Sound Bank\SubTractor Patches\. You load SubTractor patches by clicking the Browse Patch button on the top left of the SubTractor's interface to open the Reason Browser.

With a patch loaded in the SubTractor, you can use the Select Next and Select Previous buttons to choose the next and previous patches in the currently loaded patch's directory. Save any changes you make to a patch by clicking the Save Patch button and choosing a directory from the Save dialog.

The collection of included patches gives a good indication of some of the many possible uses for the SubTractor. The patches in the Bass folder demonstrate why SubTractor remains a popular choice for creating bass tracks, while scrolling through the patches in the FX folder shows off the SubTractor's ability to create off-the-wall sound effects and glitchy noises. The MonoSynths, PolySynths, and Pads folders all include a variety of useful synthesizer lead patches and ambient sounds. Finally, the Percussion folder contains an impressive array of drum sounds, which can be used individually or, as you'll see in Chapter 9, to create an entire drum kit.

The SubTractor Interface

The SubTractor's interface contains all of the elements covered in the "Synthesizer Basics" section of this chapter, as well as a number of other features drawn from a variety of synthesis techniques.

The Oscillators

The SubTractor contains two identical Oscillator sections. Figure 5.9 shows Oscillators 1 and 2.

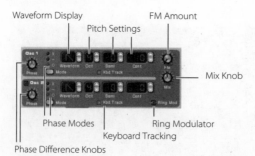

Figure 5.9

The SubTractor's Oscillators 1 and 2

When you create an initialized SubTractor patch, Oscillator 1 is always active. In order to use Oscillator 2 you must activate it by clicking the Oscillator 2 On/Off button on the top left of the section. For both oscillators, the Waveform Display shows the currently selected waveform, initially the default. You can either use the up and down arrows to scroll through the included waveforms or click and drag on the display itself.

> Each of the SubTractor's oscillators features 32 waveforms. These start with the four common waveforms covered earlier in this chapter and include 28 additional waveforms. The Reason manual has a list of all of the included wavetables as well as suggestions for how to use them.

Waveform Display Choose any waveform either by clicking and dragging in the Waveform Display or by using the Select Next and Select Previous buttons to the right of the Waveform Display.

Pitch Settings To the right of each oscillator's Waveform Display are three pitch controls. You can adjust the pitch of either oscillator by Octave, Semitone (single note), or Cent (100th of a note).

Phase Mode and Phase Difference Both oscillators contain two Phase Offset Modulation modes. Select the mode by clicking the Phase Mode switch or by clicking directly on one of the Phase Offset modes above the switch. Activating one of the Phase Offset modes creates a duplicate of the oscillator's currently selected waveform, slightly offset (out of sync) from the first waveform:

> x selects the Multiply mode, which multiplies the two waveforms.
>
> – selects the Subtract mode, which subtracts one waveform from the other.
>
> o turns the Phase Offset off.

Further adjustments to the amount of Phase Offset between waveforms can be made by adjusting the Phase Difference knobs, found on the far left of each Oscillator section.

Keyboard Tracking Turning off an oscillator's Keyboard Tracking button disables any incoming pitch information, causing the oscillator to play only one note. You can raise or lower the oscillator's pitch values to adjust the single note's pitch. This feature is especially useful for creating drum and percussion sounds.

Ring Modulator *Ring modulation* takes two waveforms and multiplies them to create harmonic overtones. To use the Ring Modulation parameter, both oscillators must be activated. This effect works best with two different waveforms, one slightly detuned.

FM Knob Frequency modulation synthesis was described earlier in this chapter. In the SubTractor's case, Oscillator 2 can be used as the modulator with Oscillator 1 as the carrier. Frequency modulation is activated by turning on Oscillator 2 and raising the FM knob.

Mix The Mix knob controls how much of each oscillator is heard. Turn the Mix knob to the far left (0) to hear only the output of Oscillator 1 and to the far right (127) to hear only Oscillator 2. The center position (64) is an equal mix of both oscillators.

Noise Generator Located just below Oscillator 2, the Noise Generator is somewhat like a third oscillator and is activated by clicking the Noise On/Off button on the top left of the Noise Generator section. True to its name, the Noise Generator creates noise. The Decay knob controls the length of the sound. The Color knob adjusts the tone from low (0) to high (127), and the Level knob controls the volume of the Noise Generator's output.

The output of the Noise Generator is routed through Oscillator 2. To hear only the Noise Generator, turn off Oscillator 2 and turn the Mix knob to the far right (127).

The Filters

The SubTractor features two Filter sections:

Filter 1 Filter 1 features Notch, High Pass 12, Band Pass 12, Low Pass 12 and Low Pass 24 filter options, which you select by clicking on the filter type or by clicking the Filter Type button. Filter 1 also has a Keyboard Tracking knob; raising it will increase the filter effect as higher notes are played on your MIDI keyboard.

Filter 2 The SubTractor also has a second Low Pass 12 filter, activated by clicking the Filter 2 On/Off button. Filter 2 can be used independently or can be linked to Filter 1 by clicking the Filter Link Freq button. With linking turned on, Filter 1's Frequency slider controls Filter 2. However, you can still adjust the Filter 2's frequency with its own slider, creating some interesting possibilities.

The Envelopes

The SubTractor features three separate envelope generators, each with the standard Attack, Decay, Sustain, and Release parameters covered earlier.

Filter Envelope The Filter Envelope section controls Attack, Decay, Sustain, and Release for Filter 1's Frequency parameter, or for both Filter 1 and 2's Frequency parameters if the Filter Link button is turned on.

Amp Envelope The Amp Envelope section controls Attack, Decay, Sustain, and Release level settings for both oscillators and the Noise Generator.

Mod Envelope The Mod Envelope section can be used to generate envelope effects for any of the available targets. These are Oscillator 1 and 2, Oscillator 2 alone, Filter 2's Frequency slider, and the Oscillator section's FM Amount knob and Phase and Mix parameters.

The LFOs

The SubTractor has two LFO sections, each with multiple destination options as well as both shared and unique functionality.

LFO 1 LFO 1 features six different waveforms, which can be routed to any of the six destinations available on the right side of the LFO 1 section. The Amount knob determines the level of the LFO effect, and the Rate knob determines the speed. Turn the Sync button on to synchronize any effects generated by LFO 1 with the current Reason song's tempo.

LFO 2 LFO 2 can be routed to Oscillator 1 and 2 together, as well as to the Phase Modulation knobs, Filter 2's Frequency slider, and the Amp Envelope. LFO 2 does not offer a Sync button. However, unlike LFO 1, it does contain a Delay knob, for delaying the start of the LFO effect, and a Keyboard Tracking knob. By raising the Keyboard Tracking knob you increase the LFO Rate as higher notes are played.

Play Parameters

The SubTractor's play parameters appear in two places. Some are found in the Velocity section on the bottom right of the SubTractor interface and the rest along the SubTractor's left side.

Velocity Section The Velocity section can be used to adjust how various parameters interact based on the velocity of incoming MIDI notes. Here you can control Amplitude, FM, the Modulation Envelope, the Phase knobs, Filter 2's Frequency slider, the Filter Envelope, the Filter Envelope's Decay parameter, and the Amplitude Envelope's Attack parameter.

The only Velocity parameter that's active in an initialized SubTractor patch is the Filter Envelope knob. Assigning a positive value to the Filter Envelope knob means that notes played with higher velocity cause the filter envelope to open wider, resulting in a clearer tone. Most of the Velocity parameters available on all Reason instruments function the same way; the only exception is the Mix Velocity Amount knob. Turning this knob to the left increases the volume of Oscillator 1 in relation to the incoming velocity. Turning it to the right increases the volume of Oscillator 2 in relation to the incoming velocity.

The Velocity controls are especially useful for creating realistic, dynamic performances, and you'll find Velocity-controllable parameters on all of Reason's instruments. For more information on how Velocity controls, work see the sidebar "About Positive and Negative Values."

ABOUT POSITIVE AND NEGATIVE VALUES

The SubTractor's Velocity section is the first example you'll see in this chapter of a common feature on many Reason instruments: the option to apply either a positive or a negative value to a parameter.

You can generally assume that whatever effect occurs when a positive value is applied, a negative value will have the opposite effect. For a clear example of this, look at the Velocity section's Amplitude knob. When you raise this knob to apply a positive value, MIDI notes triggered with higher velocities will be louder and those triggered with low velocities will be quieter. This is very much like any real-world instrument—the harder you play a piano key, the louder the sound will be; the harder you pluck a bass or guitar string, the louder it will be. If you assign a negative value to the Amplitude parameter, the opposite will be true. Notes with lower velocities will be louder, and higher velocities will be quieter.

Figure 5.10

Play parameters on the left side of the SubTractor

Figure 5.10 shows the play parameters found on the left side of the SubTractor interface.

Note On The Note On light indicates that the SubTractor is receiving MIDI input.

Polyphony The Polyphony setting determines how many notes can be played at once. The SubTractor's Polyphony range can be set between 1 and 99 simultaneous notes.

Portamento The Portamento knob is used to create pitch-gliding between notes. Higher Portamento values will result in a longer glide between notes. Turning the Portamento knob to 0 disables this function.

Legato In Legato mode triggering a new note or notes while a previous note or notes are being held will not restart any envelopes. Legato mode is most noticeable on monophonic patches. On Polyphonic patches Legato mode only begins to work on notes played after the number of notes simultaneously played exceeds the Polyphony setting. Portamento will only work in Legato mode with a Polyphony setting of 1 (monophonic).

Retrig Retrig mode is the opposite of Legato mode. In Retrig mode every new note or notes played will retrigger any envelopes.

Low BW Activating the Low Bandwidth button cuts some of the high frequencies and frees up a small amount of your processor's resources.

Pitch Bend The Pitch Bend Wheel is a feature of all of Reason's synths, as well as the sample instruments and the Dr. Rex. The Pitch Bend Wheel can be used to raise or lower the pitch of any currently playing notes. The range of the Pitch Bend is set using the Pitch Bend Range display and can be 0 (no effect) to 24 (a two-octave range). You can achieve pitch bending by clicking and dragging the wheel with your mouse or by using the Pitch Bend Wheel on your attached MIDI keyboard.

Mod Wheel The SubTractor's Mod Wheel can be assigned to control Filter 1's Frequency and Resonance settings, LFO 1, the Phase Difference parameters, and the FM amount. Like the Velocity parameters, the Mod Wheel allows both negative and positive assignable values. In this case, instead of being triggered by a difference in the velocity of individual MIDI notes, the effect is invoked by raising the Mod Wheel.

External Modulation Sources If you have an external MIDI device that can send Aftertouch, Expression, or Breath Control MIDI information, the device can be used to control Filter 1's Frequency, LFO 1, the Amp Envelope, and the FM amount.

Creating SubTractor Patches

While there are a few things that the SubTractor is especially known for, including creating bass patches and drum sounds, the instrument can create virtually unlimited sounds. Because the SubTractor offers so many optional elements, things can get confusing quickly. You don't need to use every available element to create interesting and useful SubTractor patches. In fact, you may find that simple patches are quite useful, especially for clear, straightforward instruments.

There are no rules for the process of creating your own SubTractor patches. One obvious possibility is to begin by choosing an oscillator waveform (or two oscillator waveforms by activating SubTractor's Oscillator 2) and then move on to the Filter 1 section to choose a filter and adjust the Frequency and Resolution parameters. Then again, you might just as easily start with the LFO 1 section, creating a pitch-bending effect or using one of the LFO waveforms to adjust the Filter 1's Frequency, before trying out different oscillator waveforms.

The SubTractor's basic signal flow is simple: Oscillators → Filters → Amp Envelope. But within each of these elements are many more possibilities, especially in SubTractor's Oscillator sections. The following exercises are geared toward showing you some of the possible ways to use each of the SubTractor's various sound-shaping elements. Combining these elements in your own way will be the key to creating your own original patches.

> The SubTractor's Amplitude Envelope, Filter 1, and LFO 1 sections work as described in the "Synthesizer Basics" section earlier in this chapter.

Using the FM Parameter

As described earlier in this chapter, FM synthesis is created by applying one waveform (the modulator) to another (the carrier). To activate the FM synthesis functionality of the SubTractor, you must have both oscillators going at once. Oscillator 1 will be the carrier and Oscillator 2 will be the modulator.

1. Create a new SubTractor.

2. Turn on Oscillator 2 by clicking the Osc 2 On/Off button.

3. Use Oscillator 1's Waveform Display to choose the waveform number 3, the Sine wave.

4. Use Oscillator 2's Waveform Display to choose waveform number 2, the Triangle.

5. Turn the Mix knob to 0 so you are hearing only Oscillator 1 (the carrier).

6. Raise the FM knob until you hear a noticeable effect.

7. Raise Oscillator 2's Semitone pitch parameter for an even more noticeable effect. You'll notice that raising Oscillator 2 by 4 or 7 semitones creates a more musical sound, since those intervals are the third and fifth degrees of a chord.

These waveforms can be a good starting point for creating familiar sounds if you've worked with FM synthesis before. You can experiment further by trying out different waveforms as both the carrier and modulator.

Take this even further by combining the results achieved with frequency modulation with other elements in the SubTractor to create entirely new sounds. You can also assign the Modulation Envelope and/or LFO 1 to the FM knob and create FM effects that change over time.

You can find this example as a SubTractor patch on the accompanying CD: `Examples\ Chapter 5\SubTractor\FM.zyp`.

Using Phase Offset Modulation

Phase offset modulation (explained earlier in the "Synthesizer Basics" section) is a great way to create new sounds quickly. The effect will vary from waveform to waveform and will also change depending on the settings you make with the Phase Difference knobs. Experiment with phase offset modulation by following these steps:

1. Create a new SubTractor or initialize the current patch.

2. Choose any waveform for Oscillator 1.

3. Use the Oscillator 1 Phase Mode button to select the Multiply mode (x).

4. Play a chord on your MIDI keyboard while raising and lowering the Oscillator 1 Phase Difference knob.

5. Try different waveforms to hear the effect that phase offset modulation has on each. Depending on the waveform, the selected mode, and the Phase Difference knob settings, a wide range of different sounds can be created with these parameters.

Experiment further by switching among the Multiply (+), Subtract (–), and Off (o) modes while raising and lowering the Oscillator 1 Phase Difference knob.

Turn on Oscillator 2 and add a second waveform using phase offset modulation.

You can also use the LFO 1 and 2 and the Modulation Envelope section to adjust the Phase parameter. This has the same effect as raising and lowering the Phase Difference knob in real time.

You can find this example as a SubTractor patch on the accompanying CD: `Examples\ Chapter 5\SubTractor\POM.zyp`.

Using the Ring Modulator

The Ring Modulator works by multiplying the two waveforms. However, the effect is only heard on Oscillator 2. Follow these steps to work with the Ring Modulator section:

1. Create a new SubTractor or initialize the current patch.

2. Turn on Oscillator 2.

3. Turn on the Ring Modulator.

4. Adjust the Oscillator 2's Semitone and Cent pitch controls to hear the effect. Raising Oscillator 2's pitch by a Semitone will cause a drastic effect. Using the Cent knob will be a more subtle effect.

5. To hear only the ring modulated sound (from Oscillator 2), turn the Mix knob completely to the right.

6. Experiment with different waveforms in both oscillators for different sounds and effects.

You can find this example as a SubTractor patch on the accompanying CD: `Examples\ Chapter 5\SubTractor\RingMod.zyp`.

Using the Velocity Section

The Velocity section is used to control changes in the sound of your SubTractor patches based on the velocity (Chapter 2) of the MIDI notes used to trigger the synth. The Velocity section contains nine parameter knobs, each with a range of –64 to 63, with 0 as the center value. Any knob with a setting of 0 is turned off. Assigning any knob a positive value will cause higher velocities to create a more noticeable effect. Assigning any knob a lower value will do the opposite, causing lower velocities to create a greater effect and higher velocities a less noticeable effect. This same relationship will be true for any Velocity parameter knobs, which are found on all of Reason's instruments.

By default the only Velocity parameter that's active in an initialized SubTractor patch is the Filter Envelope Velocity amount, which has a value of 32. This may not be noticeable at first, but you can experiment with this setting by playing the same note on your MIDI keyboard a few times, first softer and then gradually harder. As you play harder (with increased velocity), the filter envelope opens and the note sounds sharper and more defined. Set the Filter Envelope Velocity to 0 and try the same experiment. No matter how hard or softly you play your MIDI keyboard, the notes will sound the same.

At its most basic, the Velocity section can be used to mimic what happens when "real" instruments such as a piano or guitar are played harder, or with more velocity. When you raise the first knob, the Amplitude Velocity amount, the harder a note's velocity, the louder it will be.

Experiment with the different Velocity parameters by turning on Oscillator 2 and Filter 2, selecting a Phase Offset Mode for one or both of the oscillators, and then adjusting the various Velocity knobs.

You can find an example of Velocity effects in a SubTractor patch on the accompanying CD: `Examples\Chapter 5\SubTractor\VelocityFX.zyp`.

Creating Drum Sounds with the SubTractor

As you've seen by looking at the folder of percussion patches in the Reason Factory Sound Bank, the SubTractor works very well for creating synth drum and percussion sounds. The SubTractor's Noise Generator is especially useful for creating drum and percussion sounds, as demonstrated in the following steps:

1. Create a new SubTractor or initialize an existing patch.
2. Turn on the Noise Generator.
3. Turn the Mix Knob all the way to the right (127) so you're hearing only the output of Oscillator 2 and the Noise Generator. Because Oscillator 2 is turned off, all you'll hear for now is the Noise Generator.
4. Lower the Noise Generator's Decay knob to 80 to create a short, sharp sound.
5. Lower the Color knob to 0 to create a low sound, mimicking a bass drum. Choose higher values to mimic a snare drum or tom drum.

6. Tune your drum further using filter 1's Frequency slider.

7. Raise the Velocity section's Amp knob to add velocity/volume dynamic to the patch.

This example is just one of many possibilities. Drum sounds can also be created using different waveforms and SubTractor settings. Take a look at the `Reason Factory Sound Bank\SubTractor Patches\Percussion\` folder for even more ideas.

You can find this example as a SubTractor patch on the accompanying CD: `Examples\Chapter 5\SubTractor\BassDrum.zyp`.

SubTractor Routing Options (CV)

Figure 5.11

The SubTractor's Audio Output

Figure 5.11 shows the SubTractor's Audio Output. The SubTractor is Reason's only mono instrument device. When you create a SubTractor, it's automatically routed to the first available Left (mono) input on the session's Mixer 14:2.

You can create stereo sounds with the SubTractor by using the Spider Audio Merger & Splitter (Chapter 8) or by connecting SubTractor to any of Reason's Mono to Stereo effects (Chapter 7).

CV Routing within a Reason Device

As you've learned, many of Reason's instrument devices feature modulation effects with filters and LFOs. These parameters are generally adjusted within an instrument's interface to create variations in the produced sound. Often these parameters will also have built-in CV output and input functionality that you can access on the instrument's back panel. This kind of modulation CV routing opens up entirely new possibilities for controlling the parameters of Reason devices, some of which you saw earlier in this chapter in the section "Using an LFO to Control Panning." You'll learn even more about the exciting possibilities with CV routing in Chapters 7, 8, and 9.

This exercise uses a SubTractor's LFO (Low Frequency Oscillator) parameter to control various other parameters on the same device.

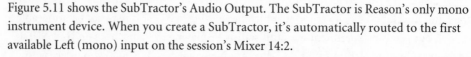

> Any CV connections you make within a device will not be saved as part of the patch. In order to save any CV routing you create, save the instrument as part of a Reason song or as a Combinator patch (Chapter 9).

1. Create a new Reason song.

2. Add a Mixer and a SubTractor.

3. Click the SubTractor's Browse Patch button and load the patch `Reason Factory Sound Bank\SubTractor Patches\CCRMA E Piano.zyp`.

4. Play a few notes to hear the unaltered patch.

5. Use the Tab key to view the back of the Reason Rack.

6. Select the LFO 1 Modulation output and route it to the Filter 2 Freq input on the back panel.

7. Play a few notes to hear the effect.

The LFO 1 section on the front panel of the SubTractor controls the LFO 1 CV output. You can create variations in the effect by making adjustments within the LFO 1 section on the SubTractor.

Try routing the LFO 1 output to the other available modulation inputs and playing a few notes on your MIDI keyboard.

> The CV modulation outputs of any Reason instrument can also be connected to the CV modulation inputs of another. You can take these experiments even further by creating new instruments and trying out various routing configurations between devices.

Using this simple CV routing, you can control two parameters at once with a single LFO. This routing also gives you the ability to control parameters not available in the SubTractor's LFO 1 section. You can also route the Modulation Envelope and Filter Envelope CV outputs to the SubTractor's other CV Modulation Inputs.

You can find more ways to work with the CV routing options available on the back panel of Reason's instrument devices in the "Spider CV Merger and Splitter" section of Chapter 8.

You can find this example as a Reason song file on the accompanying CD: `Examples\ Chapter 5\Songs\ModCV.rns`.

Combining the Elements

Everything you've learned so far in the "Synthesizer Basics" and "SubTractor Analog Synthesizer" sections of this chapter is meant to teach you some basic synthesizer concepts and to indicate some of the possibilities available within the SubTractor. As noted earlier, a typical patch that you create can contain very few or many of the elements covered. You have a great range of tools at your disposal now. At this point you should experiment further with the SubTractor by combining these elements in your own SubTractor patches.

The Malström Graintable Synthesizer

The Malström Graintable Synthesizer, introduced in Reason version 2.0, features two Oscillator sections, each with access to 82 *graintables* (sampled sounds divided into tiny increments), which are used as the starting points for creating patches. Instead of the LFO sections found on Reason's other synthesizers and sampler devices, the Malström contains two Modulator sections, which function very much like LFOs but contain a much wider range of waveforms to choose from, as well as a unique set of target options. Figure 5.12 shows the Malström interface.

Figure 5.12

The Malström
Graintable
Synthesizer

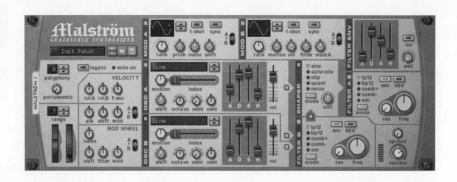

Loading, Playing, and Saving Patches

Clicking the Browse Patch button in the upper-left corner of the synth opens the Reason Browser, which you can use to locate and load Malström patches. Reason comes with a large collection of patches; they can be found in the folder `Reason Factory Sound bank\ Malstrom Patches\`.

You can also click directly on the Patch Name display to open the Browser. Once a patch has been loaded, you can use the Select Next and Select Previous buttons to browse and load patches from the currently loaded patch's directory. Click the Save Patch button and choose a patch name and location using the Save Patch dialog to save any changes you make to a patch.

The Malström Interface

Malström's two Oscillator sections are identical to each other, except for their routing options. There are two separate Filter sections, which can be connected or used separately. There is also a Shaper section that can used to further alter the sound produced by the oscillators.

Just above the oscillators are the Modulator sections, named Mod A and Mod B. These take the place of what would normally be the LFOs on another synthesizer. Modulator A works by directly modulating various parameters on either or both oscillators. Modulator B can be used to modulate parameters on either or both oscillators, either or both filters, and Modulator A. The unusual variety of target destinations and the 32 available modulating waveforms make the Malström's modulators significantly more impressive than the typical LFO sections found on other synths.

The Oscillators

As noted previously, Oscillator A and Oscillator B are essentially identical. Each can be turned on and off by clicking the Oscillator On/Off button at its top-left corner. When you create an initialized Malström patch, Oscillator A is turned on by default, while Oscillator B is turned off.

Each oscillator has 82 waveforms, known as *graintables*, that are used as starting points for your Malström patches. These are chosen from the Graintable display at the top of each oscillator, which reads "sine" in an initialized patch. By clicking on the Graintable display, you can view a list of all of the available graintables (Figure 5.13).

You can also scroll through the graintables using the Select Next and Select Previous arrows to the right of the Graintable display. The available graintables are divided into groups: Bass, FX, Guitar, Misc, Perc, Synth, Voice, Wave, and Wind. Group names are only viewable on the pop-up menu.

The Malström's oscillators also contain the following parameters, which are key to accessing the creative potential of this synthesizer:

Amplitude Envelope Each oscillator has its own amplitude envelope with Attack, Decay, Sustain, and Release parameters.

Volume Slider Each oscillator also has its own volume slider to the right of the ADSR envelope.

Pitch Controls There are three clearly marked knobs at the bottom of each oscillator that can be used to adjust the pitch in octaves, semitones, or cents.

Index The Index parameter determines where in the graintable playback begins. Sliding the index to the right will start playback later in the graintable. No matter where in the graintable playback is started from, once the waveform reaches the end it will loop back around and start from the beginning. With most of the graintables, this behavior can be used to create very different sounds. The effect will be less noticeable (or not at all) on some of the more traditional synthesizer sounds. With the sampled voices and FX graintables, the effect will be very noticeable.

Motion The Motion knob determines the speed at which any selected graintable is played back when triggered by a MIDI note event.

Shift The Shift knob raises or lowers the pitch of the individual grains within the selected graintable. This is different than raising or lowering the pitch of the entire graintable, as you can with the pitch parameter knobs; in fact, the overall pitch remains unchanged. Adjusting the Shift knob can create some very different and interesting overtones.

The Mods

The Mod, or Modulation, sections of the Malström act very much like the LFO sections found on Reason's other instruments. In the Malström's case, the Mod sections contain 32 waveforms and some interesting routing options.

Both modulators can act directly on the oscillators and will often be the first parameters you adjust after choosing an oscillator or oscillators as the starting point for your original patch. You can also drastically alter existing patches to create new and interesting variations by working with the Modulator sections of the Malström.

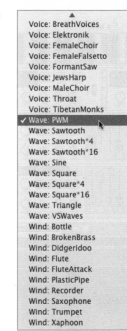

Figure 5.13

The Graintable menu list

Mod A Modulator A can be routed to either or both oscillators by choosing a destination with the Modulator A Target switch. In its default position, Mod A is routed to both Oscillators 1 and 2.

Mod A contains a Waveform Display that can be used to select from any of the 32 available waveforms. Click and drag up and down in the Waveform Display or use the Select Next and Select Previous buttons to the right of the Waveform Display to select from the different available waveforms.

Modulator A's waveforms can be routed to control the Pitch, Index, and Shift parameters found on either or both of the Malström's oscillators. In order for the Modulator A section to have any noticeable effect, one or more of the Pitch, Index, or Shift parameter knobs on an oscillator must be raised or lowered.

Clicking the Sync button syncs the Rate of the selected waveform to the current Reason song. Activating the 1-Shot button means that the waveform's effect on the target destination will happen only once and then stop.

Mod B Modulator B shares Modulator A's functionality but works on different parameters: Motion, Volume, the Filters, and Mod A. By using the Target Selector switch, you can use Modulator B to control either Oscillator A, Oscillator B, or both with the Motion and Volume knobs. You can control Filter A, Filter B, or both for the Filter knob.

Adjusting the Modulator B to Modulator A parameter knob will control Modulator A, regardless of the Target Selector switch settings. As with Mod A, activating the 1-Shot button means that the waveform's effect on the target destination will happen only once.

The Filters and Filter Envelope

Malström's Filter and Filter Envelope options are similar to those found on the SubTractor and on Reason's samplers, with some variation in filter options and how they appear in the Malström's interface.

Filter A The Filter A section contains options for a Low Pass filter, Band Pass filter, two different Comb filters (+ and −), and an AM filter. Select the Filter mode by clicking the Mode button in the bottom-left corner of the Filter section or by clicking directly on a specific type's name. The larger knob is used to select the filter's frequency, while the smaller knob adjusts the resonance. Turning on Filter A's Envelope button allows the Filter Envelope section to control Filter A.

Turning on the Keyboard Tracking button causes higher notes played on your MIDI keyboard to open the filter wider.

In order for Filter A to be activated, Oscillator A's Route Oscillator A to Shaper button must be turned on. However, the Shaper does not have to be activated in order for a signal to be routed to Filter A.

Filter B Oscillators 1 and 2 can be routed directly to Filter B independently or simultaneously using the Route Oscillator A to Filter B and Route Oscillator B to Filter B buttons.

Filter B is identical to filter A but is not routed through the Shaper. However, by clicking the Route Filter B to Shaper button, you can route the signal from Filter B to the Shaper, and then on to Filter A.

Filter Envelope The Filter Envelope section contains the standard Attack, Decay, Sustain, and Release parameters found on most of Reason's filter envelopes, along with an Amount knob for controlling how much effect the envelope has on the Filter sections and an Invert button for inverting the Filter envelope.

The Shaper Section

The Shaper alters the sound by changing the shape of the waveform. This can be used to enhance or in some cases, distort the overall sound.

Activate the Shaper section by clicking the Route Oscillator A to Shaper button, and then clicking the Shaper On/Off button in the upper left of the Shaper section. You can also route Oscillator B through the Shaper by clicking the Route Oscillator B to Filter B button and then the Route Filter B to Shaper button. Filter B does not have to be active for this routing to work.

The Shaper has five sound-shaping modes: Sine, Saturate, Clip, Quant, and Noise. Choose any mode by clicking directly on the mode name or by clicking the Mode button at the bottom of the list. Each mode has a distinct way of coloring the sound. Raise or lower the Amount knob to adjust the effect the Shaper has on the incoming signal.

Play Parameters

The following parameters control how the synth responds to notes played on your MIDI keyboard:

Polyphony Use the Polyphony display to set the number of simultaneous notes that can play in the current patch. The Malström's polyphony setting can range from 1 to 16 notes at once.

Portamento Use the Portamento knob to create pitch gliding between any notes you play. Higher values will result in a longer gliding effect. A value of zero (hard left) will turn this parameter off.

Legato Activating the Legato button on the Malström makes the synth's output monophonic, so that only one note can be heard at a time. In Legato mode, envelopes and filters are retriggered for every new note played *only* if you release the previous note.

Velocity You can use the Velocity parameter knobs to control various Malström parameters in relation to the velocity of incoming MIDI notes. The most obvious practical application for this is to create patches where greater velocities trigger louder sounds. You can control the volume/velocity effect separately for both oscillators with the Lvl:A and Lvl:B knobs. The other Velocity knobs control the Filter envelope, Attack, Shift, and Modulators.

The Attack, Shift, and Modulators knobs can be routed to Oscillator A and Modulator A, Oscillator B and Modulator B, or all four sections, using the Target selector switch on the right side of the Velocity section.

Pitch Bend Wheel Click and drag up or down on the Malström's Pitch Bend Wheel to raise or lower the pitch of any currently playing notes, or use the Pitch Bend Wheel on your connected MIDI keyboard. Use the Pitch Bend Range display just above the Pitch Bend Wheel to set the pitch bending range (up to two octaves).

Mod Wheel The Mod Wheel can be used to control Index, Shift, Filter Frequency, and the Modulators. The Target Selector switch determines which Oscillator, Modulator, and Filter sections will be controlled by the Mod Wheel.

Global Controls

In the bottom-right corner you'll find the Malström's Global controls, Spread, and Volume:

Spread The Spread knob can be used to split or combine the output of each oscillator. Turning the Spread knob to the far right (127) splits the signal, sending Oscillator A completely to the Malström's left output and Oscillator B to the right output. Turning the knob completely to the left combines the two signals.

Volume This knob controls the overall volume of the patch, ranging from 0 (silent) to 127 (maximum level).

Creating Malström Patches

The Malström contains an enormous variety of available sounds and options for editing sounds for each of the available graintables, but it is especially useful for creating off-the-wall sound effects and grainy saw-like synths. As with the SubTractor, you can hear some of the possibilities by browsing the folder of patches included with Reason, Reason Factory Sound Bank\Malstrom Patches. You'll see many of the same folder names that you saw in the SubTractor patches folder. Check out the Fx folder in particular to see how the Malström is capable of even more "out there" sounds.

Working with the Oscillators

As with all of Reason's synths, the sound of the Malström begins with the Oscillator sections. In this case you have some interesting and original options for creating sounds. You could certainly start off your patch by selecting a graintable and then moving on to the Filter or Modulator section. But you'd be missing out on some very interesting options.

MOTION, INDEX, AND SHIFT

Much of the flexibility that you can access with the Malström is found in the Oscillators' Motion Index and Shift functionality. This may not be apparent with every graintable. For this exercise you're going to use a graintable whose features lend themselves to working with these options.

1. Create a new Malström Graintable Synthesizer.

2. In Oscillator A, choose the graintable Voice: Throat.

3. Play and hold the note C3 on your MIDI keyboard.

You can hear that this particular graintable sounds like a human voice making guttural throat noises. This may not seem particularly useful for creating a musical synthesizer sound, but read on….

4. To get a clear representation of how the Index slider works, drag the slider to the right and play C3 on your MIDI keyboard again. As you move the slider to the right, you can hear that the Throat graintable starts later and later in the sample.

Working with the various graintables, you can use this parameter to create very different sounds just by adjusting the playback starting point of many graintables.

5. Next, adjust the Motion knob. Turning the knob clockwise speeds up playback of the graintable. Turning it counterclockwise slows down playback of the graintable. In this case, slowing down the graintable results in a somewhat distorted but pretty cool sound, especially when playing in the C3–C4 range on your MIDI keyboard. Leave the Motion knob somewhere around –40.

6. Finally, use the Shift knob to adjust the pitch of the individual grains. Once again, raising and lowering this parameter dramatically affects the sound coming from Oscillator A.

You can find this example as a Malström patch on the accompanying CD: `Examples\Chapter 5\Malstrom\InMoShift.xwv`.

Experiment with these parameters a while by using Oscillator A's Select Next and Select Previous buttons to choose different graintables and adjust their Index, Motion, and Shift parameters.

You can also use the various pitch controls to adjust the pitch of each oscillator.

> Each oscillator also contains its own amplitude envelope. See the "Using an Amplitude Envelope" section earlier in this chapter for instruction on how these parameters can be used to further shape and control the sound.

ADD A SECOND OSCILLATOR TO YOUR PATCH

Adding a second oscillator to your patch is as easy as turning on the Oscillator B On/Off button on the upper left side of Oscillator B.

Once Oscillator B is activated, you can use the Graintable display to select any graintable; make any Pitch, Index, Motion, or Shift adjustments; and then make any amplitude envelope adjustments with the ADSR sliders.

With both oscillators going, you can control the volume level of each oscillator independently with the Level sliders. You can also use the Spread knob on the lower right of the Malström interface to adjust the stereo field of the two oscillators' outputs.

You can find this example as a Malström patch on the accompanying CD: `Examples\Chapter 5\Malstrom\TwoOsc.xwv`.

Working with the Modulator Sections

The Malström's Modulator sections are another key to unlocking the incredible potential of this Reason synth. Follow these steps to begin working with Modulator A:

1. Create a new Malström or initialize the current patch.

2. Choose the Sawtooth*16 graintable for Oscillator A.

In an initialized Malström patch, both Modulator sections are turned on by default and routed to both oscillators. No effect from either modulator will be heard until one of the parameter knobs is adjusted.

3. For an obvious indicator of how the modulators work, raise Modulator A's Pitch knob to a value of around 15 and play a note on your MIDI keyboard. You can clearly hear how the modulator's default Sine wave is modulating the pitch up and down.

4. Turn on the Modulator A Sync button to sync the effect's tempo to the current session tempo.

5. Adjust the rate knob to set the modulation tempo in relation to the Reason song's tempo. Turn the Rate knob clockwise to choose a lower Rate value (4/4 or less) and speed up the effect to hear it more clearly.

6. Click on the up and down arrows in the Modulator A section to choose different waveforms. You will hear how each one alters the sound from Oscillator A differently.

   Using lower rate values you can clearly see how the visual representation of each waveform corresponds to the effect the Modulator has on the sound.

You can find this example as a Malström patch on the accompanying CD: `Examples\Chapter 5\Malstrom\ModA.xwv`.

Modulator B

The Modulator B section contains some very interesting options, including the ability to control a different set of oscillator parameters, as well as the Filter sections and Modulator A.

1. Create a new Malström or initialize the current patch.

2. Choose the Sawtooth*16 graintable for Oscillator A.

3. Turn on Oscillator B and choose the Sawtooth*16 graintable.

4. Raise the Spread knob to 127. This will place Oscillator A's output in the left speaker and Oscillator B's Output in the right speaker.

5. Use Modulator A's Target Selector switch to select Oscillator A.

6. Use Modulator B's Target Selector switch to select Oscillator B.

7. Raise Modulator A's Pitch knob to 40.

8. Raise Modulator B's Volume knob to 40.

You can find this example as a Malström patch on the accompanying CD: `Examples\` `Chapter 5\Malstrom\ModB.xwv`.

You can now clearly hear the effect that each modulator is having independently on each oscillator. You can experiment further with these parameters in many ways, including:

- Syncing the modulators to the current song tempo with the Sync buttons

- Turning on the 1-Shot functionality of either or both modulators

- Choosing different graintables in one or both oscillators

- Choosing different waveforms in one or both of the modulators

- Adjusting the Rate Pitch and Index of Oscillator A

- Adjusting the Rate Motion and Volume knobs on Modulator B

- Using the Spread knob to combine the output of both oscillators

- Using the Target Selectors to route the modulators to either or both of the oscillators

- Adjusting Modulator B's Mod:A knob to control Modulator A

These are just some of the ways to incorporate one or both modulators into your Malström patches.

Adding the Shaper

The Shaper can be used with any sounds from Oscillators A and/or B. Each mode has a distinct quality. It's important to note that the Shaper can quickly distort or thin out the sound of your patches, so in general it should be used lightly—unless you are specifically trying to create thin, distorted sounds.

Follow these steps to start working with the Shaper:

1. Select any graintable in Oscillator A.

2. Route the sound from Oscillator A to the Shaper by turning on the Route Oscillator A to Shaper button.

3. Turn the Shaper on by clicking the Shaper On/Off button in the upper left of the Shaper section.

4. When you route the Oscillator A to the Shaper, by default the signal then goes to Filter A, which is turned on by default in an initialized Malström patch. To get a clear idea of the Shaper's effect on the sound, turn off Filter A.

5. Use the Mode button to select a Shaper mode and the Amount button to raise or lower the amount of the Shaper effect.

You can find this example as a Malström patch on the accompanying CD: `Examples\`
`Chapter 5\Malstrom\Shaper.xwv`.

ROUTING OSCILLATOR B TO THE SHAPER

Follow these steps to route Oscillator B to the Shaper through Filter 1:

1. Turn on Oscillator B and select any graintable.

2. Click the Route Oscillator B to Filter B button located on the left side of the Oscillator B section.

3. Click the Route Filter B to Shaper button located at the top left of the Filter B section.

In an initialized Malström patch, both Filters A and B will be turned on by default. You can leave the Filter sections on or turn them off depending on the kind of sounds you are trying to create.

Routing Filter B to the Shaper sends the oscillator's output to Filter A, even if Filter A is turned off. This can be problematic in any patches with stereo separation because as you'll see later in this chapter the Malström's default output actually comes from Filter A (left output) and Filter B (right output).

Using the Filters and the Filter Envelopes

Working with the Malström's Filter sections is essentially the same as working with the SubTractor's Filter section. The main difference is that the Malström has two Filter sections that can be controlled independently and that both filters use knobs instead of sliders to adjust Frequency and Resonance settings. Follow these steps to begin working with Malström's filters and the Filter Envelope section:

1. Create a new Malström or initialize an existing patch.

2. Choose the Square wave graintable in Oscillator A.

3. Turn on the Route Oscillator A to Shaper button. Since the Shaper is turned off, it will be bypassed and the signal will be routed directly to Filter A.

4. By default the Filter A Envelope button is activated, engaging the Malström's Filter Envelope. Turn up the Filter Envelope's Amount knob to 64 and raise the Filter Envelope's Attack slider to 64 to hear the Filter Envelope's effect on Filter A.

You can use the Mode switch to switch between the available filter modes and make further adjustments with the Frequency and Resonance knobs. Turn on the Keyboard Tracking button to create a more pronounced filter effect as higher notes are played on your MIDI keyboard.

Adding Filter B

Turn on Filter B by clicking the Route Oscillator A to Filter B button.

Filter B functions in exactly the same way as Filter A. Adding a second filter to Oscillator A's output can create some cool sonic variations. Try selecting the Comb+ mode for Filter B, for example.

You can find this example as a Malström patch on the accompanying CD: `Examples\ Chapter 5\Malstrom\Filters.xwv`.

Modulating the Filters

Modulator B can be used to modulate both Filter A and Filter B simultaneously or independently. Follow these steps to try out this functionality:

1. Create a new Malström or initialize an existing patch.

2. Choose the Sawtooth*16 graintable for Oscillator A.

3. Turn on the Route Oscillator A to Shaper button (leave the Shaper turned off). This will route Oscillator A to Filter A.

4. Raise Filter A's Resonance knob to 64.

5. Turn on Modulator B's Sync button.

6. Choose Waveform # 6 in the Modulator B Waveform Display.

7. Raise Modulator B's Rate knob to 1/4.

8. Raise Modulator B's Filter knob to 40.

9. Play notes on your MIDI keyboard to hear the modulated filter effect.

Take this exercise further with one or more of the following options:

- Try different filter modes and settings with Filter A.

- Try out different graintables with Oscillator A.

- Try different rates and waveform types in Modulator B.

- Route Oscillator A to Filter B and try different settings (check out the Comb+ filter for a nice effect).

- Add Oscillator B to the patch and choose a second graintable, then route Oscillator B to Filter B.

> By default the Modulator B Target Selector switch is set to modulate both filters. You can adjust the switch to modulate only Filter A or B.

- You can find this example as a Malström patch on the accompanying CD: `Examples\ Chapter 5\Malstrom\FilterMod.xwv`.

Creating a Simulated Arpeggio

Before the RPG-8 Monophonic Arpeggiator was introduced in version 4, Reason users had to be creative if they wanted to create or simulate arpeggios. One option that's still useful for creating cool patterns and sounds is to use the Malström's pitch modulation functionality. Follow these steps to use the Malström's Modulator A to create a simulated arpeggio:

1. Create a new Malström or initialize an existing patch.

2. Choose any of the Wave graintables to start with (you can switch graintables later).

3. Turn on Modulator A's Sync button.

4. Adjust Modulator A's Rate knob to 1/8.

5. Raise Modulator A's Pitch knob to 36.

6. Choose Modulator Curve 26.

7. Play notes on your MIDI keyboard to hear the simulation of an arpeggio.

Waveforms 21–27 are all useful for creating arpeggiated-sounding patches. You can take this demonstration further by incorporating some of the other elements, including these:

- Adjust Modulator A's Rate and Pitch Settings.
- Try out different graintables in Oscillator A.
- Add a second graintable with Oscillator B.
- Adjust the Index and Shift parameters of either or both oscillators.
- You can find this example as a Malström patch on the accompanying CD: `Examples\ Chapter 5\Malstrom\SimArp.xwv`.

Malström Routing Options

The Malström also features some unique audio routing options:

Main Outputs The Malström's default stereo output is shown here. When you create a Malström, the left and right Main outputs come from Filter A (left) and Filter B (right). They are sent to the left and right inputs of the first available channel on the Reason song's Mixer 14:2.

Oscillator Outputs Using the Oscillator outputs sends signal directly from the Oscillator sections to the mixer or other connected device, bypassing the Shaper and Filter sections.

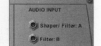

Audio Inputs The Malström also features two audio inputs that can be used to route the audio from any other Reason instrument or effect into the Malström to take advantage of the synth's Shaper and Filter sections, as well as the Filter modulation possibilities of Modulator B.

You can find an example of this kind of audio routing in a Reason song file on the accompanying CD: `Examples\Chapter 5\Songs\MalAudInput.rns`.

Combining the Elements

As with the SubTractor, learning to create complex and interesting Malström patches will be the result of combining all or some of this section's elements along with your own experimentation. Be sure to take a look at Reason's included Malström patches (`Reason Factory Sound Bank\Malström Patches`) for more inspiration and as examples of some of the creative possibilities the Malström allows for routing and patch creation.

The Thor Polysonic Synthesizer

Introduced in Reason 4, the Thor Polysonic Synthesizer brings entirely new levels of complex functionality and signal routing options to Reason. Thor's interface is made up of multiple sections, which can be used together to create incredibly intricate synthesizer patches. Each section contains numerous possibilities and options for creative exploration. In this section you'll look at each element in Thor's makeup, both individually and together.

Loading Playing and Saving Patches

The process of loading, playing, and saving patches for Thor is the same as with Reason's other instruments. You access patches by clicking the Browse Patch button or clicking directly on the Patch Name display. Once a patch is loaded, you can use the Select Next and Select Previous buttons to browse through patches in the currently loaded patch's directory. Save any changes you make to a patch by clicking the Save Patch button and choosing a directory from the Save dialog.

Thor comes with an impressive collection of included patches that give some indication of the range of possibilities found within this device. The included Thor patches are located in the folder `Reason Factory Sound Bank\Thor Patches\`.

A Quick Look at Thor

Figure 5.14 shows the entire Thor interface.

The Controller Panel   The Global Section

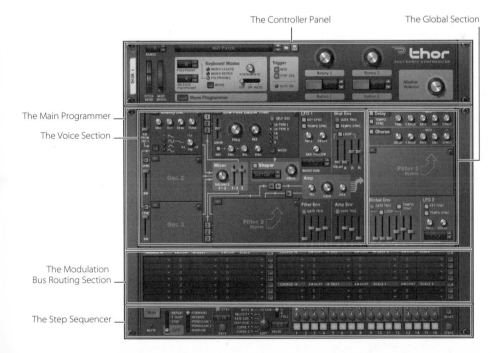

The Main Programmer

The Voice Section

The Modulation
Bus Routing Section

The Step Sequencer

Figure 5.14

The Thor Polysonic Synthesizer

In this section we'll take a look at the elements that make up the Thor interface. Click the Show Programmer button on the bottom-left side of the Controller Panel to view Thor's Programmer section.

Thor's Programmer section is where the synthesizer's patch creation and signal routing take place. The Programmer is divided into three sections: the Main Programmer, the Modulation Bus Routing section, and the Step Sequencer.

The Controller Panel

The Controller Panel is what you'll see when you first create a Thor synth. Here you'll be able to browse, load, and save patches, and you'll have the same Pitch Bend and Mod Wheel found on all of Reason's synth and sampler devices. The Controller Panel also has more in-depth functionality, including some play parameters, triggering options, and assignable rotaries and buttons.

The Main Programmer

The Main Programmer is divided into Voice and Global sections.

THE VOICE SECTION

At the top of the Programmer are all of the various elements and options for creating and routing oscillators and filters. Thor has slots for three separate oscillators. Each oscillator slot can be loaded from a choice of six possible oscillator types representing a wide range of synthesis types. Oscillators are added to a Thor patch by clicking the triangle in the upper-left corner of each Oscillator section and choosing from the drop-down menu. A Thor patch can contain lone, two, or three oscillators.

Any or all of the three oscillators can all be routed to one or both Filter sections. The filters are selected from a list of four different filter types, which you access by clicking in the upper-left corner of the Filter section.

To the right of the Filter sections are the LFO 1 section and Thor's envelope generators. Some of these sections are hardwired to specific parameters, but all of them can be routed creatively to various elements in a patch using the Modulation Bus Routing options covered in this chapter.

THE GLOBAL SECTION

To the right of LFO 1 and the envelope generators is the Global section. The Global section contains the effects Delay and Chorus, as well as a slot for an optional third filter, a Global Envelope section, and a second LFO (LFO2). The combined output of all of the elements in the Voice section is routed through the Global section.

The Modulation Bus Routing Section

Thor's Modulation Bus Routing section allows you to route an incredible number of parameters to various places within the device. The routing is accomplished via the drop-down menus that appear when any field is selected. This kind of routing is unique to this specific Reason instrument. All of Thor's envelopes, filters, LFOs and many other parameters (including audio) can be used to control an amazing range of parameters.

The Step Sequencer

Thor's Step Sequencer can be used to create patterns and melodies within the Thor synth. This has a myriad of uses, including creating synth patterns, melody lines, and rhythmic patterns. In some ways the Step Sequencer is similar to the Step Sequencer found on the Redrum Drum Computer (Chapter 3). However, Thor's Step Sequencer cannot send pattern data to tracks in the Reason sequencer.

In the rest of this section you'll take an in-depth look at each of the elements contained within the Thor interface, including how some of the elements of each section interact when you're creating Thor patches.

The Controller Panel

Thor's Controller Panel, shown in Figure 5.15, is what you'll see when Thor is added to a Reason song. The Controller panel contains many of the features that are offered as play parameters on other Reason instrument devices.

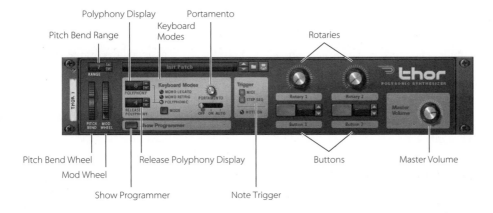

Figure 5.15
Thor's Controller panel

Pitch Bend Wheel The Pitch Bend Wheel functionality is exactly the same as that found on other Reason devices. You can adjust the Pitch Bend range using the Pitch Bend Range display just above the Pitch Bend Wheel.

Mod Wheel The Mod Wheel functionality is essentially the same for Thor as for other Reason devices. The difference here is that Mod Wheel functionality will be assigned in the Modulation Bus Routing section, covered later.

Polyphony Display The Polyphony display setting determines how many voices can be played at once. Thor's Polyphony Range is from 0 to 32.

Release Polyphony The Release Polyphony setting determines how many notes with high Release values will be allowed to continue to decay naturally after the notes are no longer being held down on your MIDI keyboard.

Keyboard Modes There are three keyboard modes, which you select with the Mode button or by clicking directly on a Mode name.

- Choosing Mono Legato will make the current patch monophonic. Triggering a new note while a previous note is being held will not restart any envelopes.

- Choosing Mono Retrig mode will also make the current patch monophonic, but triggering a new note will restart any envelopes.

- Choose Polyphonic and the patch will respond normally to your Polyphony and Release Polyphony settings.

Portamento The Portamento knob can be used to glide between notes. Three settings are available: Off, On, and Auto. In the On mode, portamento is applied to all notes. In the Auto mode, portamento is applied only when simultaneous notes are played or held on your MIDI keyboard.

Note Trigger The Note Trigger section determines whether a note played on your MIDI keyboard triggers notes from the synth (MIDI) or the Step Sequencer (Step Seq). Using the Step Sequencer requires further routing, covered in the "Using the Step Sequencer" section later in this chapter.

Rotaries and Buttons The Rotary knobs and Buttons can be assigned to parameters using the Modulation Bus Routing options, covered later in this chapter.

Master Volume The Master Volume controls the overall volume output of the Thor synth.

Show Programmer The Show Programmer button is used to show and hide the rest of the Thor interface.

The Main Programmer

This section of Thor is the heart of the synthesizer. Here you perform the basic tasks that create Thor's sounds. Before you start looking at the functionality of this section, take a look at the Filter and Oscillator options you have for creating your synths.

> The tool tips displayed by moving your mouse over various parameters will be especially useful when learning the Thor interface.

The Oscillators

Thor includes six oscillators: Analog, Wavetable, Phase Modulation, FM Pair, Multi Oscillator, and Noise. The Oscillator sections are located on the left side of the Main Programmer. A Thor patch can use a single oscillator or up to three oscillators at once.

SHARED FUNCTIONALITY

The same four knobs are found across the top of each oscillator:

Keyboard Tracking With the Keyboard Tracking's default setting of 127 notes, playing notes on your MIDI keyboard will trigger standard note values. Adjusting the knob to 0 turns off Keyboard Tracking and causing the oscillator to produce a single pitch, no matter what notes are played. Values between 1 and 126 will produce microtonal variations.

Pitch Controls Each oscillator has Octave, Semitone, and Tune (Cents) knobs for adjusting the pitch of the oscillator's output.

THE OSCILLATOR TYPES

Thor's included oscillators are:

Analog Based on simple analog synths, this oscillator features the four standard waveforms covered in the "Synthesizer Basics" section of this chapter, along with a Pulse Width Modulation knob that can be used to change the sound of the Square waveform.

Wavetable Based on Wavetable synthesis, this oscillator offers 32 wavetables to use as starting points for creating sounds. Each wavetable contains multiple waveforms. The Position knob is used to determine where in the wavetable playback begins. Choose a wavetable by clicking directly on the Table Select display or by using the Select Previous and Select Next buttons on the right of the display. Turning on the X-Fade button creates a smooth transition between the multiple waveforms in any selected wavetable.

Phase Modulation Based on Phased Offset Modulation, this oscillator works very much the Phase Offset Modulation parameters found on the SubTractor. In this case you can choose different waveforms to offset by clicking and dragging directly in either waveform display or by using the Select Previous and Select Next buttons. Make further adjustments to the sound with the Phase Modulation (PM) Amount knob.

FM Pair This is a very simple FM synthesis oscillator with a Carrier control on the left and a Modulator on the right. Select different frequency ratios by clicking and dragging directly in either the Carrier or Modulator display or by using the Select Previous and Select Next buttons. Use the Frequency Modulation (FM) knob to set the amount of frequency modulation.

Multi There are five waveforms on the left side of the Multi oscillator; they can be chosen using the button on the lower left or by clicking directly on the waveform. The selected waveform can then be altered using one of eight detune modes located on the right side, chosen by clicking and dragging directly in the waveform display or by using the Select Previous and Select Next buttons. The Detune Amount (AMT) knob determines the amount of the detuning effect that will be applied.

Noise The Noise oscillator is similar to the SubTractor's Noise Generator but with more available options. In this case there are five different types of noise, chosen by clicking directly on the name or with the Osc Noise Wave button on the lower-left corner. Further adjustments can be made with the Noise Mod knob on the lower right.

The Filters

The next elements in the Thor's signal chain are the Filter sections.

SHARED FUNCTIONALITY

Thor's options for filters all include some similar functionality.

Frequency and Resonance All of the included filter types except the Formant filter have Frequency and Resonance knobs. These knobs function exactly like the other Frequency and Resonance parameters covered in the "Synthesizer Basics" section of this chapter.

Drive The Drive slider on the left side of the filter can increase or decrease the filter's output volume.

Invert Clicking the Invert button inverts how the Filter Envelope's current ADSR settings affect the filter frequency.

Envelope Amount The Envelope Amount knob controls the amount of effect that Thor's Envelope Filter section will have on the filter.

Velocity When you raise the Velocity knob, higher-velocity MIDI notes will cause the filter to open wider, creating a more noticeable filter effect.

Keyboard Tracking Raising the Keyboard Tracking knob opens the filter more as higher notes are played on your MIDI keyboard.

Self-Oscillation Both the State Variable and Low Pass Ladder filters feature a Self-Oscillation button that can be used to generate a pitch with high Resonance knob settings.

THE FILTER TYPES

Thor offers the following filter types:

Low Pass Ladder This filter contains five Low Pass filters, with cutoffs ranging from 6dB to 24dB per octave. You select a mode by clicking directly on a filter type or by using the Mode button on the bottom-right side of the filter.

State Variable The State Variable filter has all of the standard filter types generally found on Reason's instrument devices. You select a mode by clicking directly on a filter type or by using the Mode button beneath the list of filter types. The Notch and Peak filters can be used as High Pass and Low Pass filters by adjusting the State Variable Notch (HP/LP) knob in the lower-right corner.

Comb The Comb filter works by introducing very short delays to the signal and can be used to create modulation-style effects (Chapter 7).

Formant The Formant filter mimics vocal effects. Adjustments to the Formant filter are made using the Filter X and Filter Y sliders on the top right and the Gender knob. See the patch Reason Factory Sound Bank\Thor Patches\I Am Thor.thor for an example of how this filter can be used.

The Voice Programmer Parameters

The Voice Programmer has these features:

Oscillator Slots Thor features three slots for selecting from any of the six oscillator types. Use the triangle in the right corner of each oscillator slot to view and load any of the available oscillators from the drop-down list.

In order for the sound of any oscillator to be heard, it must be routed through a Filter slot and an Oscillator to Filter Enable button must be selected. The Osc 1 to Filter 1 Enable button is activated by default in an initialized Thor patch.

Filter Slots Filter 1 and 2 slots are used to add a filter to the patch.

Click the triangle in the top-left corner to view the drop-down menu and choose one of the four available filter types.

A signal can be routed through both Filter sections even without a filter loaded. In an initialized Thor patch, the signal from Filter 1 will go directly to the Amp section and can be heard. In order to hear the signal from Filter 2, the Filter 2 To Amplifier Enable button must be activated.

Filter Enable Buttons In order for the sound of an oscillator to be heard, it has to be routed through one or both of the Filter sections, even if no filter is currently loaded. Clicking the 1, 2, or 3 button sends the signal from Oscillator 1, 2, or 3 from the mixer to the filter. You can route the signal from any oscillator to either or both Filter sections. As noted previously, the Osc 1 to Filter 1 Enable button is activated by default in an initialized Thor patch.

Mixer The Mixer controls the oscillator's volume levels before their signals reach the Filter sections. The Oscillator 1 and 2 Balance knob controls the mix of the first two oscillators. Turn all the way counterclockwise to hear only Oscillator 1, and fully clockwise to hear only Oscillator 2. The center position provides an even mix of both oscillators. The Oscillator 1 and 2 level knob controls the output volume for the combined signal from the two oscillators. The Oscillator 3 Level slider controls the volume of Oscillator 3.

Shaper Like the Shaper on the Malström, Thor's Shaper changes the shape of the waveform and can either enhance or distort the signal from Filter 1. Choose from nine different Shaper options in the LED, and then use the Drive knob to increase the amount of distortion applied by the shaper.

The Shaper can be turned on or off using the button in the top-left corner. You'll also notice that there are two arrow/buttons below the shaper. Clicking the right arrow sends the signal from the Shaper directly to the Amplifier. The left arrow, activated by default, sends the signal from the Shaper to Filter 2.

Amp Section The Amp (Amplifier) section contains three important parameters: you can increase or lower the overall volume of the patch with the Gain knob, velocity-to-volume control can be applied quickly by raising the Velocity knob, and right/left panning for the entire patch can be adjusted with the Pan knob.

LFO 1 LFO 1 can be routed to many different parameters in Thor and is activated using the Modulation Bus Routing section, covered later in this chapter. LFO 1 is polyphonic and can apply the LFO effect to individual notes.

- Key Sync resets the LFO for each note played, starting the effect at the beginning of the selected waveform.
- Activating Tempo Sync syncs the LFO speed to the current session tempo.
- The Rate knob adjusts the speed of the LFO effect.
- The Delay knob is used to delay the start of the LFO effect.
- Raising the Keyboard Follow knob increases the rate of the LFO as higher notes are played on your MIDI keyboard.

Mod Envelope The mod envelope can be routed to any number of Thor parameters using the Modulation Bus Routing options covered later in this chapter.

- When the Gate Trig button is activated, incoming MIDI notes trigger the mod envelope.
- Tempo Sync synchronizes the envelope's tempo with the Reason song tempo.
- Activating the Loop button loops the generated envelope output.
- The Delay slider can be used to delay the start of the mod envelope.

Filter Envelope The filter envelope automatically controls both Filter 1 and 2. When the Gate Trig button is activated, incoming MIDI notes trigger the filter envelope. Deactivate Gate Trig to turn the filter envelope off, silencing the patch.

Amp Envelope The Amp Envelope section contains the same Attack, Decay, Sustain, and Release parameters covered earlier in this chapter. When the Gate Trig button is activated, incoming MIDI notes trigger the amp envelope. Deactivating Gate Trig turns the amp envelope off, silencing the patch.

AM from OSC 2 This parameter can be used to create ring modulation effects by adding a second oscillator to the patch, raising the AM From Osc 2 slider, and then adjusting Oscillator 2's pitch value by semitones or cents.

Sync Buttons Activate the Sync buttons to synchronize the base frequency of Oscillators 2 and/or 3 to Oscillator 1. You can use this function to combine the output of two or more oscillators with different pitch settings. By activating the Sync buttons, you have the pitch settings of Oscillator 2 or 3 controlled by Oscillator 1, keeping the overall output in tune. However, any variations in Oscillator 2 or 3's Octave, Semitone, or Tune parameters will create an effect. Use the Bandwidth (BW) sliders to make further adjustments to the sound of the activated Sync functionality.

The Global Section

Figure 5.16 shows the Global section. Any settings made in the Global section will alter the sound of the entire patch. The Global section has the following parameters:

Delay Effect The Delay effect is activated by clicking the Delay On button and can be synced to the current Reason song's tempo by clicking the Tempo Sync button.

- Time controls the rate of the delay effect.
- Feedback sets the amount of times the sound will repeat.
- Dry/Wet controls the mix between the original signal and the effect.

The Delay can be further modified with a built-in pitch-modulating LFO. The Rate knob controls the speed of the LFO, and the Amount knob controls the stereo width.

Figure 5.16
The Global section

Chorus Effect Clicking the Chorus On button activates the Chorus effect. Chorus effects are a common feature of many synth patches. For details on using Chorus effects, see the "CF-101 Chorus/Flanger" section of Chapter 7.

As with the Delay, the Chorus can also be further modified with a built-in pitch modulating LFO. The Rate knob controls the speed of the LFO and the Amount knob controls the stereo width. Both the Delay and Chorus effect function essentially as insert effects; in this case they are built into the Thor synthesizer.

Filter 3 Filter 3 is an optional third filter that works on the combined output of the Global Envelope. You have the same options as with the other Filter slots. Filter 3's Envelope button determines how much of an effect the Global Envelope section has on Filter 3.

Global Envelope Section The Global Envelope section is connected to Filter 3, but can also be routed to multiple parameters using Thor's Modulation Bus Routing functionality.

LFO 2 A second LFO, this one is similar to LFO 1, but lacks a Keyboard Follow knob. LFO 2 is monophonic and is not capable of applying the LFO effect to multiple notes.

Modulation Bus Routing

With SubTractor, Malström, and Reason's sampler instruments, you handle routing of LFOs, modulation, and envelope generators within the individual parameter sections, usually by selecting a destination button. In Thor's interface, you control modulation routing and other parameters in the Modulation Bus Routing section, shown in Figure 5.17.

Figure 5.17
The Modulation Bus Routing section

For parameter control you have an incredible range of options that can be used to affect, alter, and control almost all of Thor's features, often in surprising and creative ways. You can think of the Modulation Bus Routing section as a kind of digital patch bay, taking the place of external CV patches.

Source To access Source parameters, click in any Source field and select a Source from the drop-down menu (Figure 5.18).

Sources are any parameter that can create an effect or control a Destination parameter. For example, by choosing an LFO as a source you could control pitch, frequency, or many of the other available parameters from the Destination list with the LFO's selected waveform and settings. Thor's list of sources includes obvious choices, such as LFOs and envelope generators, along with many other possibilities. The Source list is divided into three sections. First is simply the Off option. The second section contains parameters found in the Voice programming area, and the bottom section contains Controller, Global Section, Step Sequencer, CV, and Audio sources.

Destination To access Destination parameters, click in any Destination field and select a Destination from the drop-down menu (Figure 5.19).

The Destinations are any parameters that can be controlled by the Source parameter. The Destination list is divided into three sections: the Off option; the parameters found in the Voice programming area; and the Controller, Global Section, Step Sequencer, CV, and Audio destinations.

Figure 5.18

Selecting a Source parameter

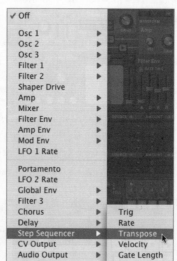

Figure 5.19

Selecting a Destination parameter

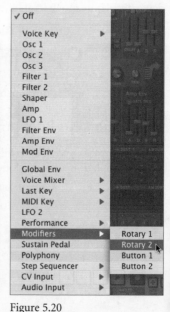

Figure 5.20

Selecting a Scale parameter

Scale Scale parameters are accessed by clicking in any Scale field and selecting a Scale parameter from the drop-down menu (Figure 5.20).

Scale parameters can be used to control the Source parameter's effect on the Destination parameter. As you'll see in the exercises, one obvious use of Scale parameter routing would be to choose an LFO as a Source, followed by an Oscillator parameter, such as pitch as a Destination. You could then choose a Mod Wheel as the Scale parameter and control the rate of the LFO with the Mod Wheel. In this case the Amount fields will be used to determine how much the LFO (Source) will control the oscillator (Destination) and how much the Mod Wheel (Scale) will control the LFO (Source).

The Scale list is also divided into three sections: the Off option; the parameters found in the Voice programming area; and the Controller, Global Section, Step Sequencer, CV, and Audio Scale parameters.

Amount In between the Source, Destination, and Scale fields are the Amount fields. Raising or lowering the Amount controls how much effect the Source will have on the Destination and how much effect the Scale parameter will have on the Source. Click on any Amount field and use your mouse to drag up or down to raise or lower the Amount values. Positive values of up to 100 and negative values as low as –100 are possible.

Clear Buttons On the right side of each Modulation Bus Routing column is a row of Clear buttons. Click any button to reset the current row's routing configuration.

Routing Configurations

The Modulation Bus Routing section features three possible types of routing configurations.

SOURCE → DESTINATION → SCALE
There are seven of these routing configurations, and they are the easiest to use.

To use this configuration:

1. Choose a Source parameter list by clicking the upside-down triangle on the right corner of any empty slot on the Source list.
2. Choose a Destination parameter from the Destination list.
3. Choose Scale parameter from the Scale list.
4. Set an Amount in both Amount fields to activate the routing.

SOURCE → DESTINATION 1 → DESTINATION 2 → SCALE

There are four of these rows available on the Modulation Bus Routing section. In this case a single source can be assigned to two destinations, and then controlled with a single Scale parameter.

SOURCE → DESTINATION → SCALE 1 → SCALE 2

There are two of these available. With this routing a single source can be routed to a single destination and then controlled by two different Scale parameters.

The Step Sequencer

Thor's Step Sequencer can be used to create pattern-based synth patches, rhythmic patterns, and effects. Take a look at some of the patches in the folder Reason Factory Sound Bank\Thor Patches\Rhythmic for examples of how Thor's Step Sequencer can be used in conjunction with the Main Programmer and Modulation Bus Routing to create intricate, exciting patches.

Figure 5.21 shows the Step Sequencer.

Figure 5.21

Thor's Step
Sequencer section

The Step Sequencer contains the following parameters:

Run Button The Run button turns the Step Sequencer on and off.

Run Mode Selector The Run Mode Selector chooses how the Step Sequencer will respond when activated:

Step Plays a single step on the Step Sequencer.

1 Shot Plays the entire pattern once.

Repeat Plays the entire pattern without stopping.

> If Repeat mode is selected, the Step Sequencer will start when you begin playback or recording of a Reason song. You can stop the Step Sequencer at any time by clicking the Run button or stopping playback of the Reason song.

Sequencer Direction Selector You have the following Sequencer Direction options:

Forward Plays the all of the active steps from start to finish.

Reverse Plays all of the active steps from finish to start.

Pendulum 1 Plays all of the active steps from start to finish and then back to the starting point, playing the step at the end of the sequence twice.

Pendulum 1I Plays all of the active steps from start to finish and then back to the starting point, playing the step at the end of the sequence only once.

Random Selects and plays steps randomly.

Sync and Tempo With the Sync button activated, the Step Sequencer playback tempo syncs to the current Reason song tempo. With the Sync button deactivated, the Step Sequencer's tempo can be adjusted independently of the Reason song's tempo.

Edit Knob The Edit knob can be used to select from the following multiple editable parameters for each step in the pattern sequencer:

Note Adjusts the note pitch value played by an individual step. The range of available notes can be selected with the Octave Range selector. Use the default −2 setting for a two-octave range, −4 for a four-octave range, and Full for the complete range of available notes (C-2 to G8).

Velocity Used to adjust the Velocity for each step from 0 to 127.

Gate Length Similar to an amplitude envelope's Release parameter. Shorter Gate lengths will cut off a note earlier.

Step Duration Sets the length of each step. This setting can be used to create rhythmic variations within Step Sequencer patterns by lengthening or shortening the amount of time the Step Sequencer stays on specific steps.

Curve 1 and 2 Can be assigned to different parameters using the Modulation Bus Routing section.

Reset Click the Reset button to reset any and all changes made with the Edit knob.

Steps The Steps knob is used to set the number of steps in the pattern. Click and drag down to reduce the number of steps. Click and drag up to increase the number.

Each Edit knob parameter can be adjusted for each individual step in the pattern sequencer. To do this, select a parameter and adjust the knob located above each individual step. The new setting will be reflected in the Value display to right of the Edit knob.

Creating Thor Patches

The Thor Polysonic Synthesizer offers a staggering range of possibilities for patch creation. It would be impossible to catalog all of the possible Voice, Global, Step Sequencer, and Modulation Bus Routing configurations available in Thor.

The good news is that once you understand a few basic routing concepts, creating amazing patches with Thor can be a fairly simple process.

> Exploring the included patches is an excellent way to see some of the possibilities contained in this instrument. In particular, the patches found in the Reason Factory Sound Bank\ Signature Patches folder were created by Thor users with extensive synth programming knowledge. These patches contain many interesting and creative uses of all of the elements that make up the Thor interface.

The exercises in the following section are designed to get you started with Thor.

Basic Patches

These first exercises will give you a look at some basic patch programming options within Thor and emphasize important things about how Thor's routing is configured. Follow these steps to create a single oscillator patch:

Follow these steps to create a simple two-oscillator patch.

1. Create a new, initialized Thor Polysonic Synthesizer.

2. Click the Show Programmer button.

An initialized Thor is created with the Analog Oscillator in the Oscillator 1 slot and the Low Pass Ladder filter in the Filter 1 slot. You can leave these default settings as they are or select a new oscillator and/or filter at any time. Even at this early stage in the game, you have a lot of options for creating sounds. Simply switching out the currently loaded oscillator and/or filter can drastically alter the sound of your patch. Making minor or major adjustments to either component can access even more creative options.

The signal path that exists now is Osc1 → Mixer → Filter 1 → Shaper (not active) → Amp → Global Section → Stereo Output.

3. Add a second filter by selecting a Low Pass Ladder filter from the Filter 2 drop-down menu.

4. Route the signal from Oscillator 1 to Filter 2 by clicking the Oscillator 1 to Filter 2 Enable button located just to the left of Filter 2.

5. Route the signal from Filter 2 to the Amplifier by clicking the Filter 2 to Amplifier Enable button. Once this is done, you'll be able to hear the output of Filter 2. You can make any adjustments you want to either filter at any time.

6. The Amp Envelope section is hardwired to the output of the Amp section. Use the Attack, Decay, Sustain, and Release parameters to control the Amplitude settings for the patch.

7. The Filter Envelope section is hardwired to both filters. Use the Filter Envelope section to create a filter envelope effect.

8. Raise the Amp section's Amplifier Velocity knob if you want higher note velocities to result in louder note volumes.

9. Turn on the Delay effect in the Global section and click the Sync button to sync the Delay effect to the current session's tempo.

CREATING A 2 OSCILLATOR PATCH

Follow these steps to create a simple two-oscillator patch:

1. Create a new Thor or initialize the current patch.

2. If the Programmer section is not currently visible, click the Show Programmer button.

3. Create a second oscillator by clicking the triangle in Oscillator 2's upper-left corner and choosing Multi Oscillator from the menu.

4. Select a filter type by clicking in the upper-left corner of Filter 2 and selecting a filter type from the drop-down menu.

5. Click the Oscillator 2 to Filter 2 Enable button.

6. Click the Filter 2 to Amplifier Enable button.

Your patch now has two oscillators generating sound, each sent to its own filter. This might be the most common routing, but it's not at all mandatory. Other possibilities include routing both oscillators through either filter or routing one or both oscillators through an empty filter slot. You can also adjust the balance between Oscillators 1 and 2 and their overall output using the Mixer section.

Use steps 6–9 from the previous exercise to work with whatever routing you've chosen to further shape the sound of your patch.

You can find an example of a two oscillator Thor patch that utilizes many of the Voice section's programming options on the accompanying CD: `Examples\Chapter 5\Thor\TwoOsc.thor`.

> You can add a third oscillator to your patch at any time with the Oscillator 3 slot. Route your third oscillator through Filter 1, Filter 2, or both by using either of the Oscillator 3 to Filter Enable buttons. Use the Mixer section to adjust the level of Oscillator 3 in relation to Oscillators 1 and 2.

Adding a Third Filter

You can add a third filter to your patch at any time in the Global section's Filter 3 slot. The third filter can be controlled with the Global Envelope and will alter the combined output of Filters 1 and 2 before routing the signal to the effects.

You can find an example of a 3 filter Thor patch on the accompanying CD: `Examples\Chapter 5\Thor\ThreeFilter.thor`.

Putting It All Together

If you've completed the preceding exercises, you've got some idea of the available options at your disposal working in the Main Programmer. Mixing and matching multiple oscillators, choosing waveforms, settings, then adding different filter types, filter settings, and routing configurations presents you with unlimited starting points for creating patches. Add the envelope generator and Global section's extra filter and effects for even more options.

You can experiment even further with the Main Programmer by working with the AM from Oscillator 2 functionality, the Sync buttons, the Mixer, and the Shaper.

Even with all of these options, this is really just the beginning of Thor's power. In the next section, you'll learn about some of the Modulation Bus Routing possibilities and how to access them for even more intricate patch creation options.

Using Modulation Bus Routing

As with everything else you've learned so far about Thor, starting to use the Modulation Bus routing section is fairly simple. Understanding the basic concepts then opens the door to virtually endless routing configurations.

Creating LFO Routing

In this first exercise you'll route the LFO 1 section to different parameters:

1. Create a new Thor or initialize the current patch.

2. Click the Show Programmer button if the Programmer is not currently visible.

3. Choose the first Source field on the Modulation Bus Routing section and choose Source → LFO 1 from the drop-down menu.

4. Click in the first Amount field and drag up with your mouse to set the Amount to 50.

5. Click in the first Destination field and Choose OSC 1 → Pitch as the Destination.

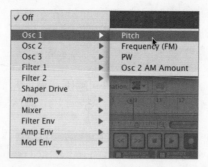

6. In the Voice Programmer's LFO section, turn on Key Sync and Tempo Sync to start the LFO with each new MIDI note played and synchronize the effect to the current Reason song tempo.

7. Play a few notes on your MIDI keyboard to hear the LFO 1 raise and lower Oscillator 1's pitch.

8. Use the LFO 1 Waveform Display to scroll through the various available waveforms to hear the various available effects.

You can assign the LFO (or any Source parameter) to any of the Destination parameters that you see in the Destination drop-down menu. This includes Oscillator, Filter, and Envelope parameters; Step Sequencer; Audio and CV parameters; and more, though not every assignment will result in a noticeable effect. Experiment with this option by assigning the LFO to various parameters to hear the results.

You are not limited to assigning the LFO to a single parameter. You can assign LFO 1 as the source to as many destinations as you have available.

You can also use one of the four Source → Destination 1 → Destination 2 → Scale slots to assign one source to two destinations.

This is Modulation Bus Routing at its most basic. Still, even within this simple routing configuration are many possibilities. Try using the various envelopes as sources and routing them to various destinations.

You can find an example of a Thor patch created with a handful of simple routing instructions on the accompanying CD: Examples\Chapter 5\Thor\ModBus1.thor.

Adding the Scale Parameter

In this exercise you'll quickly add the Scale parameter to the example you created in the previous exercise:

1. Follow steps 1–7 of the previous exercise.

2. Click the first Scale field and select Performance → Mod Wheel from the drop-down menu.

3. Adjust the Amount setting to 100.

The Mod Wheel can now be used to control the amount of effect that the LFO has on Oscillator 1's pitch parameter. Use your mouse to raise and lower the Mod Wheel on the Controller Panel or use the Mod Wheel on your attached MIDI controller.

You can select any available Scale parameter from the Scale drop-down menu. The Mod Wheel, the Pitch Bend Wheel, and the Rotary knobs are some of the more obvious possibilities for controlling sources and destinations.

Assigning a Rotary Knob

The Controller Panel's buttons and Rotary knobs are located on the Source and Scale drop-down menus in the subcategory Modifiers.

Follow these steps to assign a parameter to a Rotary knob:

1. Create a new Thor or initialize the current patch.

2. Make sure the Programmer is visible.

3. Create the following routing:

SOURCE	AMOUNT	DESTINATION
LFO 1	100	Filter1Freq
Rotary 1	100	LFO 1 Rate

4. Play notes on your MIDI keyboard while adjusting the Rotary 1 knob in the center of the Controller Panel. You'll hear the LFO 1 Rate increase as you raise the knob.

Click in the Name field just below the Rotary 1 knob to rename the parameter.

Another option for a different effect would be to assign the Rotary 1 knob as the Scale parameter. Use the following routing to try this option:

SOURCE	AMOUNT	DESTINATION	AMOUNT	SCALE
LFO1	100	Filter1Freq	100	Rotary1

You can use these kinds of routing configurations to assign either Rotary knob to any adjustable parameter.

ASSIGNING A BUTTON

You can also use these and other routing configurations to assign one of the Controller Panel's buttons to turn a parameter on and off.

Create the following Modulation Bus routing:

SOURCE	AMOUNT	DESTINATION	AMOUNT	SCALE
LFO1	100	Filter1Freq	100	Button1

As with the Rotary knobs, you can click the field just below either button and rename according to the selected parameter.

Going Deeper with Modulation Bus Routing

As you've certainly figured out by now, the configurations described in the previous examples are just the very beginning of what's possible with the Modulation Bus Routing section. Experiment further by trying out the different available Source, Destination, and Scale parameters in various configurations.

Many of the included patches found in any of the Reason Factory Sound Bank\Thor Patches folder can also serve as guides to creating the kinds of sounds and effects that you want.

Using the Step Sequencer

The Step Sequencer is a very intricate device with many possible applications. This exercise will show you how to get started using the Modulation Bus Routing options to work with the Step Sequencer:

1. Turn off MIDI in the Controller Panel Trigger section so that the incoming information from your MIDI keyboard triggers only the Step Sequencer.

2. Make sure the Programmer is visible.

3. In the Modulation Bus Routing section's first Source field, choose MIDI Key → Gate from the Source drop-down menu.

4. In the first Destination field, choose Steps Sequencer → Trig from the menu.

5. Raise the Amount to at least 10.

6. Use the Step Sequencer's Run Mode selector to choose 1 Shot mode.

With this routing in place, any incoming MIDI information will trigger the Step Sequencer, playing the entire pattern once.

In Step mode, one sequencer step would be played. In Repeat mode, the sequencer would continuously play.

Following the next steps, you'll set things up so that the Step Sequencer responds to incoming MIDI pitch information:

7. In the Modulation Bus Routing section's second Source field, choose MIDI Key → Note from the Source drop-down menu.

8. In the second Destination field, choose Steps Sequencer → Transpose from the menu.

9. Raise the Amount to 100.

While the first routing simply triggers the Step Sequencer, with this second routing in place the incoming pitch MIDI information will trigger the Step Sequencer at the same pitch as the note played on your MIDI keyboard. Play a few notes on your MIDI keyboard to try this out.

This is a very basic Step Sequencer patch that could be used as a starting point for more complex experiments. Every note you play on your MIDI keyboard will trigger the Step Sequencer for eight steps. If you play a note before the eight steps are finished, the Step Sequencer is retriggered and the pattern starts from the beginning.

You can find this example as a Thor patch on the accompanying CD: Examples\Chapter 5\ Thor\StepOne.thor.

You can create variations with this by doing any of the following:

• Change the sequencer direction.

• Change the Sync Rate to a faster or slower value.

• Use the Edit knob to select various parameters and edit one or more steps (try changing the pitch of individual steps for an immediately noticeable effect).

• Click the pink LED for any step to turn it off.

• Make adjustments to the patch in the Voice Programmer and Global section.

• Add other Modulation Bus Routing configurations.

You can find examples of some patches that utilize the Step Sequencer along with the Voice Programmer and Modulation Bus Routing concepts you've learned in this chapter on the accompanying CD in the folder `Examples\Chapter 5\Thor\Steps`.

Combining the Elements

As with all of Reason's synthesizers, the key to working with Thor is having an understanding of each of the elements that make up the synthesizer's interface. Of course, in Thor's case that covers a lot more ground than any other Reason instrument. Use what you've learned in this chapter to experiment with Thor, and be sure to look at all of the included patches in the folder `Reason Factory Sound Bank\Thor Patches` for further direction and inspiration.

Summary

The chapter you've just read contains some of the most important concepts and some of the most valuable information covered in this book. After a quick overview of the different types of synthesis used in Reason, you learned about the synthesizer parameters and components that are found on all of Reason's synthesizer instruments and how to use them. Because these same parameters are found in one form or another on many other Reason devices, this information can be utilized to help you control and create sound throughout the Reason program, with instrument, effects, and other devices.

You then looked in depth at each of Reason's synthesizers. For each device the strategy was to first survey the elements that make up each instrument's interface, and then try out the process of using the most important features of each to create patches. The SubTractor and Malström were both explained in detail, while for the more powerful Thor Polysonic Synthesizer all of the options and features were covered along with some basic lessons. The section on Thor was geared toward getting you started with Reason's most full-featured new instrument device and giving you a clear idea of some of the instrument's limitless possibilities.

What you've learned in this chapter has given you a much deeper understanding of the Reason program, as well as virtual synthesizers and digital audio in general. Following these lessons and exercises has opened up new doors and directions for working with all of Reason's devices.

CHAPTER 6

Reason's Samplers

Reason's sampler instruments, the NN-19 Digital Sampler and the NN-XT Advanced Sampler, are two of the program's most powerful devices. Both samplers are extremely versatile and can be used as virtual drum machines, pianos, or any number of synthesizers or keyboards. They can be used to trigger loops (although without the time stretching options and pitch shifting options available with the Dr. Rex), and they are both excellent tools for working with sound effects or creating sample-based vocal arrangements. The NN-19 and the NN-XT also contain editing features that can fix, distort, enhance, or mangle any sound to create new instruments, textures, and sound effects.

Topics in this chapter include:

- **Sampler Basics**

- **Using the NN-19 Digital Sampler**

- **The NN-19's Editing Features**

- **Creating and Editing NN-19 Patches**

- **Using the NN-XT Advanced Sampler**

- **Creating and Editing NN-XT Patches**

- **Drums and the NN-XT**

- **The Remote Editor's Features**

- **Creating Your Own Samples**

Sampler Basics

Traditionally, a digital sampler is a hardware device capable of recording analog audio, converting it to a digital signal, and then playing back the entire recording or a section of the recording. This is often referred to as A/D, or analog-to-digital conversion.

Digital sampling first appeared in 1976 with the Melodian, created by Computer Music Inc. Over the next few years the Melodian was followed by Fairlight CMI (Computer Musical Instrument) and the E-MU Emulator, both released in the late 1970s.

These early digital samplers were large and extremely expensive. They were also limited when it came to sound quality, usually having low bit depth and sample rate capabilities.

Throughout the 1980s and '90s, digital sampling technology improved drastically. Paralleling the same kinds of developments in personal computer technology, samplers became smaller and easier to work with. As the technology improved, bit depths and sample rates increased. Digital samplers from companies such as AKAI and Roland began appearing, providing both affordability and versatility.

Many of these sampler instruments have become extremely important over the years for different styles of music. AKAI's MPC series in particular became associated with hip-hop producers, while sampling in general became a key element in the development of Industrial music and a variety of dance and electronic music genres. Today hardware and software samplers are used in one form or another in countless recordings across the entire range of popular music.

PRE-DIGITAL SAMPLING

One of the earliest uses of a sampler-style instrument is the Mellotron. Introduced in 1965, the Mellotron used analog tape to play back recorded performances of single notes and loops when a note on a piano-like keyboard was pressed.

You can find a sampled version of the Mellotron used on many famous recordings, including the Beatles' "Strawberry Fields Forever" on Propellerhead Software's "Abbey Road Keyboards" ReFill.

Hardware vs. Software

Hardware and software samplers have some important differences. For one, software samplers such as those included with Reason are not recording devices. As you've already seen, none of Reason's devices allow you to actually record audio into the program. Reason's samplers are playback devices only, allowing you to load, play, and edit audio files from a wide range of formats (discussed in Chapter 1).

Another difference between hardware and software samplers is workflow. Although many producers prefer the hands-on approach of working with hardware samplers, there are many complex functions, such as quickly loading and editing multiple samples, that can be performed in a fraction of the time using software samplers.

The NN-19 and the NN-XT both contain many features that closely mimic popular hardware samplers. However, in a development that's similar to what's happened with virtual synthesizers, bringing sampling into the digital world has allowed for some innovations that were previously impossible with hardware devices. The NN-XT in particular is a good example of this, combining both traditional sampler features with layering, editing, and automation functionality that's only possible in the software realm.

Using Reason's Samplers

Considering all of the things that are possible with Reason's samplers, the obvious question is "Why use the other instruments at all?" The answer is that some people don't. If your background and experience are based on using hardware samplers or other software samplers, you may find that the NN-19 Digital Sampler and the NN-XT Advanced Sampler are the only tools you need to create music in Reason. This is especially true if you are creating music that requires realistic-sounding instrument performances.

For example, if you want to create a complex drum performance that truly mimics the dynamics of a live drum set and the imperfections of a human performance, then the NN-XT Advanced Sampler is easily your best bet. For many Reason users, even very experienced ones, it may be much easier to quickly create and sequence both simple and complex performances using the Redrum Drum Computer, since Redrum gives you easy access to the specific parameters most often associated with drum samples and is laid out to facilitate ease of use.

However, to create a truly realistic drum performance you'll need a much more powerful sampler, with the ability to load a drum kit made up of layered multisamples (a concept we'll be covering later in this chapter). The NN-XT offers all this and more, including the option of advanced output routing for even more control over your drum and percussion mixes.

In fact, many drum and percussion ReFills, including Propellerhead's own Reason Drum Kits ReFill, use Reason's NN-XT to take advantage of its ability to load intricately created multilayered patches and to create drum kits using more than Redrum's 10 available slots.

This is just one example of Reason's samplers that can be used to create realistic performances. Both the NN-19 and the NN-XT have been built with functionality specifically geared toward turning recorded samples of drums, keyboards, strings and any other instrument you can imagine into exciting, lifelike performances.

Which One Should I Use?

The main difference between Reason's two samplers is fairly obvious from the name of the NN-XT Advanced Sampler, which contains more complex functionality and intricate editing features than the NN-19. The NN-19 Digital Sampler is still a powerful, feature-heavy tool and well worth learning to use.

In fact, because the NN-19 uses fewer processor resources and has a much simpler interface, there will be some instances where it makes more sense to choose the NN-19 over the NN-XT.

Here are some possible uses for the NN-19, all of which will be covered in this chapter:

· Using a sampler to trigger a single loop or audio file

· Using a sampler to trigger and sequence multiple loops

· Quickly creating a sampler patch

· Sequencing a vocal track

If you're a beginning Reason user, the NN-19 will contain everything you need to get started working with samples. If you are new to sampling in general, or working with software samplers in particular, the best way to learn Reason's samplers is to use the NN-19 to cover the basics and then move on to the NN-XT to learn about more advanced functionality.

And that's exactly how this chapter is organized. Even if you are only interested in the NN-XT, I highly recommend that you start by reading the section on the NN-19.

MULTISAMPLES AND MULTILAYERED PATCHES

A multisample is a patch containing more than one sample assigned to different notes or to ranges of notes. When working with sampled instruments, the general rule is that the more samples you have in a patch, the more realistic-sounding instruments you can create.

For example, let's say you want to create a keyboard instrument patch and you have only one sampled note to work with. If you load that sample into a sampler and play it within an octave of its natural pitch, it will probably sound OK. Anything beyond that will sound increasingly unnatural, and even more so as you play higher or lower on the keyboard. This has to do with a number of factors. One reason is that the overtones created by any single piano note will vary greatly as you move up and down the keyboard. This will be true to some extent for any instrument that you sample.

So, a simple keyboard multisample patch might contain five samples, each assigned to a 12-note (one octave) key range. A more complicated patch could possibly contain a sampled note for every single key in the patch.

Another example of a popular multisample instrument would be a drum kit. In a drum kit multisample patch, each piece of the drum kit instrument is typically assigned to a single note. Playing the corresponding note on your MIDI keyboard or controller or drawing the note in the sequencer will trigger the specific sample. Both the NN-19 and the NN-XT are capable of loading, creating, and playing multisamples.

The NN-XT is capable of taking sampling a step further and can be used to create and play multilayered sample patches. A multilayered sample patch contains multiple samples mapped by velocity to the same single note or range of notes. A specific sample will be triggered based on the velocity used to trigger the specific note. For example, you may have six snare drum hits assigned to a single note. If you press down hard on the corresponding MIDI key (giving it a high velocity), a louder, sharper snare drum will sound. If you press the key with a gentler touch, then a lighter, easier sound will be triggered. This kind of functionality can be used to create incredibly realistic sample patches with drums, pianos, strings, or any other kind of instrument that can benefit from greater dynamics and realism.

Multilayered sampling is also useful for combining instruments in a single patch. With a sampler that's capable of multilayering, you can quickly combine pianos and strings, synthesizers and sound effects, percussion and noise, and so forth. Any two or more instruments or sounds can be combined in endless combinations.

Content for Reason's Samplers

Content for samplers is easy to find. Companies such as Zero-G (`www.zero-g.co.uk`), Big Fish Audio (`www.bigfishaudio.com`), and many others sell sample libraries in multiple formats.

Many sample libraries will come with patches specifically created for the NN-19 or NN-XT. If this is the case, the product's description or packaging will clearly state that these formats are included. If you want to use a sample library that doesn't come with pre-created NN-19 or NN-XT patches, after reading this chapter you'll be able to create your own. Just make sure that any sample libraries you purchase come with Wave or AIFF format files.

Many loop libraries also contain folders of "one shots" that contain the individual files used to make their included loops. If you have a collection of particularly high-quality loops, it's worth checking to see if there is a separate folder containing individual samples. Using the techniques covered in this chapter, you can load these individual samples into either of Reason's samplers and create your own loops and sequences.

ReFills

As with all of Reason's instruments, ReFills are a great way to increase your collection of sounds and patches for Reason's samplers. At `www.propellerheads.se` you'll find many resources, including links to many free, demo, and commercial ReFills with great content for both the NN-19 and NN-XT sampler.

Many older refills contain both NN-19 and NN-XT versions of sample patches, though newer ReFills will usually be geared specifically toward the NN-XT. Some commercial ReFills that contain excellent patches for either or both the NN-19 and NN-XT include:

- Abbey Road Keyboards (`www.propellerheads.se`)
- Reason Drum Kits (`www.propellerheads.se`)
- Sonic Reality (`www.sonicreality.com`)

Free Content

The Internet is an excellent resource for content for all of Reason's instruments. Because of their ability to load sound files in multiple formats, Reason's samplers in particular can benefit from the vast amounts of free samples, SoundFonts, and other compatible files available on the Web.

Here are some websites with free and demo ReFills for the NN-19 and NN-XT:

- `www.reasonbanks.com`
- `www.freesamples.breakdance.sk`

And some sites with free and demo SoundFonts:

- `www.soundfonts.it`
- `www.hammersound.net`
- `www.sf2midi.com`

And some sites with free content for samplers:

- `www.atomsplitteraudio.com`
- `www.soundsnap.com`

For more free content, try Google searches for "free Wave samples," "free Sound-Fonts," and so forth.

ReLoad: Importing AKAI Samples

Registered Reason users can download and install the ReLoad program from `www.propellerheads.se`. Unregistered users can buy the utility for $49.

ReLoad can quickly convert AKAI S1000 and S3000 sample disks to NN-XT patch files. You can also use ReLoad to convert the samples on your AKAI format discs into Wave format files for use with the Redrum and NN-19.

Create Your Own

As samplers, both the NN-19 and NN-XT are especially useful for working with your own original content. This includes simple patches created with a single note or sample, multi-samples, and multilayered samples, all of which are covered in this chapter. Source files for creating original NN-19 and NN-XT patches can come from the Reason Factory Sound Bank or Orkester ReFill, from third-party ReFills, sample or loop libraries, or your own original recordings of instruments, vocals, or any sound source. Elements from some or all of these sources can be combined in a single patch as well.

By the end of this chapter, you'll know how to create your own original sample material using a variety of methods.

Using the NN-19 Digital Sampler

The NN-19 Digital Sampler is one of the original instruments introduced in Reason version 1. As Reason has developed and as computers have become increasingly powerful, sample patches and libraries have become more complex. As a result, the NN-19 may not always be your sampler of choice. When it comes to using and creating complex, realistic sample patches, the advanced features contained in the NN-XT Advanced Sampler will usually be more appropriate.

The NN-19 still has many uses and also contains a couple of distinct advantages over the NN-XT. One advantage is in its ease of use, especially the ability to quickly create, edit, and save your own sample patches. The NN-19's interface is straightforward, and many of its parameters will already be familiar to you if you've read Chapter 3 on Reason's Dr. Rex Loop Player or the "Synthesizer Basics" and "SubTractor Analog Synthesizer" sections of Chapter 5.

The NN-19 also uses significantly less processor power than the NN-XT, so if you are working with fairly simple techniques that require the use of basic multisamples, then the NN-19 may be the best device for the job, especially in large sessions with multiple sampler devices.

The NN-19 is particularly useful as a learning tool for the Reason user who wants to learn about digital sampling devices and concepts. We'll be using the NN-19 to get a look at some basic techniques for creating and editing different kinds of sample patches.

The NN-19 Interface

The NN-19 interface, shown in Figure 6.1, contains many of the basic parameters you'll find on most virtual and hardware samplers.

Figure 6.1

**The NN-19 Digital
Sampler interface**

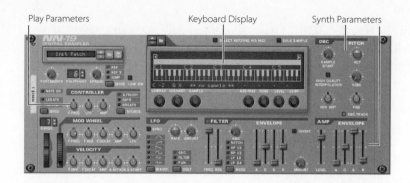

There are a number of similarities both in the functionality and signal routing of Reason's samplers and synthesizers. As you can see in Figure 6.1, the NN-19 offers many Synth parameters, including an LFO section, a Filter section, and Amplitude Envelope. We'll be looking at each of these specifically as they relate to the NN-19. For more details on the concepts behind these parameters, see the "Synthesizer Basics" section of Chapter 5.

At the top left of the NN-19 interface are the Browse and Save buttons and the LED display.

In the top center of the interface is the Keyboard display. The Keyboard display, the Browse Sample button just above it, and the seven knobs just below it are all used to create and edit sample patches.

On the left side of the NN-19 interface are the Play parameters, which are used to adjust how the NN-19 plays back the currently loaded sample or sample patch.

Content for the NN-19

The Reason Factory Sound Bank and Orkester ReFills contain a number of patches for the NN-19. There are also many third-party ReFills available with NN-19 patches, though as mentioned earlier, newer ReFills will sometimes bypass the NN-19 format altogether, instead focusing on multilayered ReFills for the NN-XT.

FILE FORMATS

The NN-19 uses the file format .smp to load and save patches. When you open the Reason Browser with the NN-19's Browse Patch button, you will also be able to see REX files and files with the NN-XT sampler format extension .sxt. If you select and load a REX file, the NN-19 will assign each slice to its own key, starting at C2.

The Browse Sample button is used to create single-sample and multisample patches with the NN-19. Using the Browse Sample button, the NN-19 can load and play Wave and AIFF files, the individual slices that make up any REX file, and the samples contained in any SoundFont file.

SAMPLE RATE, BIT DEPTH, AND THE NN-19

By default, the NN-19 will convert any samples you load individually or as part of a patch to a sample rate of 44.1 and bit depth of 16. You can bypass this automatic downsampling and use higher sample rate/bit depth samples by activating the High Quality Interpolation button in the Oscillator section of the NN-19 instrument panel.

Loading, Playing, and Saving Patches

As with many of Reason's instruments, you can get nearly endless use out of the NN-19 just by loading and playing patches, either from the Reason Factory Sound Bank, the Orkester Sound Bank, or any of the third-party ReFills that contain content for the NN-19.

Figure 6.2

The Reason Factory Sound Bank's NN-19 sampler patches

Try the following steps to quickly get started using Reason's NN-19 Digital Sampler device:

1. Create a new Reason song.

2. Choose File → Create → NN-19 Digital Sampler to add an NN-19 to the song.

3. Click the NN-19's Browse Patch button and navigate to the folder `Reason Factory Sound Bank\NN-19 Sampler Patches` (Figure 6.2).

4. Open any instrument category folder and select any NN-19 instrument patch.

5. Click OK to load the selected patch.

6. Make sure the NN-19 track is selected in the sequencer and that the track is armed to received MIDI information.

7. Use your MIDI keyboard to play the loaded patch or use the sequencer's Edit mode view to draw a performance in the Key lane using the Pencil tool.

    The Select Next Patch and Select Previous Patch buttons have the same functionality with the NN-19 as with Reason's other instruments. Clicking these will select the next or previous patch in the currently loaded patch's directory. You can also click the LED display to view all of the patches in the current directory.

8. Select and load any patch from the list or select Open Browser at the top of the list to open the Reason Browser.

If you make any changes to the current patch by adjusting any of the parameters available in the NN-19's interface, you can use the Save Patch button to save your new or edited patch.

As with all of Reason's patch formats, the .smp format does not save the actual sound files that make up your NN-19 patch. The .smp file contains "pointers" telling Reason where to locate the individual files. The patch file also contains the settings on the NN-19 interface.

Once a patch is loaded into the NN-19 and the correct sequencer track is selected and armed for recording, you can utilize all of the information and concepts found in Chapter 2 and in "The Sequencer: Advanced" section of Chapter 10 to create and edit performances.

At any time, you can choose Edit ⊕ Initialize Patch from the main Edit window to create an empty patch by returning the NN-19 to its default state. You can also right/Ctrl-click on the face of the NN-19 to initialize a patch from the context menu.

The NN-19's Editing Features

The NN-19's editing features allow you to create subtle or drastic changes to your loaded samples and patches. This can also be a great way to find unexpected inspiration by taking a "normal" sound and experimenting with it, to quickly alter the sound of a track that's been created in the sequencer to help it stand out in a mix or to come up with entirely new sound effects and instruments to work with in Reason.

Global Editing

It's important to understand early on that the editing parameters on the NN-19 interface are global. This means that any adjustments you make with the Synth or Play parameter knobs, buttons, and sliders will affect every sample in the currently loaded patch. For the ability to edit the Synth and Play parameters of individual samples within a patch, see the NN-XT Advanced Sampler.

The NN-19 Synth Parameters

Much of the NN-19's interface is taken up by what are known as the Synth parameters. If you've read Chapter 5 or Chapter 3, many of these parameters will already be familiar to you. The NN-19's Synth parameters are especially similar to the features on the SubTractor Analog Synthesizer, and these functions are covered in greater detail in the "Synthesizer Basics" section of Chapter 5.

A good way to get an idea of what each parameter can do is to load an NN-19 patch for a familiar-sounding instrument such as a piano, organ, or acoustic guitar from the Reason Factory Sound Bank and experiment with the settings as you go through the various parameters in this section.

Figure 6.3

The Oscillator section

THE OSCILLATOR

Figure 6.3 shows the NN-19's Oscillator section.

The Oscillator on the NN-19 doesn't refer to the same kind of oscillators that you would find on a Reason synthesizer, which actually generate different waveforms to create sounds. In this case it's called the Oscillator because it contains many of the same functions that are found in the Oscillator section of a synthesizer. The following parameters are found in the NN-19's Oscillator section:

Sample Start The Sample Start knob can be used to adjust the starting point for playback of the samples in a patch. The Sample Start knob can also be used in conjunction with the velocity settings covered later in this chapter.

Envelope Amount Can be used in conjunction with the Envelope Filter to create pitch effects.

The Octave Knob Lets you raise or lower the octave of the patch four octaves in either direction.

Oscillator Semitone Can be used to raise the pitch by up to 12 semitones (an octave).

Oscillator Fine Tune Can be used to adjust the pitch of the samples in a patch plus or minus 50 cents. (Cents are a unit of measure used for fine-tuning pitch. There are 100 cents to a semitone.)

High Quality Interpolation As described earlier, this setting allows you to use higher-quality samples by playing them back at their original sample rate and bit depth.

Keyboard Tracking Turning off Keyboard Tracking tells the NN-19 to always play samples at their default pitch. This can be useful if you are working with loops or sounds that don't require any pitch shifting. When you create a new NN-19, Keyboard Tracking is always turned on by default.

AMPLITUDE ENVELOPE

The Amplitude Envelope section, shown in Figure 6.4, contains the standard ADSR (Attack, Decay, Sustain, and Release) sliders found on the Amplitude Envelope section of the SubTractor and other Reason instruments.

Figure 6.4

The Amplitude Envelope

Two frequent uses for the Amplitude Envelope on the NN-19 include raising the Attack parameter to create rising, swelling sounds—for example, a more realistic violin, cello, or other string section sound. You can also quickly add sustain to an instrument patch by raising the Sustain and Release knobs.

THE FILTER AND THE FILTER ENVELOPE

The Filter section shown in Figure 6.5 has almost exactly the same parameters as the Filter section on the Dr. Rex (covered in Chapter 3) and the SubTractor (covered in Chapter 5). These include the choice of a Notch, High Pass 12, Band Pass 12, Low Pass 12, and Low Pass 24.

Figure 6.5

The Filter and Filter Envelope

The Filter Envelope has the standard ADSR sliders. Like the Dr. Rex the Filter Envelope section on the NN-19, it not only controls both the Filter but can also beused in conjunction with the Oscillator to create pitch effects by raising or lowering the Oscillator's Envelope Amount knob. You can increase the Filter effect by raising the amount knob on the lower right of the Filter Envelope. Select the Invert button to turn the envelope shape upside down.

THE LFO

Figure 6.6

The LFO section

The NN-19's LFO section, shown in Figure 6.6, is somewhat similar to the LFO section of the SubTractor and exactly the same as the LFO section of the Dr. Rex.

The LFO destination button on the lower right of the LFO section is used to choose between Oscillator (for pitch effects); the Filter, for Filter sweeps and other EQ-related effects; and Panning for creating panning effects.

When the Sync button in the upper-left corner of the LFO section is turned on, any effects generated by the LFO section will be synced to the tempo of the current session.

The Amount knob controls the amount of effect the LFO will have on the current patch. The Rate knob determines the speed of the LFO's effect.

EXAMPLE: CREATE A PANNING EFFECT

One frequent use for the LFO section is to create panning or tremolo effects. Quickly create a panning/tremolo effect by following these steps:

1. Create a new NN-19 and load any instrument patch. This effect will be especially noticeable on any guitar or piano patch.

2. Turn on the LFO Sync button.

3. Use the Waveform Select button to choose the Square wave.

4. Turn the Amount knob all the way up to 127.

5. Set the LFO Rate to 1/8.

6. Click the LFO DEST button to select Pan as the LFO destination.

7. Use your MIDI keyboard to play the instrument.

Experiment with the LFO settings first by raising and lowering the LFO Rate knob, then by switching between the different waveforms.

Take your experiments a step further by clicking the LFO DEST button to send the LFO to the Oscillator and to the Filter to create different kinds of LFO effects.

The NN-19 Play Parameters

The Play parameters are all specifically related to how the NN-19 plays back your currently loaded samples and patches. The Play and Synth parameters can also be integrated in interesting ways by adjusting some of the Mod Wheel and Velocity Play parameters to control the effects generated by the Synth parameters.

PORTAMENTO

The Portamento knob can be used to create notes that glide up or down, depending on the previous note played.

Follow any note with a higher note and the second note will rise or glide up to its normal pitch. Follow any note with a lower note and the note will descend to its normal pitch. Higher Portamento means a longer glide. Keep the Portamento knob at its default setting of 0 to leave it off.

POLYPHONY

The NN-19's polyphony setting is the same as with other Reason instruments.

Setting Polyphony to 1 means any note you play will cut off the previous note, so if you are using the NN-19 to play loops you can set Polyphony to 1 to make sure no two loops are being triggered at once. A Polyphony setting of 1 can also be used to create gate effects with drum patches or to create single-note synth lead lines.

When creating your own patches you'll want to raise the polyphony significantly from its default setting of 6, especially for piano or keyboard instruments.

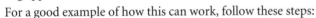

For a familiar 80's synth lead sound, try loading a synthesizer patch and then combining a high Portamento setting with a Polyphony setting of 1.

SPREAD

The Spread knob is used to create a stereo field for any instrument or sample patch. Each setting applies a different kind of stereo effect.

For a good example of how this can work, follow these steps:

1. Load any NN-19 instrument patch from the Reason Factory Sound Bank.

2. Turn the stereo Spread knob all the way up to 127.

3. Select Key mode.

4. Play some very low notes and some very high notes.

You'll notice that the low notes are panned to the left, the high notes are panned to the right, and notes in the center of the keyboard are centered in the stereo field.

Using the Key2 mode provides a similar effect, but for each 1/2 octave range. Using the Jump mode alternates every other note played between the right and left speakers.

RETRIG AND LEGATO

The Key Mode button can be used to choose between Legato or Retrig (retrigger) mode.

In Retrig mode, every new note that's played restarts any envelopes, including any Filter, LFO, or Oscillator or Amplitude settings. Retrig mode is the standard setting for most instrument patches. In Legato mode, any Filter LFO or Oscillator envelopes will complete their cycles independently, whether or not any new notes are played.

The best way to get a feel for the difference between Legato and Retrig modes is to set the Polyphony to 1 and experiment by adding LFO, Filter, and Oscillator effects, then switching between the two modes.

CONTROLLER SECTION

If your MIDI keyboard or other device supports it, this section can be used in conjunction with the device's Aftertouch, Expression Pedal, or Breath Control functionality to control Filter Frequency, LFO amount, or Amplitude Envelope amount.

PITCH BEND WHEEL AND PITCH BEND RANGE

The NN-19's Pitch Bend Range display lets you set the range of the pitch bend wheel from 0 to 24 semitones. Push the Pitch Bend Wheel forward to raise the pitch, and move backwards to lower the pitch.

The Pitch Bend Wheel can be adjusted with your mouse, or, if your MIDI keyboard has a Pitch Bend Wheel, it can be used to control the NN-19's Pitch Bend functionality.

MOD WHEEL

The Mod Wheel can be used to control these parameters with each of its knobs: Filter Frequency, Filter Resonance, Filter Decay, Amplitude, and the LFO section. Adjust any knob to a positive or negative value to activate the Mod Wheel.

The Mod Wheel can be adjusted with your mouse or, if your MIDI keyboard has a Mod Wheel it can be used to control the NN-19's Mod Wheel functionality.

VELOCITY CONTROLS

The Velocity section is one of the main keys to creating realistic and expressive patches. Each knob in the velocity section controls how the NN-19 responds in relation to the velocity of any note played on your MIDI keyboard or drawn in the sequencer.

The Filter Envelope Velocity Amount This knobs control the amount of Filter effect that's applied to a note based on velocity. This setting can be used to create realism by increasing the brightness of a note in relation to its velocity. For a good example of this, take a look at the Filter Envelope Velocity Amount knob and Filter Envelope settings in the acoustic guitar patch ACGUITAR.smp found in the Reason Factory Sound Bank/NN19 Sampler Patches/Guitar folder.

Filter Decay Velocity Amount Working in conjunction with the Filter Envelope Decay slider, this knob controls the amount of Attack. That is, it controls how much filter decay is added to the signal based on velocity. If the knob is turned clockwise, harder-hit notes have a filter decay lengthened, and soft notes are shortened. If it is turned counterclockwise, the opposite is true. This can be a difficult parameter to work with because its effect also depends on where the Filter Envelope's Decay slider is set.

Amplitude Velocity Amount For creating realistic patches, this is the most important of the Velocity settings. If you raise the Amplitude knob, notes with a higher velocity will be louder and notes with lower velocity will be quieter. Try using an Amplitude setting of 20–40 for the best results, but experiment with this setting depending on the kind of instrument patch you are working with.

Amplitude Attack Velocity Amount Working in conjunction with the Amplitude Envelope's Attack slider, this setting controls the amount of Attack each sample will have based on Velocity. When the knob is raised, triggering a note with higher velocity will increase the attack time. Lowering this knob will have the opposite effect, causing lower velocities to increase the attack time.

Sample Start Velocity Amount This can be used in conjunction with the NN-19's Sample Start functionality. By raising this knob, samples triggered with a higher velocity will start later in the sample. By lowering the knob, samples with a lower velocity will start later in the sample. Lowering the Sample Start Velocity knob slightly is another good way to reduce the attack or harshness of samples that are triggered with lower velocities.

Automating the NN-19 Parameters

Most of the parameters on the NN-19's interface can be automated. The most commonly automated sections of the NN-19 will be the LFO, Filter, and Amplitude sections. However, the Pitch Bend and Mod Wheels and any of the Play parameters knobs and sliders can all be used to create automation. Some frequent uses of automation with the NN-19 include:

- Filter sweeps (see the filter sweep exercises in Chapters 3 and 5)
- Varying the rate and amount of LFO effects
- Pitch bending with the Pitch Bend Wheel

   Conduct your own experiments with all of the parameters that can be automated on the NN-19 to come up with your own variations on the device's sample playback and synth effects options.

Creating and Editing NN-19 Patches

The NN-19 can be used to quickly create and edit sampler patches. The following are step-by-step guides to creating patches with the NN-19, starting with simple single-sample patches and moving on to more intricate and realistic-sounding multisamples. For these examples, you'll be using content from this book's accompanying CD and from the Reason Factory Sound Bank. Once you understand the basics of creating patches with the NN-19, you can start seeking out content from other sources, including ReFills and sample CDs, to create your own original sampler patches.

Terms and Concepts

Here are some terms and concepts associated with creating and editing sample patches that will be used frequently throughout this chapter with both the NN-19 and the NN-XT:

Key Zones Key zones are specific sections of the keyboard that have been assigned a sample. A key zone can be a single note, the entire keyboard range, or any group of continuous notes. Loading a single sample into the NN-19 will create one key zone. An NN-19 multisample patch will have a different key zone for every sample. As you'll see later, the NN-XT can assign multiple samples to a single key zone.

Mapping Mapping is the process of assigning samples to specific key zones. All of the key zones in any sample patch constitute the patch's Key Map.

Root Key The root key is the note on your MIDI keyboard that plays a triggered sample at its original pitch. Every key zone in the NN-19 will have an assigned a root key. Some samples will have root key information embedded in the sample file, but more often than not you'll have to assign the root key manually, which will be covered in this chapter.

Low Key The low key is the lowest note in a key zone.

High Key The high key is the highest note in a key zone.

Creating a Single-Sample Patch

There are some instances where a single sample may be all you need to create a patch. In the next three examples, you'll get a look at three different kinds of single-sample patches.

LOADING SAMPLES

All of the work for creating sample patches is done in the Keyboard display in conjunction with the Browse Sample button and the Patch Editing knobs, all shown in Figure 6.7.

The Patch Editing knobs will be covered in the multisample examples later in this chapter.

By default, when you add a new NN-19 to your Reason song you'll see the key range C1 to C5 in the Keyboard display. The scroll buttons on the top left and right of the Keyboard display can be used to view the rest of the Keyboard map by scrolling as far as C–2 on the left or C8 on the right.

Just above the Keyboard display you'll see the NN-19's Browse Sample button. Using the NN-19 Browse Sample functionality, you can load and play any sound file in Wave, AIFF, or the samples contained in any SoundFont file and the slices that make up REX format files.

Figure 6.7

The Keyboard display

Take the following steps to try out the NN-19's Browse Sample functionality:

> Make sure you've followed the instructions in Chapter 2 for setting Reason's Preferences before you begin the exercises in this chapter.

1. Create a new NN-19.

2. Click the Browse Sample button to open the Reason Browser.

3. Use the Browser to navigate to the folder `Reason Factory Sound Bank\NN-19 Sampler Patches\Piano\BrightPiano`.

4. Load the first sample on the list, `PianoBA2.wav`.

When you load a single sample into the NN-19, it automatically maps the sample across the entire keyboard. This means that this patch currently contains one key zone. Any note you play on your MIDI keyboard between C–2 and C8 will trigger the currently loaded sample.

SETTING THE ROOT KEY

The root key for any key zone is shown as the single shaded key on the Keyboard display. Unless the sample has note information embedded in the file, the NN-19 will automatically set the root key for any new sample to C3.

This means that playing the note C3 on your MIDI keyboard or drawing the note C3 on the Note lane of the NN-19's track in Reason's sequencer will play the original sample at its original pitch and length. Playing any higher note will trigger the sample at a higher pitch, and playing a lower note will trigger the sample at a lower pitch.

In this case, as with many samples, the correct root key for this sample is contained in the sample's name. You can set the root key for the sample either by using the root key knob at the bottom of the Keyboard display or by Ctrl/⌘-clicking on any key in the keyboard.

A single-sample patch can sometimes work, depending on what you trying to do, the kind of sample you are working with, and the range of notes you are going to play. If you're using the NNN-19 to trigger a single loop, as we will later in this chapter, a single sample may be all you need for your patch.

In the case of a single piano sample, if you try to play chords or notes that are much higher or lower than the root key, the sample will sound unnatural.

To get an idea of the difference between the sound of a single piano note mapped across an entire keyboard and a multisample containing multiple piano notes mapped across selected key zones, use the Browse Patch button to load the entire patch that the `PianoBA2.wav` sample comes from, located at `Reason Factory Sound Bank\NN-19 Sampler Patches\Piano\BRIGHTPIANO.smp`.

DIALOGUE/SPOKEN WORD

Follow steps 1 through 4 from the previous exercise, but instead of loading `PianoA2.wav` load the file `Examples\Chapter 6\Samples\Spoken Word\VoiceOne.wav`.

As with most dialogue or spoken word files, this one has no embedded root key information. The sample will play at its normal tempo and pitch if you press the default root key of C3.

The Reason and the NN-19 offer lots of creative possibilities for working with vocal samples, including dialogue as well as melodic vocal performances. You can create interesting effects by working with the LFO or Filter sections or adding a heavy reverb or delay by selecting the NN-19 and inserting one of Reason's effects. Radically change the pitch by triggering the sample using a higher or lower note on your MIDI keyboard.

> Save your patch at any time by clicking the Save Patch button.

SINGLE LOOP PATCHES

You can also use the NN-19 to load and play drum or instrument loops. This can have a variety of uses, including triggering repeated loops or "one-shots," which are audio files that are played once through and not automatically repeated.

Follow steps 1 through 4 from the previous exercises, this time loading the file `Examples\Chapter 6\Loops\ Beat_103.wav`.

When working with loop files in Reason's samplers, you will find it necessary to adjust the Reason song's tempo to match the loop. In this case our loop's tempo is included in the name. Use the tempo display on the Transport panel to set the Reason song's tempo to 103 BPM.

As we've seen, if you load one loop into the NN-19 it will be automatically mapped across the entire keyboard and assigned a root key of C3. Pressing the C3 note on your MIDI keyboard will play the loop at its default tempo. Pressing a higher note will play the loop back at a higher pitch and also speed the loop up so that it's no longer at the same tempo. Playing a lower note will have the opposite effect.

This can actually be used to your advantage: playing a note exactly one octave lower (in this case C2) will play the loop at exactly half the tempo. Trigger the loop an octave higher (C4), and it will play the loop back at exactly twice the speed.

> If you want to make sure that your loop is always played at its original tempo, you can turn off the keyboard tracking button at the bottom of the Oscillator section.

You are not at all restricted to using drum or percussion loops with the NN-19. Melodic instrument loops will work just as well. In fact, if you have multiple instrument loops of the same tempo, the NN-19 is a great way to sequence them.

Creating Multisample Patches

In this example you'll create a multisample patch using the Browse Sample button and the Keyboard display covered earlier, along with the seven Patch Editing knobs located just below the Keyboard display.

Figure 6.8 shows the seven patch editing knobs.

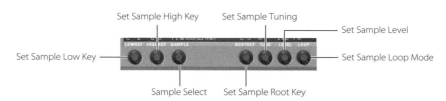

Figure 6.8

The patch editing knobs

From left to right:

Set Sample Low Key Used to set the lowest note of any selected key zone.

Set Sample High Key Sets the highest note of a selected key zone.

Sample Select Used to scroll through all currently loaded samples in order to assign them to the currently selected key zone.

Set Sample Root Key Sets the root key for the current sample.

Set Sample Tuning Used to adjust the tuning of the currently selected key zone. Can be raised or lowered by +/– 50 cents (1/2 semitone).

Set Sample Level Used to set the level of the currently selected key zone.

Set Sample Loop Mode The NN-19 has three different playback modes for looping. Off means that the sample won't loop. FW loops the sample from start to finish, and FW-BW plays the sample forward from start to finish, then backwards from end to start, then repeats.

ADDING MULTIPLE SAMPLES

The files for your multisample patches may come from any number of sources. You may load multiple loops from a loop collection, load individual instrument samples from a sample library, or create your own samples from a recording of a piano, guitar, oboe, harmonica, or any other instrument.

In the folder Examples\Chapter 6\Samples\Chorus Guitar are five guitar samples that you can use to learn the basics of creating your own multisample patches. Follow these steps to use these samples to create and save an NN-19 multisample patch:

1. Create a new NN-19.

2. Click the Browse Sample button to open the Reason Browser.

3. Navigate to the folder Examples\Chapter 6\Samples\Chorus Guitar.

4. You can select multiple samples by Shift-clicking or use the keyboard shortcut Ctrl/⌘+A to select all of the samples at once.

5. Once you've selected all of the samples, click OK in the Browser to load them into the NN-19.

Now that all of the samples are loaded into the NN-19, you'll need to assign root keys for each sample. In this case the correct root key for each sample is included in the sample's name. For example, the correct root key for the sample GTR_CH_C2.wav is the note C2.

You can scroll through all of the currently loaded samples in an NN-19 patch by using the Select Sample knob. When a sample is selected, its name will appear just above this knob.

6. Use the Select Sample knob to choose the sample GTR_CH_C2.wav, and then use the Set Root Key knob or the Ctrl/⌘-click method to assign each sample its correct root key.

7. Use the Select Sample knob to select each sample and assign the correct root key.

8. Once the root key has been assigned for each loaded sample, choose File → Edit → Automap Sample.

Reason has now created a key zone for each sample and mapped the sample out automatically. You'll also notice that the root key is roughly in the center of each key zone.

Save your new patch by clicking the Save Patch button and selecting a location for the .smp file.

AUTOMAPPING

Both of Reason's samplers contain automapping functionality that can be used to automatically create key zones for samples that have been already been assigned root keys. In some cases, if you are working with samples that have embedded root key information, you can load them into the NN-19 and select Edit Automapping without manually assigning root keys. If you use this method, it's a good idea to double-check each key zone individually because Reason will often interpret the root key as being an octave too high or too low.

ADDING REALISM TO YOUR MULTISAMPLE

As mentioned earlier, in the section "The NN-19 Play Parameters," the Velocity section of the NN-19 interface contains some of the keys to creating realistic instrument multisamples. In particular, the Amplitude Velocity Amount knob and the Filter Envelope Velocity Amount knob can be used to quickly add realism to your patches.

To quickly add velocity dynamics to your multisample, raise the Velocity section's Amplitude Envelope amount knob to between 40 and 60.

When you add velocity sensitivity to the Amplitude Envelope, the harder you play your MIDI keyboard, the louder the note will sound. The best Velocity settings will vary from patch to patch depending on the specific samples used.

You can learn more about Velocity settings by looking at other instrument patches and experimenting with different settings using the Filter and Amplitude sections and their corresponding knobs in the Velocity section.

Manually Creating Key Zones

As you've seen in the previous example, you can quickly create multiple key zones using the Automap functionality. Another way to work is to create key zones manually. Follow these steps to manually create key zones for an NN-19 patch:

1. Create a new NN-19.

2. By default any new NN-19 will have only one key zone. Create a second key zone by selecting the NN-19 in the Reason rack and choosing Edit →

   Split Zones from the main menu. You can also right/Ctrl-click any empty space on the NN-19 interface and select Split Key Zone from the context menu.

When you split any key zone, it becomes two separate key zones of equal size. The left key zone will be the MIDI notes C–2 to D#3. The right key zone will be the MIDI notes E3 to G8.

3. Next, select the key zone E3 to G8 and use the Edit → Split Key Zone functionality again. You'll need to use the right scroll button at the top of the Keyboard display in order to see the new key zone.

You now have a total of three key zones. To work with a specific key zone, use your mouse to select it in the Keyboard display. The currently selected key zone will be shaded.

You can set the low key and high key for any key zone by selecting it in the Keyboard display and using your mouse to adjust the Set Sample Low Key and Set Sample High Key knobs.

You can also resize key zones by using your mouse to move the key zone markers at the top of the Keyboard display.

Assigning Samples to Key Zones

You can quickly assign samples to a key zone by selecting it in the Keyboard display and clicking the Browse Sample button to open the Reason Browser. Any sample you select in the Browser will be immediately assigned to the currently selected key zone.

Once your sample is loaded, you'll want to assign a root key using the Select Root Key knob.

You can listen to any currently assigned sample by Alt / Option-clicking on the key zone.

You can now select another key zone and load a second sample into your patch. Switch samples between key zones by selecting a key zone and using the Select Sample knob.

Replace a sample at any time by selecting the key zone in the Keyboard display and clicking the Browse Sample button.

DIFFERENT WORKFLOW OPTIONS

The two options covered so far, loading samples and automapping them or creating key zones before loading samples, present you with two entirely different workflows for creating sample patches. How you choose to create your patches is entirely up to you.

If you are creating a melodic instrument patch from a folder of samples, you might choose to load them first, assign a root note, and let Reason choose the best key zone range for each sample. If you are creating a drum kit or loop patch and you know ahead of time exactly how many samples you'll be adding and how you want them mapped, you will probably want to create your key zones first and then assign individual samples.

In Chapter 4 you saw that Redrum could load samples from multiple sources and file types to create Redrum kits. The same is true for both of Reason's samplers.

Editing a Sample Patch

Once your patch is created, you are not locked into the specific sounds it contains. At any time in the process, you can resize key zones, reset the root key, and add or switch out samples. You can even do this with any of the included or third-party patches, using them as a starting point for your own original instruments and patches. Just make sure you click the Save Patch button to save as a new patch any changes you've made.

Sequencing Vocal Tracks with the NN-19

Since Reason doesn't allow you to record directly into the program or any of its devices, the process of creating vocal tracks with Reason can be particularly difficult. If possible, you are usually going to be better off creating your backing tracks in Reason and then using the ReWire protocol to bring your Reason tracks into Pro Tools, Logic, Cubase, or another digital audio workstation with audio recording functionality.

If you prefer to work exclusively in Reason, you can certainly use a sampler to load and sequence vocal tracks. One possibility, especially if you want to take advantage of Reason's effects, is to record vocals in another program, export multiple sections of a performance, and then bring them into a Reason song as individual samples, loaded into one of Reason's samplers.

Aside from "standard" vocal arrangements (verse/chorus/verse, etc.), there are also some cases, such as working with spoken word samples, choir, or backup singer samples, where working with a sample/sequencer configuration can make your vocal tracks more interesting.

Because most vocal tracks won't require multiple layers or access to a lot of editing functionality, the NN-19 makes a better choice than the NN-XT for sequencing a vocal track in Reason.

Here are some things to consider when working with vocal tracks and the NN-19:

- Make sure your samples don't have unnecessary "dead air" at the beginning of each sample. If this is the case, you can use the Sample Start button in the Oscillator section to adjust the start point of your sample. You could also edit out any dead air by using an audio-editing program (see the "Creating Your Own Samples" section later in this chapter).

- Break your vocal performance into individual lines wherever possible. Using the NN-19 to trigger an entire verse or chorus is a bad idea, as even minor fluctuations in timing between your Reason song and vocal track can result in noticeable problems.

- If you want to take advantage of the NN-XT's advanced functionality to edit and alter your vocal samples, these same methods can be combined with the subjects covered in the NN-XT patch creation tutorials.

Creating Drum Patches with the NN-19

Compared to working with the Redrum Drum Computer (Chapter 4), the NN-19 has both advantages and disadvantages when it comes to creating drum tracks. For creating or working with simple drum kits containing 10 or fewer individual samples, you'll always be better off using Redrum. With Redrum you'll have access to the same kinds of editing options as the NN-19 but with much more control over individual samples. You can also easily create dynamics with Redrum's Dynamic selector or by drawing velocity variations in the Reason sequencer's Velocity lane with the Pencil tool.

The obvious advantage to using the NN-19 is that instead of using only 10 samples at once you can load up to 127 individual samples to create your drum kits. This is a fairly complex process, using the same techniques as the previous example, but assigning a single sample to each key:

1. Create a new NN-19.

2. Create new key zones for each sample you intend to load.

3. Edit each key zone to be one MIDI note in length.

4. Select each key zone and load samples one at a time.

For even greater control over sampled drums and to create even more realistic performances, see the "Drums and the NN-XT" section later in this chapter.

ORGANIZING DRUM PATCHES

One thing to keep in mind when creating your own drum kits is General MIDI drum mapping. There are no hard and fast rules here, but you'll often find that specific drum samples are mapped to specific MIDI notes loosely based on the General MIDI drum bank (see the drum chart in the "Drums and the NN-XT" section in this chapter). It's a good idea to create your drum sample patches adhering somewhat to these mappings, especially if you want to use MIDI files to trigger your patches or are planning to share your kits with other Reason users.

Creating a Drum Kit from a REX File

The NN-19 can also load and automap REX loops into ready-made drum kits. The process is similar to that demonstrated in the Chapter 4 exercise on creating a REX slice drum kit for the Redrum Drum Computer. The difference here is that the NN-19 will quickly map out the slices as individual samples across your MIDI keyboard. Follow these steps to create a drum kit from a REX loop with the NN-19:

1. Create a new NN-19 and use the Browse Patch button to navigate to the folder Reason Factory Sound Bank\Dr. Rex Drum Loops\Acoustic\Hip Hop.

2. Select any REX file and click the OK button on the Browser to load it. Each REX slice will be assigned to a one-note key zone starting with the MIDI note C–1.

3. Use your MIDI keyboard to play the individual slices or draw notes in the NN-19's track in the sequencer.

The REX slices will not be automatically laid out like a standard drum patch. For example, a kick drum may be the first slice, but a snare may come at the third or fourth slice. Since you are dealing with REX slices, you'll probably also have fewer options for working with specific drum hits.

You can take this a step further and actually start with the original Dr. Rex sequence. To do this:

1. Create an NN-19 and a Dr. Rex.

2. Use the Reason Browser to load the same REX loop into both devices.

3. Make sure the NN-19 track is selected in the Reason sequencer.

4. Click the To Track button on the Dr. Rex and send the slice information to the NN-19 track.

5. Delete the Dr. Rex Loop Player.

These same methods can also be used to work with melodic REX files. You can also use these methods to work with REX files in the NN-XT Advanced Sampler.

Creating a Multisample Loop Sequence

One great way to use the NN-19 is to create a patch with multiple loops, and then use your MIDI keyboard and Reason's sequencer to create an arrangement.

One thing that's very important to this process is using loops that are all the same tempo. Loop tempos are often included as a part of the loop's name.

1. Create a new NN-19.

2. Set the tempo of your Reason song to match the tempo of the loops that you'll be using. In this case you'll want to set the song tempo to 93 BPM.

3. Use the Split Key Zone functionality to create five key zones.

4. Click and drag in the Keyboard display or use the Set Sample High and Set Sample Low Keys to create three one-octave key zones: C2-B2, C3-B3, and C4-B4.

5. Select the key zone C2-B2, then use the Browse Sample button to open the Reason Browser and navigate to the folder Examples\Chapter 6\Loops.

6. Select the loop Drum1_93.wav and click the OK button to assign it to the selected key zone.

7. Use the Select Root Key knob to assign the root key to C2.

8. Select the C3-B3 key zone, load the loop Drum2_93.wav, and leave the root key at its default C3.

9. Select the C4-B4 key zone, load the loop Drum3_93.wav, and set the root key to C4.

Play the loops using the notes C2, C3, and C4 on your MIDI keyboard. To record a live sequence with your loops, turn on Reason's click track and Precount functionality, then click the Record button on the Transport panel to begin recording after a four-note count-in.

You could also use the Pencil tool to draw a sequence using the different drum loops, as shown in Figure 6.9.

You can hear this drum sequence by opening the included Reason song named LoopSequence.rps in the folder Examples\Chapter 6\Songs.

You aren't at all limited to using drum loops for this kind of patch. In fact, this method can be a good way to sequence a group of similar melodic loops.

If you are working with longer loops, you can create loops using one section of a loop for the first measure.

Figure 6.9

A sequence of drum loops in the Reason sequencer

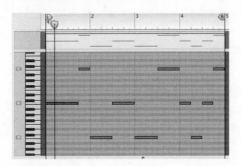

NN-19 Advanced Routing Options

Along with the standard stereo outputs, the back of the NN-19 shown in Figure 6.10 contains a number of different inputs and outputs. These can be used to both send and receive Gate and CV signals.

Figure 6.10

The NN-19's back panel

As with all of Reason's devices, the NN-19's Gate and Modulation CV inputs can be connected to and controlled by the Gate and Modulation CV outputs of any number of Reason devices, including the Matrix Pattern Sequencer, the RPG-8 Arpeggiator, and all of

Reason's instruments. The NN-19's Gate and Modulation CV routing can also be used on itself for interesting effects. Try connecting the LFO CV output to the various modulation CV inputs while playing a patch.

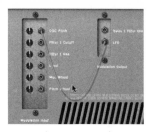

For more examples of Gate and Modulation CV routing, see Chapter 9.

Using the NN-XT Advanced Sampler

While the NN-19 Digital Sampler is a fantastic instrument for basic sampling and makes a great learning tool, the NN-XT Advanced Sampler contains lots of complex functionality that expands the range of possibilities by adding even more features.

The most important difference between the NN-19 and the NN-XT is the ability to create multilayered samples. By assigning two or more samples to the same MIDI note, triggered by different velocities, you can create more realistic sample patches. Only your computer's processor resources limit the number of samples in any NN-XT patch. Some NN-XT patches, such as those found in Propellerhead's Reason Pianos ReFill, contain more than 600 individual samples.

Other features that will be covered here include setting root keys by pitch detection, grouping multiple samples together for quick editing, and cross-fading samples based on velocity.

Content for the NN-XT

Along with ReFills created specifically for Reason, many sample libraries include NN-XT patches. The NN-XT's file format is .sxt. You can browse and load .sxt files using the NN-XT's Browse Patch button.

The NN-XT can also load and play .smp files created for the NN-19. Since the two instruments have somewhat different features and interfaces, when loading .smp files Reason will assign some parameters, such as Filter or LFO settings to the closest comparable settings on the NN-XT. The NN-XT can also load and play SoundFont files in the .sf2 format.

Using the Remote Editor's Browse Sample button, the NN-XT can load samples in AIFF or Wave format, as well as REX slices and the individual files that make up SoundFonts.

The NN-XT Interface

The NN-XT interface contains two connected sections: the Main panel, for loading and playing NN-XT patches, and the Remote Editor, for creating and editing patches.

The Main Panel

The Main panel, shown in Figure 6.11, is instantly viewable when you add an NN-XT to your Reason song.

Figure 6.11

**The NN-XT's
Main panel**

The Main panel is used to load and play patches, access Mod Wheel and Pitch Bend functionality, and make basic adjustments to NN-XT patches. This is particularly useful because it allows you to access and adjust the most common sampler features and parameters in a simple, compact interface.

THE GLOBAL CONTROLS

The Main panel contains the following Global Controls.

The Filter Section The Filter section of the Main panel can be used to quickly adjust the Filter Frequency and Resonance settings of a patch. This is a good way of quickly adding more high end or low end to a patch. You can also create filter sweeps by automating these parameters.

The Amplitude Envelope The Amplitude Envelope section can perform the basic kinds of amplitude effects you may want to access. For example, you can quickly add sustain to a patch, or adjust the attack to decrease a harsh sound or to create a rising sound.

The Modulation Envelope The Mod Envelope section contains only one knob that can be used to control the Decay parameter of the Modulation Envelope.

On the far right of the NN-XT's Main panel is the Master Volume, used to control the overall output of the instrument.

PITCH BEND AND MOD WHEELS

The Pitch Bend Wheel can be used to raise or lower the pitch of samples in the currently loaded patch. Pitch Bend parameters are set in the Remote Editor section and will be covered later in this chapter.

There are two Mod Wheels, labeled X and Y. Both can be used in conjunction with the Modulation section in the Remote Editor and will be covered later in this chapter. If your

MIDI device supports them, the wheels can also be used to work with MIDI controller messages related to Aftertouch, Expression, and Breath.

The Pitch Bend and Mod Wheel parameters are not global and can be used in conjunction both with individual samples and groups of samples, as covered later in this chapter.

High Quality Interpolation

Located near the center of the NN-XT interface is the High Quality Interpolation button.

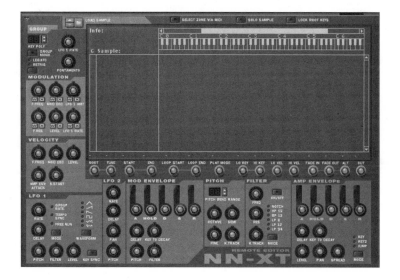

Turning this feature on will use a more complex algorithm to read any loaded samples, resulting in higher-quality playback. Apple computers with G4, G5, or Intel processors will always use High Quality Interpolation whether it's selected or not.

The Remote Editor

The second, feature-heavy section of the NN-XT is the Remote Editor, shown in Figure 6.12. You can show and hide the Remote Editor by clicking the triangle at the bottom left of the NN-XT interface.

As you can see, the Remote Editor contains a huge number of editable parameters, including Modulation and Velocity sections, two LFOs along with Pitch, Filter, and Amp Envelope sections. Many of the features will be familiar from both the NN-19 and from Reason's synthesizers. With the NN-XT many of these parameters have been expanded on, giving you more control and even more options for shaping sounds and creating patches. We'll cover the Remote Editor's features in detail later in this chapter.

Figure 6.12

The NN-XT's Remote Editor

SAMPLE RATE, BIT DEPTH, AND THE NN-XT

Unlike the NN-19, which will automatically convert samples to a sample rate of 44.1 and a bit depth of 16, the NN-XT loads and plays samples at their actual (native) sample rate and bit depth.

Loading, Playing, and Saving Patches

As with all of Reason's instruments, you load NN-XT patches by clicking the Browse Patch button to open the Reason Browser and navigating to a folder containing NN-XT patches. In the folder `Reason Factory Sound Bank\NN-XT Sampler Patches` you'll find a number of subfolders, each containing multiple NN-XT instruments (Figure 6.13).

Figure 6.13

The Reason Factory Sound Bank's NN-XT sampler patches

The Select Next and Select Previous Patch buttons can be used to load other NN-XT patches located in the same directory as the currently loaded patch. The LED displays the name of the currently loaded patch.

The obvious advantage to the NN-XT is the instrument's ability to load and play multilayered samples. As a result, one of the main uses for the NN-XT is to load and play realistic-sounding instruments. The following are some instruments you might use with the NN-XT and why:

Pianos and Keyboards For realistic-sounding pianos, organs, and other keyboards, the NN-XT is by far your best bet within the Reason program. The NN-XT's ability to load and play back complex multisamples makes it an amazing tool for creating lifelike piano performances.

For some great organ patches, download the free Electromechanical ReFill from `www.propellerheads.se`.

Synthesizers Considering the incredible range of synthesizer options in Reason, it may seem like overkill to add a Reason sampler to the list of available instruments for generating synthesizer sounds. However, there are a few great uses for the NN-XT in relation to synths. One is that the NN-XT can quickly load and play multilayered samples of classic synth sounds. Some excellent examples of this can be found on the free Analogue Monsters ReFills from `www.reasonbanks.com`. The NN-XT is also an amazing tool for creating multilayered ambient pads and soundscapes from sampled synthesizer sounds.

Reason 4 contains a number of new synthesizer-based patches for the NN-XT. Many of these include rich, excellent-sounding instruments.

Drums Working with drums is one of the ways in which the NN-XT truly outdoes the other Reason instruments. The Redrum is fantastic for creating performances that mimic drum machines and for sequencing complete performances, but the NN-XT's ability to play multilayered samples means you can use the instrument to create truly dynamic drum performances.

Creating Sample Patches with the NN-XT

The NN-XT's advanced editing features and included functionality will often make it your first choice for creating sample patches. All of the work of creating a single, multisample, or multilayered sample patch will take place in the Key Map Display section of the Remote Editor.

A Look Inside an NN-XT Patch

Before you begin creating patches, let's take a look inside one to see the kinds of ideas and concepts you'll be working with when creating your own patches:

1. Create a new Reason song and add an NN-XT Advanced Sampler.

2. Click the Browse Patch Button and locate the folder Reason Factory Sound Bank\NN-XT Sampler Patches.

3. Select and load the patch B GrandPiano 1.0.sxt.

4. Open the Remote Editor to view the Key Map display for the patch B GrandPiano.sxt patch, shown in Figure 6.14.

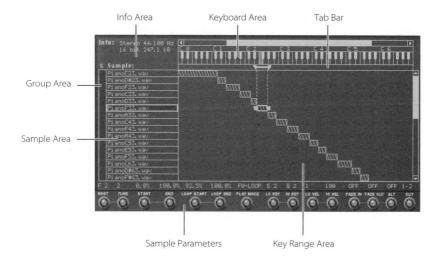

Figure 6.14
The Key Map display

The components of the Key Map display are:

The Info Area Displays sample rates and the bit depth of selected samples as well as stereo/mono information and file size. If no samples are selected, this area remains blank.

The Sample Area Displays the names of the currently loaded samples. Clicking the name of any sample in the sample area gives the selected sample *edit focus* (see the sidebar "Edit Focus").

The Keyboard Area Used to set the root key for any selected sample.

The Tab Bar Shows the key range for any selected key zone.

The Key Range Area Shows each samples key zone. Click any empty space in the Key Range area to deselect any of the currently selected samples or groups. Use the scroll bar on the right side of the Key Range area to view all of the patches' included samples.

The Group Area Click the Group area to select any group of samples. If there are no groups, clicking here selects all samples.

By looking at the Key Map display for this patch, you can learn a few important things about the elements that go into making an NN-XT patch.

If you use the scroll bar on the right side of the Key Range area to scroll down and view the rest of the samples in the patch, you'll see that the patch is divided into two sets of samples, separated by a horizontal line across the Key Range area. This means that the patch contains multiple Groups of samples. Creating Groups allows you to quickly adjust the parameters of multiple samples at once.

As you can see in Figure 6.15, you can select an entire group of samples by clicking in the narrow column on the left side of the Sample Area.

Selecting a group gives all of the samples in the group edit focus.

Figure 6.15

Select a group of samples in the Key Map display.

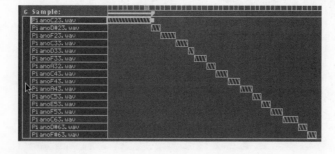

EDIT FOCUS

The concept of *edit focus* refers to the sample or samples that are currently selected in the Key Map display. When a sampler or multiple samples are selected, they have what's known as edit focus. This means that they are currently capable of being edited, both in relation to the Remote Editor's Synth and Play parameters as well as the key zone, root note, and key mapping functionality in the Key Map display.

When you are creating patches made up of groups, selecting the group will give the entire group edit focus. Selecting an individual sample within or outside a group will give edit focus to the individual sample.

Figure 6.16

The Sample parameter knobs

THE SAMPLE PARAMETER KNOBS

The Sample parameter knobs, shown in Figure 6.16, are used to adjust the sample mapping parameters. Some of this functionality can also be accessed with the mouse in the Key Map display.

The Parameter knobs from left to right are:

Root Key Sets the root key for the sample or group with edit focus. The root key for any key zone can also be set by Ctrl/⌘-clicking on any key in the Keyboard area.

Sample Tune Can be used to adjust the pitch of any selected sample or group up or down by 50 cents.

Sample Start Sets the point within the sample at which playback will begin when the sample is triggered.

Sample End Sets the point within the sample at which playback will end once the sample has been triggered.

Loop Start Sets the point in the sample at which the sample will begin looping, according to which Play mode is set.

Loop End Sets the point in the sample at which the sample will return to the Loop Start point and begin the loop cycle again.

Play Mode Sets the looping or nonlooping functionality for the selected sample or samples. Play modes include:

>   **FW** Triggering a sample plays it forward from the Sample Start point to the Sample End point.

>   **FW-BW** Triggering a sample plays it forward from the Sample Start point to the Sample End point, then in reverse from the Sample End point to the Sample Start point.

FW-Loop Triggering a sample plays it forward from the Sample Start point to the Sample End point, then returns to the start point and repeats.

FW-SUS This is the same as FW-Loop but plays the looped section of the sample while the MIDI key is held down. When you release the key, the actual end of the sample will be heard.

BW Triggering a sample play it backwards from the Sample End point to the Sample Start point.

Low Key Sets the lowest note of the sample range on the keyboard.

High Key Sets the highest note of the sample range on the keyboard.

Low Velocity Sets the minimum velocity that will cause the sample to be triggered.

High Velocity Sets the maximum velocity that will cause the sample to be triggered.

All new samples loaded in the NN-XT will automatically be assigned a low velocity of 0 and a high velocity of 127. Defining the high and low velocity is an important part of creating multilayered samples, as you'll see in the "Creating a Multilayered Instrument Patch" section later in this chapter.

The key zone for each sample is displayed under the Tab bar.

The root note for the current key zone with edit focus is the shaded note on the Keyboard area.

Creating a Single-Sample Patch

The NN-XT is certainly capable of creating complex multilayered sample patches, but it can also be used to quickly and easily create very simple patches, using a single sample or loop.

You load a single sample (or multiple samples) via the Browse Sample button. Clicking the Browse Sample button will open the Reason Browser, allowing you to navigate to any folder that contains sample files recognizable by the NN-XT. Samples for the NN-XT can be loaded from ReFills, including the Reason Factory Sound Bank, from folders on your hard drive, or from CD or DVD-ROM discs. If you load samples or patches from a DVD or CD, you should always copy the files to your hard drive first. This will speed up the loading process, as well as reducing the load on your CPU when playing the NN-XT.

To create a single-sample patch, follow these steps:

1. Create a new NN-XT.

2. Open the Remote Editor.

3. Click the Browse Sample button in the Remote Editor to open the Reason Browser.

4. Navigate to any folder that contains an AIFF or Wave sample. For example, try the folder `Reason Factory Sound Bank\Other Samples\FX-Vox`.

5. Make sure that the Browser's Autoplay functionality is turned on and preview samples by selecting them.

6. Once you've found a sample that you like, click the OK button at the bottom of the Browser window to load it into the NN-XT.

Unlike the NN-19, the NN-XT automatically maps the sample across a five-octave range, not across the entire keyboard. Once a sample is loaded, you can resize the key zone by clicking and dragging the left or right end of the key zone or using the Low Key and High Key parameter knobs.

Unless the sample has specific information embedded into the file to tell the NN-XT otherwise, the root key for any new sample will be set to C3 by default. You can change the root key for your sample in three ways:

- Ctrl/⌘-click the keyboard in the Key Map display with your mouse.

- Use the Set Root Key parameter knob on the bottom left of the Key Map display.

- Select File → Edit → Select Root Notes From Pitch Detection.

AUTOMAPPING AND PITCH DETECTION

Automapping with the NN-XT is very similar to automapping with the NN-19, with one important difference: the NN-XT can set root notes via pitch detection. You can access this functionality by selecting a single sample or multiple samples in the Key Map display and choosing File → Edit → Set Root Notes From Pitch Detection.

This process will sometimes assign a root key that is an octave too high or too low, so be sure to double-check any automapping for mistakes.

SWITCHING OUT SAMPLES

Double-clicking on a sample's name in the Sample area will open the Reason Browser, allowing you to search for new samples. If you use this method to open the Browser, any sample you select will replace the currently loaded sample.

ADD MORE SAMPLES

To add more samples to the patch, deselect the current sample by clicking any empty space in the Sample area or Key Range area, then click the Browse Sample button to open the Reason Browser and locate, preview, and load another sample.

CREATING A MULTISAMPLE

Creating a basic multisample patch with the NN-XT is a very simple process. Follow these instructions to create a multisample patch from the samples used in the NN-19 multisample patch exercise:

1. Create a new NN-XT and open the Remote Editor.

2. Click the Browse Sample button and navigate to the folder Examples\Chapter 6\ Samples\Chorus Guitar.

3. Select all of the samples and click the OK button on the Browser to load them.

4. Select each file individually and set the root key (remember, the root key is contained in the file name).

5. Select all of the currently loaded samples either by using the keyboard shortcut Ctrl/⌘+A or by clicking in the Group area.

6. Select File → Edit → Automap Zones.

   Figure 6.17 shows the mapped zones.

   Save your new patch by clicking the Save Patch button on the NN-XT's Main panel.

Figure 6.17

Mapped zones in the NN-XT

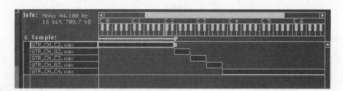

Editing an NN-XT Sample Patch

There are a number of options for editing NN-XT patches in the Key Map display. Here are some frequently used techniques:

- Adjust the key zone for any sample by selecting in the Key Range area and dragging to the left or right. In the NN-XT, key zones can overlap, triggering two sounds at once with the same MIDI note.

- Delete a sample from your patch at any time by selecting it in the Sample area or in the Key Range area and pressing the Delete key.

- You can copy and paste a sample by using the keyboard shortcuts Ctrl/⌘+C and Ctrl/⌘+V.

- Add more samples at any time by deselecting the current samples and clicking the Browse Sample button. Patches can be made up of files from multiple sources, including any of the different file types that the NN-XT is capable of loading.

Creating a Multilayered Ambient Texture

One interesting use for the NN-XT is to quickly create your own original layered sound effects and pads. This is a very simple process that can be used to quickly create lush soundscapes and ambient textures. The Reason Factory Sound Bank has many sounds that can be used as starting points for this, though you are not at all limited to using Reason's included sounds.

Here are a few of the folders in the Reason Factory Sound Bank that contain excellent samples that can be combined to create ambient textures:

```
NN-XT Sampler Patches\Pads\MKS Euphorium Samples

NN-XT Sampler Patches\Sound FX\Sound FX Samples

NN-XT Sampler Patches\Textures and Musical Effects

Other Samples\Chords-Phrases-Stabs

NN-19 Sampler Patches\Synth and Keyboard
```

To use the NN-XT to create ambient sounds, follow these steps:

1. Create a new NN-XT and open the Remote Editor.

2. Click the Browse Sample button to open the Reason Browser.

3. Preview, select, and load a sample from one of the suggested folders.

4. Repeat the previous two steps, loading multiple samples from different folders.

5. Use your MIDI keyboard to play the sample patch.

Create variations by reversing some samples using the Play Mode knob and setting higher or lower root keys for others.

Figure 6.18 shows the Key Map display for the included AmbientNoise.sxt patch, which you can find in the folder Examples\Chapter 6\NN-XT Patches.

> Combine this technique with velocity crossfading, covered later in this chapter, for some very nice results.

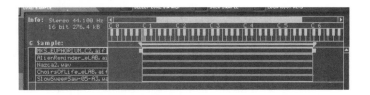

Figure 6.18

The Key Map display for an ambient patch

Creating a Multilayered Instrument Patch

In this exercise you're going to use the NN-XT to create your own basic multilayered sample patch. You'll take two sets of samples and assign them to different velocities. This is one of the keys to creating realistic instrument patches with the NN-XT. The multilayered patch that you'll create is simple, containing only two layers of seven samples each, but the concepts you learn in this exercise can be taken much further and used to create multilayered patches with as many sample layers as your computer is capable of loading.

1. Create a new NN-XT.

2. Open the Remote Editor

3. Use the Browse Sample button to navigate to the folder `Examples\Chapter 6\Samples\KB Synth`.

4. Select all of the samples at once and load them into the NN-XT.

5. Each sample is named according to its pitch. Use this name to choose the root key for each sample. For example, the root key for the sample `Syn_HiVel_C2.wav` will be C2. Select each sample, one at a time, and set the root key by using the Set Root Key parameter knob or Ctrl/⌘-clicking the correct root key in the Keyboard area.

6. Once you've assigned root keys, click any empty space in the Key Range area to make sure all samples are currently deselected.

The samples you've loaded include both high-velocity and low-velocity samples. The files named "HiVel" are high velocity; the files named "LoVel" are low velocity.

7. Select all of the high-velocity samples at once by Shift-clicking them, then create a group by selecting Edit → Group Selected Zones from the menu bar.

By creating one new group out of the high-velocity samples, you've actually created two separate groups, one containing the high-velocity samples and another containing the remaining low-velocity samples.

If you've missed any of the samples when creating your group, you can select and drag samples between groups at any time (Figure 6.19).

Figure 6.19

A selected group in the Key Map display

8. Use the keyboard shortcut Ctrl/⌘+A to select all of the samples in both groups, then choose Edit → Automap Zones from the main menu bar (Figure 6.20).

The point of creating multilayered samples is to have lower MIDI velocities trigger the low-velocity samples and higher MIDI velocities trigger the high-velocity samples. Select the low-velocity group and set the High Velocity parameter knob to 80. As soon as you adjust the Velocity Range for a selected sample or group, you'll see the sample or group change from clear to shaded in the Key Range area.

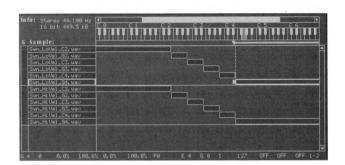

Figure 6.20

Automapped zones in the Key Map display

Select the high-velocity group and set the Low Velocity parameter knob to 81.

What you've done here is set up a simple velocity-mapped multilayered sample. Any time you play a note on your MIDI keyboard with a velocity of 80 or lower, the quieter sample will be triggered. Any time you play a note on your MIDI keyboard with a velocity of 81 or higher, the louder sample will be triggered.

Play any note on your MIDI keyboard, once very softly and once very hard to hear the difference between a higher and lower MIDI velocity.

> Quickly add more dynamic realism to this patch by raising the Level knob in the Velocity section to 50%.

This is velocity mapping for multilayered samples in its simplest form. To get a closer look at a more complex multilayered sample, open some of the NN-XT piano patches and scroll through each group. You'll see that these patches are often made up of many groups, each with a small Velocity Range.

Velocity Crossfading

Another element you can add to your tracks is to use velocity crossfading to create interesting transitions between velocity-mapped multilayered samples.

Here's an example of how to create an interesting patch combining two sampler patches and velocity crossfading.

> This exercise also utilizes the ability to copy and paste between NN-XT instruments.

1. Create a new NN-XT.
2. Open the Remote Editor and use the Browse Sample button to locate and load the file
   `Reason Factory Sound Bank\Other Samples\Chords-Phrases-Pads-Stabs\AlienReminder_`
   `eLab.aif`.

3. Create a second NN-XT.

4. Click the Browse Patch button on the NN-XT's Main panel and load the NN-19 sampler patch `Reason Factory Sound Bank NN-19 Sampler Patches\Mallet and Ethnic\Vibraphone`.

5. Open the second NN-XT's Remote Editor.

6. Select the entire group of samples by clicking in the group area and choose File → Edit → Copy Zones.

7. Select the first NN-XT and select File → Edit → Paste Zones.

8. Select the second NN-XT and press the Delete key on your computer's keyboard to delete it from the session.

9. Select the `AlienReminder_eLab.aif` sample in the Key Map display and adjust the Low Velocity knob up to 70.

10. Select all of the samples in the Key Map display and choose File → Edit → Create Velocity Crossfades or right/Ctrl-click on the NN-XT and choose Create Velocity Crossfades from the context menu.

With velocity crossfading, the samples in the patch will respond differently to notes played harder or softer on your MIDI keyboard. In this case, notes played softly will trigger only the vibraphone. The harder you play, the more you'll hear the AlienReminder sample and the less you'll hear the vibraphone. Combining different instrument and samples with velocity crossfading can create very expressive patches.

Velocity crossfades can also be adjusted manually using the Fade In and Fade Out parameter knobs.

MULTIPLE PARAMETERS

Along with editing entire groups of samples at once, with the NN-XT you can edit parameter settings for individual samples in the Remote Editor. When you select any sample or group in the Key Map display (giving it edit focus), the parameter knobs and sliders will reflect any changes you've made for the selected sample or group.

If two or more selected samples have different settings for the same parameter, the NN-XT lets you know this by adding an "M" icon next to the parameter in question.

Drums and the NN-XT

Reason includes a number of excellent options for creating drum tracks, including the Redrum Drum Computer and the Dr. Rex Loop Player. Even Reason's synthesizers can be used to create drum sounds. But when it comes to creating truly realistic drum performances, the NN-XT is the only Reason device with the ability to get the job done.

In some cases the intricacy of the multilayered sampler patches combined with the higher sample rates and bit depths will create some of the most processor-intensive instrument/ patch combinations. This can cause glitches in both recording and playback of your Reason songs, especially if you have multiple multilayered sampler instruments in a single session.

The Reason Factory Sound Bank has some included drum kits that can be found in the folder `Reason Factory Sound Bank\NN-XT Sampler Patches\Drums and Percussion`.

Sequencing Drum Patterns

Creating a drum performance with the NN-XT will require either using a MIDI keyboard or drum pads to play a sequence or drawing drum patterns in the sequencer.

USING A MIDI KEYBOARD

To create a drum track by playing your MIDI keyboard:

1. Create a new NN-XT and load any drum kit from the `Reason Factory Sound Bank\ NN-XT Sampler Patches\Drums and Percussion\Drums and Kits` folder.

2. Set the song's Tempo in the Transport panel.

3. Turn on Reason's click track and Precount functionality (see Chapter 2).

4. Make sure the NN-XT track is selected in the sequencer and armed for recording.

5. Click the Record button on the Transport panel to begin recording after a four-beat count-off. If you're not sure which MIDI notes will trigger which drums, see the list of assigned samples in the next section.

6. Use the Tool window's Quantize and Note Velocity functionality (see Chapters 2 and 10) to clean up or adjust your performance.

USING THE PENCIL TOOL

If you don't have a MIDI keyboard or you prefer to work in the sequencer, you can follow these steps and use the Pencil tool to create a drum performance:

1. Create a new NN-XT and load a drum kit from the Reason Factory Sound Bank.

2. Click the Switch To Edit View button on the top left of the sequencer.

3. Set the Snap To Grid function to 1/8 (you can change this to another value for more intricate drum patterns). You may also want to zoom in on the sequencer to get a better view.

4. Use the Pencil tool to create a two-measure clip.

5. Use the Pencil tool to draw notes in the Note lane to create your performance.

Figure 6.21 shows a drum performance in the Reason sequencer.

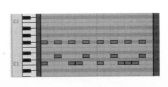

Figure 6.21

A drum performance in the Reason sequencer

General MIDI

You'll notice when you load and play NN-XT drum kits that when you switch between kits some of the same drums are assigned to the same MIDI keys. Here's a list of some of the most common MIDI note/drum assignments for NN-XT kits:

KEY #	NOTE	INSTRUMENT
36	C3	Kick Drum
37	C#3	Side Stick
38	D3	Snare
41	F3	Rack Tom
42	F#3	Closed Hi-Hat
44	G#3	Pedal Hi-Hat
45	A3	Floor Tom
46	A#3	Open Hi-Hat
49	C#4	Crash Cymbal

More often than not, this provides just a rough sketch of how drums are mapped across a multisample. The drums that are most important are those most commonly found in just about every drum kit: kick drum, snare drum, open hihat, closed hihat. These are closely followed in importance by the crash cymbal and toms.

Importing MIDI Files

Different samplers and patch formats will often use different mapping for their drum kits. As a result, MIDI drum performances created for other samplers such as Native Instruments' Kontakt, Steinberg's HALion, and virtual drum programs such as FXpansion's BFD or Toontrack's EZPlayer may not work well if you import them into Reason and use them to trigger NN-XT drum patches. It is possible to import MIDI files meant for other samplers and manually move MIDI notes to trigger the correct sounds, but this can be very time consuming.

Some MIDI loop libraries exist that create loops specifically mapped to work with the NN-XT. You can find good examples of this in collections from Smart Loops (www.smartloops.com) and Groove Monkee (www.groovemonkee.com).

There are two types of MIDI files that you can use with Reason: Type 1 and Type 0. Type 1 MIDI files are single track and Type 0 MIDI files are multitrack. When you import a Type 1 MIDI file into Reason, it creates one new track. Importing a Type 0 MIDI file will create multiple new tracks.

To import a MIDI file for use with the NN-XT:

1. Create a new NN-XT and load the Brush kit from the Reason Factory Sound Bank.

2. Select File → Import MIDI File to open the Reason Browser.

3. Use the Browser to navigate to the folder `Examples\Chapter 6 \MIDI Files`.

4. Select the file `BeatOne.mid` and click OK.

5. Reason will create a new track and an empty Combinator device for the imported MIDI file. Use your mouse to select and drag the MIDI file from the new track to the NN-XT track.

Reason will automatically adjust the tempo of the session based on information contained in the MIDI file.

SWITCHING DRUM KITS

It's a pretty safe bet that if you program a beat using just kick, snare, and hihat, and then use the Browser to select and switch kits, you'll hear the beat played back correctly on the new kit. This may or may not be true with intricate patterns that have been created using more samples, especially percussion. Sometimes switching kits can result in interesting and unexpected performances.

Using the ReGroove Mixer

Combining the NN-XT with Reason 4's new ReGroove mixer is an good way to create new rhythms and to further enhance the human feel of a sampler-created drum performance.

The Remote Editor's Features

The NN-XT's Remote Editor has some of the most advanced sound-shaping functionality in Reason. The specifics of using the various parameters are covered in Chapter 5 "Synthesizer Basics" section and in "The NN-19 Digital Sampler" section earlier in this chapter. The following section covers the similarities and differences between the NN-19 and NN-XT editing features.

Group The Group section has some of the same functionality seen on the NN-19, but instead of globally altering an entire patch these settings can be adjusted for individual groups or individual samples within a patch.

Here you can choose between Legato and Retrig modes as well as set Portamento. The Group section also includes a knob for adjusting LFO1's rate in relation to a specific group.

Modulation The NN-XT's Modulation lets you control various parameters with the two Mod Wheels in the Main panel. You can choose which Mod Wheel is used by selecting the w or x button under each parameter knob.

Assigning a Mod Wheel and adjusting any of the knobs give you Mod Wheel control over Filter Frequency, Modulation Decay, LFO 1 Amount, Filter Resonance, Level, and LFO 1 Rate settings.

Velocity In the Velocity section you can control how the NN-XT will alter the sound of a sample in relation to the note velocity data coming from your MIDI keyboard or the Velocity lane in the Reason sequencer.

This is similar to the Velocity section in the NN-19 but contains some slightly different parameters. The NN-XT's Velocity parameters are Filter Frequency, Modulation Decay, Level, Amplitude Envelope Attack, and Sample Start.

LFO 1 The LFO 1 section of the Remote Editor can be used to create LFO effects with the pitch, filter, and volume level of individual samples or groups.

The NN-XT's LFO 1 contains parameters similar to those found on other Reason instruments, including the NN-19 and the Dr. Rex Loop Player. Unlike those instruments, the NN-XT's LFO section can control the pitch, filter, and level simultaneously using the corresponding knobs at the bottom of the LFO section.

The Delay knob can be used to delay the start of the LFO.

LFO 1 has three modes: Free Run, Tempo Sync, and Group. Select the Group mode to apply the LFO effect to a group of samples, using the LFO Rate knob in the Group section to control the LFO speed.

LFO 2 The LFO 2 section can be used to create panning and pitch effects. LFO2 section also has a Delay knob, allowing you to delay the start time of the LFO2 effect.

Mod Envelope The Mod Envelope section can be used to control Filter and Pitch parameters using the two knobs at the bottom of the Mod Envelope section. The Mod Envelope contains ADSR knobs as well as an "extra" parameter called Hold. The Hold knob is used to define how long the envelope will stay at the Attack level before going to the Decay parameter.

Pitch The Pitch section is similar to the Oscillator section of the NN-19.

The Pitch Bend Range setting controls the range of pitch bending for individual samples using the Pitch Bend Wheel. Octave, Semi, and Fine tuning parameters can be used to adjust the pitch of an individual sample or selected group of samples.

Using the Keyboard Tracking knob allows you to adjust the intervals between notes in a patch.

Filter The Filter section of the NN-XT is similar to the Filter section on the NN-19 and other Reason devices. However, the NN-XT's Filter adds an extra low pass filter option (LP6) and a keyboard tracking option. Turning the Keyboard Tracking knob to the right will raise the filter frequency as you play higher up on your MIDI keyboard. Turning the knob to the left will have the opposite effect.

The Amplitude Section The NN-XT's Amplitude section contains the standard ADSR envelope features and also adds a Hold knob.

As with the Mod Envelope, the Hold knob here is used to define how long a sample will stay at the Attack level before going to the Decay parameter.

The Amplitude Envelope section also contains Level and Panning knobs that can be used to adjust the volume and stereo placement of individual samples or groups.

The lower-right corner features Spread mode functionality identical to the same functionality found on the NN-19, except that here it can be applied to individual samples and groups.

AUTOMATING THE NN-XT

In spite of its many editing options, the NN-XT actually has significantly fewer automation options than Reason's other instrument devices. This is because the many adjustable parameters in the Remote Editor can be used to adjust both individual samples and groups of samples. While just about all of the parameters on the NN-XT's Main panel can be automated, none of the parameters on the Remote Editor can be automated.

NN-XT Advanced Routing Options

Another major difference between the NN-19 and the NNXT is that the NN-XT features up to 16 individual outputs, or 8 stereo pairs. This can be useful in any number of ways, both obvious and creative. Figure 6.22 shows the back panel of the NN-XT accessed by pressing the Tab key on your computer's keyboard.

Figure 6.22

The back panel of the NN-XT

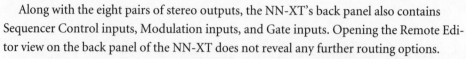

Along with the eight pairs of stereo outputs, the NN-XT's back panel also contains Sequencer Control inputs, Modulation inputs, and Gate inputs. Opening the Remote Editor view on the back panel of the NN-XT does not reveal any further routing options.

The NN-XT's advanced routing options are accessed by combining the Sampler parameters of the Remote Editor with the instrument's back panel. Any sample or group of samples loaded into the NN-XT and given edit focus can be assigned to any stereo pair of outputs using the Output knob on the bottom right of the Key Map display.

Outputs must then be routed manually from the back of the NN-XT to the session's Mixer 14:2 or another Reason device.

You'll notice that when assigning an output from the NN-XT's back panel you will not be able to rename the track in the mixer. The track's name in the mixer will always correspond to the specific NN-XT output.

Creating a Submix with the NN-XT

One common use of the NN-XT's extra routing options is to send the elements of a drum kit to different inputs on a Mixer 14:2 for greater control. This is similar to the submix that we did with the Redrum in Chapter 3. We'll use one of Reason's included NN-XT Drum kits to check out some submix routing options and how to access them.

1. Create a new Reason song.

2. Create an unconnected Mixer 14:2 by holding the Shift key down and choosing Mixer 14:2 from the Create menu.

3. Name the first Mixer 14:2 **MainMix** and the second Mixer 14:2 **SubMix**.

4. Route the output of SubMix manually to inputs 1 and 2 on MainMix.

5. Hold down the Shift key and create a new unconnected NN-XT.

6. Route the outputs of the NN-XT to the individual inputs on the SubMix: 1–2 to track 1 left and right, 3–4 to track 2 left and right, as shown in Figure 6.23.

7. Use the Browse Patch button to open the Reason Browser and navigate to the folder Reason Factory Sound Bank\NN-XT Sampler Patches\Drums and Percussion\Drums and Kits.

8. Load the kit Jazz Kit.sxt.

9. Open the NN-XT's Remote Editor.

10 Alt / Option-click any sample in the Sample area to preview it, then select samples by group and assign them by instrument to different outputs. For example, assign all of the snare samples to outputs 3–4, then assign all of the hihat samples to outputs 5–6, etc.

Figure 6.23

Output routing on the back panel of the NN-XT

Once you've created a submix, you'll have much greater control over your final drum mixes. Aside from having quick access to the volume and EQ levels for individual drum kit pieces, you can also add up to four send effects to your submix Mixer 14:2 and add compression, reverb, delay, or other effects to single or multiple tracks in your submix.

Creating Your Own Samples

As you learned earlier in this chapter, the main difference between Reason's software samplers and traditional hardware is that Reason's samplers don't record audio.

That doesn't mean that the NN-19 and NN-XT can't be used to play your own original samples and loops. It just means that you'll have to create them outside of Reason. Creating your own samples and loops to use with Reason is one of the best ways to work with entirely original elements.

To create your own samples, the main things you'll need are a source for creating your audio files and a way to edit those files. The most common way to create audio files for use with software samplers is to record into a DAW program such as Logic, Pro Tools, Sonar, or Acid.

Using a DAW program, you can record directly from an instrument, microphone, connected turntable, or other audio source. The sounds you record can be edited directly in your DAW program and then exported to Wave or AIFF format for use in Reason's samplers.

> Wave and AIFF files can also be opened in ReCycle and converted to REX format for use with the Dr. Rex Loop Player.

Audio-editing software is another option. You can export files from your DAW software and use programs such as BIAS' Peak and Audiofile Engineering's Wave Editor to edit, enhance, and perfect sample content. You can also record directly into most audio-editing programs, though usually only to one mono or stereo track at a time.

If you don't have the ability to record vocals or instruments into your computer, you can also create sample content by extracting audio from CDs inserted into your computer's CD drive or from downloaded MP3 or AAC files, which can be opened in just about any audio-editing program. (But see the sidebar "Copyright Issues" if you plan to take this route.)

Recording

If you have a hardware audio interface, then you are already set up to record your own original sample material. Recording your sample material directly into your computer has a number of advantages. Obviously, it's the only way to go if you will be creating samples from your own vocals or instrumental performances. Recorded performances of vocals, guitars, or other instruments can be easily exported from any DAW program as Wave or AIFF files.

Figure 6.24 shows a performance of four individual guitar chords in Pro Tools. Each individual chord has been divided into its own region. Each region will then be selected and exported as an individual file, creating four individual samples that can be loaded into either of Reason's samplers, assigned a root key and key zone, and saved as a patch.

Figure 6.24

Guitar chord performances in Pro Tools

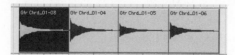

Another possible use for your DAW program would be to create the individual samples needed to create a multilayered sample. For example, if you wanted to create a multilayered guitar sample, you would record multiple performances of individual notes, gradually increasing the volume and/or attack of each note. You can then export the individual notes for further audio editing or import them directly into the NN-XT.

Yet another option is to hook up a turntable, tape deck, or other audio device to your audio interface and record samples from records, tapes, or other sources to create loops and samples. (Again, be aware of copyright issues here.) You can then edit your recordings directly in your DAW or export them for further tweaking with an audio-editing program before loading them into the NN-19 or NN-XT.

Ripping

Almost everyone is aware these days of the process of converting CDs to MP3 or AAC format. This can be quickly and easily accomplished using iTunes, the Windows Media Player, or Winamp or other free or inexpensive music-management software.

The process is simple. Insert a CD into your computer's CD drive, launch iTunes or another application, and follow the basic instructions. Once a file has been "ripped," it resides on your hard drive as a digital audio file, usually in MP3 or AAC format. Although most DAW programs and audio editors can easily import MP3 and AAC format files, they are not the highest-quality audio files that your ripping software can create. I recommend using MP3 or AAC format files as source material only as a last resort.

If possible it's a good idea to use the import settings for your ripping software to create high-quality WAV or AIFF files with bit depth/sample rate settings of 16/44.1 or higher to edit.

I'm going to use iTunes for this example because it's free and cross-platform. You can just as easily use other audio-ripping software by locating and changing the program's import settings.

Here's how to use iTunes to create a high-quality audio file that's ready for sample extraction:

1. Choose File → iTunes → Preferences.

2. Click Advanced, then click the Importing tab.

3. Select either Wav Encoder or AIFF Encoder from the Import Using drop-down menu.

4. Click OK to save your settings.

Now, when you import any tracks from an audio CD in your CD drive, the files created will be higher-quality Wave or AIFF format files. Locate the file or files on your hard drive or in your iTunes collection and create a copy of the file, or move the file to your desktop or to another folder.

You can now open your Wave or AIFF song file in your DAW or audio-editing program and edit the file to extract any loop or sample from the recording.

COPYRIGHT ISSUES

As a direct result of the popularity of digital samplers, creating music from samples taken from other artists' commercially available songs has caused some of the biggest changes in the music business in recent memory. In some well-known cases, artists have sued other artists for appropriating their work; in other instances, the original songwriters sometimes receive co-writing credits for songs created using sampled material.

In order for you to use sampled material from a commercially available song, the sample must be "cleared," giving you the legal right to use it. The process of clearing samples involves dealing with the record label, artist, or both, as well as the song's publisher. Depending on the artist being sampled, you may have to pay a flat rate, a percentage of royalties, or possibly even a percentage of royalties with an advance upfront. The process of clearing samples is often expensive and probably not worth doing unless you've got financial backing (such as a record company) to do it.

If you are a producer or an artist looking to showcase your skills with material that incorporates uncleared samples, you could consider creating a limited number demo discs or MP3s to give to record companies, potential clients, or other producers. Making your work available commercially or on the Internet without legally clearing samples is generally not a good idea.

Editing Your Samples

Once you created an AIFF or Wave file, you'll often need to perform some kind of editing to optimize the file for use in Reason's samplers. Your DAW may have this kind of functionality built in. While each audio-editing program will have a different interface and workflow, most will contain some common functionality specifically related to sampling. Here are some important things to keep in mind when editing samples:

- Remove any "dead air" or silence from the beginning of your sample.

- Make sure your sample fades out completely or has a clearly defined end point. Most audio-editing programs and DAWs will have an option for fading audio.

- Normalizing an audio file is the process of making it as loud as possible without distorting. Most audio-editing programs and DAWs will have normalizing functionality.

- Crossfading is the process of making sure your sample or loop starts at a "zero-crossing" point in the audio file. This is very important, especially in relation to looping, and will eliminate unwanted pops or clicks at the beginning and end of a sample. Most audio-editing programs and DAWs will have crossfading functionality.

Audio Editors

There are many audio-editing programs available for both Mac and Windows operating systems. For a free audio editor, try the open source Audacity program, available for both platforms from `http://audacity.sourceforge.net`.

Other audio-editing programs include:

- BIAS' Peak (Mac/Windows): `www.bias-inc.com`

- WaveLab (Windows): `www.steinberg.net`

- Sound Forge (Windows): `www.sonycreativesoftware.com`[AU: This is for Sony Creative Software ED]

- TwistedWave (Mac): `www.twistedwave.com`

- Sound Studio (Mac: `www.freeverse.com/apps`

- Wave Editor (Mac): `www.audiofile-engineering.com`

Summary

In this chapter you learned about two of Reason's most powerful devices: the NN-19 and NN-XT sampler instruments. Learning to use either or both of these samplers opens up entirely new possibilities when you're working with Reason, including creating realistic-sounding instrumental tracks and utilizing the sound-sculpting options available on both instruments, particularly the NN-XT's advanced functionality.

The first part of this chapter gave you an overview of the history of digital sampling and some basic concepts related to the sampling process. You then learned how to use the NN-19 to load, play, and edit sampler patches. Next, you learned how to create and edit your own NN-19 sample patches.

As you've seen, learning to create and edit your own patches opens up entirely new creative possibilities when working in Reason, giving you access to a huge range of available sounds, both included with Reason and found outside of the program, as building blocks for instruments and patches.

Next, you learned about the NN-XT Advanced Sampler, first covering the instrument's Main panel functionality, then how to use the Remote Editor to create and work with multilayered sampler patches. Working with and creating your own multilayered sample patches further increases your ability to create realistic, human-sounding musical performances with Reason and to experiment with creative sound-sculpting, including combining multiple samples and instruments in a single patch.

The last section of this chapter covered some of the things that go into creating and editing your own original sample material, either by recording your own original performances or by extracting audio from existing recordings. Creating your own sounds and samples gives you even more possibilities to choose from when creating sounds, tracks, and complete performances with Reason's samplers.

CHAPTER 7

Reason's Effects

Effects and signal processing devices are used in just about every modern recording and are an important element in any studio, whether hardware or software based. For example, a typical Reason song might contain a subtle reverb effect applied to drums and keyboards to give the illusion of natural space, various instances of EQ used to shape the individual sounds, and one or more of the MClass devices placed between the mixer and the hardware device and applied to the stereo mix.

In other cases, Reason's effects can be put to even more dramatic uses and become a part of an instrument's performance. A delay might be added to a synthesizer arpeggio or a percussion track in order to create rhythmic complexity, or sweeping effects may be applied to synthesizer or guitar tracks with a chorus, phaser, or flanger. You can use effects like these to completely change a track's sound.

Reason's effects are an integral part of the program and are extremely versatile. Combined with the program's automation, external MIDI control, and flexible audio and CV routing, adding the effects devices to your Reason workflow opens up new worlds of creative possibilities.

Topics include:

- **Using Reason's Effects**

- **The Half-Rack Effects**

- **The Scream 4 Sound Destruction Unit**

- **The RV7000 Advanced Reverb**

- **The MClass Effects**

- **Effects Chains**

- **External MIDI Control**

Using Reason's Effects

Reason's effect devices can be added to songs as either insert or send effects. Chapter 1 covered the basic information you need to know about insert and send effects, including how they are created and the automatic routing that takes place in Reason when you add effects to the Reason rack.

To recap briefly: you create an insert effect by selecting a Reason instrument in the rack, and then using the Create menu, a context menu, or the Tool window to create an effect. This creates automatic routing, sending the signal from the selected instrument to the newly created effect, and then to the Reason song's Mixer 14:2.

Send effects are created by selecting the Mixer 14:2 and then creating the effect. This sets up automatic send and return routing, connecting the newly created device to the mixer's Aux Send and Aux Return functionality. Using the four Send knobs at the top of each channel in the Mixer 14:2, you can apply send effects to any or all of the instruments currently connected to the mixer.

Reason includes the entire range of available signal processing options found in any studio, including reverb, delay, modulation (chorus, flanger, phaser) and distortion effects, along with EQs and various dynamics processors (compressor/limiter devices).

In this chapter we're going to look at all of Reason's effects: the half-rack effects, mostly introduced in Reason version 1; the advanced effects—the Scream 4 Sound Destruction Unit and the RV7000 Advanced Reverb, introduced in Reason version 2.5; and the MClass mastering effects, introduced in Reason version 3. Although the effects are often radically different from each other, Reason's tools for controlling them have a lot in common, so we'll begin with those tools.

Shared Functionality

Figure 7.1

The Input meter and the Power/Bypass switch

Each of Reason's effects devices includes some basic shared functionality. Figure 7.1 shows the Input meter and the Power/Bypass switch found on all of Reason's effects.

The Input meter shows the level of the audio signal coming into the device and that an effect is currently in use. The Bypass/On/Off switch found in the upper-left corner of each effect is used to turn the effect on and off and has three modes:

Bypass Turns off the effect but allows signal to pass through.

On Turns the effect on.

Off Turns the effect off and does not allow any signal to pass through.

Any effect in Bypass or Off mode will show no level on the Input meter since no signal will actually be going to the effect.

Parameter Values

The knobs found on Reason's half-rack effects devices mostly use standard MIDI values of 0–127 or –64–63 with 0 as the center value.

Some of Reason's half-rack effects contain LFO (low-frequency oscillator) sections. Just like the LFOs found on Reason's instruments, these LFOs can be synced to the current Reason song's tempo by activating a Sync button. When sync is activated, values are represented by time signatures.

Some of the values found on the MClass and the RV7000 are measured in other increments, including dB (decibels), milliseconds, and percentages, allowing more precise control of these parameters.

Stereo and Mono

Each of Reason's effects contain is capable of multiple types of stereo and mono routing. Which particular routing configurations are available to a specific device can be determined by looking at the graphs found on the left side of the back panel of each of Reason's effects devices.

Mono to Mono Effects with mono-to-mono functionality take a mono signal input, process it, and then send it out of the effect as a mono signal. Mono-to-mono functionality is accessed by connecting an instrument device to an effect's left input and the effect's left output to the Mixer 14:2. Most of Reason's half-rack effects feature mono-to-mono functionality, the exceptions being the DDL-1 Digital Delay and the RV7 Reverb.

Mono-to-Stereo Mono-to-stereo effects can take a mono signal, process it, and send it out as a stereo signal. This is accomplished by connecting an instrument's mono or left output to the left input of the effect, then connecting the stereo outputs to the Mixer 14:2 or another effects device. Mono-to-stereo effects can be useful for adding a stereo feel to mono tracks.

The functionality is available on many Reason effects, including the DDL-1 Digital Delay, both the RV7 and RV7000 Reverb effects, and all of Reason's modulation effects.

When added as send effects, Reason effect devices that feature mono-to-stereo functionality will be routed out of the mixer in mono and returned in stereo.

Dual Mono is the most common signal routing option and is available on most of Reason's effects. A stereo signal from the left and right outputs of a Reason device instrument is actually treated as two separate mono inputs.

The only Reason effects that don't feature dual mono routing are the DDL-1 Digital Delay and the RV7 Reverb, which feature mono to stereo and stereo summing, and the RV7000, which features mono to stereo and true stereo signal processing.

Stereo Summing 🔲 Stereo summing effects combine the left and right signals before processing them, and then output a stereo signal. The RV7 Reverb and the DDL-1 Delay are Reason's only two stereo summing effects.

True Stereo 🔲 The RV7000 Advanced Reverb is Reason's only true stereo effect. When a stereo signal is routed to the effect, it's then processed in stereo, meaning that both channels are processed individually, outputting a true stereo signal.

CV Routing

Reason's half-rack effects and the RV7000 Advanced Reverb and the Scream 4 Sound Destruction Unit all include basic CV input functionality, allowing you to control one or more parameters by connecting the CV outputs of any Reason device to the effect's CV inputs. Using this CV input functionality means that the filters, LFOs, and gates found on Reason's instrument devices, as well as the Matrix Pattern Sequencer and the RPG-8 Arpeggiator, can all be used to control various available parameters on Reason's effects devices. This CV control opens up even more effects routing options, and we'll be looking at these features later in this chapter and in Chapters 8 and 9.

> None of the MClass effects have CV inputs, but the MClass Compressor does have Gain Reduction CV Output.

Saving Effects

None of the half-rack effects or MClass effects offer the ability to save patches with any settings you make. You do have a few options for saving effects settings and multiple effects configurations, which are also known as "effects chains." The easiest way to save your effects is as a Combinator device.

If you've made settings to an effect that you want save and recall later, follow these steps:

1. Select the effect or multiple effects in the Reason rack. You can select multiple effects at once by holding down the Shift key.

2. Right/Ctrl-click on the device or devices and choose Combine from the context menu.

3. Name and save your new Combinator patch.

To add your effect to future sessions you can either create an empty Combinator (choose Create → Combinator from the menu bar) and then use the Browse Patch button to locate your patch or choose Create Effect from the Create menu on the menu bar and use the Browser to locate and load your Combinator patch.

Once your Combinator is added to the new Reason song you can right/Ctrl-click any blank area on the Combinator or effect interface and choose Uncombine from the context menu. You'll now have your effects and any settings you've made available in the new session.

You can also use the Combinator to save instrument and effect configurations, which you'll learn more about in Chapter 9. This method will also work with multiple effects chains, which are covered later in this chapter.

COPYING AND PASTING EFFECTS BETWEEN SONGS

Another option is to copy and paste effects and tracks between Reason songs. Reason allows you to have multiple songs open at once, so if you already know that you have an effect or chain of effects that you'd like to replicate from one song to another, you can open the original song and follow these steps:

1. Select the effect in the original song or select multiple effects by holding down the Shift key.

2. Right/Ctrl-click to view the context menu and select Copy Devices And Tracks or choose Edit → Copy Devices And Tracks from the menu bar. This will copy both the effects devices and any sequencer tracks containing automation data.

3. Select the location in the rack that you'd like to paste your effects and devices, then right/Ctrl-click and choose Paste Devices And Tracks from the context menu or choose Edit → Paste Devices And Tracks from the menu bar.

If you are copying and pasting multiple connected effects devices, any routing will remain in place between the copied and pasted effects. However, once they are pasted in the new session, Reason will not create automatic routing, connecting your effect or effects to any specific instrument or the song's Mixer 14:2. You'll have to use the Tab key to view the back of the Reason rack and manually route the effects either to a specific instrument, for insert effects, or to the mixer's Aux Send and Return inputs and outputs to create send effects.

The Half-Rack Effects

Reason's half-rack effects are relatively straightforward and both easy to use and to understand. If you are familiar with guitar effects pedals, any of the hardware or software signal processors found in most recording studios, or with digital audio plug-ins found in other DAW programs, then some or all of these effects and their available parameters will be familiar to you.

Most of the half-rack effects were introduced in Reason version 1, although the UN-16 Unison was added in version 2.5. As often happens when software evolves, devices added in more recent versions of Reason have overshadowed some of these original effects. In particular, the features of the D-11 Foldback Distortion and the RV7 Digital Reverb have been expanded on greatly by the Scream 4 Sound Destruction unit and the RV7000 Advanced Reverb, respectively. Both the D-11 and the RV7 still have their uses in Reason, so I'll cover them in this chapter. You may find that their simplicity is actually a benefit in some circumstances.

RV7 Digital Reverb

While the RV7 Digital Reverb (Figure 7.2) may have been upstaged by the much more full-featured RV7000 Advanced Reverb, it's still a powerful and useful effect. It contains a nice selection of reverb types, combined with an easy-to-use interface. The RV7 also uses considerably less processor resources than the RV7000, making it a good choice if you

Figure 7.2
**The RV7 Digital
Reverb**

need to add one more reverb effect to an already crowded Reason song.

Parameters

The RV7 has a straightforward interface featuring an LED display, three of the basic parameters found on most reverb effects, and a Dry/Wet knob for controlling the amount of the effect being used at any time. The RV7 contains the following parameters:

Algorithm Display The LED display on the right side of the interface shows the currently selected algorithm, the processing method that produces a particular style of reverb. You can choose a different algorithm by clicking and dragging up or down on the LED or by using the Select Next and Select Previous buttons on the right side of the display. The next section briefly describes each of the RV7's algorithms.

Size The Size knob controls the size of the room whose ambience you're simulating, within the selected algorithm. Turning the knob to the right increases the room size; turning to the left makes the room smaller.

Decay The Decay setting is very much like the Decay parameter found on Reason's envelope generators. It sets the time it takes for the reverb effect to fade out. Raise the Decay knob for a longer decay, resulting in a longer and more noticeable effect.

Damp The Damp knob is used to adjust the high frequencies of the reverb effect. Lowering the Damp knob allows more high frequencies to pass through, resulting in a brighter effect. Raising it cuts the high frequencies, resulting in a darker, "dampened" sound.

Dry/Wet The Dry/Wet knob controls the mix of the original signal with the effect. Choose a value of 0 by turning the knob all the way to the left and you'll hear only the original signal. Turn the knob all the way to the right (a value of 127) and you'll hear only the effect. At a center value of 64, you'll hear both the original and effect equally.

When adding reverb as a send effect through the main mixer, you'll generally keep the Dry/Wet at its default value of 127, controlling the amount of reverb using the specific channel's Send knob. To use it as an insert, you'll want to experiment with lower values, starting in the middle and raising and lowering depending on the circumstances.

The Algorithms

A reverb algorithm is a set of instructions and calculations used to simulate the sound of a specific room or area. The RV7 offers nine algorithms, each representing a different-sized and -shaped room, hall, or reverb effect.

Halls Hall, Large Hall, and Hall 2 algorithms all represent various sizes and shapes of concert halls. These are generally used to create noticeable ambience and give the effect of larger open space.

Rooms Large Room, Medium Room, and Small Room are useful for creating sounds that emulate real recording situations, such as a studio's "live" room used for recording or a smaller room such as a vocal booth.

Gated The Gated reverb algorithm creates a reverb that is abruptly stopped, as if it were passing through a gate signal processing unit.

Low Density This is a thin sounding reverb with noticeable echoes.

Stereo Echoes This algorithm is a more of a delay effect than a reverb. With this algorithm selected, the Size knob controls delay time and the Decay controls the delay feedback.

Pan Room Somewhere between a reverb and a delay effect. As with the Stereo Echoes, with this algorithm selected the Size knob controls delay time and the Decay knob controls the delay feedback.

The RV7's Decay parameter can be controlled using the CV input on the device's back panel.

Using the RV7

Reverb is one of the most frequently used effects in recording and is particularly important to virtual music creation, since you won't be recording instruments in live rooms. Using reverb correctly can add a sense of space, distance, and realism to your tracks. Reverb can be used to good effect on just about any acoustic instrument, including guitars, pianos, and strings, and on complete drum mixes or individual pieces of a drum kit. Kick and snare drums in particular can be greatly improved by adding reverb. Any track that you would like to add a sense of acoustic space to can benefit from the RV7 Digital Reverb. Reverb is also useful in creating ambient sounds such as synth pads and is used in conjunction with sound effects.

USING THE RV7 ON AN INSTRUMENT TRACK

Follow these steps to try out the RV7 Digital Reverb on an instrument patch:

1. Create a new Reason song and add an NN-XT Advanced Sampler.

2. Locate and load the patch Reason Factory Sound Bank\NN-XT Sample Patches\Baritone Sax.sxt. Use your MIDI keyboard to play a few notes before adding the effect in the next step.

3. Select the NN-XT in the rack and create an RV7 Digital Reverb.

4. Lower the Wet/Dry significantly; experiment in the 10 to 40 (percent) range for the best results.

You can hear immediately that the reverb has the effect of adding realism and space to the saxophone sound. This is useful in getting a sound or performance to fit more naturally into an overall mix.

You can learn more about the RV7 by experimenting with the various algorithms and settings. Use the NN-XT's Patch Load button to locate and load some other instrument patches and try them out with the NN-XT.

You can find this example on the accompanying CD in Examples/Chapter 7/Songs/SaxVerb.rns.

USING THE RV7 ON A DRUM KIT

Adding reverb to specific elements of a drum kit is also useful. Follow these steps to use the RV7 as an insert effect with a Redrum drum kit:

1. Create a new Reason song.

2. Select the mixer and an RV7 Digital Reverb as a send effect.

3. Choose the Medium Room algorithm in the RV7's Algorithm display.

4. Create a Redrum Drum Computer and use the Browse Patch button to load the kit Reason Factory Sound Bank\Redrum Drum Kits\Heavy Kits\Dublab HeavyKit2.drp.

5. Program a performance in the Step Programmer using the kick drum on Channel 1, the snare drum on Channel 2, and the closed hihat on Channel 8.

6. Use the S1 knob at the top of the channel strip to add different amount of the reverb effect to all three channels.

Experiment with different amounts of reverb and with different algorithms and parameter settings.

You can find this example on the accompanying CD in Examples\Chapter 7\Songs\DrumVerb.rns.

For more detailed information on reverb parameters and how to create and work with more advanced reverb effects in Reason, see the section "The RV7000 Advanced Reverb" later in this chapter.

DDL-1 Digital Delay Line

One of the most useful of Reason's original effects devices, the DDL-1 Digital Delay Line (Figure 7.3) is a great device to add to your Reason songs as either an insert or a send effect. Unlike a reverb effect, which simulates the sound of a specific room, a delay effect duplicates and repeats a signal based on the settings you make on the device's interface.

Figure 7.3

The DDL-1 Digital Delay Line

Setting the Delay Time

The LED on the left side of the DDL-1 displays the current delay value, either in steps or in milliseconds. Click the Unit button to choose between working in steps and milliseconds.

Steps The default mode, this will sync the delay effect to the current session's tempo automatically. Delay times from 1 to 16 steps can be chosen.

Milliseconds This setting allows you to set the delay by time, not necessarily synced to the current session tempo. Delay times from 1 to 2000 milliseconds can be chosen.

Use your mouse to click the up or down arrow, or click and drag directly on the LED to adjust the delay value in either mode.

To the right of the Unit mode selector is the Step Length selector. In Steps mode you can choose between step lengths of 1/16th note and 1/8th note for a triplet feel.

Feedback The Feedback setting determines how many times the echo will repeat. This is a very important setting; with the feedback too low, the effect may not be noticeable; with the feedback too high, the effect can go on too long and interfere with other tracks.

Pan The Pan knob sets where in the stereo field the delay effect will be placed. The Pan knob has no effect on the original signal, only on the delay effect.

Dry/Wet The Dry/Wet knob determines the mix of the original signal (dry) and the processed signal (wet). When using the DDL-1 as a send effect, you should leave the Wet/Dry knob at its default value of 127. When using the DDL-1 as an insert effect, you'll want to adjust the Wet/Dry knob to hear both the original and delayed signal.

The DDL-1 has two CV inputs that can be used to control the Pan and Feedback Parameters.

Using the DDL-1 Digital Delay

Delay is an endlessly useful effect in recording and creating music. Small amounts of delay added to a vocal track can beef up a performance. Adding delay to a synthesizer track can create entirely new sounds. Used in conjunction with the RPG-8 Arpeggiator, a delay effect can become an interesting composition tool.

Entire genres of music such as reggae/dub, psychedelic rock, and many electronic genres make frequent use of delay, sometimes as an integral part of a composition.

TRY OUT THE DDL-1 DIGITAL DELAY

Follow these steps to experiment with the DDL-1 and an NN-XT Advanced Sampler:

1. Create an NN-XT Advanced Sampler.

2. Load the patch `Reason Factory Sound Bank\NN-XT Sampler Patches\Vibes II.sxt`.

3. Add a DDL-1 as an insert effect.

4. Lower the Wet/Dry to 64 for an even mix between the original signal and the effect.

5. Use the Select Next Patch and Select Previous Patch buttons to try out other instruments with the DDL-1.

CONTROLLING PANNING WITH CV

The CV inputs found on many of Reason's effects can be used some interesting and unexpected ways. Follow these steps to use the DDL-1's panning CV input to create a panning effect.

Using the same NN-XT and DDL-1 configuration from the previous example:

1. Use the NN-XT's Browse Patch button to load the patch `Reason Factory Sound Bank\NN-XT Patches\Vibes II.rns`.

2. Next, hold down the Shift key and create an unconnected NN-19 in the Reason rack.

3. Select the NN-XT's track in the track list to return Master Keyboard Input (as described in Chapter 1).

4. Press Tab to view the back of the Reason rack and connect the NN-19's LFO output to the DDL-1's panning input.

5. Beneath every Reason CV input there's a CV value knob. Adjust the CV panning value knob to 127.

6. In the NN-19's LFO section, turn on the LFO Sync button.

Create variations in the effect by clicking the NN-19 LFO Wave button to select a different LFO waveform and by adjusting the LFO speed with the Rate knob.

You can also experiment further by loading different NN-XT patches and trying out different delay times and parameter settings on the DDL-1.

You can find this example on the accompanying CD in `Examples\Chapter 7\Songs\CVDelay.rns`.

USING THE DDL-1 AS A SEND EFFECT

A common use for the DDL-1 is as a send effect, applied to multiple tracks wherever needed in a mix. You can apply the effect constantly throughout a track, or use automation to add the effect to specific instruments at different times in a song. Add a DDL-1 to your Reason song as a send effect by selecting the mixer before creating the effect.

D-11 Foldback Distortion

Distortion can be a crucial element in digital mixes, adding grit and bite to otherwise tame-sounding performances. The D-11 Foldback Distortion (Figure 7.4) is the simplest of Reason's effects devices. Compared to Reason's other distortion device, the Scream 4 Sound Destruction Unit (covered later in this chapter), the D-11 is pretty limited. Still, you may find that its available sounds are appealing and it is worth experimenting with the device to see what you can come up with.

Figure 7.4

The D-11 Foldback Distortion

The D-11 has two adjustable parameters:

Amount Controls the amount of distortion that will be applied

Foldback Controls the shape of the distortion

Using the D-11 Foldback Distortion

The D-11 Foldback Distortion will always be used as an insert effect. These are some possible uses for the D-11:

- Adding it to a clean guitar loop or sampler performance, using it as a virtual distortion pedal

- Quickly creating lo-fi drums with a Dr. Rex or a Redrum

- Adding distortion to synthesizer patches

You can get a good idea of how the D-11 works by creating a Dr. Rex Loop Player and adding a D-11 as an insert effect. Raise the D-11's Amount and Foldback knobs, and then use the Dr. Rex instrument's Browse Loop button to browse and preview the various REX drum and instrument loop files found in the Reason Factory Sound Bank to hear the distortion effect on different types of performances.

For more advanced uses of distortion, see the section "The Scream 4 Sound Destruction Unit" later in this chapter.

ECF-42 Envelope Controlled Filter

The ECF-42 Envelope Controlled Filter (Figure 7.5) is the stand-alone device equivalent of the Filter and Filter Envelope sections you've seen on all of Reason's synths and sampler devices.

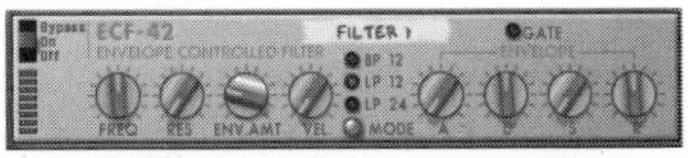

Figure 7.5

The ECF-42 Envelope Controlled Filter

The ECF-42 has the following parameters:

Modes The ECF-42 has three modes: BP12 (band pass filter), LP 12, and LP 24 (both low pass filters). As explained in Chapter 5, low pass filters cut high frequencies, allowing low frequencies to pass through the filter. Band pass filters cut both high and low frequencies, allowing a narrow band of frequencies to pass through the filter.

Frequency The Frequency knob controls which frequencies are allowed to pass through the filter. In the low pass modes, raising this knob allows more frequencies to pass through. In band pass mode, the Frequency knob determines whether a high or low band of frequencies is selected.

Resonance The Resonance knob is used to select frequencies within each mode's frequency range, and is similar to the Resonance slider found in the Filter sections of Reason's instruments.

Envelope Amount The Envelope Amount knob works in conjunction with the Gate CV input on the back panel of the ECF-42. Gate CV can be sent from another Reason device, such as a Matrix Pattern Sequencer, and used to trigger the ECF-42's filter envelope. This functionality will be covered in the "Matrix Pattern Sequencer: Advanced" section of Chapter 8.

Velocity The Velocity also works in conjunction with the Gate functionality, allowing you to control the Envelope based on the velocity of the Gate signal.

Envelope The Envelope contains the standard Attack, Decay, Sustain, and Release parameters found on most of Reason's envelope generators, which were covered in Chapter 5. In this case, the Envelope can only be triggered by Gate CV input.

The ECF-42 has four CV inputs for Frequency, the Envelope's Decay parameter, the Resonance knob, and Envelope Gate input to trigger the Envelope.

Using the ECF-42

The ECF-42 is most useful as an insert effect; it is very much like having an extra filter and filter envelope section at your disposal. Follow these steps for a quick look at one possible use for the ECF-42:

1. Create a SubTractor.

2. Select the SubTractor and create an ECF-42 as an insert effect. Play a few notes on your MIDI keyboard to hear the result.

3. Use the Tab key to flip to the back of the Reason rack.

4. Connect the SubTractor's LFO1 output to the ECF-42's Res CV input. The LFO will raise and lower the resonance, creating a vibrating sound.

You can also try connecting the LFO1 to the Frequency CV input to raise and lower the Frequency parameter. Try various LFO1 settings, including turning on the LFO1 Sync button, adjusting the Rate knob, and selecting different waveforms for different results.

You'll learn more about Gate triggering, CV routing, and the ECF-42 in the "Matrix Pattern Sequencer: Advanced" section of Chapter 8.

CF-101 Chorus/Flanger

The CF-101 Chorus/Flanger (Figure 7.6) is two separate effects in one unit: a chorus effect and a flanger effect. Chorus and flanging are closely related. Both are modulation effects

that work by creating a second version of an audio signal and then slightly delaying and altering the duplicate to create the effect. Chorus creates the

Figure 7.6

The CF-1-1 Chorus/Flanger

illusion of two instruments at once by slightly delaying and detuning the second signal.

Flanging was originally created by playing the same audio on two tape machines and slightly adjusting playback of one machine. Digital flanging works by delaying one signal and adjusting the speed of the delayed signal slightly with an LFO.

The CF-101 replicates this by using an LFO to alter the second signal. The following parameters are found on the CF-101:

Delay The Delay knob is used to set the delay time between the original and the processed signal.

Feedback The Feedback parameter controls the amount of the processed signal that is routed back into the effect.

Rate The Rate knob controls the speed of the LFO. With the Sync button off, the value range is 0 to 127. When the Sync button is activated, the Rate knob values are 16/4 to 1/32.

Sync The Sync button, when activated, syncs the LFO to the current session's tempo.

Mod Amount The Mod Amount knob controls the amount of modulation that will be applied using the LFO. In this case, the modulation is the speeding up and slowing down of the delayed signal.

Send Mode When the CF-101 is used as a send effect, turning on the Send mode will output only the processed signal. Mixing the processed signal with the original by using the channel strip's level fader and Send knob creates the effect.

The CF-101 has two CV inputs that can be used to control the Delay and Rate parameters.

Using the CF-101

Chorus and flanger effects can be very interesting on strings, synthesizers, vocals, and guitar. Chorus effects are frequently included in synth patches (the Thor Polysonic Synth has its own built-in chorus effect). Follow these steps to use the CF-101 on a guitar performance, one of the effect's frequent uses:

1. Create a new Dr. Rex Loop Player.

2. Load the REX loop `Reason Factory Sound Bank\Dr. Rex Instrument Loops\Guitar Loop\AC Guitar Strum 115\AcGt_Pop_C_115.rex`.

3. Select the Dr. Rex and create a CF-101 as an insert effect.

4. Click the Dr. Rex Preview button to hear the loop.

5. Try various adjustments to the effect's parameters. For more subtle effects, use lower LFO Rate and LFO Modulation amounts.

6. To create a stereo effect, use the Tab key to flip the Reason rack and disconnect the CF-101's right audio input.

USING THE FLANGER WITH A SYNTH

To see how the CF-101 works with a synth, try the following:

1. Add a Malström Graintable Synthesizer to your session.

2. With the Malström selected, add a CF-101 as an insert effect.

3. In the Malström's Osc 1 section, select the Square waveform in the waveform display.

4. Turn on the CF-101's Sync button and raise and lower its LFO Rate knob to experiment with the effect.

TAKING IT FURTHER

Take this effect configuration further by following these steps:

1. Flip the Reason rack and connect the Malström's MOD A CV output to the CF-101's Delay CV input.

2. On the Malström, turn on the MOD A Sync button.

3. Adjust the Malström's MOD A section's rate knob for different effects.

4. Try out different waveforms in the Malström's OSC 1 and MOD A sections.

   An example of this configuration can be found on the accompanying CD in `Examples\Chapter 7\Songs\MalsFlange.rns`.

PH-90 Phaser

Phasing is another modulation effect and is related to both chorus and flanging. As you've seen, chorus effects are created by delaying and detuning a second signal, and flanger effects are created by delaying and adjusting the speed of a second signal. Phasing is accomplished by creating a second signal and cutting frequencies, then altering the cut frequencies with an LFO.

Figure 7.7

The PH-90 Phaser

The PH-90 Phaser (Figure 7.7) uses a four-band filter to cut frequencies from an audio signal, and then applies an LFO to adjust the frequencies,  creating a sweeping sound as the LFO moves the selected frequencies.

The following parameters are found on the PH-90 interface:

Frequency The Frequency knob chooses the selected frequencies that will be cut.

Split The Split knob controls the distance between the four frequency bands that are being cut. Higher values result in a greater distance between the frequency bands.

Width The Width knob sets the width of the four frequency bands.

Rate The Rate knob controls the speed of the LFO.

Sync The Sync button allows you to sync the LFO Rate setting to the current Reason song.

Frequency Modulation The Frequency Modulation knob controls how much of the LFO will be applied to the signal.

Feedback The Feedback knob controls how much of the processed signal will be routed through the effect.

The PH-90 has two CV inputs, one to control frequency and one to control LFO rate.

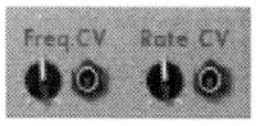

Using the PH-90

Phasing is another effect with a lot of possible applications. In many ways the sound of a phaser is similar to that of a flanger, though slightly less harsh. As a result you'll find that it is useful on similar effects. Long, sweeping phaser settings are particularly appealing on strings, guitar, bass, or any performance with long, sustained notes.

1. Create an NN-XT Advanced Sampler.

2. Load the Reason patch Orkester\Strings\String Combinations VSS-BSS f.sxt.

3. With the NN-XT selected, add a PH-90 as an insert effect.

4. Raise and lower the LFO Rate and Frequency Modulation parameters to hear some possible variation on the phaser effect.

This example can be found on the accompanying CD Examples\Chapter 7\Songs\ StringPhase.rns. Try loading other patches into the NN-XT, such as basses or synthesizers, to hear how they sound with the PH-90.

UN-16 Unison

The UN-16 Unison (Figure 7.8) creates multiple versions of any signal it receives and then makes slight tuning, timing, and panning adjustments to create the illusion of multiple instruments playing at once. The Unison can also create stereo and chorus-like effects.

Figure 7.8

The UN-16 Unison

Voice Count Sets the number of times the UN-16 will multiply the signal. The choices are 4, 8, and 16.

Detune Sets the amount the duplicated signals will be detuned from the original.

Dry/Wet Controls the mix of the original signal with the detuned signal. Leaving it at its default of 127, you'll hear only the detuned signal.

The UN-16 has a single CV input that can be used to control the Detune parameter.

Using the UN-16

The UN-16 is similar to the chorus effect. You can quickly create a stereo sound from a mono instrument, such as the SubTractor or a mono Dr. Rex loop, by adding the Unison as an insert effect and choosing four voices, then setting Detune to 0 and Dry/Wet to 64 or close to the center value. The UN-16 can be used to create strange piano and guitar sounds, fat synth sounds, and more.

CREATING A STEREO SUBTRACTOR SOUND

You can get a quick idea of how the Unison works by adding it as an insert effect with a SubTractor:

1. Create a new SubTractor.

2. With the SubTractor selected, create a UN-16 Unison.

3. Lower the Wet/Dry knob to the middle value of 64 for an even mix of the original and processed signal.

4. Create more pronounced, chorus-like effects by raising the Detune value and selecting a higher voice count.

Create some interesting sounds by routing one of the SubTractor's CV outputs to the Detune CV input.

Try the UN-16 Unison out on various piano, strings, and synthesizer sounds for interesting, chorus-like effects.

Comp-01 Compressor

The Comp-01Compressor (Figure 7.9) is one of three compression/limiting devices in Reason, along with the MClass Compressor and the MClass Maximizer, both of which you'll learn about later in this chapter.

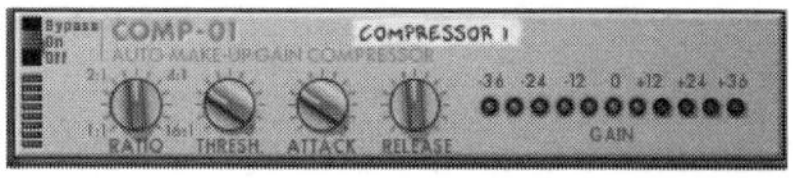

Compression is one of the most frequently used signal processing components in record-ing and mixing. Compression is used on vocals, drums, and many instrument perform-ances as well as on complete mixes as a mastering effect. Few modern recordings are made that don't include some kind of compression.

In Reason you'll find that compression can have all sorts of uses. Compression is used on individual instruments to level out performances, to help a specific instrument stand out in a mix and also to dramatically alter a sound.

Figure 7.9

The Comp-01 Compressor

How Compression Works

At its most basic, compression is applied to a performance to even out the dynamic range by lowering the volume of the loudest sounds and/or raising the volume of the quietest sounds.

For example, many vocal performances contain a wide dynamic range with noticeably louder and quieter sections. Instead of having to constantly raise and lower the volume of the vocal track in the mix, by applying compression you can even out the entire perform-ance and keep it within a consistent dynamic range.

Compression also has many other uses. Heavy compression settings can be used to cre-ate distortion. Subtle or drastic compression is often used to alter the sound of perform-ance, enabling it to stand out in a mix. Compression is also used on the combined stereo output of complete mixes (see the MClass Compressor) as a mastering effect.

The Comp-01 Parameters

The Comp-101 has the following parameter knobs:

Ratio The Ratio knob sets the amount of compression that will be applied to the incoming signal. A ratio of 1:1 means that no compression will be applied; gradually raising the Ratio knob will apply more and more compression to the signal. The Comp-01's maximum com-pression ratio is 16:1.

A ratio of 2:1 reduces every decibel above the compressor's set threshold by half. This means that ½ of the level above the threshold passes through. At a ratio of 4:1, every deci-bel above the threshold is reduced to ¼ of its original level. At the Comp-01's maximum ratio of 16:1, every decibel above the threshold is reduced to 1/16th of its original level.

Threshold The Threshold setting sets the volume level at which compression will begin to be applied. Selecting lower Threshold knob values will lower the level at which the compressor starts to work, resulting in a more noticeable effect.

Attack The Attack knob controls how quickly the compression will take effect. Faster attack settings are crucial when dealing with quick, unexpected volume spikes. Slower attack rates will create a more subtle effect but may also completely miss quick, loud noises.

Release The Release parameter controls how quickly the compression will end once the volume level drops below the Threshold setting. The appropriate setting for the Release parameter depends on the kind of performance that is being compressed and the desired effect.

Gain Meter The Comp-01 also has a built-in automatic makeup gain functionality, which compensates for any signal that has been reduced in volume by the applied compression. The Gain meter shows the amount of makeup gain that's being applied to the signal.

Using the Comp-01

The Comp-01, like most compressors, will almost always be used either as an insert effect or as a mastering effect. Compression as a mastering effect will be covered in "The MClass Effects" section later in this chapter. Follow these steps to use the Comp-01 as an insert effect with a Dr. Rex drum loop:

1. Add a Dr. Rex Loop Player to a Reason song.
2. Create a Comp-01 as an insert effect.
3. In order for compression to have any effect, the incoming signal must reach the threshold level. Lower the Threshold and Attack settings and raise the Ratio to create a noticeable effect.

For a more subtle effect, try higher Threshold settings and lower Ratio settings. The appropriate settings for the Release knob will depend both on the specific performance and the desired result. You may want to set the Release knob so that the compression effect on one event has ended before the next audio event begins, or you may want a higher Release value to create a consistently compressed performance.

Perform further experiments with the Comp-01 by loading different types of instrument loops and experimenting with the Attack, Ratio, and Threshold settings.

Before the introduction of the MClass effects, the Comp-01 was frequently used to add compression and limiting to complete mixes by inserting it between the mixer and the Reason Hardware Device. For more on limiting and mastering, see "The MClass Effects" section later in this chapter.

PEQ-2 Two Band Parametric EQ

Reason has multiple options for equalization. The most basic EQ options are the high and low EQ knobs found on each channel strip of the main mixer, and the most advanced is the MClass Equalizer covered later in this chapter. Falling somewhere in the middle of these two is the PEQ-2 Two Band Parametric EQ (Figure 7.10).

Figure 7.10

The PEQ-2 Two Band Parametric EQ

The PEQ-2 is in many ways similar to the Filter sections found on Reason's synth and sampler instruments. The PEQ-2 contains the following parameters:

The Display The Display on the left side of the PEQ-2 shows the results of the adjustments made with the device's parameter knobs. This is a visual representation of the EQ's functionality.

Frequency The Frequency knobs select the specific frequency that will be cut or boosted. The Frequency parameter is very similar to the Filter slider found on Reason's filter sections.

Q The Q knob sets the width of the band of frequencies selected in conjunction with the Frequency knobs and is similar to the Resonance slider on most Reason instruments' Filter sections. A lower Q value selects a wider range of frequencies. A higher Q value selects a tighter range, allowing you to zero in on specific frequencies for cutting and boosting.

Gain The Gain knob controls how much the selected frequencies are raised or lowered. Turning the Gain knob to the left cuts the selected frequencies; turning the knob to the right boosts them.

Filter B On/Off By default, when a PEQ-2 is created only Filter A is activated. This button turns the second EQ band, Filter B, on and off.

The PEQ-2 has two CV inputs, one for each Frequency knob.

EQ Basics

Equalization is an important part of any mix. Reason's virtual studio "atmosphere" can change some of the usual considerations involved when working with EQ to create a mix. For example, in a live recording studio if your acoustic piano track is too dull, you may want to boost some of the high-end frequencies with a hardware EQ device or software EQ plug-in. With a Reason sampler device, you could just as easily use the Filter frequency knob to boost high-end frequencies. Another example would be the kick drum found on Channel 1 of many Redrum kits.

Whereas in other DAW programs or in a hardware-based studio a dull or unclear kick drum track might be routed to an EQ hardware device or software plug-in, in Reason you could just as easily raise the Channel 1 Tone knob to boost the kick drum's high end.

For greater control over cutting and boosting specific frequencies, the PEQ-2 (and Reason's other EQ, the MClass Equalizer) can be used as an insert effect. Keep in mind that EQ is definitely something that is best used sparingly and only as necessary, unless you are specifically using it to create a dramatic effect.

Using the PEQ-01

After you've created your complete Reason song, you may find that some instruments sound too bright, or too dull, or are not cutting clearly through the overall mix. The mixer's EQ section with its Treble and Bass knobs can certainly help, but for more precise equalization tasks, adding the PEQ-2 as an insert effect on specific instruments can give you greater control over your mixes. In these cases you'll select the device and then create a PEQ-2. Use the A Frequency band to select and cut or boost the desired frequencies. For more control activate the B Frequency band and make a second selection of frequencies to cut or boost.

THE PEQ-2 AS AN EFFECT

Because you can automate the PEQ-2 through CV routing, it's useful as an effect as well. Follow these steps to create a filter effect with the PEQ-2:

1. Create a SubTractor. You can use the SubTractor's default settings or load any patch.

2. Select the SubTractor in the rack and create a PEQ-2 as an insert effect.

3. Raise the Filter A Gain knob on the PEQ-2 to the maximum value (63).

4. Connect the LFO 1 output of the SubTractor to the PEQ-2's Freq. 1 input.

5. Set the SubTractor's LFO 1 to Sync and lower the Rate knob to 8/4.

You can make further adjustments by raising and lowering the LFO 1 Rate knob. You can find this example on the CD in `Examples\Chapter 7\Songs\PEQ2.rns`.

Reason's other EQ device, the MClass Equalizer, has even more EQ functionality and is covered later in this chapter.

The Scream 4 Sound Destruction Unit

The Scream 4 Sound Destruction Unit (Figure 7.11) takes the basic concept of the D-11 Distortion effect and expands on it. Its uses range from the obvious, such as heavy distortion and complete sonic mayhem, to more subtle applications, such as adding a touch of analog-style warmth to a single track or to a complete session by inserting the effect between the mixer and the hardware device as a mastering effect.

Figure 7.11

The Scream 4 Sound Destruction Unit

The Master Volume knob located to the right of the Body section controls the overall output of the Scream 4.

Loading Patches

Along with the RV7 Advanced Reverb, the Scream 4 is one of two Reason effects devices capable of loading and saving patches. This functionality works in exactly the same way as with Reason's patch-loading instruments. The patch loading and saving section at the lower left contains a display that shows the currently loaded patch, Select Next Patch and Select Previous Patch buttons, a Browse Patch button that opens the Patch Browser, and a Patch Save button for saving any new or altered Scream 4 patches.

You can find a large collection of included Scream 4 patches by clicking the Browse Patch button and using the Browser to locate the folder `Reason Factory Sound Bank\Scream 4 Patches\`. These included preset patches run the entire range of possible Scream 4 effects and are a great way to become familiar with some of the effect's possible uses.

Damage

The left side of the Scream 4 contains the Damage section. This is the heart of the effect and where much of the Scream's sonic action takes place. The Damage section is turned on and off using the Damage On/Off button in the upper-left corner.

The Damage Type knob is used to select from any of the 10 types of distortion that Scream has to offer. Each of these distortion types has its own unique sound and features two adjustable parameters, which are controlled by the two knobs at the bottom of the Damage section, marked P1 and P2. The Damage Control knob raises and lowers the amount of the distortion effect.

The following are the different available distortion types and their adjustable parameters:

Overdrive Overdrive simulates a guitar amplifier turned up to the point where distortion is created by "overdriving" the amp. Its two adjustable parameters are Tone and Presence. The Tone parameter is used to adjust the high and low frequencies of the effect. Raising the Presence parameter adds more clarity and definition to the sound by boosting specific frequencies. Raise these parameters with the P1 and P2 knobs for a clearer, brighter effect. Lower them for a more muted effect.

Distortion The Distortion setting is similar to the Overdrive setting but features a more pronounced and compressed distortion effect. Its adjustable parameters are also Tone and Presence.

Fuzz The Fuzz setting is the equivalent of "Fuzz Box" distortion pedals. Its adjustable parameters are also Tone and Presence.

Tube The Tube setting replicates the sound you'd get by running your signal through an overdriven tube amplifier. Its two adjustable parameters are Contour and Bias.

Tape Tape distortion creates the kind of sounds you'd hear by pushing the signal in an analog tape machine. Different tape speeds result in different types of distortion. The Tape distortion setting features Speed and Compression parameters.

This setting is very useful and is explored further in the "Using the Scream 4" section later in this chapter.

Feedback Holding an instrument, such as an electric guitar, too close to a speaker cabinet creates feedback. You can use this setting to create "screaming" feedback effects. The adjustable parameters are Size and Frequency.

Modulate The Modulate distortion doubles the signal, creating overtones similar to the ring modulation effect found on the SubTractor. The two adjustable parameters for this setting are Ring and Frequency. Increase the P1 knob for a more noticeable ring modulation effect.

Warp Warp creates distortion by multiplying the input signal. This setting contains sharpness, and raising the Bias parameter with the P2 knob creates a very thick distortion.

Digital Creates the kind of distortion you'd hear by reducing a sound's bit depth and sample rate. The Resolution and Rate parameters can be used to increase or decrease the effect.

Scream The Scream setting is another thick distortion, very much like the Overdrive, Distortion, and Fuzz settings. Raise the Tone and Frequency knobs for a biting sound; lower both parameters for a more muted distortion.

Cut

The Cut section of the Scream 4 is a straightforward three-band EQ. The Cut section is turned on and off by clicking the button. The three sliders can be used to cut or boost Low, Mid, or High Range frequencies. As with any EQ you can quickly create "thinner" sounds by boosting the high end and/or lowering the low end. You can thicken the sound of the Scream's output by doing the opposite.

> Cranking the mid-range on the Scream 4's Cut section is a great way to quickly create a CB radio–style effect.

Body

The Body section of the Scream 4 is used to further shape the sound by simulating different types of output, including speaker cabinets and various speaker configurations and enclosures.

Type The Type selector lets you choose from five types of speaker/enclosure configurations, each with its own distinct sound.

Resonance Resonance of the selected Body type can be raised and lowered with this knob.

Scale The Scale parameter determines the size of the Body's speaker or enclosure. This knob is actually "backwards"; turning it to the left increases the Body size, and turning to the right decreases the Body size.

Auto Auto can be used to create envelope effects with the Scale parameter. Raising the Auto knob is the equivalent of manually adjusting the Scale knob back and forth. A higher Auto value results in a faster effect. For a more pronounced effect, try raising the Resonance knob.

CV Routing

The Scream 4 contains four CV inputs—the Damage Control P1, P2, and Scale—and it also has a CV output for the Body section's Auto parameter. These CV routing options open up many sound-shaping possibilities, including controlling the Scream 4's parameters with LFOs, envelope generators, and the Matrix Pattern Sequencer, as well as routing the Auto CV output back into one of the Scream 4's CV inputs.

Using the Scream 4

The Scream 4 will almost always be used as an insert effect and can be applied to any instrument in your Reason songs for subtle or drastic effect. Reason users working in hard rock, industrial, or noise genres may find the Scream 4's more dramatic possibilities particularly useful, while other Reason users will be more likely to take advantage of the less obvious parameters to add warmth to tracks.

Some Reason users will place the Scream 4 between the mixer and the hardware device and use the tape compression.

Damaging a Drum Loop

The Scream 4 can be used to quickly change the sound of any drum loop by adding various amounts of distortion. Follow these steps to try out the Scream 4 with a Dr. Rex drum loop:

1. Create a Dr. Rex Loop Player and load the drum loop RFSB\Acoustic\Straight\ 125 Stones\Acs03_Stones_125.rx2.

2. Select the Dr. Rex in the rack and create a Scream 4 as an insert effect.

3. Raise the Damage Control knob to full value (127).

4. Start playback of the loop and use the Damage Type knob to scroll through the different distortion types.

You can hear very clearly that while each distortion type serves essentially the same function (blowing the heck out of the sound) each one has its own individual tone and sound qualities. You can experiment further by shaping these qualities using the P1 and P2 knobs.

To get an idea of how each damage type can be further altered, try reducing the Damage Control knob to 64 (the middle value) and scrolling through each damage type, once again using each damage control parameter knob to experiment with the distortion's qualities.

Use the Dr. Rex's Browse Loop button to load different drum and instrument loops, then try scrolling the various distortion types again to see which kinds of distortion work best for your music.

Tape Compression

A common complaint about Reason and about digital audio software and digital recording in general is a lack of "analog warmth." For example, in studios that use analog tape machines as their recording medium, "tape compression" is the sound created by an audio signal being recorded at a high volume to analog tape.

Tape compression has a pleasant and distinctive way of coloring the sound of a recording, which is missed by many people who create music digitally.

Tape compression is still widely used, especially for drum recording. Many software-based recording projects will record drums to tape, and then send the audio into a DAW program for editing and overdubbing.

The Scream 4 has a damage type specifically for creating the effect of a signal being recorded to analog tape that can be useful as both an insert and a mastering effect used on complete mixes.

> You'll find the Scream 4's Tape setting used in the Bass & Drum Mastering Combi patch.

Try these settings as a starting point to create your own patch using the Scream 4's Tape setting:

1. Using the same Dr. Rex loop as in the previous example, initialize the Scream 4 (Edit → Initialize Patch) to start with a clean slate.

2. Use the Damage Type knob to select the Compression Damage type.

3. Raise the Compression parameter (P2) to a value of 100.

4. Turn on the Cut section and raise the Lo slider slightly to add some low end to the drum loop.

5. Adjust the Damage Amount knob to higher and lower values to hear the difference.

At this point you can make adjustments to the various parameters, including Tape Speed and Compression as well as the Cut settings, to find a sound that works for you. Save your patch by clicking the Patch Save button and choosing a location for your new patch.

A version of this example can be found on the accompanying CD in `Examples\Chapter 7\Songs\TapeComp.rns`.

The RV7000 Advanced Reverb

The RV7000 Advanced Reverb (Figure 7.12) is one of the most interesting and complicated of all of the Reason effects. Along with the Scream Distortion it's one of two effects that allow you to load, edit, create, and save patches. The Reason Factory Sound Bank comes with a number of RV7000 patches, which can be found in the folder `Reason Factory Sound Bank\RV7000 Patches` along with some free demo versions of commercially available ReFills. The RV7000's interface consists of the main panel, shown in Figure 7.12, and a Remote Programmer panel with advanced features that will be covered here as well.

Figure 7.12

**The RV7000
Advanced Reverb**

Loading and Saving Patches

The RV7000's patch loading and saving functionality works in exactly the same way as in the Scream 4 and Reason patch-based instruments.

The patch loading and saving section contains a display that shows the currently loaded patch, Select Next Patch and Select Previous Patch buttons, a Browse Patch button that opens the Patch Browser, and a Patch Save button for saving any new or altered RV7000 patches.

You can find a large collection of included RV7000 patches by clicking the Browse Patch button and using the Patch Browser to locate the folder Reason Factory Sound Bank\RV7000 Patches\. Experimenting with these patches will give you an idea of the range of available reverb and delay effects available with the RV7000.

> See the "RV7 Digital Reverb" section earlier in this chapter for other ideas on using reverb as insert and send effects.

RV7000 Main Panel Parameters

When you create an RV7000, only the device's main panel will be visible. Working only with RV7000's main panel you can load and save patches and access some important functionality.

EQ Enable and Gate Enable Buttons Clicking the EQ On/Off turns on and off functionality that you'll learn about in the "RV7000 Advanced Parameters" section later in this chapter.

Decay The Decay parameter controls the decay time for the reverb effect. Turn the knob to the right for longer decay times, resulting in a more noticeable effect.

HF Damp HF stands for High Frequency. The HF Damp is similar to the damping parameter found on the RV7 Reverb, but in this case it controls the amount of high-frequency content in the reverb signal.

Hi EQ Use the Hi EQ knob to raise and lower the high frequencies of the EQ effect.

Dry/Wet The Dry/Wet knob controls the mix between the original signal and the reverb effect. The default setting of 127 should be left as is when using the RV7000 as a send effect. To use the RV7000 as an insert, lower the Dry/Wet as needed for a specific application.

RV7000 Advanced Parameters

The RV7000's Remote Programmer contains advanced functionality for editing the included reverb algorithms, and also for adding EQ and gate effects to the device's output. To display the Remote Programmer, click the Show/Hide Remote Programmer button on the bottom left of the RV7000's main panel.

Reverb Mode

Reverb mode is where you'll make most of the main adjustments to your reverb effects. The RV7000 Reverb mode gives you access to multiple algorithms. The algorithm is a mathematical representation of the room. Each algorithm contains its own set of adjustable parameters. Some of these are familiar settings, such as the Room and Hall algorithms. Some are more experimental, such as the Multi Tap delay and Reverse algorithms. Figure 7.13 shows the Reverb mode for the Spring Reverb algorithm.

Figure 7.13

The Advanced Programmer in Reverb mode

THE ALGORITHMS

You can access the RV7000's different algorithms by turning the Algorithm knob in the top-left corner.

Small Space The Small Space algorithm can be used to simulate a closet, bathroom, or other small enclosure. Room size and shape can be adjusted.

Room This algorithm emulates a small-to-large room, such as a studio main room or a bedroom. The settings available include options for adjusting the size and shape of the room.

Hall The Hall algorithm can be used to simulate a small, medium, or large concert hall. Among the available parameters are the room size and shape.

Arena The Arena algorithm is used to emulate larger venues such as a sports arena. Among its parameters is the ability to set left and right delay times for a stereo effect.

Plate The Plate algorithm replicates plate reverbs, which use a transducer connected to a sheet of metal to create the reverb effect. The Plate algorithm is easy to use and features only predelay and Low Frequency damping parameters.

Spring Spring reverbs create their effect by capturing the sound of a signal vibrating a metal spring. Spring reverbs are most commonly found on guitar amplifiers, making this a good starting point for reverb effects used in conjunction with guitar loops or samples.

Echo The Echo algorithm gives Reason users another excellent delay effect. The Echo Time parameter can be synced to the current session tempo using the Tempo Sync On/Off knob on the bottom left.

Multi Tap This is another delay effect, even more complex than the Echo algorithm. The Multi Tap algorithm features four separate delays, which can be chosen by using the Edit Select knob at the top right of the Remote Programmer. Once you specify a Delay setting, you can use the three knobs below the Edit Select to set delay time, level, and panning.

Reverse This is a very cool algorithm that simulates the effect of a taped performance being played backwards while reverb is applied, and then played forward. This results in a reverse reverb effect that can be simulated with this algorithm.

EQ Mode

The Edit Mode button on the left side of the Remote Programmer can be used to select the EQ mode, shown in Figure 7.14. The EQ mode must be turned on in the main panel by clicking the EQ Enable On/Off button.

Figure 7.14

The Remote Programmer in EQ Mode

The EQ mode can be used to change the sound of your reverb patches by cutting or boosting selected frequencies. The EQ mode contains parameters similar to those found on the PEQ-2 Two Band Parametric EQ and the MClass Equalizer. The EQ sections parameters are:

Low Gain Used to cut or boost low frequencies with a shelving filter shape.

Low Frequency Used to select which low frequencies will be cut or boosted.

Parametric Gain Used to cut or boost frequencies selected by the parametric Frequency knob with a parametric style EQ shape.

Parametric Frequency Selects the specific frequencies that will be cut or boosted.

Parametric Q Used to select a narrow or wide range of frequencies. Higher Q values will result in a narrower band on selected frequencies.

Gate Mode

The RV7000's Gate mode is accessed by clicking the Edit Mode switch and selecting Gate Mode. Turn Gate mode on and off using the Gate mode Enable button on the RV7000's main panel. Figure 7.15 shows the Gate mode in the Remote Programmer. Using the Gate mode you can both trigger and stop the reverb effect based on audio levels or incoming MIDI note or Gate CV information.

Figure 7.15

The Remote Programmer in Gate Mode

The RV700's Gate mode parameters are:

Threshold Sets the level at which the gate will open, allowing the effect to be heard

Decay Modulation Can be used to control the effect's decay time as the gate closes

Trigger Source Lets you choose between Audio and MIDI/CV as the trigger for the Gate parameters

High Pass Can be used to set which frequencies will open the gate

Attack Sets how soon the gate will open once the signal reaches the threshold level

Hold Sets how long the gate will remain open after the signal drops below the threshold level

Release Determines how long it will take the gate to fully close

CV

The RV7000 features Delay, High Frequency damping, and Gate CV inputs. Earlier in this chapter you saw how panning could be controlled with CV on the DDL-1 Digital Delay. The same techniques can be used to control the Delay and High Frequency Damping parameters of the RV7000 via their CV inputs. In the "Matrix Pattern Sequencer: Advanced" section in Chapter 8, you'll learn more about Gate CV and Reason's effects.

Creating RV7000 Patches

To get a better understanding of what's possible with the RV7000, follow these steps to experiment with creating your own patches:

1. Start by adding an NN-XT Advanced Sampler to a Reason song.

2. Load the patch `Reason Factory Sound Bank\NN-XT Sampler Patches\Guitar and Plucked\A-coustic Steel.sxt`.

3. Select the NN-XT in the Reason rack and create an RV7000 as an insert effect.

4. Set the Wet/Dry knob to the middle value (64) to get an even mix of the original signal and the processed signal.

5. Open the Remote Programmer and select any algorithm.

The best way to become familiar with the RV7000 is to try out each of the available algorithms, experimenting with the different parameters. Once you've found some settings that sound interesting to you, use the NN-XT's Browse Patch functionality to open the Browser and preview different instruments by selecting them in the Browser and playing notes with your MIDI keyboard.

> Try setting a lower Wet/Dry value for a more subtle effect and higher values for more dramatic ambience. Different kinds of instruments and performances will benefit from different amounts of reverb.

After you've spent some time with the various algorithms, try enabling and incorporating the EQ and Gate modes into your patches. To save a patch, click the Save Patch button on the main panel and choose a name and location for your patch.

You'll learn more about working with the RV7000 in both the "Matrix Pattern Sequencer: Advanced" section in Chapter 8 and in Chapter 9.

The MClass Effects

Before the introduction of the MClass mastering effects in version 3, Reason users had limited options for mastering their completed songs. For many users, it was standard operating procedure to go outside Reason for final mixes, taking advantage of the ReWire protocol to access the software plug-ins and outboard routing capabilities available in Pro Tools, Digital Performer, Cubase, and other DAW programs. The MClass mastering effects were introduced to give Reason users the opportunity to take care of all of their mastering needs within the program itself.

> Mixing and mastering via ReWire are covered in the "ReWire" section in Chapter 10.

MClass consists of four separate effects: the MClass Equalizer, the MClass Stereo Imager, the MClass Compressor, and the MClass Maximizer. These devices are virtual recreations of the hardware devices that make up the core of any mastering studio. These devices can all be used as mastering effects, placed between your session's Mixer 14:2 and the Reason Hardware Device. You'll also find that the MClass effects can be quite useful as insert effects with any of Reason's instrument devices.

The MClass Equalizer

The MClass Equalizer (Figure 7.16) contains functionality that can be useful for working with your overall mixes or with individual instruments. EQ almost always be used as an insert effect, either on an instrument or inserted between a Reason song's mixer and hardware device.

Figure 7.16

The MClass Equalizer

Lo Cut Cuts all frequencies below 30Hz. This parameter has only on and off.

Low Shelf Can be used to lower or raise low frequencies in the 30Hz to 600Hz range.

Parametric 1 Can be used to lower or raise frequencies in the 39Hz to 20kHz range.

Parametric 2 Can also be used to lower or raise frequencies in the 39Hz to 20kHz range.

Hi Shelf Can be used to lower or raise frequencies in the 3kHz to 12kHz range.

The Lo Cut section cuts the low frequencies from an instrument when used as an insert or an entire mix when used as a mastering effect. The other EQ sections have adjustable parameters:

Frequency Determines which specific frequencies will be lowered or raised.

Gain Knob Determines how much the selected frequencies will be lowered or raised. Turning the knob to the left will lower the selected frequencies. Turning the knob to the right will raise the selected frequencies.

Q Determines the slope of the EQ's shape on the Low Shelf and High shelf sections. With the Parametric sections, Q determines how wide or narrow the selected frequency band will be.

> The function of the Q knob is similar to the Resonance slider found on the Filter section of many of Reason's instruments.

Using the MClass Equalizer

As a mastering effect, the MClass Equalizer is best used lightly. You may want to use the Lo Cut and Lo Shelf to remove low-end rumble and noise, or the High Shelf to boost the high-end of the entire mix for more clarity. EQ as a mastering effect is meant to enhance a mix. Wherever possible it's a good idea to use EQ on individual instruments in your mix instead of relying on mastering EQ to fix the overall sound.

For example, instead of cutting all of the low end out of a muddy mix with a mastering EQ, try using the MClass Equalizer's Lo Cut or Lo Shelf settings on just your bass tracks or drum tracks, especially on heavy kick drum sounds. Always try taking advantage of Reason's other EQ options to work with specific instruments before you add mastering EQ.

The MClass Stereo Imager

The MClass Stereo Imager is primarily for use on complete mixes and is used to enhance the listener's perception of a mix's stereo separation. It can also be used to do the opposite. The MClass Stereo Imager splits the signal into low and high frequencies, allowing you to adjust the low or high frequencies of a mix independently.

Figure 7.17

The MClass Stereo Imager

Lo Band The Lo Band section is used to adjust the width of the stereo field of the low frequencies. Turn the Lo Band's Mono/Wide knob to the left to decrease the stereo width of the low frequencies; turn to the right to increase it.

Hi Band The Hi Band section is used to adjust the stereo field of the high frequencies. Turn the Hi Band's Mono/Wide knob to the left to decrease the stereo width of the high frequencies, or turn to the right to increase it.

X-over Freq This knob set the crossover frequency, which determines the frequencies that will be adjusted by the low frequency and high frequency knobs. Turn the knob to the left to lower the crossover point or to the right to raise it.

The Solo Section The Solo section has three buttons, one for soloing the high frequencies (Hi Band), one for soloing the low frequencies (Lo Band), and a Normal setting for hearing both at once. The Solo section is used primarily for auditioning just the lows or just the highs.

The MClass Stereo Imager also features an extra stereo output that can be used to send either the low or high band to a separate stereo channel on the mixer or to another effect device.

As a general rule, when working on a complete mix you'll probably want to use the Stereo Imager to decrease the stereo image of the low end and increase the stereo image of the high end. What each mix needs and whether or not the mix can benefit from this device will vary from song to song. Along with increasing or decreasing the stereo field for an entire mix, the Stereo Imager can be used on individual instruments.

Using the MClass Stereo Imager

Follow these steps to try out the Stereo Imager on a synthesizer/echo effect configuration:

1. Create a New SubTractor Analog Synth.

2. With the SubTractor selected in the Reason rack, create an RV7 Digital Reverb as an insert effect.

3. Choose the Stereo Echoes algorithm and play a few notes with your MIDI keyboard to hear the stereo effect.

4. With the RV7 selected, create an MClass Stereo Imager.

Experiment by raising and lowering both the Hi Band and Lo Band Mono/Wide knobs while playing notes on your MIDI keyboard. Because spatial effects are better perceived at higher frequencies, you'll hear a distinct difference in how the effect sounds when each band is increased or decreased.

Try experimenting with the Stereo Imager's settings on different types of mixes to find the results that best work for your music.

The MClass Compressor

The MClass Compressor (Figure 7.18) is a more advanced compression device than the half-rack Comp-01 compressor, but contains many similar features and essentially the same functionality.

Figure 7.18
The MClass Compressor

The Input Gain The Input Gain knob controls the level of signal coming in to the compressor. You can use this knob to raise the volume of a quiet signal before applying compression.

Threshold The Threshold knob determines the volume level at which the device will begin to apply compression to the incoming audio signal.

Soft Knee Turning on the Soft Knee button will apply a more gradual compression to any signal that reaches the Threshold level. This is similar to the Attack parameter and is used to create a smoother-sounding, less harsh compression when using high ratio/low Threshold settings.

Ratio The Ratio determines the overall amount of compression that is applied to the incoming audio signal. A ratio of 1:1 applies no gain reduction. Higher ratios will apply more gain reduction to signals that are passing through the threshold. Use high ratios and low threshold settings to achieve more noticeable compression effects.

Gain Meter The Gain meter displays the amount of volume reduction that is taking place in the compressor.

Sidechain/Solo The Sidechain is used in conjunction with the sidechain inputs. Using the sidechain inputs, you can send a second signal into the compressor. This second signal essentially takes over for the Threshold knob and can be used to trigger compression on the original signal. The Sidechain light will go on every time the sidechain signal is active. Click the Solo button to hear only the sidechain inputs.

Attack The Attack setting specifies the amount of time it takes for compression to begin once the signal reaches the Threshold level. The MClass compressor lets you set this in milliseconds.

Release Release sets the amount of time it takes for the compressor to stop applying compression once a signal has dropped below the Threshold setting.

Adapt Release With the Adapt Release button activated, the MClass Compressor will adjust the release value automatically as needed for longer spikes in volume.

Output Gain Unlike the Comp-01, the MClass Compressor does not feature Auto Makeup Gain. The Output Gain knob can be used to raise the volume level to make up for any compression-related volume reduction.

Using the MClass Compressor

The MClass compressor is useful as a mastering effect and also as an insert effect on individual instruments. See the "Comp-01 Compressor" section earlier in this chapter for ideas and suggestions for using compression as an insert effect in your Reason songs.

The MClass Maximizer

The MClass Maximizer (Figure 7.19) is a limiter and soft clipper. Limiting is considered compression with a ratio of 10:1 or higher. Soft clipping is used to smooth the distortion created by a signal that's too loud, making it less harsh to the ear. The Maximizer's main function is as a mastering effect, and is used to give your final mixes the maximum possible volume levels without distorting.

Figure 7.19
The MClass Maximizer

The Limiter Section

Turn the Limiter on by clicking the On/Off button in the upper-left corner of the Limiter section. The Limiter section contains the following parameters:

Input Gain The Input Gain knob controls the level of signal coming in to the Maximizer. You can use this knob to raise the volume of quiet signal before applying limiting.

Look Ahead Enable   Turning on Look Ahead Enable adds a 4ms delay to the audio coming into the Maximizer. The Maximizer then uses this 4ms to "look ahead" and prepare itself for any upcoming volume spikes, creating a smoother limiting.

Gain Meter   The Gain meter displays the amount of volume reduction being applied by the Maximizer.

Attack   The Attack setting is the same as the Attack feature found on the Compressor devices. In this case, instead of a knob that can be used for setting specific values you are limited to choosing between Fast, Mid, and Slow attack times.

Release   Again, this is the same functionality as the Release parameters found on Reason's compressors. In this case you can choose between Fast, Slow, and Auto. Use the Fast setting for a more dramatic effect and a slow setting for more subtle limiting. Select the Auto setting and the Maximizer will automatically set the Release time based on the incoming signal.

Output Gain   The Output Gain controls the overall output of the Maximizer. The normal setting for this is 0dB.

The Soft Clipper Section

Turn the Soft Clipper on and off using the Soft Clip Enable button in the top-left corner. The Amount knob adjusts the amount of clipping that will be applied and ranges from 0 (no soft clipping applied) to 127 (maximum soft clipping applied).

Use the Peak and VU buttons to switch between viewing peaks in volume as they happen or viewing the average volume level of your limited mix.

Using the MClass Maximizer

The MClass Maximizer is generally used as a mastering effect on complete mixes but can also be used as an insert effect. As an insert, the Maximizer can be used on Rex loops, for any instrument performance, or on a drum submix like the one you created in Chapter 3. To do this, create the Maximizer and place it between the Submix Mixer and the main mixer; route the stereo output of the Submix to the stereo inputs of the Maximizer; and then route the Maximizer to a channel on the session's main mixer.

As a mastering effect, the MClass Maximizer should always be the last device in your mastering chain. The settings you choose with the other mastering devices will often be geared specifically toward getting the maximum amount of volume from your tracks.

"Brick Wall" Limiting

One of the most common uses for a limiter is creating what is known a "brick wall" limiting. This is heavy compression with a high ratio and a set volume level that cannot be exceeded.

Insert the MClass Maximizer or the MClass Mastering Combi between your Reason song's mixer and the Hardware Device. The MClass Mastering Combi will already be in place if you have already set up your preferences according to the instructions at the end of Chapter 2.

1. Turn on the Limiter section of the Maximizer.

2. Turn on the 4ms Look Ahead Enable button.

3. Set the Attack and Release settings to Fast.

4. Make sure the Output Gain knob is at 0.0 dB.

5. Turn the Soft Clipper on and raise the amount knob to 127.

Brick wall limiting is used to get the maximum volume from your mixes without exceeding the set Output Gain of 0 dB. In the MClass Mastering Combi preset folder you'll find an example of brick wall limiting in the patch called Brick Wall + Hi Band Spread Mastering.cmb.

The Mastering Combi

The Mastering Suite Combi shown in Figure 7.20 combines all of the MClass effects in one easy to use the Combinator patch. The Mastering Combi comes with a collection of mastering presets, which you can find in Reason Factory Sound Bank\MClass Mastering Patches\.

The Mastering Combi presets also give you good examples of some of the standard signal flow options used for the mastering process and makes a great starting point for learning about mastering.

Figure 7.20

The MClass Mastering Combi

Using the Mastering Suite Combi

At the end of Chapter 2 you chose `Mixer and Mastering.rns` to use as the template file for creating Reason songs and working with the exercises in this book. This template includes the MClass Mastering Combi, and places it between the song's Mixer 14:2 and the Hardware Device.

> The Maximizer in the default MClass Mastering Combi is set to On by default.

Follow these steps to get a look inside the MClass Mastering Combi:

1. Click the Device Unfold button to view the Combinator's interface.
2. Click the Show Devices button to view the devices that make up the default Mastering Combi. You'll see one instance of each MClass device.
3. Click the Browse Patch button and locate `Reason Factory Sound Bank\MClass Mastering Patches`.

This folder contains a set of preset patches designed to help in the mastering process. You'll find a number of patches created to work with specific genres (`Hard Rock.cmb`, `Hip Hop.cmb`, `Dance.cmb`) and you'll also find some more general mastering presets, such as the Gentle Mastering and Acoustic patches.

Try these various options out on your completed songs or works in progress to see which ones best suit your music in general and specific songs in particular. Any Mastering Combi preset can be altered and saved for later use by clicking the Combinator's Save Patch and choosing a name and location for your patch.

Effects Chains

An effects chain is any two or more effect devices routed together. Effects chains are easy to create and manage in Reason. Creating multiple effects will also create automatic routing, depending on which device is selected. To get an idea of how effects routing works, follow these steps:

1. Create a Malström Graintable Synthesizer.
2. Use the Tab key to view the back of the Reason rack.
3. With the Malström selected, create a DDL-1 Digital Delay line.
4. Next, create an RV7 Digital Reverb with the Malström selected. The RV7 will be placed before the DDL-1 in the effects chain.
5. Select and delete the RV7. The Malström and DDL-1 effects routing returns to what it was before the RV7 was created.

6. Now select the DDL-1 and create a new RV7 with the DDL-selected instead of the Malström. This time the RV7 will be placed after the DDL-1 in the effects chain.

7. Play a few notes on your MIDI keyboard to hear the results of this effects chain.

By selecting specific devices before creating new effects, you can create any routing you want, then change it at any time. Working on the back of the Reason rack, you can also use your mouse and the context menus to create new routing configurations between instruments and effects.

> The last device in any chain of effects will be the name of the channel on the Mixer 14:2.

Rules of the Road

There are some commonly accepted rules about how effects are placed in a chain. These suggestions are made to get the maximum results out of each effect, but they aren't hard and fast rules. In fact, rearranging effects out of order can result in new and unexpected sounds. When creating effects chains, use this order of effects as your starting point:

Distortion > Compression/Limiting > Modulation effects > Delay or Reverb

If you are going to include both delay and reverb on a track, try adding them as individual send effects and not inserts. This way, your delays and reverb will work independently.

> Using the RV7000's Echo or Multi Tap algorithms can be a great way to combine reverb and delay in a single effect.

Reason's instrument devices that feature audio inputs, such as the Malström and Thor, can also be included in effects chains. See the sidebar "Combinator Effects Chains" for more details about Reason's included effects chain Combinator patches.

COMBINATOR EFFECTS CHAINS

Reason's Combinator device is a great way to create and save effects chains to use both as sends and inserts. The Reason Factory Sound Bank contains lots of effects chain patches. To get an idea of some of the possibilities:

1. Create any Reason synthesizer or sampler instrument and load a patch.

2. Play a few notes on your MIDI keyboard to hear the original patch, without any added effects.

3. Select Create → Create Effect from the menu bar.

4. Use the Browser to navigate to the folder Reason Factory Sound Bank\All Effects Patches\. In this folder are eight individual folders, each containing a different type of effect. Open the Delay or Modulation Effects folder, and select a patch. Playing notes on your MIDI keyboard, you'll now hear both the instrument and the Combinator effects chain.

5. Select a patch and click the Browser's OK button to load it.

To view the devices contained in any Combinator, click the Show Devices button. See Chapter 9 for specific examples including creating your own Combinator effects chains.

External MIDI Control

Just like Reason's instrument devices, all of Reason's effects have multiple parameters that can be controlled by external MIDI devices. You can view the controllable parameters by choosing File → Options → Remote Override Edit Mode. Any parameters with downward-facing arrows can be mapped to your external MIDI keyboard or other controller device.

Figure 7.21

The DDL in Remote Override Edit Mode

Clicking any arrow changes it to a spinning lightning bolt. Adjust any knob or slider to map the parameter to your MIDI keyboard. Any parameter that has been assigned to your external MIDI controller will be represented by a stationary lightning bolt symbol. Moving your mouse over the assigned parameter will show you the which knob or slider can be used to control it.

Summary

In this chapter you learned about all of Reason's effects devices, including specific applications for each device. First, you worked with each of Reason's "half-rack" devices and learned about each device's parameters and CV routing options. An understanding of these parameters and similarities in how devices can be routed and controlled means you now have all of the information you need to experiment further with these simple but powerful Reason devices.

Next, you learned how to use the two patch-loading effects devices, the Scream 4 Sound Destruction Unit and the RV7000 Advanced Reverb, including each device's many features and uses. This was followed by the MClass mastering effects, which you learned could also be used as insert effects on single-instrument devices, as well as on your complete mixes.

After reading this chapter, you have a better understanding of Reason's signal flow, including the many options you have for controlling multiple devices and parameters. You've also looked at some of the unlimited ways in which you can combine Reason's instrument and effects devices. You can use the things you've learned in this chapter in many ways, including creating new original sounds, improving the sound of specific instruments and performances in your mixes, and mastering the final mixes of your Reason songs. Much of what you learned in this chapter will be further expanded on when you create even more complex combinations of instruments and effects using the Combinator device in Chapter 9.

CHAPTER 8

Other Devices and Features

Along with its many instruments and effects, Reason includes a number of devices that don't fit neatly into either specific category. These devices can be used for creative routing, enhancing your ability to create and play back performances. In this chapter you'll learn about all of these devices and how they can enhance your ability to create music with Reason 4. This chapter will also cover a new feature in Reason 4 called the ReGroove mixer. Each individual lane on any track in a Reason song can be routed through the ReGroove mixer to create rhythmic adjustments and variations. This is especially useful with drum and percussion tracks but is not limited to any specific type of instrument or performance.

Topics in this chapter include:

- **The Matrix Pattern Sequencer: Advanced**
- **The Spider Audio Merger and Splitter**
- **The Spider CV Merger and Splitter**
- **The BV512 Digital Vocoder The RPG-8 Monophonic Arpeggiator**
- **The ReGroove Mixer**

The Matrix Pattern Sequencer: Advanced

You've seen some basic uses for the Matrix Pattern Sequencer (Figure 8.1) in earlier chapters, beginning with an introduction to the sequencer in Chapter 2, and continuing with its use with Redrum in Chapter 4 and with Reason's effects in Chapter 7.

Figure 8.1

The Matrix Pattern Sequencer

In this section we'll take an even closer look at this amazing device. The Matrix is a great tool for triggering notes to create bass lines and melodies, especially with Reason's synthesizers, but there's even more creative power available with this device. Learning how to create and edit the different types of CV (control voltage) in the Matrix and then send that CV to Reason's instruments, effects, and other devices opens up endless options for control and creativity.

CV Types and Their Uses

The Matrix Pattern Sequencer can control Reason devices with three types of CV information: Note CV, Gate CV, and Curve CV. Each CV type has standard uses; the most obvious connections create relatively predictable results. Reason's CV types can also be accessed for less conventional uses as well, which you'll learn about in the "Making Unusual Connections" sidebar later in this chapter. This section describes each of the three CV types and both their standard and their less obvious possible uses.

ABOUT CV INPUTS

Most of Reason's devices feature one or more CV inputs. In most cases these inputs will respond to different types of CV messages. How the device's input responds to CV is determined by certain factors: the CV types and values sent from the device that is creating the CV information and the CV input value settings on the device receiving the CV input. The CV input value settings are controlled by CV Input Value knobs found to the left or below most CV inputs.

The CV Value knob determines the extent to which the incoming CV will affect the parameter. All CV Input knobs have a range of 0–127 and a default center value of 64. At a setting of 0, the incoming CV will have no effect. At a setting of 127, the incoming CV will have the maximum possible effect. You can reduce or increase the effect of the incoming CV information by raising and lowering this knob at any time.

Note CV

Note CV sends specific pitch information to Reason's instruments to set the pitch of a specific sound. Notes are triggered in conjunction with Gate CV, which determines the note's velocity. Note CV is sent from the Matrix using the Note CV output on the back panel. The Matrix Note CV output can also be used to send CV to other parameters, creating interesting effects.

Note CV is programmed in the main window of the Matrix Pattern Sequencer shown in Figure 8.2.

Figure 8.2

Note CV in the Matrix Pattern Sequencer

Figure 8.3

The Gate CV lane

Gate CV

The most common use for Gate CV is in conjunction with Note CV. As noted earlier, the Note CV determines the note value (pitch) while the Gate CV controls the velocity. Figure 8.3 shows the Gate CV lane of the Matrix Pattern Sequencer.

Gate CV is edited by using your mouse. Click any Gate event in the Gate lane and drag up or down to raise or lower the gate value. You can edit multiple Gate events by clicking and dragging across the Gate lane.

You can tie Gate events together by clicking the Gate Tie button to the left of the Gate lane, and then drawing with your mouse in the Gate lane. You can "untie" notes by turning off the Gate Tie button and clicking any notes that you've tied together.

Gate CV is sent from the Matrix using the Gate CV output on the back panel. The standard routing configuration that is created when you select a Reason instrument device and then create a Matrix sends the Note CV output from the Matrix to the instrument's Note CV input and the Gate CV output to the instrument's Gate CV input.

By using the Gate Tie functionality, you can make Gate CV function exactly like Curve CV, discussed next.

Gate CV can be used to open and close filters and trigger LFOs, and can also be used to trigger the Gate input of the ECF-42 and the RV7000, as you'll see in the exercises later in this chapter.

Curve CV

Curve CV is generally used to control parameters that benefit from gradual changes (also known as continuous controllers) such as envelopes and LFOs, and can also be used to control panning. You access Curve CV by selecting Curve mode with the Matrix's Edit mode switch.

You define Curve CV by clicking and dragging your mouse across the programmer interface. There are two different types of Curve edit views: Unipolar and Bipolar. Figure 8.4 shows the default Unipolar view.

The Unipolar Curve mode has a value range of 0–127, which makes it especially useful for controlling parameters such as level faders and envelope amounts.

The Curve CV view mode can be changed using the Unipolar/Bipolar Curve button on the back panel of the Matrix.

The Bipolar Curve mode has a value range of –64 to 63, which makes it useful for controlling panning, velocity parameters, or any other knobs that have positive and negative values with a center value of 0.

Figure 8.5 shows the Bipolar Curve mode.

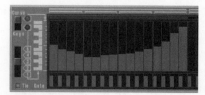

Figure 8.4

The Unipolar CV curve

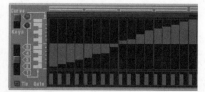

Figure 8.5

The Bipolar CV curve

Creating and Editing Patterns with the Matrix

One of the main uses for the Matrix Pattern Sequencer is to create performances by programming and sequencing multiple patterns. The Matrix can be used to trigger any Reason instrument, including the Dr. Rex Loop Player and Redrum. However, since the Matrix itself replicates a method used to control synthesizers, the best and most frequent use will be to trigger Reason's synthesizers and any synth patches loaded into Reason's samplers.

Not all patches will work well with the Matrix, though decisions about specific patches may be made based on the type of performance you are creating. For example, in many cases a synthesizer or instrument patch with a slow attack is not the best choice for creating patterns with the Matrix. However, if you are working with slower tempos and using the Gate Tie functionality, the Matrix can work with these types of sounds as well. For the examples that follow, you'll load specific patches from the Reason Factory Sound Bank.

Steps, Resolution, and Shuffle

Each pattern can have its own Steps, Resolution, and Shuffle settings. Figure 8.6 shows these parameters on the right side of the Matrix Pattern Sequencer.

Figure 8.6

The Steps, Resolution, and Shuffle parameters

Each pattern can range in length from 1 to 32 steps. Pattern length can be adjusted by clicking and dragging up or down in the Pattern Length LED or by using the up and down arrows to the left of the LED.

The Resolution knob can be used to set the speed of the pattern. You can increase the default resolution of 1/16 by using your mouse to turn the knob to the right or decrease it by turning the knob to the left.

Turning on the Shuffle button will change the rhythm of your patterns, adding a shuffle feel. The amount of shuffle that's added to your patterns is determined by the Global Shuffle Amount knob on the ReGroove mixer, covered later in this chapter.

When a Matrix is created, a few default settings that will always be in place:

- Bank A Pattern 1 is selected.

- The Matrix is in Key Edit mode; Note CV is visible in the pattern window.

- Resolution is set to 1/16.

- A 16-step pattern of MIDI note 60 (middle C).

- The range of notes currently visible is C3 to C4.

These settings are the same for all 32 patterns, and are a useful starting point for creating your own Matrix patterns. Clicking the Run button with these default settings will play the default pattern.

> You can create and edit patterns with the Matrix running.

Creating Multiple Matrix Patterns

Follow these steps to start creating your own multiple patterns:

1. Create a Thor Polysonic Synthesizer and load the patch `Reason Factory Sound Bank\Thor Patches\Bass\Bass Knuckles.thor`.

2. With the Thor selected in the Reason rack, create a Matrix Pattern Sequencer.

3. Click the Run button to start playback.

4. Use your mouse to program notes in the Note Value display. To program notes higher or lower than the C3–C4 range, use the Octave switch to select a different octave range.

5. Use your mouse to adjust the velocity of some of the notes in the Gate lane.

6. Click the Gate Tie button and tie a few notes together to hear the effect.

You've now created a pattern in Bank A Pattern 1. Once you've created Pattern A1, go to the Bank and Pattern section and click the 2 button to select Pattern 2.

The currently selected pattern is now Bank A Pattern 2. You can select a different bank of patterns at any time by clicking the A, B, C, or D Bank Select buttons.

As with all of the Matrix's empty patterns, Bank A Pattern 2 has the same default settings as Bank A Pattern 1.

7. Use your mouse to create a new pattern in Bank A Pattern 2 with different Note and Gate CV values.

You can use your mouse to select the notes and octave range, adjust the gate values, the resolution, and the number of steps for each individual pattern.

Random Patterns

The Matrix has random pattern functionality that can be accessed by right/Ctrl-clicking the Matrix and selecting Randomize Pattern from the context menu or by selecting the Matrix in the rack and choosing Edit → Randomize Pattern. This creates random Note, Gate, and Curve CV and can be a good starting point for creating patterns. You can edit and alter random patterns with your mouse or by using the Alter Pattern functionality described in a moment.

Altering Patterns

You can use keyboard commands and context menus to alter and adjust existing patterns. Shifting patterns up, down, left, and right takes existing events and moves them incrementally. Altering a pattern moves the existing Note, Gate, and Curve CV values in a pattern, but doesn't create any new CV events. Altering a pattern is different from the Randomize feature, which creates new random CV events. You can shift and alter patterns using the Edit menu, the Matrix's context menu, and keyboard shortcuts, as listed in Table 8.1.

Table 8.1

Commands and Keystrokes for Adjusting Patterns

COMMAND	KEYBOARD SHORTCUT	RESULT
Shift Pattern Left	Ctrl/⌘+J	Moves all CV events one step to the left
Shift Pattern Right	Ctrl/⌘+K	Moves all CV events one step to the right
Shift Pattern Up	Shift+Ctrl+U/Shift+⌘+U	Moves all Note CV events up one semitone
Shift Pattern Down	Shift+Ctrl+D/Shift+⌘+D	Moves all Note CV events down one semitone
Alter Pattern	Ctrl/⌘+T	Moves existing CV values around in the pattern but doesn't create any new events

Sequencing Patterns

As a pattern device, the Matrix Pattern Sequencer works very much like the Redrum Drum Computer (Chapter 4). Once you've created multiple patterns, you can then arrange and play them back in any order using Reason's automation functionality by drawing patterns in the sequencer or by sending patterns as MIDI notes to any track in the sequencer.

Sequencing Patterns with Automation

After completing the steps in the "Creating Multiple Matrix Patterns" section, follow these steps to arrange your patterns with automation:

1. Select the Matrix track on the sequencer's track list and make sure that Record Enable Parameter Automation is turned on.

2. Click the Record button on the Transport panel and then use your mouse to select different patterns and/or banks on the Matrix Pattern Sequencer. Every time you select a new pattern, a new clip is created on the Matrix's track.

After you're done creating your arrangement, click the Stop button on the Transport panel. The Bank and Pattern Select sections of the Matrix will now have a green outline around them, indicating that automation has been created.

Reason's automation functionality has now created a new Pattern Select Track lane containing all of the clips you've created. You can the use the sequencer's editing functionality to move, resize, and edit your clips.

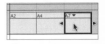

Drawing Patterns in the Sequencer

Starting again at the end of the steps outlined in the "Creating Multiple Matrix Patterns" section, follow these steps to draw your pattern sequence directly in the sequencer:

1. Select the Matrix track on the sequencer's track list.

2. Click the Create Pattern Lane button at the top of the sequencer.

3. Use your mouse to select the Pencil tool. The Time Signature and Pattern drop-down menus will appear to the left of the Pattern Lane button.

4. Choose a pattern from the Pattern drop-down menu and draw a clip on the sequencer's Matrix track.

5. Create your arrangement by selecting different patterns from the Pattern drop-down menu and drawing clips in the sequencer.

Once a clip is drawn, you can use your mouse to select, move, and resize clips at any time.

Copying Patterns to a Sequencer Track

Another option for sequencing tracks is to use the Copy to Track function. This is similar to copying Rex files to tracks (Chapter 3) and the Copy to Track on Redrum (Chapter 4).

To copy a Matrix pattern to a sequencer track:

1. Set the left and right locators to determine the length of the copied pattern.

2. Select the instrument or Matrix that you want to trigger on the track list.

3. Select the Matrix in the Reason rack.

4. Right/Ctrl-click and choose Copy Pattern To Track from the context menu or choose Edit → Copy Pattern To Track from the menu bar.

You've now created a new clip in the sequencer containing your pattern. Once the pattern has been copied, be sure to turn off the Matrix's Pattern Enable button. If the instrument is triggered both by the MIDI notes on the track and by the sequence in the Matrix, a "washy" sound will occur.

> Make sure you've sent the pattern to the instrument's track and not to the Matrix's track. If you've sent the pattern to the Matrix's track, use the Selection tool to select it in the sequencer and manually drag it to the instrument track.

You can select a new pattern and send it to a track, creating a new lane, or move the left and right locators to a new position in the sequencer and send the pattern to a different location on the same track.

Using Curve CV to Control Reason's Devices

Follow these steps to add Curve CV to a pattern sequence:

1. Create a Malström Graintable Synthesizer and load the patch `Reason Factory Sound Bank\Malstrom Patches\MonoSynths\Antilator.xwv`.

2. With the Malström selected in the rack, create a Matrix Pattern Sequencer.

3. Click the Run button on the Matrix to start playback of the default pattern.

4. Use the Matrix's Mode switch to select Curve Edit mode.

5. Drag your mouse across the Matrix programmer to draw a Curve CV pattern.

6. Press the Tab key to view the back of the Reason rack.

7. Try routing the Curve CV from the Matrix to the various Modulation inputs on the back of the Malström one at a time to hear the effect that Curve CV has on each of the parameters.

You can increase or decrease the effect by adjusting the CV Modulation Input knobs to the right of each CV input. Try drawing different Curve CV patterns in the Matrix to create different effects. Switch to Bipolar mode on the back of the Matrix for different results.

With the Matrix running, disconnect the Note and Gate CV routing between the Matrix and the Malström. Then select the Malström track in the sequencer's track list and use your MIDI keyboard to play the Malström while the Matrix Curve CV changes the connected parameter.

Curve CV is not the only option for working with the CV inputs of Reason devices. You can also try routing the Note and Gate CV to the Modulation inputs on the back of the Malström.

As you'll see later in this chapter and in Chapter 9, this kind of CV routing with the Matrix can be used to control, alter, and experiment with multiple parameters found on many Reason devices, including all of the instruments and, as you'll see in the next section, many of the effects.

MAKING UNUSUAL CONNECTIONS

As mentioned earlier, you are not restricted to using Note CV to trigger notes, Gate CV to set velocities, and Curve CV for panning or other obvious uses. When working with the exercises in this chapter, try creating different connections along with the suggested connections. Not all connections will work, and some will create undesirable and distinctly unmusical results. However, one of the best ways to become familiar with the inherent possibilities of the Matrix Pattern Sequencer is to create exactly these kinds of unconventional routing connections and experiments.

Using the Matrix to Control Effects

The CV outputs of the Matrix can also be used to control Reason's effects devices via their CV inputs. As you saw in Chapter 7, most of the half-rack effects, the RV7000 Advanced Reverb, and the Scream 4 Sound Destruction unit all have CV inputs and therefore can be controlled in one way or another by the Matrix's CV outputs. The following are just two possible examples of how you might combine the Matrix Pattern Sequencer with Reason's effects.

The ECF-42 Envelope Controlled Filter

Follow these steps to control the ECF-42 Envelope Controlled Filter with a Matrix Pattern Sequencer:

1. Create an NN-19 Digital Sampler and load the patch `Reason Factory Sound Bank\ NN19 Sampler Patches\Organ4.smp`.

2. Select the NN-19 in the rack and create an insert ECF-42.

3. With the ECF-42 selected in the rack, create a Matrix Pattern Sequencer. This creates automatic Curve CV and Gate CV routing from the Matrix to the ECF-42's Frequency and Env. Gate inputs.

4. Select the NN-19 on the sequencer's track list to give it Master Keyboard Input.

5. Click the Run button on the Matrix (the Matrix must be running in order for the effect to work).

6. Lower the Frequency knob on the ECF-42 slightly.

7. Use your MIDI keyboard to play the NN-19.

As you learned in Chapter 7, the ECF-42 is a gate-controlled envelope filter. The effect that you are hearing now is the Gate CV from the Matrix opening and closing the filter. The Gate LED on the ECF-42 interface indicates when this happens.

You can create different and even more noticeable effects by experimenting with the settings:

- Raise or lower the Matrix Resolution knob.
- Switch the Matrix into Curve Edit mode and draw Curve CV.
- Raise the Resonance and Env. Amount knobs on the ECF-42.
- Flip the Reason rack and make different CV connections, such as routing the Matrix Curve CV output to the Resonance CV input.

These are just some of the possibilities for working with the Matrix and the ECF-42. Try your own experiments along with different NN-19 patches or other Reason instruments.

The RV7000 Advanced Reverb

Follow these steps to use the Matrix Pattern Sequencer to control the RV7000 Advanced Reverb's Gate CV input:

> If you aren't already familiar with the RV7000's interface and functionality, be sure to read the section "The RV7000 Advanced Reverb" in Chapter 7 before proceeding with this exercise.

1. Create a Dr. Rex Loop Player and load the loop `Reason Factory Sound Bank\Dr Rex Drum loops\Acs01_StrghtAhead_130.rx2`.
2. With the Dr. Rex selected, create an RV7000 Advanced Reverb as an insert.
3. With the RV7000 selected, create a Matrix Pattern Sequencer. This will create automatic routing from the Matrix Curve and Note CV outputs to the RV7000's Decay and Gate Trigger inputs.
4. Adjust the RV7000's Dry/Wet knob to create an even mix of the original signal and the reverb effect.
5. Click the Gate Enable button on the RV7000's main panel to turn on the Gate effect.
6. Click the Remote Programmer button on the left side of the RV7000's main panel to open Remote Programmer, and then use the Edit Mode button to select the Gate mode.

7. Use the Gate mode's Trig Source input knob to select MIDI/CV as the input. Now Gate CV from the Matrix will trigger the effect.

8. Start playback of the Dr. Rex by clicking the Preview button on the Dr. Rex interface.
9. Start the Matrix by clicking the Run button on the Matrix interface.

From here you can make a number of adjustments on the RV7000 and the Matrix to control the effect. Some possibilities include:

- Raising or lowering the Resolution setting on the Matrix interface

- Using the Gate tie enable button to tie Gate events together, keeping the reverb open

- Raising and lowering the Attack and Release parameters on the RV7000

- Using the Remote Programmers Edit Mode switch to choose Reverb Edit mode and trying out the Gate triggering configuration you've created with different algorithms and settings

The RV7000 also features Decay and High Frequency Damping CV inputs. Experiment with these to create even more CV related effects with the Matrix.

The method described in this exercise can be used to create Gate CV effects with any of the RV7000's included presets found in the folder `Reason Factory Sound Bank\RV7000 Patches\`.

The Spider Audio Merger and Splitter

The Spider Audio Merger and Splitter (Figure 8.7) is a half-rack device that can be used to combine (merge) or split audio signals from any Reason device. You can use the device in the Reason rack or as part of a Combinator patch. For creating, naming, deleting, and routing, the Spider Audio device functions just like any other Reason device.

Some common uses for the Spider Audio device include splitting the output of an instrument and sending it to two or more different effects, and combining the output of multiple instruments and/or effects as a single stereo or mono signal.

Because the Spider Audio device is for routing rather than modifying a signal, its front panel contains no controls, but only the LEDs shown in Figure 8.7 that indicate that the device is receiving and/or outputting a signal. The back panel is where you'll do your work. It is divided into two sections (Figure 8.8). The left side is used for merging audio signals and the right for splitting audio signals.

Figure 8.7

The Spider Audio Merger and Splitter

Figure 8.8

The back panel of the Spider Audio Merger and Splitter

Splitting Audio

Splitting the audio output of an instrument or effect is just one way to begin to create new and original sounds. The Spider Audio device can be used to split an audio signal many times over, routing it through multiple effects.

For example, Figure 8.9 shows the Splitter section of the Spider Audio device in a configuration where stereo output from the Malström synth is routed through the Splitter as input to both the DDL-1 Digital Delay and the RV7000 Advanced Reverb devices.

Figure 8.9

The Splitter section with audio connections

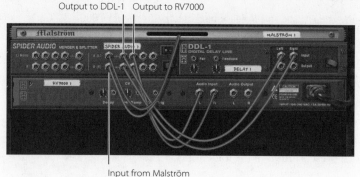

Output to DDL-1   Output to RV7000

Input from Malström

A stereo or mono signal from any Reason instrument or effect can be routed to the inputs on the left side of the Splitter section. Mono signals must be routed to the left input only. The signal can then be split into as many as four stereo or mono signals that are routed out of the Spider Audio device using any of the four stereo outputs of the Splitter section.

You can actually split the signal endlessly by routing any one of the four Split outputs to another Spider Audio device.

Follow these steps to send the output of a sampler device to three separate audio effects:

1. Create an NN-XT Advanced Sampler.

2. Load the patch `Reason Factory Sound Bank\NN-XT Sampler Patches\B Grand Piano 1.0.sxt`.

3. Create a Spider Audio Merger and Splitter.

4. Hold down the Shift key while creating a DDL-1 Digital Delay Line. (Holding the Shift key while creating a device places it in the rack unconnected.)

5. Create an unconnected PH-90 Phaser.

6. Create an unconnected CF-101 Chorus/Flanger.

7. Route the output of the NN-XT to the input of the Spider's Splitter section.

8. Route the Spider's Split Output 1 left and right to the DDL-1.

9. Route the Spider's Split Output 2 left and right to the PH-90.

10. Route the Spider's Split Output 3 left and right to the CF101.

At this point you have a lot of cables visible and some pretty complex routing going on. Press the L key on your computer's keyboard to hide the cables for a clearer view of the back of the Reason rack.

11. The last step is to connect each of the effect's outputs to individual channels on the Mixer 14:2.

With all of these connections in place, you now have complete control over the output of each effect. Play the NN-XT with your MIDI keyboard to hear the results of all of your splitting and routing. You may want to try raising and lowering the levels and adjusting the panning for each channel.

Figure 8.10

The Spider Audio device's merge inputs and outputs

You can find a version of this Spider Audio routing on the accompanying CD in the Reason song Examples\Chapter 8\Songs\SpiderAudio.rns.

You've still got another Split Output available on the Spider. You could take the Spider's Split Output 4 and route it directly to the mixer for a clean channel with no effect or route it to another Spider Audio device and split the signal again!

This example is provided as an illustration of one way to use the Spider Audio device and to familiarize you with its inputs and outputs. When working in Reason with a similar configuration, you'll be most likely to create this kind of routing within a Combinator device, as covered in Chapter 9.

Merging Audio

The left side of the Spider Audio device shown in Figure 8.10 contains the four stereo merge inputs and the left and right stereo merge outputs, which send the merged signal to the mixer or to another device.

The stereo output from up to four Reason devices can be connected to the four stereo inputs. Mono signals can be routed into the Spider Audio device by using only the left input of any stereo pair.

The merged signals can then be sent out of the Spider by connecting the Merge Output Left and Right to the Mixer 14:2 or to another Reason device with audio input functionality. A mono signal can be sent from the Spider Audio device by connecting only the left output to the left input of another Reason device.

Since only one Reason instrument can have Master Keyboard Input at one time, merging is often best accomplished as part of a Combinator patch or by using the CV Splitter to trigger two instruments.

The Spider CV Merger and Splitter

While the Spider Audio Merger and Splitter is used to split and merge audio signals into new routing configurations, the Spider CV Merger and Splitter is used to split and merge CV information that can be used to trigger and control Reason devices.

The Spider CV Merger and Splitter (Figure 8.11) is one of Reason's most useful devices for getting creative with Reason's routing. Splitting CV can be used to control multiple devices or parameters at once. Merging CV is also an interesting option, though less practically useful.

Figure 8.11

The Spider CV Merger and Splitter

Figure 8.12

The Spider CV device's splitter section

Splitting CV

Splitting CV is a great way to control multiple devices at once, and to control multiple parameters on the same or different devices at one time. The following examples demonstrate some of the possibilities. The front of the Spider CV device (Figure 8.11) displays LEDs that let you know if the device is receiving CV input. The Spider CV device's splitter section (Figure 8.12) is found on the right side of the device's back panel.

Splitting Envelopes and LFOs

Follow these steps to start controlling multiple parameters with the Spider CV device:

1. Create a SubTractor and load the patch `Reason Factory Sound Bank\SubTractor Patches\CCRMA E Piano.zyp`.

2. Hold down the Shift key and create an unconnected Spider CV device.

3. Use the Tab key to view the back of the Reason rack.

4. Route the SubTractor's LFO1 Modulation Output to the Split A input in the Spider's splitter section.

5. Route the CV from the first three Split A outputs to various Modulation CV inputs on the SubTractor.

Use your MIDI keyboard to play the SubTractor while experimenting with different CV input routing. Some of the connections will result in very noticeable effects (OSC Pitch and Pitch Wheel in particular) while others will be less obvious or not at all noticeable.

You can control the LFO1 CV by flipping the rack to view the front panel and adjusting the LFO1's Rate knob and selecting different waveforms with the LFO1 Wave button. Turn on the LFO Sync button to sync the LFO to the current session's tempo.

TAKE IT FURTHER

You can take this experiment even further by trying one or more of the following:

- Connect the Mod Envelope and Filter Envelope outputs to the Spider's Split B input and create more CV routing.

- Use this same method to route CV from the SubTractor to another instrument device or between any of Reason's instrument devices.

- Route the CV from a Reason instrument to itself, another instrument, and/or an effect device simultaneously.

- Send one of Split A's output's to a second Spider CV device and split the CV further to control even more parameters or devices.

You'll find more examples of CV splitting in Chapter 9.

INVERTED CV

Each of the CV Splitter sections on the Spider CV device has three "normal" outputs that send exact copies of the input CV to the connected devices. Interestingly, there's also a fourth CV output, labeled Inv, that sends inverted CV to the connected input:

This sends an inverted or backward version of the CV signal to any connected CV input. For example, an inverted version of an LFO will move in the opposite direction and can be used to create interesting variations of the CV output signal.

Merging CV

The Spider CV device's merging functionality, shown in Figure 8.13, is found on the left side of the device.

Merging CV is an interesting concept, but it can be hard to control. It can be useful for creating unexpected, unpredictable results. Follow these steps to merge CV and create some noise:

Figure 8.13

The Spider CV device's Merge section

1. Create a Malström Graintable Synthesizer and load the patch Reason Factory Sound Bank\Malstrom Patches\Dystant Strings.xwv.

2. Create an unconnected Spider CV device.

3. Use the Tab key to view the back of the Reason rack.

4. Route the Malström's Mod A and Mod B to the Spider Merge inputs.

5. Connect the Spider's Merge output to the Malström's OSC Pitch input.

6. Use Tab to view the front of the Malström so you can control its Mod A and Mod B waveforms.

7. Use your MIDI keyboard to play long sustained notes.

You'll hear the effect of the merged CV from both Mod A and Mod B's waveform shapes on the pitch of the notes you're playing. To get an even clearer idea of how the two CV outputs are being combined, try raising the Mod A's Rate knob and lowering Mod B's Rate knob while playing notes on your MIDI keyboard.

Try out different waveforms at various rates for different kinds of effects. You can find a version of this merged CV routing on the accompanying CD in the Reason song Examples\ Chapter 8\Songs\MergeCV.rns.

Experiment

The previous descriptions and examples are meant only to suggest what you can do with the Spider Audio and Spider CV. Both devices can be used in all sorts of different ways with all of Reason's devices. Take some time to experiment with routing audio and CV and trying things out even when you think they might not work. Sometimes, seemingly crazy ideas can lead to interesting and useful sounds. Both of the Spider devices are particularly useful within Combinator patches, so be sure to read Chapter 9 for more examples of how to put both Spiders to good use in Reason.

The RPG-8 Monophonic Arpeggiator

An arpeggio is a series of notes that make up a chord, played sequentially instead of simultaneously. The RPG-8 Monophonic Arpeggiator (Figure 8.14) is a monophonic device that creates arpeggio patterns from multiple notes played simultaneously on your MIDI keyboard or drawn in the Reason sequencer. An arpeggiator is a feature Reason users have long wished for, and the RPG-8 is one of the key new features of Reason version 4.

Figure 8.14

The RPG-8 Mono-phonic Arpeggiator

Creating an RPG-8

To add an RPG-8 to a Reason song, you'll first want to select the instrument and patch that will be arpeggiated in the Reason rack, and then choose Create → RPG-8 Monophonic Arpeggiator from the menu bar. You can also create the RPG-8 from the Tool window or use the right/Ctrl-click method to create an RPG-8 from a context menu.

> The RPG-8 is not capable of saving patches. However, as you'll see in Chapter 9, you can save an RPG-8 and its current settings as part of a Combinator device.

Although this is the same method you'd use to create an insert effect, the RPG-8 is not an effect device. The RPG-8 is more like the Matrix Pattern Sequencer in that it uses Note and Gate CV to create arpeggios.

Figure 8.15 shows the default routing created when an RPG-8 is connected to a Reason instrument, in this case the Malström Graintable Synthesizer.

Figure 8.15

The RPG-8's default CV routing

These automatic connections include the same Note and Gate CV routing that Reason creates for the Matrix Pattern Sequencer, along with Pitch Bend and Mod Wheel CV connections.

When you create an RPG-8 connected to a Reason instrument, a track is created on the Reason sequencer and given Master Keyboard Input. Playing simultaneous notes on your MIDI keyboard or drawing notes on the RPG-8's sequencer track will trigger the RPG-8, which then converts the incoming MIDI information to an arpeggiated pattern. Different kinds of arpeggiated patterns can be created based on the settings made on the RPG-8's interface.

The RPG-8 also has Aftertouch, Expression and Breath, Start of Arpeggio Trig, and Sustain pedal CV outputs.

The CV inputs include Gate Length, Velocity, Rate/Resolution, Octave shift, and Start of Arpeggio. You can control these parameters with the CV outputs found on the Matrix Pattern Sequencer or any of Reason's instrument and effects devices.

The RPG-8 Interface

The RPG-8 interface is made up of multiple parameters, many of which interact with each other in order to create a wide range of possible variations using the arpeggiated notes.

Velocity The Velocity knob controls the velocity of the individual notes that make up the arpeggio. With the Velocity knob's default Manual setting, the velocity of each note will be determined by the velocity you play on your MIDI keyboard. Adjusting the Velocity knob from 0 to 127 will set a uniform velocity for every note in the arpeggio.

Hold With the Hold button activated, you can create arpeggios by playing and releasing chords on your MIDI keyboard. The arpeggio will continue after the notes have been released. You can change the arpeggio at any time by playing and releasing a different chord.

Octave Shift The Octave Shift buttons can be used to change the pitch of the RPG-8's output up to three octaves higher or lower. In the default position, any notes triggered by the sequencer or your MIDI keyboard will play at their normal pitch. Use the left and right arrows to lower or raise the arpeggio's pitch.

Mode The Mode knob is used to choose the note sequence of the arpeggio:

> **Up Mode** Plays notes from lowest to highest.
>
> **Up + Down Mode** Plays notes from lowest to highest and then back down to the lowest note.
>
> **Down Mode** Starts the arpeggio with the highest note and descends to the lowest note.
>
> **Random Mode** Creates an arpeggio by selecting played notes randomly.
>
> **Manual Mode** Creates arpeggios from notes in the order that they are triggered.

Octave The Octave buttons are used to set the range of the arpeggio. Choosing the 1 OCT button sets a one-octave range. Only the notes triggered by the sequencer or your MIDI keyboard will be used in the arpeggio. Selecting the 2 OCT button sets a two-octave range; the arpeggio will contain the original notes triggered and the notes one octave higher. The 3 OCT and 4 OCT buttons will create three-octave and four-octave range arpeggios, respectively.

Insert The insert functionality is used to create variations and patterns by repeating or inserting notes into the arpeggio:

> **Off** Turns the insert function off.
>
> **Low** Inserts the lowest note in the arpeggio between each successive note.
>
> **High** Inserts the highest note in the arpeggio between each successive note.
>
> **3-1** Creates patterns of notes by playing three forward, one back, and then repeating the cycle.
>
> **4-2** Creates patterns of notes by playing four notes forward, taking two steps back, playing a note, and then repeating the cycle.

Rate Sets the rate of the arpeggio. In the default Sync mode, the Rate can be adjusted from 1/1 to 1/128. The default setting of 1/16 is a good starting point.

In the Free mode, the rate can be adjusted independently from the song's tempo, from .01 Hz to 250 Hz.

Gate Length The Gate Length knob sets the duration of the Gate CV output. The gate knob has a value range of 0–127 and a default setting of 95. Lowering the Gate knob will result in a more staccato, clipped arpeggio. Raising the Gate value will result in longer sustained notes. Higher Gate values can be especially useful for slow arpeggios.

Single Note Repeat With the Single Note Repeat button activated, a single note played on your MIDI keyboard or drawn in the sequencer will trigger the RPG-8. With the Single Note Repeat button deactivated, only two or more notes played simultaneously on a MIDI keyboard or drawn in the sequencer will trigger the RPG-8.

The Pattern Editor This tool can be used to create patterns by lowering the number of steps in the arpeggio and to create rests by turning off individual steps within a pattern.

You can turn the Pattern Editor on and off by clicking the Pattern Enable Button in the upper-left corner. Remove steps from the arpeggio by clicking the Steps– button on the upper right of the pattern section. Add steps to the pattern by clicking the Steps+ button.

You can also insert rests into your arpeggios by clicking on any of the 16 steps to deactivate them. Click a deactivated step a second time to reactivate it.

The Grid Display In the Grid Display, you can view the arpeggio as it's happening. Each note is visible as an LED, and you can view the motion of the arpeggio as it's happening in real time.

Shuffle Turning on the Shuffle button will change the rhythm of your arpeggios, creating a different rhythmic feel. As with the Matrix Pattern Sequencer, the amount of shuffle that's added to your arpeggios is determined by the Global Shuffle Amount knob on the ReGroove mixer, covered later in this chapter.

Using the RPG-8

Choosing the right sound to work with is important when using the RPG-8. Some synthesizer and instrument patches will not work well with arpeggiation or may require different settings to be used effectively. Instruments with slow attack times will not be good candidates for fast arpeggiator tracks.

Long release times may also present a problem when creating mid-tempo and faster arpeggios because you don't want notes bleeding into each other. Aside from making adjustments to the settings on the specific instrument, you also have the option to use the Gate Length knob to control the release time of your arpeggiated patch.

Creating and Playing an RPG-8

To get started using the RPG-8, follow these steps:

1. Create a Thor Polysonic Synthesizer.
2. Load the patch Reason Factory Sound Bank\Lead Synths\Big Club Lead.thor.
3. Select the Thor synth in the Reason rack and create an RPG-8 Arpeggiator.

Play three or four simultaneous notes on your MIDI keyboard. Try out a few different chords and note combinations to hear the changes as they are happening.

Working with the Default Settings

When you create an RPG-8, the device has some default settings in place:

- Up Mode
- One Octave Range

- Insert Off

- 1/16 note Rate/Resolution

- Gate length: 95

You can start to become familiar with the RPG-8's functionality by making adjustments to these default settings. Hold down any three notes on your MIDI keyboard and try out each parameter:

1. Adjust the Mode switch, trying out different modes and chords.

2. Increase and lower the octave range.

3. Cycle through each of the insert buttons.

4. Raise and lower the Gate Length.

5. Raise and lower the Rate/Resolution Knob.

6. Select the Free mode and adjust the Rate/Resolution knob.

The combinations of these settings will all have an effect on your arpeggios, and each setting interacts with the next. For example, choosing Down mode and a two-octave range with a 3-1 insert setting will create a very different pattern than choosing Up mode with a three-octave range and a 4-2 insert setting.

Creating Patterns

Clicking the Pattern Enable button turns on the Pattern Editor. The default RPG-8 pattern is 16 notes long. Once the Pattern Editor is on, you can remove notes from the pattern by clicking the Steps button.

Create rests in a pattern by clicking any of the pattern buttons to deactivate the note. This doesn't actually silence the deactivated note, it just inserts a one-note rest; the arpeggiated pattern picks up again after the rest.

Recording Arpeggios

The RPG-8 is similar to the Matrix Pattern Sequencer in that it sends Note and Gate CV to another device to trigger monophonic patterns.

The RPG-8 is more like an instrument device than the Matrix. When you are recording with the RPG-8, you are recording onto the RPG-8 track. The RPG-8 then takes the MIDI note information and converts it to Note CV (pitch) and Gate CV (velocity).

Follow these steps to record a performance with the RPG-8:

1. Create an NN-XT Advanced Sampler.

2. Load the patch NN-XT Sample Patches\Synth Leads\Mini Popcorn.sxt.

3. With the NN-XT selected in the Reason rack, create an RPG-8. The RPG-8 now has Master Keyboard Input. You may want to experiment for a while, trying different chords and notes on your MIDI keyboard and various settings on the RPG-8 interface.

4. Turn on Click and Precount on the Transport panel.

5. Click the Record button.

6. After the Precount count-off, play multiple simultaneous notes on your MIDI keyboard to create and record arpeggiated patterns.

You can also make changes to the parameters found on the RPG-8 interface as you are recording. These changes will be recorded as automation and can become a part of your performance.

The RPG-8 Arpeggiator responds very precisely to the MIDI input it receives. Small amounts of latency and slight imperfections in a performance can vary the results.

If you are not getting the exact results you want, try recording with Record Quantization enabled or use the techniques described in the next exercise to create arpeggios by drawing notes in the sequencer.

Creating Arpeggios in the Sequencer

Creating arpeggios by drawing the notes in the sequencer is a good way to get more precise control over your performance and create exactly the kinds of patterns you want with the RPG-8. Follow these steps to draw arpeggiated patterns in the sequencer:

1. Create your Reason instrument and a connected RPG-8.

2. Select the RPG-8 track on the track list.

3. Click the Edit Mode Select button.

4. Select the Pencil tool and create an empty clip by clicking and dragging across any lane in the sequencer.

5. Click once in the Velocity lane. This will allow you to set the Grid value for the notes you are going to draw before you actually begin drawing them.

6. Set the Grid Value to a low setting; try Bar or 1/2 to start with. You can select a higher grid value later for more precise note drawing and editing.

7. Create your arpeggio by drawing multiple simultaneous notes in the sequencer's Note lane, as shown here:

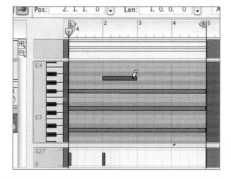

Use the arrangement and editing techniques covered in Chapters 2 and 10 to edit and arrange your arpeggios.

You can also create your arpeggios in real time by using the left and right locators to set the loop length, and then turning on Reason's loop playback functionality on the Transport panel.

Sending Arpeggio Notes to a Track

Whether you've created your arpeggio by recording or by drawing the notes used to trigger the RPG-8, you can send the individual notes of your arpeggios to any instrument track for editing and arranging. Follow these steps to send an arpeggiated performance to an instrument track:

1. Select the Reason instrument that you want to send the notes to in the Main sequencer's track list.

2. Select the RPG-8 Arpeggiator in the Reason rack.

3. Click the RPG-8 interface and choose Edit → Arpeggio Notes To Track from the context menu, or choose the same option from the menu bar.

Once you've sent the arpeggiated notes to an instrument's track, you'll have to either mute the RPG-8 track or delete the original clip or clips. Having both the MIDI notes and the RPG-8 triggering the same devices will result in a washy, unclear sound.

The BV512 Digital Vocoder

The BV512 Digital Vocoder (Figure 8.16) is among Reason's more interesting devices. Technically, it's one of Reason effect devices, but its unique functionality and signal routing set it apart from the program's other effects.

Figure 8.16

The BV512 Digital Vocoder

The term *Vocoder* is a combination of the words *voice* and *encoder*. The original idea behind the concept was to create a way to encode human voices for secure radio transmissions. The Vocoder as an electronic music device has been used for many years in a wide range of recordings, from 70s funk artists like Roger Troutman of Zapp and electronica pioneers Kraftwerk to modern-day artists like Daft Punk.

Getting started with the BV512 is a bit difficult, but once you understand the connections and some basic concepts, getting good and useful sounds out of it can be less challenging. Along with creating familiar vocoding effects, the BV512 also doubles as an EQ device.

Carriers and Modulators

The main idea you need to understand to use the Vocoder is the concept of how the carrier and the modulator interact. This is very much like the *carrier/modulator* concept discussed in the "FM Synthesis" section of Chapter 5, where a carrier oscillator is changed or altered by a modulator oscillator.

With the BV512, the carrier contains the musical notes and/or the sound of the synthesizer, while the modulator contains the rhythmic or vocal performance that triggers the actual sound produced by the Vocoder.

In Reason, if you want to create the classic "robot voice" sounds most commonly associated with a Vocoder, you'll use a synthesizer patch for the carrier and a sampler device with a loaded vocal sample as the modulator. You'll see exactly how that's done in one of the exercises at the end of this section.

The Vocoder Interface

The following are the various parameters found on the BV512 Vocoder's interface:

On/Off/Bypass The Vocoder has the same On/Off/Bypass functionality as Reason's effects devices. In the On position, the Vocoder is active. In the Off position, no sound will pass through. In the Bypass position, the signal passes through the Vocoder with no effect.

Level Meters The two level meters show the input levels of both the carrier and modulator.

Band Selector The Band Selector lets you choose among the different EQ band options. These range from a simple 4-band EQ to the 512-band FFT option.

Equalizer/Vocoder The Vocoder has two modes. Use this knob to switch between the Equalizer and Vocoder modes.

Modulation Levels This display shows the incoming levels from the modulator source.

Frequency Band Level Adjust In the Frequency Band Level Adjust display, you can use your mouse to adjust the levels of individual frequency bands.

Hold Clicking the Hold button freezes the modulator source at its current settings.

Attack Raising the Attack will slow the Vocoder's reaction time in relation to the incoming signal from the carrier.

Decay Raising the Decay knob increases the length of the Vocoder effect.

Shift The Shift knob adjusts the filter frequencies and can change the sound of the Vocoder effect. You can automate the Shift knob by sending Curve CV from a Matrix Pattern Sequencer to the Shift CV input on the back of the BV512.

HF Emphasis The HF (high frequency) Emphasis knob does exactly what the name implies: it emphasizes the higher frequencies, resulting in a clearer sound.

Dry/Wet The Dry/Wet knob controls the mix of the dry (original) signal and Wet (vocoded) signal.

Using the BV512

Any sound-generating device can be either a carrier or a modulator. It's important to note that in order for the BV512 to work, at least one of them must be generating sound at all times. The easiest way to make this happen is to use a Matrix Pattern Sequencer. The following two examples are two possible uses for the BV512.

Percussive Vocoding

In this example, you'll create a familiar Vocoder effect using a Thor Polysonic Synthesizer as the carrier and a Dr. Rex Loop Player as the modulator.

1. Create a Malström Graintable Synthesizer and load the patch `Reason Factory Sound Bank\Malstrom patches\MonoSynths\Digisaw.xwv`.

2. With the Malström selected, create a Matrix Pattern Sequencer.

3. With the Matrix selected, create a BV512 Digital Vocoder. Reason has now created automatic routing connecting the Matrix to the Malström and the Malström to the BV512 as the carrier.

4. Hold down the Shift key and create an unconnected Dr. Rex Loop Player.

5. Flip the rack and connect the left audio output of the Dr. Rex to the modulator input of the BV512.

6. Load the loop `RFSB\Dr Rex Drum Loops\Elc29_RadioActive_eLAB.rx2`.

7. Select the Dr. Rex track on the sequencer's track list and click the To Track button to send the loop between your left and right locators in the sequencer.

8. Turn on Reason's Loop playback functionality and then click the Start button on the Transport panel to begin playback.

From here you can experiment with a number of possibilities:

- Try using the Malström's Browse Patch functionality to load different patches to use as the carrier. This can result in very different sounds.

- Adjust the settings on the Vocoder interface. Raising the HF Emphasis knob or lowering the low EQ bands will often improve a muddy Vocoder effect.

- Try loading and playing different loops in the Dr. Rex, including instrument loops.

- Program different notes into the Matrix interface to create Vocoder melodies.

- Use the Matrix Gate Tie functionality to tie notes together for a consistent Vocoder effect.

- Bring the original loop into the mix by lowering the Dry/Wet knob.

> You don't have to use a Matrix Pattern Sequencer to trigger the carrier. You could delete the Matrix in this exercise and draw or record a performance on the Malström's track in the sequencer.

Experiment with these and other settings to create new and unusual sounds with percussion and instrument tracks. You can find a version of this Vocoder routing on the accompanying CD in the Reason song `Examples\Chapter 8\Songs\PercVoco.rns`.

Classic Vocoding

Follow these steps to create a classic "robot voice" vocoding effect with a spoken word sample patch from the accompanying CD:

1. Create a new Reason song.
2. Add a SubTractor Analog Synthesizer and load the patch `Reason Factory Sound Bank\ SubTractor Patches\Obie Brass.zyp`.
3. With the SubTractor selected, create a Matrix Pattern Sequencer.
4. Turn on the Matrix's Gate Tie button and tie all of the Gate notes together.
5. With either the SubTractor or the Matrix selected, create a BV512. Reason will automatically route the SubTractor as the carrier.
6. Create an unconnected NN-19 Digital Sampler.
7. Load the NN-19 patch `Examples\Chapter 8\Patches\Voices.smp` from this book's CD.
8. Flip the rack to view the routing.
9. Connect the NN-XT's left audio output to the BV512's modulator input.
10. Click the Run button on the Matrix or click the Start key on the Transport panel.
11. Select the NN-19 track on the track list to give it Master Keyboard Input.
12. Play the MIDI note C3 NN-19 with your MIDI keyboard to trigger the voice sample.

    You can make various adjustments to the BV512 to improve the sound:

    - Raise the HF Emphasis knob to increase the high frequencies, creating a clearer tone.
    - Raise the higher frequency bands on the Band adjustment view to create a clearer sound.
    - Make further adjustments with the SubTractor's Low Pass filter to clarify the voice.
    - Bring the original vocal sample into the mix by lowering the Dry/Wet mix knob.

Using different synthesizer patches as a carrier will result in different sounds. Many Thor, Malström, and SubTractor patches will work well, while others will not. Experiment by using this same configuration with different synth patches to find the best effect for your music.

> You may have to stop and restart the Matrix after you've loaded a new patch.

As with the previous exercise, you don't have to use a Matrix Pattern Sequencer to trigger the carrier. You could delete the Matrix in this exercise and draw or record a performance on the SubTractor's track in the sequencer. This can be a good way to create a better musical performance with the Vocoder effect.

You can also use you own original voice samples or voice samples from any source to trigger the BV512 Vocoder. Refer to Chapter 6 for information on creating your own original samples.

You can find a version of this Vocoder routing on the accompanying CD in the Reason song Examples\Chapter 8\Songs\RoboVoco.rns.

The BV512 as EQ Device

Along with the PEQ-2 Two Band Parametric EQ and MClass Equalizers covered in Chapter 7, you can also use the BV512 as a graphic-style EQ device. Follow these steps to use the BV512 as an equalizer with any Reason instrument:

1. Create any Reason instrument.

2. With the instrument selected, create a BV512.

3. Switch the Vocoder/Equalizer knob to Equalizer.

Use the Band Count knob to choose between 4, 8, 16, and 32 Band EQ or choose the FFT (512) setting. Use your mouse to raise or lower the band setting for whichever EQ Band setting you've chosen.

In Equalizer mode, adjusting the Shift knob will still cause a change in the signal output of the BV512. The rest of the parameter knobs on the right side of the device's interface will have no effect on the signal.

The ReGroove Mixer

The ReGroove mixer (Figure 8.17) is Reason 4's new quantization-based groove maker. In Chapter 2 you saw how quantization can be used to align an imperfect performance. In a sense, the ReGroove uses quantization in the opposite way, taking a performance and using quantization to add imperfections and rhythmic variations to create groove, shuffle, or other concepts associated with human drum and percussion performances.

How the ReGroove Mixer Works

The ReGroove mixer applies quantization in real time to the MIDI data on any track in a Reason song.

Figure 8.17

The ReGroove mixer

You can show and hide the ReGroove mixer by clicking the ReGroove Mixer button on the Transport panel.

You select a groove by clicking the Browse Groove patch on the any ReGroove Mixer channel. This opens the Groove Patch Browser. Reason comes with a large collection of grooves that can be found in the folder Reason Factory Sound Bank\ReGroove Patches\.

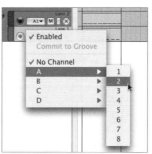

As you saw in Chapter 2, every Reason instrument track has multiple lanes. Each instrument track lane has its own ReGroove drop-down menu, which allows you to assign a ReGroove channel to the selected lane.

You can make adjustments to the groove, such as the amount of effect it has, on the assigned channel on the ReGroove mixer. Make adjustments to the patch itself using the Groove tab of the Tool window. You can edit, create, and save groove patches in the Tool window.

The ReGroove Interface

The ReGroove mixer is divided into two sections: the Global controls on the left side of the mixer and the eight visible channels. The Tool window's Groove tab is an important part of the ReGroove mixer's functionality and is included here as well.

Global Controls

The Global Controls work with features both within the ReGroove mixer and with Reason devices that contain Shuffle functionality.

Channel Banks On the left side of the ReGroove mixer are the four bank selectors. This functionality is similar to Reason's pattern devices. There are four banks, each with eight available ReGroove channels. Selecting bank A, B, C, or D makes that bank available on the ReGroove mixer.

Anchor Point The anchor point determines where in the song the ReGroove settings will start to be applied. If your song starts off with one or more measures before the drum or percussion track starts, you can set the anchor point accordingly. This allows your ReGroove patches to begin with a performance.

Global Shuffle The Global Shuffle knob controls the amount of Shuffle applied to any Reason devices with Shuffle parameters activated. The Reason devices with the Shuffle option are the RPG-8 Arpeggiator, the Matrix Pattern Sequencer, and the Redrum Drum Computer. Each channel of the ReGroove also has a Shuffle knob.

Channel Strip Parameters

The ReGroove mixer has eight visible channel strips (one bank) at any one time. You can select a different bank by clicking one of the Bank selectors in the Global Control section.

On Button The On button turns the ReGroove channel on and off. When a channel is deactivated, the loaded groove will have no effect.

Edit Button Clicking the Edit button opens the channel's currently loaded groove patch in the Tool window's Groove tab. Adjustments to the groove can then be made in the Tool window.

Bank/Channel Display The LED to the right of the Edit button shows the current bank and channel information.

LED Display The LED display shows the currently loaded groove. Clicking directly on the LED will display of the patches in the current patch's directory and can also open the Browser. Right/Ctrl-click the LED display to initialize the channel or to copy and paste channel settings between channels.

Groove Amount Slider The Groove Amount slider controls how much of an effect the loaded patch will have on the assigned track. The value ranges from 0% (no effect) to 100% (the maximum possible effect). The parameter sliders in the Tool window's Groove tab set the individual parameters, while the Groove Amount Slider applies their combined effect to the track.

Slide The Slide knob can be used to move notes slightly forward or backward, creating a rushed or relaxed feel. Raise the Slide knob to play notes later; lower the knob to play notes earlier. This knob is especially useful on a single piece of a drum kit—for example, an isolated kick or snare drum performance.

Shuffle The Shuffle knob can be used to add a swing or shuffle feel to the channel. The default Shuffle knob value is 50%. Raising the Shuffle knob increases the shuffle amount, with a value of 66% creating a triplet feel. Values below 50% work the opposite way and can also be used to remove a shuffle or triple feel from an existing beat.

Pre-Align Turning on the Pre-Align functionality aligns any stray MIDI notes to the grid before applying the groove effect of the loaded patch.

Global Shuffle Turning on Global Shuffle deactivates the channel strip's Shuffle knob and applies the shuffle settings.

The Groove Tab in the Tool Window

The Tool window's Groove tab (Figure 8.18) contains important functionality that determines the overall effect of the overall groove patch. The four parameter sliders work in conjunction with each channel's Groove Amount slider to create the overall effect.

> If the Tool window is not currently visible, press the F8 key to view it or choose Window →
> Show Tool Window on the menu bar. Click the Groove tab to view the Tool window's
> ReGroove's functionality.

Groove Channel   Select the channel to edit the channel's currently loaded patch or to assign it a new patch.

Groove Patch   Here you'll find the same functionality as the LED display on the ReGroove's channels. You can use this drop-down menu to view all of the patches in the current directory or to open the Groove Patch Browser. The up and down arrows to the right of the drop-down menu can be used to select the next or previous patches in the current directory.

Browse and Save Patch Buttons   The Browse Patch button opens the Groove Patch Browser. The Save Patch button can be used to save new or edited groove patches.

Patch Info   The Patch Info display shows the patch's length and time signature. The time signature of any loaded patch should match the time signature of your Reason song, displayed on the Transport panel.

Timing Impact   The Timing Impact slider determines how much the timing of your MIDI performance will be altered by the currently loaded groove. Higher values will result in a more noticeable effect.

Velocity Impact   The Velocity Impact slider determines how much variation in velocity will be applied to the MIDI notes of your performance.

Note Length Impact   The Note Length Impact slider determines how much variation in note length will be applied, based on the settings contained in the Groove patch. This is most relevant when working with instrument performances, such a bass track with one of the Bass-Comp Groove patches applied.

Random Timing   The Random Timing slider is used to move notes randomly in your grooves. Adding some randomness can increase the "human element" of your tracks, but adding too much will make your tracks sound sloppy.

Using the ReGroove Mixer

The best way to get a quick idea of what's possible with the ReGroove is to try it out with a drum performance. Chapter 3 contains a quick look at using the ReGroove mixer with the Redrum Drum Computer.

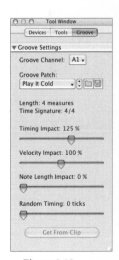

Figure 8.18

The Tool window's Groove tab

Follow these steps to create and edit a more intricate drum performance with the Redrum Drum Computer and the ReGroove mixer:

1. Create a Redrum and load the kit `Reason Factory Sound Bank\Redrum Kits\Rock Kit RDK.drp`.

2. Use the left and right locators to create a two-measure loop in the sequencer.

3. Turn on Reason's looping functionality by activating Loop On/Off on the Transport panel.

4. Click the Start button on the Transport panel to begin playback. The rest of this exercise will take place in real time, with Reason playing the audio as you create the drum track.

5. Select Channel 1 on the Redrum and create a kick drum pattern.

6. Choose Edit → Copy Pattern To Track to send the kick drum pattern to the Redrum's sequencer track.

7. Choose Edit → Clear Pattern to clear the pattern.

8. With the kick drum pattern playing, select Channel 2 on the Redrum and create a snare drum pattern.

9. Choose Edit→ Copy Pattern To Track to send the snare drum pattern to the Redrum's sequencer track. A new lane will be created for the snare drum pattern.

10. Choose Edit→ Clear Pattern to clear the pattern.

11. Select Channel 8 on the Redrum and drag your mouse across the step programmer from left to right to create a hihat pattern using every step. You'll be able to hear the ReGroove effect much more clearly on this lane.

12. Choose Edit → Copy Pattern To Track to send the hihat pattern to the Redrum's sequencer track.

13. Choose Edit → Clear Pattern to clear the pattern.

14. You've now created a drum track with three separate lanes, each with its own editable clip. Using each lane's Select Groove drop-down menu, assign the lanes to ReGroove channels A1, A2, and A3.

15. Now open the ReGroove mixer and use each of the assigned channel's Browse Groove Patch buttons to navigate to the `Reason Factory Sound Bank\ReGroove patches\` folder and assign a different groove patch to each channel.

Once you've assigned a groove patch to each channel, the best way to familiarize your-self with the ReGroove mixer's functionality is to experiment with the various settings, lis-tening for the effect each one—or each combination—has on the rhythm and timing in each lane.

> With many groove patches, you may not notice much difference in sparse drum perform-ances containing only a few hits, such as a snare hit that only takes place on beats 2 and 4. The ReGroove will have a much more noticeable effect on intricate drum patterns.

For specific details of each knob and slider, return to the section in this chapter on the various ReGroove mixer and Groove tab parameters while working with them in real time.

COMMIT TO GROOVE

Once you've found a Groove patch that suits your track, you can make its effect a perma-nent part of your drum performance by opening the Select Groove drop-down menu and choosing Commit To Groove.

> Using the Commit To Groove function is an optional step and may not always be a good idea because it results in a permanent change.

Editing Patches

You can save any changes you make to a groove patch by clicking the Save Groove Patch button in the Tool window. This only saves changes you've made to the patch in the Tool window, not any changes made on the ReGroove channel.

Extracting Grooves from REX Loops

The ReGroove can be used to extract timing variations from REX loops. These extracted grooves can be applied to tracks in the current Reason song, including other REX loops or Redrum tracks. Extracted grooves can also be saved and applied to other tracks in other sessions.

Follow these steps to extract a groove from a REX loop:

1. Create a Dr. Rex Loop Player and load any drum loop and send it to the sequencer (instrument loops will also work).

2. Select one of the newly created Rex clips in the sequencer.

3. If you want to apply the groove to a track in your current Reason song, select a groove channel from the drop-down menu at the top of the Tool window's Groove tab.

4. Click the Get From Clip button at the bottom of the Tool window's Groove tab.

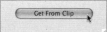

A new groove patch is created, named User 1, and assigned to the selected ReGroove channel. You can make any adjustments you want to the patch in the Tool window.

Extracting the groove information from one clip and applying it to another is a great way to tighten up your tracks, especially with multiple performances that contain slight timing variations. Try applying an extracted groove to another REX or Redrum track, a bass track, or any instrument track to create compatible grooves.

> REX files make the easiest starting point for creating grooves, but you can use any Reason clip as a starting point. Select any instrument performance clip in the sequencer and click the Get From Clip button in the Tool window.

To save the patch for future use, click the Save Patch button in the Tool window and choose a name and location for your new patch.

Summary

In this chapter you have increased your knowledge of the inner workings of Reason 4, and the topics covered here will open up new avenues of creativity with Reason's audio and CV routing functionality, as well as the rhythmic variations available with the ReGroove mixer.

Learning in-depth how to use the Matrix Pattern Sequencer gives you access to creating patterns and complete song arrangements along with using CV to create new sounds and control Reason's instruments and effects in exciting and original ways. The Spider Merger and Splitter devices open up new possibilities for virtually infinite routing combinations with audio and CV connections. Combining the Spider CV device with the Matrix or with any Reason instrument's CV output options gives you the ability to control multiple parameters on multiple devices in endless combinations.

The BV512 Vocoder gives you access to a classic yet malleable sound effect and another EQ option, while Reason 4's new RPG-8 Arpeggiator adds entirely new possibilities for performance and improvisation techniques. Working with two devices has taught you more about Reason's audio and CV routing functionality.

Finally, the new ReGroove mixer adds the ability to create locking grooves and timing variations and to add human randomness into your tracks, all designed to increase the vibe and realism of your Reason songs.

All of the devices and features covered in this chapter can interact with each other at varying levels. Utilizing what you've learned about each device so far and exploring on your own will deepen your understanding of ways to use Reason to create your own original workflow. Combining this chapter's lessons with the remaining chapters in this book will further solidify your knowledge and increase your creative output with Reason 4.

CHAPTER 9

The Combinator

In some ways the Combinator device is like a miniature rack within the Reason rack. It allows you to save and recall simple or complex configurations of Reason devices, including instruments, effects, and routing devices. Along with saving and recalling these patches, the Combinator also contains its own key mapping and modulation routing functionality, which can be used to further expand the device's creative possibilities.

In this chapter you'll look at all the elements found in the Combinator's interface, learn about the uses and routing for some of Reason's included Combinators, and start creating your own instrument and effect Combinator patches.

Topics in this chapter include:

- **Combinator Basics**

- **The Combinator Interface**

- **The Programmer**

- **Inside Combinator Patches**

- **Creating Combinator Patches**

Combinator Basics

The Combinator was introduced in Reason version 3, immediately expanding the instrument and effect routing options for Reason users. In earlier versions of the program, in order to save or share a complex routing setup it was necessary to save or exchange entire song files. Having the ability to creatively route, experiment with, and save combinations of Reason devices in an easily recalled patch unleashed a great tide of creativity. Combinators are now a part of many free and commercial ReFills, including the Flatpack series (www.1apjockey.com), in free ReFills on the Propellerhead Software site, and on websites like Combinator HQ (www.combinatorhq.com) and ReasonBanks (www.reasonbanks.com).

Combinators (or Combinator patches; the two terms are used interchangeably) make an excellent tool for learning about Reason routing techniques. A look inside a well-constructed Combinator can provide a window into exploring new concepts for working within Reason. And just as with Reason's instrument and effect patch devices, you are not limited to keeping existing Combinator patches as they are. You can create Combinator patches from scratch or by working with existing patches, adding new instruments, settings, samples, and effects, and then saving the results.

Loading, Playing, and Saving Combinator Patches

There are two kinds of Combinators: instrument Combinator patches and effect Combinator patches.

Instrument Combinators are patches that include any of Reason's instrument devices. An instrument Combinator patch can contain as many instruments, effects, or other Reason devices as you want. Only your own imagination and your computer's available processing power limit you. The instrument Combinator category can also include pattern device Combinators with Redrum kits, Thor Synthesizers, or Matrix Pattern Sequencers (see the sidebar "Pattern Device Combinator Patches"). Instrument Combinators function exactly like Reason's other instrument devices and can be triggered by a MIDI keyboard or by notes drawn in the Reason sequencer.

Effect Combinators function just like Reason individual effect devices and can be added to your Reason songs as insert or send effects (Chapter 2). Effect Combinator patches can be made up of multiple effects and pattern devices. It's also possible to use Reason instrument devices as signal processors and CV generators in effect Combinator patches.

Loading an instrument or effect Combinator patch is exactly the same process as loading any of Reason's other patch devices. Create a new Combinator from the menu bar's Create menu, and then use the Patch Browse button to open the Reason Browser and locate any Combinator patches. Combinator patches use the file extension .cmb.

Included with Reason version 4 are 20 folders containing many different types of Combinator patches. These are located in the directory Reason Factory Sound Bank\Combinator Patches.

PATTERN DEVICE COMBINATOR PATCHES

Any Combinator patch on the Reason Factory Sound Bank that contains a pattern device will include [Run] in the patch's name.

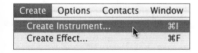

This is to indicate that the Reason song should be playing back or recording in order to properly use the device. In some cases pattern device Combinators will be playable as instruments or will work as effect processors even when they aren't running, but in order to access the pattern device functionality you must either start playback of the Reason song or click the Run Pattern Devices button on the Combinator's Main panel.

There are different types of pattern device Combinators, including both instrument and effect patches. An instrument pattern device Combinator may contain a Matrix Pattern Sequencer to trigger Note and Gate CV or to control a modulation parameter. Another possibility would be a Redrum Drum Computer with preprogrammed patterns.

You can find many pattern device Combinators throughout the subfolders in the Reason Factory Sound Bank\Combinator Patches directory. A collection of pattern device effects Combinators can be found in the folder Reason Factory Sound Bank\Combinator Patches\ Effect Device Patches\Pattern Based.

Once a Combinator patch is loaded, you can use the Select Next Patch and Select Previous Patch buttons to select different patches in the current directory. Clicking on the Patch name display will open a context menu showing you all of the available patches in the current directory. You can also choose Open Browser from the top of the context menu to open the Reason Browser.

Previewing Combinator Patches

One of the fastest ways to access an existing instrument Combinator patch is to choose Create → Create Instrument from the menu bar:

Use the Browser to navigate to the folder Reason Factory Sound Bank\Combinator Patches. You can then open any folder, select any instrument Combinator in the Browser, and preview it by playing notes on your MIDI keyboard.

Using the Create menu, you can also quickly preview any effect Combinator. Follow these steps to preview an effect Combinator as an insert effect:

1. Select an instrument in Reason's main sequencer track list and make sure the instrument has Master Keyboard Input.

2. Choose Create → Create Effect from the menu bar or select the instrument in the Reason rack and right/Ctrl-click and choose Create → Create Effect from the context menu.

3. Use your MIDI keyboard to play the instrument and hear how the effect Combinator patch will sound as an insert effect.

> Once you've added the effect Combinator to your Reason song, you'll have lots of options for further editing the patch's included effect or effects.

You can also select the Reason song's Mixer 14:2 and add any effect Combinator to your Reason song as a send effect.

The Combinator Interface

The Combinator has three separate sections, which will all be covered here. These are the Main panel, the Programmer, and the Device area. Figure 9.1 shows the Combinator's Main panel.

Figure 9.1

The Combinator's Main panel

The Main Panel

The Combinator's Main panel features the following parameters:

Pitch Bend Wheel and Mod Wheel The Combinator's Pitch Bend and Mod Wheel will automatically control the Pitch Bend and Mod Wheel functionality of any Reason instruments in a Combinator patch. You can set the specific Pitch Bend range and Mod Wheel routing for any instrument in a Combinator patch on each individual instrument's interface. As you'll see in "The Modulation Routing Section" later in this chapter, you can also route the Combinator's Pitch Bend Wheel and Mod Wheel to control individual parameters on any device in a Combinator.

Run Pattern Devices Button If your Combinator contains any pattern devices (Redrum Drum Computers, Matrix Pattern Sequencers, and in some cases Thor Polysonic Synthesizers), clicking the Run Pattern Devices button will start and stop them. Starting and stopping playback or recording of your Reason song will also automatically start and stop playback of any pattern devices.

Bypass All FX Button Clicking the Bypass All FX button automatically puts all of the effects in any Combinator into Bypass mode, deactivating the effects but allowing the audio to pass through.

Show Programmer Button Clicking the Show Programmer button opens the Combinator's Programmer window. As discussed in the next section, using the Programmer you can create key range mapping, velocity mapping, and modulation routing.

Show Devices Button Clicking the Show Devices button opens the Combinator's device window, showing all of the Reason devices included in the patch. This button is activated by default when you create a new empty Combinator.

Rotary Knobs The Rotary knobs can be assigned to control single or multiple parameters on any device or multiple devices in a Combinator patch using the Modulation Routing section of the Programmer. Once you've assigned parameters, you can then rename any knob by clicking the name field below the knob and typing a new, relevant name.

Buttons Like the Rotary knobs, these four buttons on the Combinator's main panel can be assigned to single or multiple parameters on any device in the Combinator patch using the Modulation Routing section of the Programmer. Once you've assigned a parameter or parameters, you can then rename any button by clicking the name field below the button and typing a new, relevant name.

The Programmer

The Programmer contains some very useful functionality that can turn your Combinator patches from simple device and effect configurations into your own completely original instruments and effects. To display the Programmer, click the Show Programmer button.

The Programmer Interface

The Programmer interface is divided into two sections: the Key Mapping section is used for creating key ranges and velocity mapping, and the Modulation Routing section is used for assigning parameters to the Rotary knobs and buttons, the Pitch Bend and Mod Wheels, and any external MIDI performance controllers.

The Key Mapping Section

The Key Mapping section contains functionality that's very similar to the key mapping of the NN-XT Advanced Sampler's Remote Editor (Chapter 6), though with the Combinator it is somewhat simpler to use. If you need a refresher on any of the terminology used here, see the section "Terms and Concepts" in Chapter 6. Figure 9.2 shows the Key Mapping section.

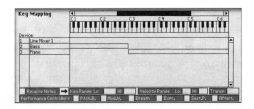

Figure 9.2

The Key Mapping section

Device List   The Device list shows all of the Combinator's currently loaded devices. Select-ing a device in the Device list gives you the ability to make adjustments to the device in the Key Map display, by using the settings at the bottom of the Key Mapping section or with the Modulation Routing section on the right side of the Programmer.

Key Map Display   The Key Map display shows the current key range mapping for the instru-ments in the Combinator patch. By default any new instrument added to a Combinator patch is given a key range of C–2 to G8 (the complete range). Click and drag the scroll bar at the top of the display to view the complete range of available notes.

If a Combinator patch contains more than nine devices, you'll also see a scroll bar on the right side of the Key Map display.

You can select any instrument in the Device list and click and drag with your mouse to manually set the key range.

However, the easiest way to set key ranges for devices in a Combinator patch is to use the Key Range Lo and Hi fields (discussed in a moment).

Receive Notes   Selecting an instrument in the Device list and clearing the Receive Notes check box will turn off the device's ability to respond to incoming MIDI note information.

Key Range   Set the Key Range for any instrument device in the Combinator by selecting the device in the Device list and clicking the Key Range Lo field, and then dragging up or down to set the lowest note in the key range. Click and drag in the Key Range Hi field to set the highest note in the key range.

Velocity Range   The Combinator makes it easy to create velocity-mapped instruments with different MIDI note velocities triggering different sounds. Choose a velocity range for any instrument device in the Combinator by selecting it in the Device list and then click-ing and dragging in the Velocity Range Lo field to set the low velocity and the Hi field to set the high velocity.

Transpose   By clicking and dragging up or down in this field, you can transpose the output of any instrument device selected in the Device list by up to 36 semitones (three octaves) higher or lower.

Performance Controllers   You can deactivate any of the Performance Controllers for an instrument device by selecting the device in the device list and unchecking any of the boxes. This includes the Pitch Bend Wheel and Mod Wheel as well as any of the external MIDI Performance Controllers, such as Breath, Expression, Sustain Pedal, or Aftertouch.

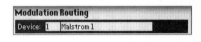

Figure 9.3

The Modulation Routing section

The Modulation Routing Section

Selecting a device in the Key Mapping section's Device list enables you to route the control of various parameters on the selected device to the Rotary knobs and buttons on the Combinator's Main panel.

Figure 9.3 shows the Modulation Routing section with routing in place.

Device The Device field displays the name of the device currently selected in the Key Mapping section's Device list. Any Reason device can be selected in the Device list and assigned modulation routing.

Source The Source list shows the knobs and buttons available for assignment. The default view shows Rotary knobs 1–4, followed by Buttons 1–4 and then two blank fields.

Click any Source field to view the complete list of available sources (Figure 9.4).

You are not locked into any Source list configuration. For example, if you wanted to, you could choose Rotary 1 or the Mod Wheel as the source for more than one field and assign multiple parameters to it.

Target The Target is the parameter that will be controlled by the source.

This is where things get quite interesting as most Reason devices have an incredible range of parameters that can be controlled. Figure 9.5 shows just some of over 80 available Target parameters on the Malström synth.

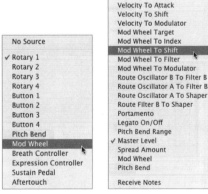

Figure 9.4

Select a Source from the drop-down menu.

Figure 9.5

Some of the available Target parameters on the Malström synth

Min/Max In the Min and Max fields, you'll set the value range for controlling the selected parameter. The available value ranges will differ among parameters and will reflect the same values you'd see when adjusting them on a device's interface. For example, ADSR sliders will have a default range of 0 to 127, whereas other parameters, such as panning knobs, will have a default range of –64 to 63. Still others will display other default values depending on the parameter's available options.

By adjusting the Min and Max settings, you can set the value range that the assigned source can control on the Target parameter. Click and drag up or down to set the minimum and maximum values in these fields. This can be useful in many ways. For example, suppose you want to create a filter sweep by controlling a filter's Frequency slider. Instead of including the lowest (0) value and the highest (127), which would be too drastic an effect, you could set the Min and Max settings to work only with the middle range, containing only the value range that is actually used in creating the effect.

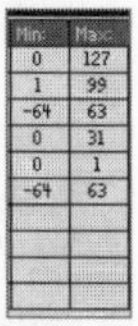

For practical examples using both the Key Mapping section and the Modulation Routing section, see the "Using the Key Mapping Section" and "Using the Modulation Routing Section" exercises later in this chapter.

The Device Area

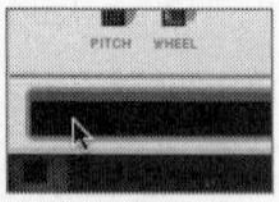

The Device area is shown and hidden using the Show Devices button. The empty Device area and the red Insertion line are visible by default when you create a new empty Combinator.

As long as the Insertion line is visible, any new devices you create will automatically be placed inside the Device area. If you do any work in Reason outside of the Combinator as you create your patch, you'll have to click inside the Device area again and make the Insertion line visible before you can add more devices to the Combinator patch.

To create new Reason devices outside the Combinator, click anywhere outside of the Combinator interface on the Reason rack before creating the device.

Combinator Routing

The Combinator's back panel, shown in Figure 9.6, contains all of the device's input and output routing as well as its CV input functionality.

In an instrument Combinator patch, the signal from the output of the combined instruments and effects is usually routed to a Mixer 6:2. The mixer's output then goes to the From Devices input and from there to the Combi Output outputs.

Figure 9.6

The Combinator's inputs and outputs

In an effect Combinator patch, the signal from the instrument or mixer enters the Combinator with the Combi Inputs, and is then routed to the included effects via the To Devices connection. The output of the included effects is then routed to the From Devices input and from there to the Combi Output outputs.

CV Routing

The Combinator features the same standard Note and Gate CV inputs found on Reason's other instrument devices. For example, select an instrument Combinator and create a Matrix Pattern Sequencer outside of the Combinator, and Note and Gate CV routing will be automatically created as they would with any Reason instrument.

The Combinator also features six CV Modulation inputs.

These CV inputs open up some interesting possibilities. By connecting a Matrix or any CV-generating Reason device, you can control the Pitch Bend and Mod Wheels or any of the four Rotary knobs. You'll learn about assigning a Rotary knob to a target parameter and then controlling it with CV in "Using the Modulation Routing Section" later in this chapter.

Inside Combinator Patches

If there's one point that you should be clear on, it's this: Combinators have absolutely no rules. A Combinator patch can be as simple as a single instrument and effect, combined, or even one instrument or effect by itself.

> Creating a single-instrument Combinator patch can be useful for saving CV routing within an instrument, which is never saved as part of a patch. A single-effect Combinator can be useful for saving effect device settings for effects that don't feature patch-saving functionality.

Of course, Combinators are generally complex patches, often containing multiple instruments and/or effects, layered or routed together creatively.

In the following exercises you'll take a look at a few of the Combinator patches that are included with the Reason program to see some of the instrument, effect, and modulation routing techniques that are possible with this device. Follow these steps to take a first look inside a Combinator patch:

1. Create a new Reason song.

2. Choose Create → Create Instrument from the menu bar.

3. Use the Reason Browser to load the patch Reason Factory Sound Bank\Combinator Patches\Guitar and Plucked\Acoustic Guitar\Intimate Steel String Guitar.cmb.

4. Use your MIDI keyboard to play a few notes to hear how this instrument Combinator sounds.

5. Click the Show Devices button to view the Combinator's included devices (Figure 9.7).

6. Press the Tab key to view the Combinator's routing (Figure 9.8).

This is a fairly simple Combinator patch containing a single NN-XT Advanced Sampler connected to an MClass Stereo Imager, which is then routed to the Patch's Line Mixer 6:2 (See "The Line Mixer 6:2" section later in this chapter). Finally, an RV7000 Advanced Reverb is connected to the Line Mixer 6:2 as a send effect.

Figure 9.8

**The Intimate
Steel String Guitar
Combinator's device
routing**

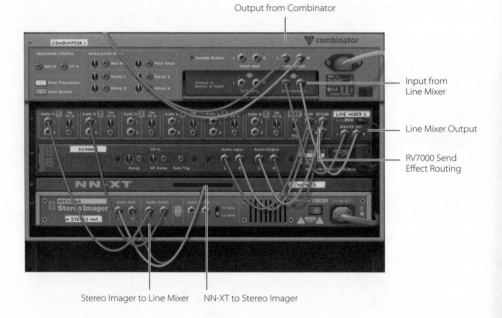

By looking at the renamed Rotary knobs and buttons, you can see that modulation routing has been created and assigned for this patch using the Programmer.

7. Click the Show Programmer button to view the Programmer section.

8. Select each device in the Device list one at a time to view its assigned Modulation Routing setting.

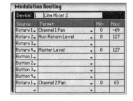

As with all instrument Combinators, you can use your MIDI keyboard or draw notes in the Reason sequencer to play this patch as it is. But you're not at all limited to using any Combinator patch in its saved state. Some possibilities include:

- Loading any patch into the RV7000
- Making adjustments to the RV7000, Stereo Imager, or NN-XT
- Using the NN-XT's Browse Patch button to load different sampler instrument patches

Any changes you make can be saved at any time by clicking the Save Patch button and choosing a name and location for your altered Combinator patch. You can now recall the new version of your patch at any time, using it in any new song you create.

Inside an Effect Combinator Patch

Follow these steps to view the routing of an effect Combinator.

1. Create an NN-19 Digital Sampler and load the patch Reason Factory Sound Bank\NN19 Patches\ORGAN4.smp.

2. Select the NN-19 in the rack and choose Create → Create Effect from the menu bar.

3. Use the Browser to locate and load the patch Reason Factory Sound Bank\ALL Effects Patches\Delay\Analog Modulation Delay.cmb.

4. Play notes on your MIDI keyboard to hear the delay effect.

5. Click the Show Devices button on the Combinator's Main panel to view the included effects (Figure 9.9).

6. Press the Tab button to view the routing, shown in Figure 9.10.

Figure 9.9

The Analog Modulation Delay Combinator's included devices

Figure 9.10

The Analog Modulation Delay Combinator's device routing

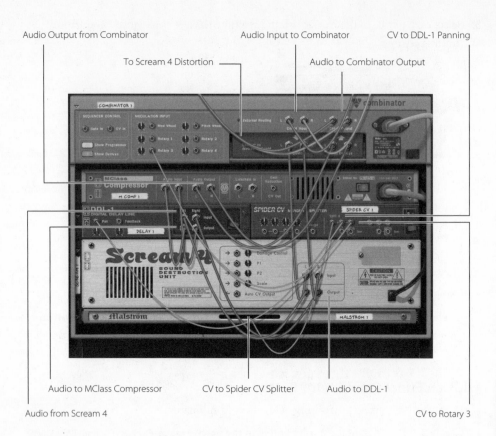

Audio Output from Combinator

To Scream 4 Distortion

Audio Input to Combinator

CV to DDL-1 Panning

Audio to Combinator Output

Audio to MClass Compressor

CV to Spider CV Splitter

Audio to DDL-1

Audio from Scream 4

CV to Rotary 3

In this Reason song, the sound from the NN-19 is routed into the Combinator via the Combi Input routing inputs. From there the Combinator's signal flow is the To Devices input → Scream 4 Sound Destruction Unit → DDl-1 Delay Line → MClass Compressor → From Devices input → Combi Output.

There's another interesting bit of routing included here as well. The Malström's Mod A output is routed to send CV to the Spider CV Merger and Splitter. The CV is then split and used to control the DDL-1's panning knob *and* the Main panel's Rotary knob 3. As you'll see in a minute, the Rotary 3 knob is connected to the DDl-1's Feedback knob via modulation routing. In order for this to work you'll have to turn on the Malström's Mod A.

Once you've turned on the Mod A section, you'll see the DDL-1's Feedback knob moving in real time as it's controlled by the Malström's CV output.

As you can further see from the renamed Rotary knobs and Buttons, some modulation routing has been configured for this patch.

7. Click the Show Programmer button to view the Programmer's Key Mapping and Modulation Routing sections.

8. Select each device one at a time in the Device list to view the assigned modulation routing for this patch.

Taking a look at the Malström's routing in particular, you can see that three buttons have been assigned. One button is assigned to turn on Mod A's sync functionality, one to turn Mod A on and off, and one to switch between the waveforms shapes that are used to control the effect. Rotary 1 has been assigned to Mod A's Rate knob and Min and Max values have been set to limit the range of available Rate values that the Rotary can control.

Inside a Pattern Device Combinator Patch

Pattern device Combinators can be either instrument or effect Combinators. Follow these steps to take a look inside and work with an instrument pattern device Combinator.

1. Choose Create → Create Instrument from the menu bar.

2. Use the Reason Browser to locate and load the patch Reason Factory Sound Bank\ Combinator Patches\Drums and Percussion\Machines Electronic Research [Run].cmb.

3. Click the Show Devices button to view the Reason devices that make up this Combinator (Figure 9.11).

Figure 9.11

The Devices in the Electronic Research [Run] Combinator patch

4. Click the unfold arrow to view the patch's Redrum Drum Computer device.

5. Use the Tab key to view the Combinator's routing.

In this patch, the Redrum's CV Gate outputs on Channels 1,2, 8, and 10 are triggering drum sounds created by each of the four synthesizer instruments. Three of the drum sounds are then routed to individual channels on the Line Mixer 6:2. A fourth drum sound (the hihat created with a Thor synth) is routed to the Spider Audio Device, and then split. The hihat is then sent separately to Channels 2 (left) and 3 (right) on the Line Mixer 6:2 and also to the DDL-1 Delay, then through the CF-101 Flanger and finally to Channel 6 on the Line Mixer 6:2.

Further routing includes an RV7000 connected to the Line Mixer 6:2 as a send effect and an MClass Maximizer connected as an insert effect between the Line Mixer 6:2 and the Combinator outputs.

In some ways this instrument can be used just like any Redrum Drum Computer (Chapter 4):

- This particular patch contains some preprogrammed Redrum patterns. Use the Pattern select buttons to choose from any of the eight preprogrammed patterns, or take advantage of the patch's modulation routing and use Rotary knob 1 to select any of the eight patterns.
- Edit the existing patterns or create your own patterns at any time using the methods covered in Chapter 4.
- Start playback by clicking the Play button on the Transport panel or by clicking the Run button on the Redrum's interface.
- Sequence patterns by selecting the Redrum inside the Combinator and choosing Edit → Copy Pattern To Track from the menu bar or right/Ctrl-clicking and choosing Copy Pattern To Track from the context menu.

When a Redrum or any pattern device is part of a Combinator device, you can't access the device's pattern lane sequencing functionality as you would working with the device outside of a Combinator patch. In this case, because the Redrum's pattern selection is modulation-routed to Rotary 1 of the Combinator, you could create a pattern sequence by recording automation of Rotary 1.

Just as you could with any Redrum, you can also draw MIDI notes in the sequencer to trigger the device or play the device with your MIDI keyboard.

The Electronic Research [Run] Combinator is only one type of pattern device Combinator. Take a look inside of some other pattern device Combinator patches to get a better understanding of how pattern device Combinators work. You can find many more pattern device Combinators, including both instrument and effect pattern device patches, throughout the Reason Factory Sound Bank\Combinator Patches subfolders.

Inside Other Combinator Patches

To learn more about Combinator routing, use the same steps as in the preceding exercises to try out the device and modulation routing of some of Reason's other included instrument Combinator patches. You'll find interesting patches throughout the folders. In particular there are some good, complicated instrument patches in the subfolders located in the Reason Factory Sound Bank\Combinator Patches\Performance Patches\ directory. You can find lots of effect Combinators in the subfolders located in the Reason Factory Sound Bank\Combinator Patches\Effect Device Patches directory.

Working with existing patches by making adjustments to various parameters, choosing different patches for any of the Combinator's patch loading devices, switching out instruments and effects, and reconfiguring routing are all excellent ways to become familiar with some of the inner workings of Combinator patches.

Creating Combinator Patches

The Combinator is a particularly exciting Reason device to work with because of its ability to create and recall complex configurations, but even very simple Combinator patches can be extremely useful when working in Reason. Throughout the rest of this chapter, you'll learn about creating different kinds of Combinators, starting with some basic patches and then moving on to more complex configurations.

The Line Mixer 6:2

An important element in many Combinator patches will be the Line Mixer 6:2, also known as the MicroMix, shown in Figure 9.12.

The Line Mixer can also be used outside of the Combinator, but it's included in this chapter because its primary use is within Combinator patches.

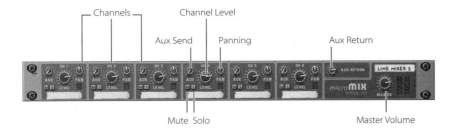

Figure 9.12
The Line Mixer 6:2

The Line Mixer 6:2 is sort of a miniature version of the Mixer 14:2. It has six stereo input channels and left and right (stereo) outputs. It's capable of routing a single send and return effect.

Each channel has Mute, Solo, Level, Aux Send, and Panning functionality as well as a level meter. Here are some useful tips for working with the Line Mixer 6:2 inside a Combinator patch:

- When you create a Combinator and add a Line Mixer, the mixer's output is then automatically routed to the Combinator's From Devices input, and then to the Combi Output.

- When you create an instrument inside a Combinator patch that contains a Line Mixer 6:2, it will be automatically routed to the Line Mixer's first available channel.

- If you select the Line Mixer 6:2 inside a Combinator patch and create a single effect, it will automatically be routed as a send effect.

- If you select the Line Mixer 6:2 inside a Combinator patch and create a second effect, it will automatically be routed as an insert effect between the Line Mixer 6:2 and the Combinator's output.

Create a Simple Patch

There are multiple ways to create a Combinator device in Reason:

- You can create an empty Combinator device by choosing Create → Combinator from the menu bar.

- You can right/Ctrl-click any empty area on the Reason rack and choose Combinator from the context menu.

- You can hold down the Shift key and use your mouse to select multiple instruments, devices, and/or effects in the Reason rack, and then choose Edit → Combine from the menu bar or right/Ctrl-click on any of the selected devices and choose Combine from the context menu.

In these next few exercises, you'll start off by creating a few simple Combinator patches. Follow these steps to combine an instrument and effect as a Combinator:

1. Create a new Reason song.

2. Create a Malström Graintable Synthesizer. Load any patch from the `Reason Factory Sound Bank\Malstrom Patches\MonoSynths` folder.

3. With the Malström selected, create a PH-90 Phaser.

4. Hold down the Shift key and select both devices at once.

5. With both devices selected, choose Edit → Combine from the menu bar or right/Ctrl-click on any of the selected devices and choose Combine from the context menu.

6. Click the Save Patch button on the Combinator's Main panel, and then choose a name and location for your new patch.

You can save any changes you make to the Malström or the PH-90 as part of your Combinator patch by clicking the Save Patch button and overwriting the patch or creating a second version of the patch with a different name.

The preceding exercise is a good way to quickly save any instrument/effect configurations you come up with when working in Reason for use in future projects.

You can also create the same patch much more quickly by using the Create menu. Just choose Create → Combinator, then Create → Malström Graintable Synth, then Create → PH-90 Phaser.

> When you create a new Combinator, any new Reason devices you create after it will be automatically placed in the Combinator's Device area. To create devices outside of the Combinator, click any blank space on the Reason rack.

You could also use the Devices tab on the Tool window to create the same patch by double-clicking the Combinator and then double-clicking first the Malström, then the PH-90.

Create a Multi-Instrument Combinator

Follow these steps to create a multi-instrument Combinator patch.

1. Create a new Combinator.

2. Create a Line Mixer 6:2 inside the Combinator.

3. Create two NN-XT Advanced Samplers.

4. Load the patch `Reason Factory Sound Bank\NN-XT Sampler Patches\B Grand Piano.sxt` into the first NN-XT.

5. Load the patch `Reason Factory Sound Bank\NN-XT Sampler Patches\Strings\String Orch.sxt` into the second NN-XT.

6. Select the Line Mixer and create an RV7000 as a send effect.

7. Load any patch from the `Reason Factory Sound Bank\RV7000 Patches` and use the Channel 1 and Channel 2 Aux Sends knob to bring the Reverb effect into the mix.

8. Save the patch to a location on your hard drive. You'll be using this patch later, in the "Using the Key Mapping Section" exercise.

   You can find this patch on the accompanying CD:

   `Examples\Chapter 9\Patches\MultIns.cmb`

You've now created a multi-instrument Combinator. Playing notes on your MIDI keyboard triggers both NN-XT instruments simultaneously and their output is routed through the Line Mixer 6:2. You can take this much further by working the elements contained in the patch:

- Control the levels of each instrument with its Channel Level knob.

- Adjust the panning of each instrument.

- Raise and lower the effect amount.

- You can also easily add up to four more instruments to the patch and then adjust volume, panning, and reverb effect levels for each instrument.

- Select any instrument in the Combinator and create any effect as an insert.

Take It Further

Using this method you can quickly create Combinator patches with up to any six Reason instruments, a single send effect, and as many insert effects as you'd like. You're not at all limited to six instruments, though. You could add five instruments to a patch and use the Line Mixer's sixth input for another line mixer.

You can also add even more instruments by merging audio within a Combinator with the Spider Audio device or add more instruments and up to four send effects by using a Mixer 14:2 in place of the Line Mixer 6:2.

CHANGING THE LOOK OF YOUR COMBINATOR PATCHES

Combinators are the only Reason device whose appearance you can change. You can do this by selecting the Combinator in the Reason rack and either choosing Edit → Select Backdrop from the menu bar or right/Ctrl-clicking and choosing Select Backdrop from the context menu.

This will open the Reason Browser, which you can use to navigate and select any JPEG image file on your hard drive to use as a backdrop. A Combinator backdrop should be 734 × 138 pixels. Template Combinator backdrops, including a Photoshop template and a JPEG version, are included with Reason and located in your Reason folder Reason\Template Documents\Combi Backdrops.

Using the Key Mapping Section

Along with accessing the Modulation Routing functionality, which you'll learn about shortly, the Key Mapping section can be used to create split instrument Combinator patches and velocity-layered patches.

Split Instrument Combinator Patches

Using the Programmer, you can assign different instruments to different note ranges. This functionality is very similar to the Key Zone mapping functionality of the NN-XT Advanced Sampler (Chapter 6).

In this exercise you'll create a basic split layered patch with a bass sound in the lower note range and a piano in the higher note range:

1. Use any method to create a new empty Combinator.

2. Create a Line Mixer 6:2 inside the Combinator.

3. Add an NN-XT Advanced Sampler and load the patch Reason Factory Sound Bank\NN-XT Sampler Patches\Upright II.sxt.

4. Name the NN-XT **Bass**.

5. Create a second NN-XT Advanced Sampler and load the patch Reason Factory Sound Bank\NN-XT Sampler Patches\B Grand Piano 1.0.sxt.

6. Name the second NN-XT **Piano**.

7. Click the Show Programmer button to view the Combinator's Programmer section.

8. Select the Bass NN-XT in the Device List.

9. In the Key Range Hi field, click and drag downward with your mouse to set the highest note in the key range to B2. The key range for the Bass instrument will now be C-2 to B2.

10. Select the Piano in the Device list and set the Lo key to C3. The key range for the  Piano instrument will now be C3 to G8.

Playing any notes below C3 with your MIDI keyboard will trigger the Bass instrument. Playing the note C3 or any notes above C3 will trigger the Piano instrument. You can use this functionality to create Combinator patches with as many instruments as you want by adding new instruments and setting key ranges for each one.

Take this further by adding an RV7000 as a reverb send effect or as an insert on either device.

You can find this patch on the accompanying CD:

    Examples\Chapter 9\Patches\SplitIns.cmb

You can find more split instrument Combinator patches in the folder Reason Factory Sound Bank\Combinator Patches\Performance Patches\Splits.

Velocity Layered Combinator Patches

Also similar to the NN-XT's functionality is the Combinator's velocity-layering functionality. In a velocity-layered patch, the device will trigger different sounds depending on the velocity of the incoming MIDI note.

Follow these steps to create a velocity-layered Combinator patch:

1. Create a new Combinator and load the patch you created in the "Create a Multi-Instrument Combinator" exercise or load the patch from the accompanying CD: Examples\Chapter 9\Patches\MultIns.cmb.

2. Click the Show Programmer button to view the Combinator's Programmer.

3. Select the NN-XT 2 instrument in the Device list and use your mouse to set a value of 80 in the Velocity Range Lo field.

Any notes you play on your MIDI keyboard with a velocity of 79 or lower will trigger only the Piano patch loaded into NN-XT 1. Any MIDI notes with a velocity of 80 or higher will trigger both the NN-XT 1 and NN-XT 2 patches.

You can find this patch on the accompanying CD:

    Examples\Chapter 9\Patches\Velocity1.cmb.

You can also use the key Mapping sections velocity layering functionality to create simple to extremely complex combinations of velocity-triggered instrumentation.

> Combine the techniques covered in the previous two exercises to create split instrument, velocity-layered Combinator patches.

Using the Modulation Routing Section

The Modulation Bus Routing section can add new levels of creative possibility and routing complexity to your Combinator patches. Follow these steps to create a Combinator patch that utilizes modulation routing with a mixer, an instrument, and an effect.

1. Create a new Combinator.

2. Add the following in order:

   > A Line Mixer 6:2

   > A DDL-1 Delay

   > A Malström Graintable Synthesizer

3. Load the patch `Reason Factory Sound Bank\Malstrom Patches\Rythmic\ArpBells.xwv` into the Malström.

4. Click the Show Programmer button to view the Combinator's Programmer.

5. Select the Line Mixer in the Device list.

6. In the Modulation Routing section's Target menu, assign Channel 1 Aux Send as the Target and Rotary 1 as the Source.

7. Use your mouse to adjust Rotary 1 and thus activate the Modulation Routing.

Raising and lowering the Rotary 1 knob now controls the Channel 1 Aux Send on the Line Mixer, raising and lowering the amount of delay effect heard when the patch is played using your MIDI keyboard. As you raise and lower Rotary 1, you can see the mixer's Channel 1 Aux Send knob responding.

8. Select the Delay in the Device list and assign Rotary 2 to the Feedback knob.

9. Assign Button 1 to the Wet/Dry Balance knob.

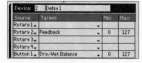

Raising and lowering Rotary 2 will now control the delay effect's Feedback knob, while button 1 will control the Wet/Dry knob. Button 1 will switch between a value of 0 (completely dry signal) and 127 (completely wet signal), effectively turning the delay effect on and off.

10. Select the Malström in the Device list and assign Rotary 3 to Modulator A Rate and Rotary 4 to Modulator A To Pitch.

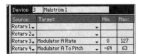

Figure 9.13

Select the Pitch Wheel from the Source list.

11. With the Malström selected in the Device list, deselect the Pitch Bend Performance Controller box. This will deactivate the Malström's Pitch Bend Wheel's pitch bending functionality.

12. Click the first empty field on the Modulation Routing section's Source list and select Pitch Bend Wheel from the pop-up menu (Figure 9.13).

13. Assign the Malström's Pitch Bend Wheel to the Target Oscillator A Octave.

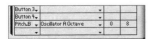

14. Name the Rotary knobs and Button 1 to reflect their modulation routing assignments.

15. Click the Save Patch button and choose a name and location for your patch. You'll be using this patch again in the section "Controlling the Rotary Knobs with CV."

You've now created a Combinator patch with a good selection of modulation routing assignments. Use your mouse to adjust the various Rotary knobs and the Pitch Wheel while playing notes and chords on your MIDI keyboard.

You can find this patch on the accompanying CD:

```
Examples\Chapter 9\Patches\ModRout.cmb
```

If your MIDI keyboard or controller features adjustable knobs, see the sidebar "External MIDI Control" for instructions on how to utilize them with the Combinator.

Controlling the Rotary Knobs with CV

Another way to work with the Main panel's Rotary knobs is to create automation by using the CV output of a Matrix Pattern Sequencer, Reason instrument, or other device to control them, and by extension their assigned parameters. In "Using the Modulation Routing

EXTERNAL MIDI CONTROL

If you have a MIDI keyboard that includes adjustable knobs, there's a good chance that Reason has automatically routed them to the Combinator's four Rotary knobs. You can try this out by making sure the Combinator is selected in the Reason rack and adjusting knobs on your MIDI keyboard. If the automatic routing is in place, you'll see the Combinator's knobs respond accordingly.

If this automatic external control is not in place, do the following:

1. Choose Options → Remote Override Edit Mode from the main menu.

2. Double-click any Rotary knob. You'll see a rotating lightning bolt appear over the parameter.

3. Adjust any knob on your external keyboard to assign it to the selected Rotary knob.

Section" earlier, you created modulation routing within your Combinator patch. Follow these steps to further control that modulation routing with CV.

1. Open the Combinator patch you created in "Using the Modulation Routing Section" or use the patch Examples\Chapter 9\Patches\ModRout.cmb.

2. Click the Show Devices button to view the included devices.

3. Click in the bottom of the Combinator's device area to make the red insertion line visible.

4. Hold down the Shift key and create an unconnected Matrix Pattern Sequencer inside the Combinator's Device area.

5. Press the Tab key to view the Combinator's device routing.

6. Route the Curve CV output of the Matrix to the Rotary 1 Modulation Input on the back of the Combinator's Main panel.

7. Choose Bipolar Curve Mode on the back panel of the Matrix.

8. Press the Tab key to view the front of the Combinator.

9. Use the Matrix's Mode switch to choose Curve Edit mode.

10. Draw a Curve CV in the Matrix's interface.

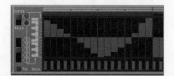

Start playback or recording of your Reason song or click the Run Pattern Devices button on the Combinator's Main panel. Keep an eye on the Line Mixer's Channel 1 Aux Send button and you'll see it moving in real time as the Curve CV is sent from the Matrix to Rotary 1, which is controlling Aux Send 1.

> This patch is now a pattern device Combinator and should be resaved with [Run] added to its name.

You can find this patch on the accompanying CD:

```
Examples\Chapter 9\Patches\CVControl [Run].cmb
```

Arpeggiator Combinators

Since the RPG-8 Arpeggiator is not capable of saving and recalling settings, creating an arpeggiator Combinator patch can be a good workaround for this, as well as a way to create RPG-8, instrument, and effect configurations that you'll be able to recall later.

1. Create a new Combinator and add a Line Mixer 6:2 and a SubTractor Analog Synthesizer. You can use the instrument's default initialized settings for this exercise.

2. Select the SubTractor in the Combinator Device area and create an RPG-8 Monophonic Arpeggiator.

3. Click the Show Programmer button.

4. In the Key Mapping area, select the SubTractor on the Device list and deselect the Receive Notes box.

Figure 9.14 shows the devices in this RPG-8 Combinator patch.

Figure 9.14

The devices in an RPG-8 Combinator patch

With both devices receiving MIDI notes, the SubTractor would be triggered twice—once by the notes played on your MIDI keyboard and again by the RPG-8. Now only the RPG-8 will receive MIDI notes, which will in turn trigger the SubTractor.

5. Select the Line Mixer 6:2 and add a CF-101 Chorus/Flanger to the patch as a send effect.

6. Click the CF-101's Send Mode button.

7. Raise the Channel 1 Aux Send knob to hear the effect.

8. Make any adjustments you want on the RPG-8's interface.

9. Use your MIDI keyboard to play the Arpeggiator Combinator patch.

    You can use this patch as a starting point for creating more RPG-8 patches. Some possibilities include:

- Create different settings in the RPG-8 interface such as adjusting the Mode, Octave, and Insert settings to create new arpeggio patterns, and save individual, recallable Combinator patches.

- Assign modulation routing to parameters on the RPG-8 or any included devices. For example, assign a Rotary knob to control the RPG-8's Rate or Mode knobs.

- Replace the Chorus/Flanger with another effect.

- Create a chain of effects by selecting the Chorus/Flanger and adding more effects to the patch.

- Use the SubTractor's Browse Patch button to load a different SubTractor patch.

- Replace the SubTractor with a different Reason instrument.

    You can find this patch on the accompanying CD:

    ```
    Examples\Chapter 9\Patches\RPG8.cmb
    ```

> You can also use the RPG-8 to trigger a Combinator patch with multiple instruments by selecting the Combinator in the rack and creating the RPG-8 outside of the Combinator.

Create a Dr. Rex Combinator

A Dr. Rex Combinator patch can be used to create your own original sounds from existing REX loops, and also a way to save Dr. Rex settings for use in multiple Reason songs.

1. Create a new empty Combinator patch.

2. Add a Line Mixer 6:2.

3. Select the Line Mixer and create an RV7000.

4. Add a Dr. Rex and load any Rex loop from the Reason Factory Sound Bank.

5. Select the Dr. Rex and create a Scream 4 Sound Destruction Unit as an insert effect.

6. Raise the Channel 1 Aux Send knob to add the reverb effect to the patch.

7. Adjust settings on the Scream 4 to add distortion/compression to the loop.

8. Click the Preview button on the Dr. Rex interface to hear the patch. Unlike pattern device Combinator patches, starting playback of the sequencer will not automatically start your Dr. Rex Combinators.

9. You can send the REX loop to the sequencer at any time by selecting the Dr. Rex in the Combinator and choosing Edit → Copy REX Loop To Track from the menu bar or right/Ctrl-clicking and choosing Copy REX Loop To Track from the context menu.

Figure 9.15 shows the devices in this Dr. Rex Combinator patch.

Figure 9.15

The devices in a Dr. Rex Combinator patch

From here you have lots of possibilities:

- Make adjustments to any of the parameters on the Dr. Rex interface, including the LFO, Filter, Filter Envelope, and pitch setting.

- Click the Dr. Rex's Browse Loop, Select Previous Loop, or Select Next Loop buttons at any time to load a different REX loop.

- Load different patches into the RV7000 and Scream 4.

- Replace the RV7000 and/or the Scream 4 with different effects or add more effects to the patch to create a chain.

- Create modulation routing for any of the included devices.

- Add CV control to any modulation routing.

Any changes you make to your patch can be saved by overwriting the existing patch or by creating a new patch with a different name.

You can find this patch on the accompanying CD:

```
Examples\Chapter 9\Patches\DrRex.cmb
```

Create a SubTractor Drum Kit

Another potential use for the Combinator device is to combine percussion sounds from Reason synthesizers. Follow these steps to create a drum kit using four SubTractor Analog Synthesizers:

1. Create a new Combinator.

2. Add a Line Mixer 6:2.

3. Create four SubTractor synths and name them (in order) Kick, Snare, Hihat, and Clap.

4. "Load the following patches from the Reason Factory Sound Bank into the four Sub-Tractors, one at a time.

> Reason Factory Sound Bank\SubTractor Patches\Percussion\BassDrums\BassDrum1.zyp
>
> Reason Factory Sound Bank\SubTractor Patches\Percussion\SnareDrums\nareDrum.zyp
>
> Reason Factory Sound Bank\SubTractor Patches\Percussion\HiHats\Hihat.zyp
>
> Reason Factory Sound Bank\SubTractor Patches\Percussion\Claps\Clap2.zyp

5. Click the Show Programmer button to view the Programmer window.

6. Select each SubTractor one at a time and use the Key Range Lo and Hi fields to set the following one-note key ranges for each SubTractor:

DRUM	MIDI NOTE #
Kick	C1
Snare	D1
Hihat	E1
Clap	F1

To keep this exercise simple, you've just assigned four drum sounds to four consecutive "white keys" on your MIDI keyboard. When creating your own Combinator drum kits, consider using conventional MIDI drum assignments, as covered in the "Drums and the NN-XT" section of Chapter 6.

You can now use your MIDI keyboard to play the SubTractor drum kit or draw MIDI notes in the Combinator's sequencer track. Figure 9.16 shows the patch's included devices in the Device area.

Figure 9.16
The SubTractor drum kit devices

7. Click the Combinator's Save Patch button and choose a name and location for your patch.

In the next exercise, you'll use the drum kit you've just created as a starting point for creating a Pattern Device Combinator patch.

Create a Pattern Device Combinator

Follow these steps to take the previous exercise further by turning the SubTractor Drum Kit Combinator patch into a Pattern Device Combinator:

1. Starting with the patch you created in the previous exercise, create a Redrum and route the Gate CV output of channels 1–4 to the Gate input of each SubTractor.

   You can now use Channels 1–4 of the Redrum Drum Computer to trigger the drum sounds of each SubTractor. This opens up some very cool options that you saw earlier in the "Inside a Pattern Device Combinator Patch" section's look at the Electronic Research [RUN] Combinator patch: you can create multiple patterns in the Redrum and assign a Rotary knob to switch between patterns.

2. Using the Redrum's Bank and Pattern select buttons, program different beats on patterns A1 through A4.

3. Open the Programmer and select the Redrum in the Device list.

4. Use the Modulation Routing section and choose Rotary 1 as the Source and the Redrum's Selected Pattern as the Target.

5. Set a Min value of 0 and a Max value of 4.

You can now use Rotary 1 to switch between the Redrum's programmed patterns. By recording automation of Rotary 1, you can create pattern sequences.

TAKE IT FURTHER

You can take this further by adding effects or pattern devices to the patch.

- Select the Line Mixer 6:2 and create a send effect.

- With an insert effect in place, select the Line Mixer 6:2 again and create any MClass effect or a Scream 4 Sound Destruction unit to use as an insert effect on the overall mix.

- Select individual SubTractors within the patch and add insert effects.

- Use different synth percussion sounds, including Thor and Malström percussion patches.

- Delete the Redrum, create four Matrix Pattern Sequencers, and route the Gate CV output of each to a SubTractor. Use the Gate CV lane on each Matrix to create patterns with each SubTractor.

You can find examples of the previous two exercises, including a pattern device version of the patch with a Redrum routed to trigger the individual drum sounds on this book's accompanying CD:

```
Examples\Chapter 9\Patches\STDrumKit1.cmb

Examples\Chapter 9\Patches\STDrumKit2.cmb

Examples\Chapter 9\Patches\STDrumKit [Run].cmb
```

Create Effect Combinators

Effects Combinators are best created while connected to an instrument and being used in real time as an insert effect. You can do this with any Reason instrument. Follow these steps to create an effect Combinator in real time with a Dr. Rex Loop Player:

1. Create a Dr. Rex Loop Player and load any loop from the Reason Factory Sound Bank.

2. Click the Preview button on the Dr. Rex interface to begin playback of the loop.

3. Hold down the Shift key and create an unconnected Combinator.

4. Press the Tab key to view the back of the Reason rack.

5. Connect the Dr. Rex's Left and right Audio Outputs to the left and right Combi Inputs.

6. Connect the left and right Combi Outputs to the first available channel on the Reason song's Mixer 14:2 (Figure 9.17).

Figure 9.17

Connections for an effect Combinator patch

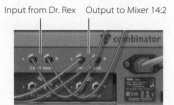

This is all of the manual routing you'll need to create for basic effects chains. From here you can create simple effects chains by adding effects to the Combinator in any order. The input and output will automatically be routed from the first effect to the last in your chain. Of course, it's also possible to be much more creative with your effects routing.

With the Dr. Rex and Combinator routing in place from the previous exercise, follow these steps to create an effect patch with a Line Mixer 6:2 and a Spider Audio Device:

1. Add a Line Mixer 6:2 to the Combinator patch.

2. Add a Spider Audio Device.

3. Manually route the Combinator To Devices jacks to the left and right inputs of the Spider's Audio Splitter section (Figure 9.18).

Figure 9.18

Connect the Spider Audio Device to receive audio input.

4. Connect the Spider's first pair of splitter outputs to Channel 1 on the Line Mixer 6:2. This channel will be your Dry (no effect) signal.

5. Hold down the Shift key and create an unconnected DDL-1 Digital Delay Line inside the Combinator.

6. Connect the Spider's second pair of Splitter outputs to the left and right inputs of the DDL-1.

7. Connect the DDL-1's stereo outputs to Channel 2 to on the Line Mixer 6:2.

8. Hold down the Shift key and create an RV-7 Digital Reverb.

9. Connect the Spider's third pair of Splitter outputs to the left and right inputs of the RV-7.

10. Connect the RV-7's stereo outputs to Channel 3 on the Line Mixer 6:2.

11. Make sure the Dr. Rex is generating sound by clicking the Preview button on the Dr. Rex interface or by sending the currently loaded REX file to a sequencer track and starting playback of the Reason song.

This patch now contains three separate volume controls for the attached Dr. Rex. Use the Line Mixer's Channel 1's Level knob to raise and lower the Dry signal. Use Channel 2's Level knob to raise and lower the delayed signal, and use Channel 3's Level knob to raise the reverb effect.

12. Assign Channels 1, 2, and 3 on the Line Mixer 6:2 to Rotary knobs 1, 2, and 3.

13. Name each Rotary to reflect its function: Dry Amount, Delay Amount, and Reverb Amount.

You can find this patch on the accompanying CD:

```
Examples\Chapter 9\Patches\Effects1.cmb
```

You can find the Dr. Rex and Combinator routing with this patch in the Reason song file:

```
Examples\Chapter 9\Songs\REXFX.rns
```

Take It Further

Here are some possibilities for using the previous example as a starting point for effect Combinator patches:

- Create modulation routing to control the Line Mixer 6:2 or any included effects.

- Switch out the Combinator effects with other effects.

- Create a second Spider Audio Device, connect it to the first, and split the signal further, adding more effects.

- Add any CV-generating device to control effects parameters.

- Create a pattern device effect Combinator by adding a Matrix to control parameters or Rotary knobs.
- Add a Spider CV device and split the CV.

You can find examples of these suggestions the accompanying CD:

```
Examples\Chapter 9\Patches\Effects2.cmb

Examples\Chapter 9\Patches\Effects3.cmb

Examples\Chapter 9\Patches\Effects4[Run].cmb
```

Summary

More than any other chapter in this book, the one you've just read gives you a clear indication of the innumerable ways in which Reason's various instrument, effect, and routing devices can work together. You now have practical, hands-on experience working with the entire range of Reason's included devices and a better understanding of how the features and functionality of all of these devices are both complementary and often interrelated.

As mentioned at the beginning of this chapter, the Combinator is in some ways like a miniature rack within the Reason rack. By working extensively with this device, in this chapter you have solidified and increased your knowledge of both audio and CV signal routing within Reason. These lessons can be utilized not just with the Combinator device, but also throughout your Reason songs.

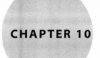

CHAPTER 10

Arranging, Mixing, and Exporting

In Chapter 2 you learned some of the basics to start working with Reason's sequencer, including important terms and concepts. In Chapters 3 through 9 you learned about Reason's instruments, effects, and other devices, and you learned about the sequencer in relation to specific devices.

In this chapter you'll combine everything you've learned so far with all of the things you need to know to arrange, mix, and export your Reason sessions. This will include the advanced features and functionality of the Reason sequencer, working with and editing Reason's different clip types, automating all of Reason's devices, and creating final mixdowns. You'll also learn some important information about utilizing ReWire to connect Reason to other digital audio programs, and we'll explore some advanced options for saving and publishing Reason song files, as well as exporting loops and complete songs.

Topics in this chapter include:

- **The Sequencer: Advanced**

- **Advanced Automation**

- **Arranging in the Sequencer**

- **Mixing in Reason**

- **Using ReWire**

- **Saving and Exporting**

The Sequencer: Advanced

Before you begin the lessons and exercises in this chapter, be sure to read "The Sequencer: Basics" in Chapter 2, where you'll find basic information on the various elements that make up the Reason sequencer and definitions of important concepts and terminology.

The Reason sequencer has undergone a major overhaul between Reason versions 3 and 4. In addition to a completely new look, there are many new sequencer features, including multiple-lane recording for MIDI performances, new pattern sequencing functionality, and both streamlined and enhanced automation functionality.

In Chapter 2 you learned the basics of working with track lanes and Reason clips, which are used to create performances with MIDI notes. Chapter 2 also contains basic information about working with automation and creating pattern device sequences.

Reason offers two views of the sequencer: Arrange and Edit. You'll use the Arrange view for arranging clips, while you can edit clips in both the Arrange and Edit views. Which view you use will depend on the type of clip you are working with and the kind of editing you wish to accomplish. In these next exercises you are going to learn how to utilize the in-depth functionality available for working with lanes and clips in both sequencer views.

Working with Lanes and Clips in the Arrange View

Three types of lanes are available on Reason tracks in the Arrange view, and each lane has its own type of clip. Here are the lane and clip types that you will work with in the Arrange view:

Note Lanes Note lanes contain Note clips and are available on all Reason instrument tracks and RPG-8 Monophonic Arpeggiator tracks. Figure 10.1 shows multiple note lanes and clips in the Arrange view. Note lanes can also be created for Matrix Pattern Sequencer tracks. Note clips are made up of MIDI notes that have been recorded by playing a MIDI keyboard, drawn in the Edit view, or created by sending MIDI information to a track from a Redrum Drum Computer, Dr. Rex Loop Player, Matrix Pattern Sequencer, or RPG-8 Monophonic Arpeggiator. You'll use Note lanes in the Arrange view to record and arrange Note clips, as well as perform some editing functions.

Figure 10.1

Note lanes in the Arrange view

Automation Lanes Automation lanes are available on all Reason tracks and contain Automation clips. You create Automation clips by adjusting Reason device parameters while recording or by drawing clips and automation breakpoints in the Arrange or Edit views. Automation clips are the only clips that can be entirely created from scratch and edited by drawing in the Arrange view. Automation lanes and clips are covered in the "Advanced Automation" section of this chapter. Figure 10.2 shows multiple Automation lanes and clips in the Arrange view.

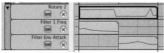

Figure 10.2
Automation lanes in the Arrange view

Pattern Select Lanes Pattern Select lanes contain Pattern clips, which are used to sequence patterns programmed into Reason's Pattern devices: the Matrix Pattern Sequencer and the Redrum Drum Computer. You create Pattern clips either by drawing with the Pencil tool or by recording pattern automation in real time. This process of creating and sequencing patterns was covered in detail in the "Creating Arrangements" section of Chapter 4 and the "Sequencing Patterns" section of Chapter 8. Figure 10.3 shows a Pattern Select lane in the Arrange view.

Figure 10.3
A Pattern Select lane with a sequence of Pattern clips

Working with Tools in the Arrange View

The tools found in the Toolbar at the top of the Reason sequencer have different functionality depending on whether you are working in the Arrange or Edit view. The following are uses for each tool in the Arrange view.

> Some of the basic uses for each tool are discussed in the section "The Sequencer Interface" in Chapter 2.

The Selection Tool

The Selection tool's functions in the Arrange window include the following:

- Selecting and moving Note, Pattern, and Automation clips.
- Selecting multiple clips on a track in order to combine, move, or delete them. Hold down the Shift key to select multiple clips with the Selection tool one at a time, or use the selection rectangle technique (see "Selection Rectangles" later in this chapter).

- Resizing clips by selecting them and then clicking and dragging the clip handles on either end.

- Selecting clips for cutting, copying, and pasting.

- Selecting banks and patterns by clicking on Pattern clips and choosing a bank and a pattern from the Pattern Select drop-down menu, located in the upper-right corner of the sequencer or the upper-left corner of each individual Pattern clip.

The Pencil Tool

Select the Pencil tool and click and drag with your mouse across any lane in the Arrange view to create a new clip.

The Pencil tool's functions in the Arrange window include the following:

- Drawing empty Note clips on Note lanes. Once a Note clip is created in the Arrange view, you can double-click the clip with the Selection tool to open the Edit view, and then draw MIDI notes with the Pencil tool.

- Drawing empty Automation clips on Automation lanes and creating automation breakpoints within Automation clips (see the "Advanced Automation" section of this chapter).

- Drawing Pattern clips on Pattern Select lanes.

The Erase Tool

The Erase tool is very simple to use:

- With the Erase tool selected, any Note, Pattern, or Automation clip you click on will be deleted.

- You can also select and delete multiple clips at once with the Erase tool by using the selection rectangle technique (see "Selection Rectangles").

The Razor Tool

The Razor tool is used to split clips. With Snap To Grid disabled you can split a clip at any place within the clip. With that option enabled, edit points are determined by the Snap To Grid drop-down menu.

> For more on Snap To Grid functionality, see the "About Snap To Grid" sidebar in the "Creating a Performance in the Edit View" section of this chapter.

Enabling Snap To Grid and choosing a value is a good way to ensure that your Razor tool edits will take place on the beat.

In the Arrange view, you can use the Razor tool to do any of the following:

- Click anywhere on a clip to split it.

- Click and drag anywhere on a clip to create a clip within a clip.

- Select multiple clips at once across tracks and lanes to split them.

- Click and drag across the top of the sequencer to split all of the clips in any section of a Reason song at once.

The Magnify Tool

The Magnify tool is used to zoom in and out in the Arrange view. In the Arrange view with the Magnify tool selected, you can do any of the following:

- Zoom in by clicking and dragging around a clip or a small section of the arrangement.

- Zoom out by clicking and dragging multiple clips and tracks or a larger area of the arrangement within a selection rectangle.

- Click any spot on the arrangement with your mouse to zoom in.

- Ctrl/Option-click with the Magnify tool to zoom out in the Arrange view.

The Hand Tool

The Hand tool is used to manually navigate in the Sequencer. Select the Hand tool and then click any clip or empty area in the Arrange view window and drag up or down, left or right to navigate to different locations in the Arrange view.

The Hand tool and the Magnify tool are complementary. See the section "Key Commands for Tools" in a moment.

Selection Rectangles

The Selection tool, the Erase tool, the Razor tool, and the Magnify tool can all be used to select multiple clips or large areas in the Arrange view by creating a "selection rectangle" encompassing multiple clips.

Any clip touched by the selection rectangle will be included in the selection.

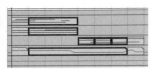

Key Commands for Tools

You can speed up your workflow in the Reason sequencer significantly by utilizing keyboard shortcuts when working with the tools. As you learned in Chapter 2, the letters Q W E R T Y can be used to select each of the tools individually, from left to right.

Because so much of the work you'll be doing with clips in both the Arrange and Edit views involves switching (toggling) between the Pencil and the Selection tools, Reason has some great keyboard shortcut functionality for this:

- With the Selection tool selected, hold down Alt/⌘ to switch to the Pencil tool.
- With the Pencil tool selected, hold down Alt/⌘ to switch to the Selection tool.

Other toggling key commands include:

- With the Erase tool selected, hold down the Alt/⌘ key to switch to the Pencil tool.
- With the Razor tool selected, hold down the Alt/⌘ to switch to the Pencil tool.
- With the Magnify tool selected, hold down the Alt/⌘ key to switch to the Hand tool.
- With the Hand tool selected, hold down the Alt/⌘ key to switch to the Magnify tool.

In order for any selected or toggled tool to be visible, your cursor must be hovering over a lane where those tools can be used.

Using Tools in the Arrange View

Follow these steps to get a look at using each tool in the Arrange view:

All of this chapter's exercises require that you set Reason's Preferences according to the instructions at the end of Chapter 2.

1. Create a New Reason song.
2. Add any Reason synthesizer.
3. Select the Pencil tool and draw an empty clip on the synthesizer's Note lane.
4. Choose the Selection tool, and then click anywhere on the clip.
5. Holding your mouse down, drag the clip to the left or right.
6. Using your mouse, move the cursor to the left or right edge of the clip, select one of the clip handles, and then click and drag to the left or right to resize the clip.
7. Choose the Razor tool and click anywhere inside the clip to split it.

You now have two separate clips that can be moved to any location in the sequencer. You can use the Razor tool to create multiple clips by clicking on different locations with your clip or by clicking and dragging across a section of any clip.

8. Select the Erase tool and click either of the clips to delete it. You can also click and drag across multiple clips and lanes and use the selection rectangle technique to delete multiple clips.

9. Select the Magnify tool and create a selection rectangle around a single clip to zoom in.

10. Select the Magnify tool and hold down the Ctrl/Option key, and then click anywhere in the Arrange view to zoom out.

You now have a clear indication of some of the ways in which Reason's tools will be used together in your Arrange view workflow.

Working with Lanes and Clips in the Edit View

The sequencer's Edit view mode is used to access more in-depth editing functionality for all of Reason's different clip types. You can access the Edit view from the Arrange view by:

- Clicking the Edit view button in the upper-left corner of the sequencer
- Double-clicking any Note clip or Pattern clip
- Using the Shift+Tab key command to toggle between the Arrange and Edit views
- Pressing Ctrl/⌘+E

In the Edit view, each track in a Reason song can be accessed one at a time for editing by selecting it in the track list. Selecting different types of tracks will show a different set of available lanes, each with specific functionality. The following are the different lanes available in the Edit view and their uses:

Overview Lane The Overview lane (Figure 10.4) will be visible for all instrument tracks and the RPG-8 Monophonic Arpeggiator. You can also create an Overview lane for the Matrix Pattern Sequencer with the device's Copy Pattern To Track functionality. The Overview lane can be used for creating and moving clips, much like the Note lanes in the Arrange view.

Figure 10.4

The Overview lane

Note Edit Lane The Note Edit lane is where you'll do all of your creating and editing of specific MIDI note events. Note Edit lanes only exist on tracks for Reason's instrument devices, the RPG-8 and the Matrix Pattern Sequencer. If your track has clips on more than one Note lane, only the Note lane currently selected in the track list will be visible in the

Edit view. The Note Edit lane will contain different views for different types of Reason devices. Figure 10.5 shows the Note Edit lane for a Reason synth, NN-19 or NN-XT sampler, the RPG-8, or Matrix Pattern Sequencer, which contains a keyboard display along the left side of the lane.

Figure 10.5

The Note Edit lane for a Reason synth, sampler, RPG-8, or Matrix device

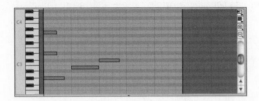

Figure 10.6 shows the Note Edit lane view for a Redrum Drum Computer, which contains a list of the individual drum samples currently loaded in any selected Redrum.

Figure 10.6

The Note Edit lane for a Redrum Drum Computer

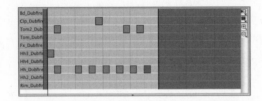

Figure 10.7 shows the Note Edit lane for a Dr. Rex Loop Player, which contains a list of the individual slices that make up the device's currently loaded REX loop.

Figure 10.7

The Note Edit lane for a Dr. Rex Loop Player

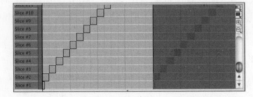

You can switch between these views for any Reason device by clicking the Change Note Edit Mode button at the top right of the Note Edit lane and choosing a different mode from the drop-down menu.

Velocity Lane The Velocity lane (Figure 10.8) is visible for any Reason device with a Note Edit lane. On this lane you can edit velocity values for every note event on the Note Edit lane.

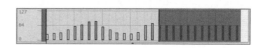

Figure 10.8

The Velocity lane

Performance Controller Automation Lanes Performance Controller Automation lanes (Figure 10.9) are used to create and edit the performance automation parameters contained within Note clips in the Arrange view. Performance Controller automation will be covered in the "Advanced Automation" section of this chapter.

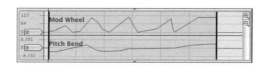

Figure 10.9

Performance Controller Automation lanes

You can show and hide Performance Controller lanes by using the Note Lane Performance Parameter Automation pull-down menu in the upper-right corner of the Note Edit lane.

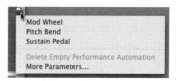

Pattern Select Lanes Pattern Select lanes can be used to sequence pattern devices in the Edit view mode, exactly as they can be used in the Arrange mode. Figure 10.10 shows a Pattern Select lane.

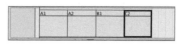

Figure 10.10

Pattern Select Lane

Track Parameter Automation Lanes Track Parameter Automation lanes (Figure 10.11) are found at the bottom of the Edit view and are the equivalent of the automation lanes in the Arrange view. You can also create Automation lanes in the Edit view using the Automation drop-down menu. For tracks created for effects devices, only Automation lanes will be visible in the Edit view. Track Parameter automation will be covered in the "Advanced Automation" section of this chapter.

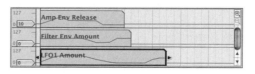

Figure 10.11

Track Parameter Automation lanes

If your Track Parameter Automation lanes are not visible when you switch from Arrange to Edit view, or if you create them in the Edit view, move your cursor to the divider at the bottom of the Edit view, and then click and drag upward with your mouse.

> You can select multiple clips at once in the Edit view in order to move, delete, or access functionality from the clip Edit or context menus. However, only one clip at a time can be edited in the Edit view using the Selection, Pencil, Erase, or Razor tools.

Resizing the Edit View

By default, any time you switch to the Edit view for a Reason instrument track, your Overview, Note Edit, and Velocity lanes should all be visible. If any of these lanes are not visible, drag the divider at top of the sequencer to increase the sequencer view. If any or all of your Automation lanes or Pattern Select lanes are not visible, you can either resize the entire sequencer window by clicking and dragging the divider at the top of the sequencer or resize the Performance Controller Automation and the Track Parameter Automation sections by clicking and dragging at the top of each section.

When working with multiple tracks in the Edit view, you may also find it helpful to detach the sequencer, moving it to its own window. You can detach the sequencer at any time by selecting Window → Detach Sequencer Window from the menu bar or by clicking the Detach Sequencer button in the top-right corner of the Reason rack.

Working with Tools in the Edit View

The tools on the Reason sequencer Toolbar have similar but different functionality when working in the Edit view.

The Selection Tool in the Edit View

In the Edit view the Selection tool has these uses:

- Selecting and moving entire clips or multiple clips in any visible lane
- Selecting and moving individual notes in the Note Edit lane
- Selecting and moving multiple notes in the Note Edit lane
- Adjusting individual breakpoints in Automation clips
- Selecting and moving multiple breakpoints in Automation clips

The Pencil Tool

In the Edit view the Pencil tool has these uses:

- Drawing new clips by clicking and dragging in any visible lane
- Drawing notes in the Note Edit lane

- Editing velocity values in the Velocity lane
- Drawing Automation clips and breakpoints on Automation lanes

The Erase Tool

In the Edit view the Erase tool has these uses:

- Erasing complete clips in any lane
- Erasing single or multiple MIDI notes in the Note Edit lane or the Velocity lane
- Erasing single or multiple automation breakpoints in an Automation clip

The Razor Tool in the Edit View

In the Edit view the Razor tool has these uses:

- Splitting Note clips by clicking anywhere in the Overview, Note, Velocity, Pattern, or Note Lane Performance Parameter Automation lanes. This will split the clip across all lanes, except Automation lanes, which are independent.
- Creating multiple clips by clicking and dragging anywhere in the Overview, Note, Velocity, Pattern, or Note Lane Performance Parameter Automation lanes. This will also affect the clip across all lanes, except Automation lanes.
- Splitting Automation clips by clicking inside any Automation clip.
- Creating multiple Automation.

The Magnify Tool

In the Edit view the Magnify tool has these uses:

- Zooming horizontally on the Overview, Velocity, Pattern Select, and Automation lanes
- Zooming horizontally and vertically on the Note Edit lane

To resize the Overview, Velocity, Pattern Select, and Automation lanes vertically in the Edit view, you can click and drag up or down on the dividers between lanes. You can resize the Note Edit lane by selecting the divider at the bottom and dragging downward.

The Hand Tool

In the Edit view the Hand tool has these uses:

- Dragging horizontally (left or right) on the Overview, Velocity, Pattern Select, and Automation lanes to view different sections of an arrangement
- Dragging horizontally and vertically on the Note Edit lane to view a different selection of clips or MIDI notes

Creating a Performance in the Edit View

Using the Toolbar you can create a MIDI performance entirely from scratch in the Edit view. Follow these steps to create a Note clip in the Edit view:

1. Create a new Reason song.

2. Create any Reason synth or sampler instrument and load any patch.

3. Switch to the Edit view by using the Shift+Tab key command or by clicking the Switch To Edit View mode button.

4. Make sure the new instrument's track is selected in the track list.

5. Select the Pencil tool.

6. Click and drag with the Pencil tool in the Overview, Note, or Velocity lane to create a new clip.

7. Use the Pencil tool to draw MIDI note events in the new clip.

If you want to preview notes before you add them to a clip, move your cursor to the keyboard display on the left side of the Note Edit lane. As it moves over the keyboard display, the cursor becomes a speaker icon and you can click any note to hear it.

You can use the previous steps to create multiple clips on one or more instrument device tracks in the Edit view.

Create a second clip by selecting the Pencil tool; clicking any empty space on the Overview, Note Edit, or Velocity lanes; and drawing a new empty clip. Again, use the Pencil tool to draw MIDI notes in the clip.

ABOUT SNAP TO GRID

In Chapter 2 the section "The Sequencer Interface" covered some of the functionality accessed by activating the Snap To Grid button and choosing a value from the Snap To Grid value menu.

Enabling Snap To Grid and choosing a value affects many aspects of your Reason song when working in both the Arrange and Edit views.

The exercise you've just performed, "Creating a Performance in the Edit View," demonstrates this very well. When you create a new clip with the Pencil tool, the default Snap To Grid value is one bar. This means you can use the Pencil tool to create clips as large as you want in one-bar increments with a minimum size of one bar. If you'd like more control over the size of the clips you draw, you can use the Snap To Grid value drop-down menu to select a smaller value before you begin drawing your clip.

When you begin drawing MIDI notes inside the clip, the Snap To Grid default value changes to 1/16 note. You can change this setting by using the Snap To Grid value drop-down menu to select a new (higher or lower) value for drawing MIDI notes before you begin drawing your clip. To do this, click in the Velocity lane or to the left of the Keyboard display in the Note Edit lane and choose a new value from the drop-down menu.

The following sequencer functions, among others, are also affected by Snap To Grid settings:

- Where clips can be moved around in the sequencer. Clips will always "snap" to the closest value as set by the Snap To Grid value drop-down. For example, if the setting is Bar, when you move clips in either view they will always snap to the closest bar.

- How clips are resized in the sequencer. With Snap To Grid enabled, clips can only be resized in increments equal to Snap To Grid value.

- How the Left, Right, and Play Position locators and the End marker can be moved.

When you are new to working in Reason 4, you should, as a rule, select relatively low Snap To Grid values. As you progress with Reason 4, you may find various situations where both higher and lower Snap To Grid values will be helpful, depending on how precise your editing and note creation need to be.

Editing Note Clips

The Edit view's Note Edit lane gives you very precise control over editing MIDI notes that trigger your Reason instruments. Follow these steps to edit any Note clip:

1. Open any Reason song with multiple clips, or create multiple clips on a single Reason instrument track using the methods described in the previous exercise.

2. Choose the Selection tool.

3. Click any clip once to select it. The clip will be outlined and the resizing arrows will be visible on both ends of the clip. In this state you can move or resize the clip in the Overview lane, but the individual MIDI notes and note velocities will be grayed out and not accessible for editing.

4. Clicking the clip a second time will give you access to the MIDI notes in the Note Edit lane and velocity values in the Velocity lane.

5. If necessary, zoom in on the clip using the Magnify tool, or use the Zoom buttons in the upper-left corner of the Note Edit lane and the bottom left of the sequencer.

6. Use the Selection tool to select and move single or multiple notes around or to lengthen or shorten notes by clicking and dragging the note handle on the right side of any selected MIDI note.

7. Use a selection rectangle to select multiple MIDI notes to move, lengthen, or shorten.

You can also delete individual or multiple notes by selecting them and pressing the Delete key.

8. Select the Pencil tool to draw new MIDI notes or to adjust the velocity of individual notes.

9. Select the Erase tool to erase individual notes by clicking them or use the selection rectangle method to delete multiple notes at once.

This exercise has given you a look at the note editing options that are available in Reason's Edit view. Taking the time to develop your note editing skills will greatly enhance your ability to create music by working with clips and tracks for all of Reason's instruments.

Velocity Editing

As you've seen, velocity values for note events are edited with the Pencil tool and the basic process is simple. Every MIDI note in a clip has a corresponding Velocity bar in the Velocity lane.

Click on or above any Velocity bar in the Velocity lane and drag up or down to raise or lower the velocity of the corresponding event.

When multiple MIDI events start at the same time, such as the notes of a chord or the different pieces of a drum kit in a drum performance, you can edit each MIDI event's velocity individually by selecting a specific individual note in the Note Edit lane with the Selection tool and then pressing and holding down the Shift key before editing the velocity value with the Pencil tool.

Because editing the individual velocities of simultaneous MIDI notes requires switching between the Selection and Pencil tools, it's a great opportunity to practice using the Ctrl/⌘ key to switch between the two.

The Line Tool

You can quickly create rising or decaying velocities across an entire clip by using the Line tool. Access the Line tool by selecting the Pencil tool and then Ctrl/Option-dragging across the Velocity lane.

Velocity Editing with the Tool Window

Reason 4's new Tool window also contains velocity editing options. If the Tool window is not currently visible, press the F8 key or choose File → Window → Show Tool Window.

Edit the velocity values of MIDI notes in a clip by selecting a single note or multiple notes and using one of the fields in the Note Velocity section to adjust velocities. Figure 10.12 shows the Note Velocity section of the Tool window's Tools tab.

Figure 10.12

Note Velocity options in the Tool window

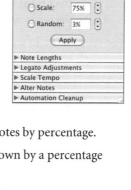

To adjust an option, select it, type a value, and click the Apply button at the bottom of the Note Velocity section, or use the arrows on the right to raise and lower values and then click the Apply button.

- Use the Add option to add or subtract the same amount to or from the selected MIDI notes.

- Use the Fixed option to adjust all selected MIDI notes to a uniform velocity.

- Use the Scale option to reduce the velocity of selected MIDI notes by percentage.

- Use the Random option to adjust velocities randomly up or down by a percentage value.

> You can access this same functionality in the Arrange view by selecting entire clips, choosing a field, setting a value, and clicking the Apply button.

The Clip Edit and Context Menus

You can access much of the functionality you'll use to work with clips in Reason 4 from the Edit menu or a clip's context menu. Select any clip or multiple clips in either the Arrange or Edit mode and choose the Edit menu on the menu bar or right/Ctrl-click to view the clip's context menu, shown in Figure 10.13.

A clip's Edit menu and its context menu will both offer the same options, which will depend on the type of clip you have selected (Pattern, Automation, or Notes).

In some cases you can also use the clip Edit and context menu on individual notes and events within clips. If an option is unavailable for the selected clip(s) or event(s), it will remain grayed out on the clip's Edit menu and context menus.

Figure 10.13

The context menu for a clip

These functions are visible but will not be available from the clip Edit and context menus:

- Duplicate
- Commit To Groove
- New Note Lane
- Create Pattern Lane
- Parameter Automation
- Merge Note Lanes on Tracks

See the section titled "The Track List Edit/Context Menu" later in this chapter for descriptions of these functions.

The following functions are available from the clip Edit and context menus:

Cut Choosing Cut will remove an entire selected Note, Pattern, or Automation clip or multiple clips from a track. It can also be used to remove individual MIDI notes and automation breakpoints from a clip. Cut clips and MIDI events can be pasted to new locations using the Paste function. You can also perform this function by pressing Ctrl/⌘+X.

Figure 10.14

Setting the left and right locators

Copy Choosing Copy will copy an entire selected Note, Pattern, or Automation clip; multiple clips; individual automation breakpoints; or MIDI notes. Copied clips and MIDI events can be duplicated in new locations using the Paste function. You can also perform this function by pressing Ctrl/⌘+C.

Paste Selecting Paste will paste any copied or cut Note, Pattern, or Automation clip; multiple clips; individual automation breakpoints; or MIDI notes. You can also perform this function by pressing Ctrl/⌘+V.

Delete Choosing Delete will permanently remove any selected Note, Pattern, or Automation clips from your Reason song. It can also be used to remove individual or multiple MIDI notes and events from a clip. If you accidentally delete clips or MIDI events, you can get them back by choosing Edit → Undo or by pressing Ctrl/⌘+Z.

Select All In the Arrange view this option selects all of the clips in the Reason song. In the Edit view this option selects all of the clips on a track or, if a single MIDI note or multiple notes are selected, all of the MIDI notes in the currently selected clip. You can also perform this function by pressing Ctrl/⌘+A.

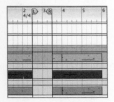

Figure 10.15

Bars inserted between the left and right locators

Insert Bars Between Locators The Insert Bars Between Locators function creates empty space in the arrangement between the current location of the left and right locators. If the left and right locators are placed inside any clips, the clips will be split. Figures 10.14 and 10.15 show before and after images of this process.

Remove Bars Between Locators The opposite of the Insert Bars Between Locators function, choosing Remove Bars Between Locators removes any events currently residing between the left and right locators. This function will split and contract any clips that start or end outside of the current placement of the left and right locators. Any MIDI notes or automation data contained in the deleted sections of clips will be deleted as well.

Get Groove From Clips Use this function to extract Groove information from any Note clip. This option automatically creates a User groove in the Tool window's Groove tab. For details on editing and saving extracted grooves, see the section titled "The ReGroove Mixer" in Chapter 8.

Join Clips Choosing Join Clips combines any selected multiple clips on a single lane into one clip. Clips cannot be joined across lanes or tracks. You can also perform this function by pressing Ctrl/⌘+J.

Mute Clips (M) Choosing this function mutes any selected clip or clips. Selecting any muted clips will change this option to Unmute Clips. You can also mute or unmute clips by selecting them and pressing the M key.

Crop Events To Clips Choosing this function deletes any note or automation events that exist outside of a clip. In the Arrange view events that exist outside of a clip will not be visible. You can see events that exist outside of clips in the Edit view.

Add Labels To Clips Select any clip or multiple clips and choose this option to give names to individual clips.

Clip Color Choose from any of the included colors. This option is useful for organizing Reason songs. You can easily differentiate between different types of instruments or sections of an arrangement by assigning different colors to clips or tracks.

Quantize Notes Choosing this function quantizes any selected clip in the Arrange view in conjunction with the Quantize settings in the Tool window's Tools tab. In the Edit view you can quantize a selected clip in the Overview lane or a selected note or group of notes in the Note lane. See the "Note Quantization in the Tool Window" section later in this chapter.

Create and Edit Note Clips in the Arrange and Edit Views

You've had a look at working independently in both the Arrange and Edit views. Ultimately your workflow in Reason will involve a combination of the two views. Using the information covered in the previous sections, follow these steps to create and edit clips using both the Arrange and the Edit views, speeding up your workflow using tool selection key commands:

1. Create a new Reason song.
2. Create a Thor Polysonic Synthesizer.

3. By default the Selection tool is selected when you create a new Reason song. Hold down the Ctrl/⌘ key to switch to the Pencil tool to draw a Note clip on the Thor track's Note lane.

4. Release the Ctrl/⌘ key to return to the Selection tool.

5. Double-click the new clip with the Selection tool to open the clip in Edit view.

6. Hold down Ctrl/⌘ to switch to the Pencil tool to draw individual notes in the Edit view's Note lane. For a better view of the available notes in the Note lane, detach the sequencer (or click and drag at the top of the sequencer to increase the vertical view).

> As you learned in the "About Snap To Grid" sidebar, by default the Note lane in the Edit view will have a Snap To Grid value of 1/16 note. You can change the Snap To Grid value at any time by choosing a new value from the Snap To Grid Value menu.

Working with the Track List

As you saw in Chapter 2, the track list contains its own functionality. Tracks in track list can contain any of the following lanes:

Note Lanes Used for recording and editing performances

Automation Lanes Used for recording, manually creating, or editing automation of Reason devices

Pattern Select Lanes Used for sequencing patterns with Reason's pattern devices, the Redrum and the Matrix

In the Arrange view all lanes will be visible at all times.

Creating New Tracks

A new track will be automatically created in the track list for any Reason instrument, the Matrix Pattern Sequencer, and the RPG-8 Arpeggiator.

You can also create tracks for other reason devices, such as effects and mixers by selecting the device in the Reason rack and choosing Edit → Create Track For (device name) or by right/Ctrl-clicking any blank spot on the device's interface and choosing Create Track For (device name) from the context menu.

Creating New Lanes

You can create new Note lanes in the track list for any track in either the Arrange or Edit view in any of the following ways:

- By selecting a track in the track list and clicking the New Note Lane button at the top of the track list

- By selecting a track and choosing Edit → New Note Lane from the main menu

- By right/Ctrl-clicking any track on the track list and choosing New Note Lane from the context menu

> You can select multiple tracks in the track list by holding down the Shift key. This can be useful, for example, if you want to create new Note lanes on multiple tracks at once.

- New Automation lanes can be created in any of the following ways:

- By recording automation

- By selecting a parameter from the Track Parameter Automation list or Track Parameter Dialog window (covered in the "Advanced Automation" section of this chapter)

New Pattern Select lanes can be created by recording pattern automation on a Matrix or Redrum or by clicking the Create Pattern Lane button at the top of the sequencer.

The Transport Panel Track

The Transport panel track is created automatically with every new Reason song and will always be located at the top of the track list. Tempo and Time Signature automation lanes can be created for the Transport panel.

Track View Options

You have some options for changing the look and order of tracks on the track list:

- You can rearrange tracks (except the Transport panel track) in the track list by selecting a track's handle located on the far-left side of the track and dragging it up or down in the list.

- You can rename a track by clicking the track name in the upper-left corner and typing a new name.

- You can change the color of the track handle and the default color of any newly created clips by using the Track Color option on the track Edit and context menu (discussed in a moment).

- You can minimize a track by clicking the track handle arrow in the upper-left corner.

- You can minimize all of the tracks in the track list at once by Alt/Option-clicking any track handle arrow. Figure 10.16 shows minimized tracks in the track list.

Figure 10.16

Minimized tracks in the track list

- Automation lanes can also be minimized by clicking the arrow in the upper-left corner of the top Automation lane on any track.

The Track List Edit/Context Menu

The track Edit and context menus are similar to the clip Edit and context menus and contain some of the same functionality. As with the clip's Edit and context menus, certain options will be grayed out, depending on the kind of track you select. Figure 10.17 shows the track context menu.

Figure 10.17

The context menu for a track

Cut Track And Device Selecting this option will cut the track and its associated Reason device and store it in the Clipboard. You can then use the Paste function to return it to the session in a different location on the Track list. The Ctrl/⌘+X key command performs the same function.

Copy Track And Device This option copies both the track and the associated Reason device to the Clipboard. You can then use the Paste function to create a copy of the device and track in the session. This function can also be performed using the Ctrl/⌘+C key command.

Paste Use this to paste any cut or copied track and associated device. Pasted devices will have to be manually routed to the song's Mixer 14:2 or other devices. This function can also be performed using the Ctrl/⌘+V key command.

> Select multiple devices to cut, copy, or paste by holding down the Shift key and selecting each track on the track list.

Delete Track And Device Permanently deletes the selected track and associated Reason device from the Reason song.

Delete Tracks Deletes the track in the Track list but not the device. You can create a new track for it by selecting Edit → Create New Track For (device name) from the main menu or by right/Ctrl-clicking any blank area on the device and choosing New Track For (device name) from the context menu.

Select All Selects all tracks in the track list. This function can also be performed using the Ctrl/⌘+A key command.

Duplicate Tracks And Devices Duplicates any selected tracks and devices. The newly created duplicate devices must be manually routed to the Reason song's Mixer 14:2. You can also duplicate a track and device by holding down the Ctrl/Option key and selecting the track handle and moving the track to a new location in the track list. You can also perform this function by pressing Ctrl/⌘+D.

Insert Bars Between Locators Serves the same function it does in the clip context menu, creating an empty space on all tracks in between the left and right locators in the sequencer.

Remove Bars Between Locators Also serves the same function as in the clip context menu, deleting any empty space, clips, or sections of clips in between the left and right locators in the sequencer.

Convert Pattern Track To Notes Available only when a Pattern Device track is selected. Choosing this option creates a new Note lane and converts all patterns on the track to MIDI notes. The Pattern lane is then disabled. See the "Converting Pattern Device Tracks to Notes" section of this chapter for more details.

Commit To Groove Commits all clips on a track to the currently assigned ReGroove mixer settings. See the section titled "The ReGroove Mixer" in Chapter 8.

Parameter Automation Opens the Track Parameter Automation dialog window. See the "Advanced Automation" section of this chapter for details on the Track Parameter Automation dialog.

New Note Lane Creates a new Note lane for any Reason instrument track.

Create Pattern Lane Creates a new Pattern lane for any Reason pattern device.

Merge Note Lanes On Tracks Merges all of the Note lanes on any track into a single Note lane, deleting any unused lanes that result.

Track Color Can be used to change the color of the track's handle, which is useful for creating groups of similar tracks or identifying specific track types quickly. Changing the track color also changes the default color of any new clips created on the track. Regardless of the track's default clip color, you can manually change the color of any clip at any time by using the clip context menu.

Crop Events To Clips This option becomes visible when you have Note clips and Automation clips that contain MIDI notes and Automation breakpoints outside of the clips. Using the Crops Events To Clip option deletes any information that exists outside of clips on your track.

Quantize Notes Quantizes all of the notes on the selected track to the current settings in the Tool window's Quantize section.

Advanced Automation

In Chapter 2 you learned some of the basic information you need in order to create automation with Reason's instruments and effects. Specific automation techniques for various Reason devices have also been touched on throughout this book, including the automation functionality used to create pattern sequences with the Redrum Drum Computer (Chapter 3) and the Matrix Pattern Sequencer (Chapter 8).

As you've already seen, the process of recording automation by adjusting knobs, sliders, and other parameters while Reason is recording is very easy to understand and implement. Just make sure a track's Record Enable Parameter Automation button is active, click the Record button on the Transport panel, and make adjustments to automation capable parameters.

In this section you're going to learn about some of Reason's more advanced automation options and functionality.

Creating Automation Lanes in the Sequencer

Working in either the Arrange or the Edit view, you can see many of the parameters available for automation by clicking the Track Parameter Automation button at the top of the sequencer and viewing the list shown in Figure 10.18.

Selecting any parameter on the list will automatically create a new Automation lane, where you can draw and edit Automation clips. You can create as many automation lanes as you like, one each for any available parameter.

Some devices will have more parameters available that are not on the list. You can view these parameters by selecting More Parameters from the bottom of the list to open the Track Parameter Automation dialog (Figure 10.19).

You can create Automation lanes for any parameters in the Track Parameter Automation dialog by putting a check mark in any box.

> You can also open the Track Parameter dialog at any time by selecting a track and choosing Parameter Automation from the Edit menu or context menu.

Figure 10.18

The Track Parameter Automation list

Figure 10.19

The Track Parameter Automation dialog

Drawing Automation in the Arrange View

Aside from recording parameter moves in real time on Reason devices, another method for creating automation is to use the Pencil tool to draw Automation clips and breakpoints. You can do this in both the Arrange and Edit views.

Automation is created by drawing *breakpoints*. Breakpoints are the dots you'll see inside of Automation clips, whether you've recorded automation or drawn it manually. Each 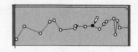 breakpoint represents a specific value on the parameter that's being automated. By creating multiple breakpoints, you set the values to change over time as the clip progresses from breakpoint to breakpoint.

Follow these steps to create automation on a Reason synthesizer in the Arrange view:

1. Create a new Reason song.

2. Create a SubTractor synth.

3. Select Filter Freq from the Track Parameter Automation menu. A new Automation lane will be created in the sequencer.

4. Select the Pencil tool.

5. Draw a four-bar empty clip in the new Automation lane.

6. Select the Selection tool and double-click the clip to open it in the Arrange view.

Unlike double-clicking Note clips or Pattern clips, double-clicking an Automation clip will not open the Edit view. Instead the clip will open in its lane in the Arrange view, allowing you to create and edit automation there. You can use the Magnify tool or the sequencer's Zoom functionality to zoom in on the clip for more precise breakpoint creation. All of the Arrange view navigation techniques, tools, and key commands for zooming in and out work for individual Automation lanes in the Arrange view as well.

7. Select the Pencil tool and draw automation in the clip by clicking and dragging up and down across the clip.

8. Click any lane other than the current Automation lane or press the Enter/Return key to return to the regular Arrange view.

You can see your automation in action by clicking the Play or Record button on the Transport panel. Just as it would with recorded automation, a green line will appear around the automated parameter (which in this case is the Sub-Tractor's Filter 1 frequency slider).

You can now work with your Automation clip exactly as you would with any Note or Pattern clip, cutting, copying, pasting, and duplicating the clip within the Arrange or Edit view.

Whether you choose to create automation before or after recording a performance is up to you. If you do choose to create automation first, you can still create or record Note clips on the SubTractor track as you would without the automation present.

You can also turn off individual Automation clips by muting them. To mute an Automation clip, select it in the sequencer and press the letter M or choose Mute Clips from the clip Edit or context menu.

Drawing Automation in the Edit View

Drawing automation in the Edit view is essentially the same process as drawing automation in the Arrange view:

1. Select the track for the Reason devices you'd like to automate.

2. Choose any parameter from the Track Parameter Automation list to create an Automation lane. The new lane will appear at the bottom of the Edit window.

3. Use the Pencil tool to draw an empty Automation clip.

4. Use the Pencil tool to draw automation breakpoints. Unlike drawing automation in the Arrange view, you won't have to select the clip first with the Selection tool.

Editing Automation

You can edit automation in both the Arrange and Edit views by any of the following methods:

- Choosing the Selection tool and moving individual or multiple automation breakpoints. You can select multiple breakpoints by using the selection rectangle method or by using the keyboard shortcut Ctrl/⌘+A to select all of the breakpoints in a clip.

- Adding more breakpoints or redrawing the automation with the Pencil tool.

- Using the Erase tool to erase individual or multiple breakpoints.

- Using the Razor tool to split clips and create multiple clips.

Automation Cleanup

The Tool window's Tools tab has a feature called Automation Cleanup that you can use to create smoother automation by eliminating unnecessary breakpoints. Automation Cleanup features four amounts to choose from: Minimum, Normal, Heavy, and Maximum. Figure 10.20 shows the Automation Cleanup section in the Tool window.

Figure 10.20

The Automation Cleanup section in the Tool window

To use Automation Cleanup, follow these steps:

1. Choose the Selection tool and select a minimized clip in the Arrange or Edit views or multiple breakpoints inside a clip.

2. Choose an amount from the Amount menu.

3. Click the Apply button to clean up the selected automation.

Different Types of Automation

Different parameters will present you with different types of automation. The process of creating clips and drawing automation breakpoints will be the same; however, the types of breakpoints you can create will vary.

Switches such as the Malstrom's Mod Wheel Target automation or simple On/Off buttons for oscillators and filters will have a limited number of available breakpoints.

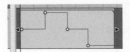

Automation for parameters with bipolar numeric values such as a panning knob from –64 to 63 and parameters with positive values from 0 to 127 can be drawn as curves, as you saw in the previous exercise.

Performance Controller Automation

Performance Controller Automation is included by default in Note clips in the Note lane. When you create automation with performance controllers (these include the Pitch Wheel, Mod Wheel and, where available, Aftertouch, Sustain, Breath, and Expression), this automation will be visible within the Note clip and will be copied and pasted along with note and velocity information when you copy and paste Note clips between tracks and Note lanes. Figure 10.21 shows a Note clip with Mod Wheel and Pitch Bend Wheel automation.

You can edit Performance Controller Automation in the Edit view by clicking the Note Lane Performance Parameter Automation button on the upper-left corner of the Note Edit lane and choosing a parameter to create a separate lane.

Separate Automation lanes can be created for Performance Controller Automation in the Arrange view by selecting the More Parameters option from the bottom of the Track Parameter Automation list.

Figure 10.21

A Note clip with Performance Controller Automation

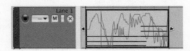

Automation As Performance Controller

You also have the option to create all automation on Note lanes as part of Note clips. This allows you move automated clips between different locations in your arrangement and even different device tracks without having to copy or re-create your individual Automation lanes.

To do this, click the Automation As Performance Controller button on the Transport panel.

You can do the same thing in the Edit view by selecting the Note Lane Performance Parameter Automation button and choosing More Parameters from the bottom of the

drop-down menu. This opens the Note Lane Performance Parameter Automation window shown in Figure 10.22.

Figure 10.22

The Note Lane Performance Parameter Automation window

Putting a check mark next to any parameter will create a Performance Controller Automation lane for the parameter. In the Edit view you can create and edit automation clips as you would with any Automation lane. When you view the clip in the Arrange mode, you'll see that the automation has been created as a part of the clip.

Arranging in the Sequencer

Up until this point we've been working mostly with individual clips. Now let's take a look at some of the options available for creating complete songs and arrangements.

Cutting, Copying, and Pasting Clips

In the previous sections you've seen some of the options for cutting, copying, and pasting clips via the clip Edit and context menus. You can also use these key commands:

Cut Ctrl/⌘+X

Copy Ctrl/⌘+C

Paste Ctrl/⌘+V

You can also duplicate a clip to a new location by selecting the clip and Ctrl/Option-dragging.

Any single clip or multiple clips can be selected with the Selection tool, and then cut or copied and then pasted in the sequencer. You can select multiple clips at once by holding down the Shift key and selecting the desired clips or by using the selection rectangle method.

When you select and cut or copy a single clip, the Play Position locator moves to the end of the clip.

Use one of the Edit or context menu paste options or press Ctrl/⌘+V to paste the clip starting at the Play Position locator's current location.

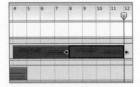

The Play Position locator will then move to the end of the newly pasted clip.

Selecting and then cutting or copying multiple clips will move the Play Position locator to the end of the last selected clip.

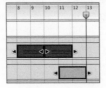

Using the Paste functionality, you can then paste all of the cut or copied clips in the sequencer, starting at the Play Position locator's current location.

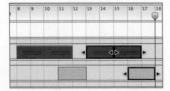

Joining Clips

Any two or more clips in the same lane can be selected and joined. Choose the Selection tool and either use a selection rectangle or Shift-click multiple clips.

Then choose Join Clips from the clip Edit or context menu. You can press Ctrl/⌘/+J to join clips.

Moving Clips between Tracks and Lanes

Clips can easily be moved between tracks and lanes. Any Note clips can be moved to any Note lane for any instrument. This means, for example, that you could easily create a clip or entire track for a Reason synthesizer, and then select and drag it on to an NN-XT or NN-19 track to trigger that device instead.

You can't cut or copy and then paste clips between different tracks and lanes, but you can duplicate them by Ctrl-/Option-dragging from one track or lane to another, thereby triggering both devices at once.

Alien Clips

A clip that has been moved to a track where it has no function is called an *alien* clip. For example, try moving a Pattern clip on to a Note lane or a Note clip onto an Automation lane. The result will look like this:

Some Automation clips can be moved between Automation lanes, provided they are of similar types of automation. If, for example, you tried to move a clip that's being used to automate an On/Off switch to a lane containing panning automation, it would be displayed as an alien clip and have no effect on the parameter.

The Inspector Bar (Position and Length)

Select any clip in the Arrange or Edit view and you'll see its position and length represented in the Inspector bar at the top of the sequencer.

As you manually move or resize clips with the Selection tool, you'll see the values displayed in the Inspector bar change. You can also click and drag up and down, or type a new numeric value in any field in either the Position or Length inspector to move or resize clips.

When you select multiple clips on different tracks, you'll see an equal sign appear next to the Clip Position locator field (Figure 10.23). This is the Match Values symbol and can be used to align and uniformly resize clips in the sequencer.

Clicking the Match Values button next to the Position inspector will align any selected clips on any tracks to the first selected clip on the track that's currently highest on the track list. Clicking the Match Values button next to the Length inspector will resize all selected clips to match the first clip on the top selected track on the track list. Figures 10.23 and 10.24 show the Position and Length Match Values buttons in action.

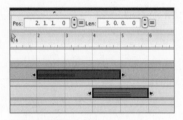

Figure 10.23

Multiple clips selected in the Arrange view

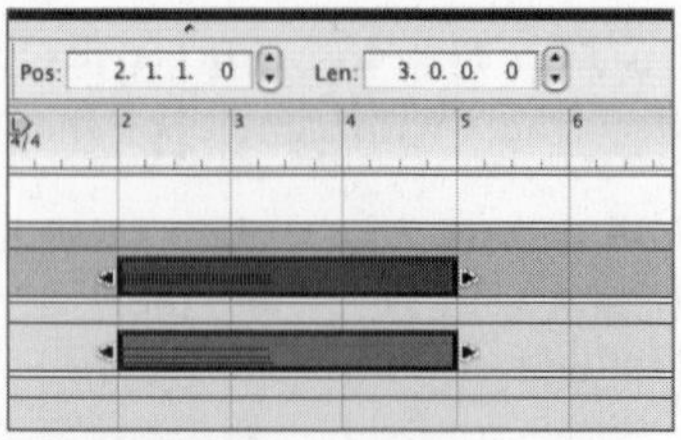

Figure 10.24

The same clips aligned and resized by clicking both of the Match Values buttons in the Arrange view

If you select multiple clips on the same track, they'll be aligned to the earliest clip on the track.

Recording Options with Instrument Tracks

The basic information about recording Reason's instrument devices is covered in "The Sequencer: Basics" section of Chapter 2 and in Chapters 3 through 6 on the individual instrument devices.

Whether you are creating a single loop or an entire track from start to finish, Note lanes offer some excellent features for creating instrument tracks.

Alternative Take Recording

Reason's track, clip, and lane functionality gives you some extra choices for creating complete recordings. Follow these steps to try out Alternative Take recording:

1. Create a new Reason Synth or Sampler instrument.
2. Select the instrument's track in the track list to make sure the track has Master Keyboard Input.
3. Click the Record button on the Transport panel to begin recording.
4. Play a performance using your MIDI keyboard.

5. Click the New Alternative Take button on the Transport panel to mute the first take and create a new Note lane.

6. Use the Rewind button on the Transport panel.

7. Click the Record button to begin recording a new performance.

Using these steps, you can create as many different takes of a performance as you want. After you've settled on a specific performance, delete any unwanted takes by clicking the Delete Note Lane button (the X with a circle) on the right side of each Note lane.

Overdub Recording

Overdub recording is similar to Alternative take recording, but instead of muting the previous take, both your new and previous performances will be heard simultaneously. Follow these steps to use Reason's overdub functionality:

1. Create a new Reason Synth or Sampler instrument.

2. Select the instrument's track in the track list to make sure the track has Master Keyboard Input.

3. Click the Record button on the Transport panel to begin recording.

4. Play a performance using your MIDI keyboard.

5. Click the New Overdub button on the Transport panel to create a new Note lane.

6. Return the Play Position locator to the beginning of the song.

7. Click Record to begin recording a new performance on top of the original.

This method is particularly useful when working with a sampler device or Redrum to create beats by recording one drum at a time.

Note Quantization in the Tool Window

Quantization is used to take a performance or sequence of MIDI notes and adjust them in relation to the tempo settings of a Reason song. The most frequent use of quantization is to align imperfectly played notes in a performance.

In Chapter 2 you learned about the Quantize During Recording feature on the Transport panel. Because this functionality creates pre-quantized clips without the possibility of undoing any unwanted quantization, you may prefer to apply quantization after recording.

The Tool window's Quantize section (Figure 10.25) can be used to quantize entire clips and individual or multiple notes after recording.

Figure 10.25

Quantization options in the Tool window

To quantize all of the notes contained in a Note clip:

1. Use the Selection tool to select the clip in the Arrange view or in the Edit view's Overview lane.

2. Choose a quantization value from the Value drop-down menu.

3. Choose a percentage amount from the Amount drop-down. This option can be used to avoid quantization that sounds too perfect or mechanical by moving notes close to the selected quantization value by percentages.

4. Create randomness by clicking the up and down arrows to set a value for slightly or greatly randomizing quantization. This can also be used to avoid an overly mechanical sounding performance.

5. Click the Apply button.

6. Listen to your quantized performance.

7. If you are unhappy with the results, use the clip Edit or context menu or press Ctrl/⌘+Z to undo the quantization and start the process over again.

In the Edit view, you can use the Selection tool to select single or multiple notes for quantization, and then follow steps 2 through 7 to quantize only the selected notes.

Converting Pattern Device Tracks to Notes

You can create arrangements with Reason's pattern devices in two ways. In Chapter 4, the section "Creating Arrangements" covers the process using the Redrum Drum Computer, which is also identical to the options available for sequencing patterns with the Matrix Pattern Sequencer.

A quick way to access all of the individual notes in your pattern device tracks is to utilize the Convert Pattern Track to Notes function. This can be especially useful on Redrum tracks, which contain limited options for note velocity variation and improvisation. Follow these steps to convert a pattern sequence to MIDI notes:

1. Select any Reason Pattern Device track in the track list that has a Pattern Select lane containing a clip or multiple clips.

2. Choose Edit → Convert Pattern Track To Notes or right/Ctrl-click and select the command from the context menu.

3. The Pattern Lane button on the pattern select track will be turned off, deactivating the pattern arrangement and making the original patterns irrelevant. A Note lane with a single 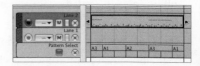 clip containing all the MIDI notes will be created, which will now trigger the pattern device.

4. Double-click the Note clip to open it in the Edit view.

You can now use the Selection and Pencil tools to move and add new MIDI notes in order to create pattern variations and fills or to edit the velocity of individual notes. Or you can split the performance into individual clips for rearranging and further editing.

Mixing in Reason

Once your arrangement is complete, you can begin the process of creating a final mix-down of your song.

Signal Processing and Effects

As you saw in Chapter 7, Reason contains lots of resources for signal processing and audio effects. Here are some of the Reason effects and signal processing options that will be particularly useful in the mixing process:

EQ As you learned in Chapter 2's section on the Mixer and in Chapter 7, you have a range of options for equalization in Reason 4. Start with the EQ section on the Mixer, which features basic high and low EQ knobs. Use these knobs or add a PEQ-2 Parametric EQ or an MClass Equalizer as an insert effect on any track that needs high or low frequencies cut or boosted.

Compression Using compression on individual instruments is a good way to help a particular track stand out in a mix. Because you are working in a virtual environment, many of the frequent uses for compression (fixing uneven performances) can be accomplished in other ways, such as working with velocity values. However, tracks that are traditionally compressed in a mix including bass, guitar, vocals, drums, and others can still benefit from the MClass Compressor and the Comp-01 Compressor/Limiter used as insert effects.

Reverb Reverb effects are easy to go overboard with, especially considering the excellent reverb options available in Reason. Multiple reverb effects on different tracks can compete with each other, producing a muddled, unclear mix. If your mixes sound muddy or too reverb-heavy, try replacing multiple reverb effects with a single send effect RV7000 or RV7 reverb.

Automating the Mixer 14:2

One way to take advantage of Reason's automation functionality in a mix is to automate the mixer. In the Mixing and Mastering template file, a Reason track has already been created for the mixer. You can use this track to create automation on the mixer as you would for any Reason device, either recording adjustments to various parameters in real time or using the sequencer to create Automation lanes and then drawing Automation clips and breakpoints with the Pencil tool.

In Reason songs created without this template, you can create a track for the mixer by selecting any blank area on the Mixer, right/Ctrl-clicking and choosing Create Track For Mixer from the context menu or selecting the mixer in the rack and choosing Edit → Create Track For Mixer from the menu bar.

To view all of the Mixer's parameters that are available for automation, select the Mixer's track in the track list and click the Automation button.

Here are some options for automating the mixer:

- Muting and soloing tracks
- Raising and lower individual channel levels
- Creating panning effects with individual channels
- Raising and lowering Aux send effects
- Creating a fadeout on the Master Level fader at the end of a song

Mixing a Song

The best way to become familiar with the mixing process is to work with Reason songs containing multiple tracks and instrumentation. To get you started, this book's CD contains a Reason song file with a number of Reason instrument tracks. Follow these steps to begin the process of creating your own mix from the included Reason song file:

1. Open the Reason song file `Examples\Chapter 10\Songs\UnMixed.rns`.

2. Press the Play button to hear playback of the song.

3. Start the mixing process by clicking the Browse Patch button on the MClass Mastering Combinator at the top of the Reason rack and choosing a Mastering preset. You'll hear an immediate difference in the overall sound of the song.

4. Try out the different mastering presets and choose one that sounds good to you.

One of the side effects of adding the Mastering Combinator or, as in this case, selecting a preset, is that while your overall mix may sound better some instrument levels may become out of balance. Always keep an ear out for any adjustments you may need to make after adding or changing the settings of the MClass Mastering Combinator.

Using the included instrument tracks, you can try some of the following suggestions to improve the overall sound of the mix:

- Adjusting the stereo placement of specific instruments. For example, try separating the two synthesizer sounds by panning them in opposite directions.
- Add an MClass compressor or COMP-01 Compressor/Limiter as an insert effect on either of the Dr. Rex Drum tracks.
- Pan either of the Dr. Rex Drum tracks to separate them.

- Add an MClass compressor or COMP-01 as an insert effect on the Bass track.

- Use the Channel Aux Send knobs on the Mixer 14:2 to add the RV7000 Reverb to selected tracks.

- Use the individual Channel EQs on the Mixer 14:2 to adjust the highs and lows of some tracks.

- Add PEQ-2 Parametric EQs or MClass Equalizers to any tracks you think need more precise EQ adjustments.

- Automate the Mixer to bring instruments in and out of the mix.

- Automate the Master Level of individual instruments to bring them in and out of the mix.

- Utilize the Filters and other sound-shaping parameters on instrument devices.

To help specific instruments stand out even further in your mixes, try these options:

- Use the Scream 4 Sound Destruction unit.

- Add noticeable effects such as the CF-101 Chorus/Flanger.

- Utilize more drastic EQ settings with the Channel EQs, the PEQ-2, and the MClass Equalizer.

You can find an example of a final mix of this Reason song on the book's CD in `Examples\Chapter 10\Songs\SampleMix.rns`.

Any or all of these elements can be used to enhance a final mix-down. Try experimenting with these and other devices and settings. Remember that it's not necessary to use every option at your disposal for every mix. Depending on the specific song, you may want to use more or less of these or other options. You can find out more about the mixing process, including information and tips on working with specific types of instrumentation, in books such as *The Mixing Engineer's Handbook* by Bobby Owsinski (Artistpro, 2nd ed. 2006) and *Basic Mixing Techniques* by Paul White (Sanctuary, 2004). For a great book on the mastering process, check out *Mastering Audio: The Art and the Science* by Bob Katz (Focal Press, 2nd ed., 2007).

Using ReWire

ReWire is the protocol developed by Propellerhead Software for using Reason in conjunction with other digital audio programs (see the "ReWire" sidebar in Chapter 1). In recent years ReWire has become the industry standard not just for working with Reason but for connecting various digital music creation and recording programs together. As a result, ReWire can be used not just with Reason, but also to some degree with most of the digital audio programs available today. Some programs that contain ReWire functionality include:

> Pro Tools (www.digidesign.com)
>
> Ableton Live (www.ableton.com)
>
> SONAR (www.cakewalk.com)
>
> ACID (www.sonycreativesoftware.com)
>
> Cubase (www.steinberg.net)
>
> Logic Studio (www.apple.com)
>
> Digital Performer (www.motu.com)
>
> FL Studio (www.flstudio.com)

How ReWire functionality works will vary somewhat from program to program. In some cases the process of using ReWire is similar to using plug-in virtual instruments such as those found in the VST, Audio Units, and Real-Time Audio Suite (RTAS) formats. In other cases ReWire functionality is implemented differently. For example, with the FL Studio program, you need to use specifically included ReWire tracks.

> It's also possible to use ReWire to connect more than two programs at once. For example, a Pro Tools user can create a session using both Ableton Live and Reason as client/slave programs in the same session.

You can find tutorials on the Propellerhead website for working with Reason, ReWire, and some specific digital audio programs. However, these tutorials may not always represent the most current release of both Reason and other ReWire compatible software. For specific details about using ReWire, you should check the documentation that comes with your digital audio software.

Uses for ReWire

ReWire offers the Reason user some exciting possibilities for working in conjunction with other digital audio programs:

- Add vocals or live instrumentation to a Reason song by using ReWire to connect the Reason song's output to a digital audio program capable of audio recording.

- Use specific instruments in Reason as part of a song in another digital audio program. For example, you could use Redrum or the NN-XT for a drum track, and/or one or more synthesizers or samplers.

- Use plug-in effects from other digital audio programs on individual Reason tracks.

- Send a stereo output of a finished Reason song to another digital audio program for final mastering.
- Using the MIDI sequencing functionality of other programs to control Reason's instruments.

Hosts and Clients

When using ReWire and any two (or more) digital audio programs, one program will be the host (or master). The other program or programs will be the client (slave). Reason will always be the client program in any ReWire configuration. Host programs will always be started first, and the client programs second. When you close programs in a ReWire session, the reverse will be true. You'll want to close your client program first and then the host program.

> Most digital audio programs with ReWire capability can function as either a host or a client, but not both. There are exceptions to this, such as Ableton Live, which can act as either a host or a client, allowing you to insert Reason and other ReWire-compatible programs into Ableton Live sessions and to insert your Ableton Live sessions into other programs.

When Reason and another digital audio program are connected via ReWire, both programs' interfaces will be available. If you have two monitors connected to your computer, you can view one program on each monitor. You can also use press Alt/⌘+Tab to switch between programs.

Depending on which digital audio program you are working with, how the transport control functionality works will vary. You will generally have access to simple starting and stopping functionality. You may also have access to functionality in Reason such as turning looping on and off and setting the left and right locators for playback. It's also possible that playback functionality will only be accessible from the host program.

Stereo Output

Most programs that make use of ReWire will allow two possible options: sending your Reason song as a stereo mix or as individual tracks.

The easiest way to use ReWire is to send a stereo output of an entire Reason song or instrumentation to another digital audio program. This is an easy task to accomplish in most programs that support ReWire.

On the Reason side, if you are sending your tracks out to another program as a single stereo track you can operate as you've been working in Reason all along. By default Reason sends a stereo output to outputs 1 and 2 (left and right) on the Hardware Audio Device at the top of the Reason rack.

Under normal circumstances this stereo output is sent to whatever audio output you've chosen in Reason's Audio Output preferences. Using ReWire "hijacks" this audio signal and routes it to the Host program. In order to hear Reason's output, you'll almost always need to create a track for Reason within the Host program. The type of track (audio, MIDI instrument, auxiliary) will vary from one Host program to another.

The general procedure for using Reason and ReWire is as follows:

1. Start your host program.

2. Start Reason.

3. Create the kind of track your host program uses for ReWire.

4. Add Reason to the track.

Figure 10.26 shows Reason on an Ableton Live Audio track.

Figure 10.27 shows Reason as a plug-in on a Pro Tools instrument track.

Figure 10.26

Reason on an Ableton Live Audio Track

Figure 10.27

Reason as a plug-in on a Pro Tools instrument track

In creating your session in Reason, you don't have to do anything different. Reason automatically sends the output of your Reason sessions to Audio Out 1 and 2 on the hardware device.

Different programs will have slightly different ways of implementing ReWire. For example, since Reason will always be a slave program you may or may not be able to set looping or control playback in Reason.

When sending a stereo output to a host program, it's a good idea to take advantage of the MClass Mastering Combi (Chapter 8) by placing it as an insert effect between the mixer and the Hardware Audio Device, as it is with the Mixer and Mastering template used for the exercises in this book.

Individual Track Outputs

For even more control over your individual Reason tracks, another option available with many digital audio programs that support ReWire is to send your entire session out as individual tracks.

To do that follow these steps:

1. Delete the session's Mixer 14:2 or create your Reason song without a mixer. If you are using the Mixer and Mastering template, you'll have to delete the MClass Mastering Combi as well.

2. Route the output of each instrument to its own mono or stereo output in the hardware device (Figure 10.28).

3. Create individual tracks for each instrument in your host program.

This is an excellent way to take advantage of another digital audio program's plug-in effects and mixing capabilities.

> To quickly access your ReWired Reason sessions, it's a good idea to get in the habit of saving the Reason session in the same location or folder as the host program's session file.

Figure 10.28

Individual instrument output routing in the hardware device

Saving and Exporting

Finished Reason songs or works-in-progress can be exported and saved in both AIFF and .wav formats, as can sections of songs or individual instrument loops.

Exporting Songs

Exporting complete songs in Reason requires setting the End marker to tell Reason where to stop exporting. If the End marker is not currently visible, use the scroll bar at the bottom of the sequencer to scroll to the end of the song.

Take the following steps to export a complete song:

1. Use your mouse to set the End marker to the end of the last measure of your Reason song.

If your tracks contain effects such as delay or reverb, you'll want to make sure that these are not cut off prematurely. It's always a good idea to set the End marker and then listen to the last few bars of your song before exporting to make sure any effects completely trail off before the End marker.

2. Select File → Export Song As Audio File from the menu bar.

3. Use the Save dialog to choose a name and location for your audio file.

4. Select a file format from the Format drop-down menu.

5. Click the Save button. Now you'll see the Audio Export dialog.

6. Choose a sample rate and bit depth from the Audio Export Settings dialog. If you are unsure which settings to choose, leave them at their default setting of 44.100Hz and 16 bits.

7. Click the Export button.

Your audio file will be created in the location you selected in the Save dialog. Reason does not include the option to export files to MP3 or AAC format, but you can easily use iTunes or another digital audio program to convert your .wav or AIFF files to either format.

Exporting Loops

Reason can also be used to create loop files that can be used in other DAW programs or converted to the REX format using ReCycle, and then loaded into the Dr. Rex Loop Player and used in your Reason sessions.

> The Loop On/Off button does not need to be enabled to export a loop.

To export a loop file from Reason, follow these steps:

1. Set the left locator to the beginning of your loop and the right locator to the end. If you are exporting a single track, make sure the track is soloed in the mixer or on the track list.

2. Choose File → Export Loop As Audio File from the menu bar.

3. Use the Save dialog to choose a location for your loop file.

4. Select a file format from the Format drop-down menu.

5. Choose a sample rate and bit depth from the Audio Export Settings dialog. If you are unsure which settings to choose, leave them at their default settings of 44.100 Hz and 16 bits.

6. Click Export to save your loop to the location you selected in the Save dialog.

Reason makes an excellent tool for creating loops. If necessary, you may want to perform some extra editing on your exported loops using an audio-editing program such as the ones discussed at the end of Chapter 6.

Saving Songs

In Chapter 2 you learned the basics of saving songs as Reason song files (.rns) by choosing File → Save As from the menu bar and creating Reason published songs (.rps) format by choosing File → Publish Song. With both of these strategies, you have more available options.

Self-Containing Reason Songs

If you are sharing Reason songs between users or computers, or moving files to a new session, you have the option within Reason to save any samples or REX files as a part of the song file. This works for both published songs and regular songs. This is an important step when sharing Reason songs with users who may not have the same ReFills, sample collections, or REX libraries that you have. By self-containing the song, you'll ensure that end users have access to all of the necessary content they'll need to listen to and work with the song.

Follow these steps to self-contain a Reason song:

1. Create a Reason song containing samples and/or REX loops that exist outside of any ReFills. Samples and REX loops that are contained within ReFills will not be available for self-containing.

2. Choose File → Song Self-Contain Settings.

3. The Song Self-Contain Settings dialog will appear (Figure 10.29). Put a check mark next to any samples or REX files you want to self-contain within the Reason song.

Reason song files that are not self-contained are usually very small. Self-containing files will increase the song file's size by the combined size of the included samples and REX files.

Figure 10.29

The Song Self-Contain Settings dialog

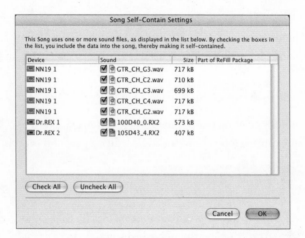

Including Song Information

Both Reason Song formats allow you to include information displayed in the form of a splash window. This is the same window you'll see when opening any of Reason's included demo songs. Follow these steps to include song information in your Reason song:

1. Choose File → Song Information to open the Song Information dialog.

2. Type any information in the Text In Window Title field that you want to appear at the top of the Reason song, next to the song's name.

3. Type any information in the More Information field to include a message to the Reason user who is opening the song, including specific instructions or personal details or any relevant song info.

4. Click the Song Splash folder icon to load an image that will appear on the splash window. The image must be a JPEG with a size of 256 × 256.

5. Put a check mark in the Show Splash On Song Open box to have the splash screen open automatically with the Reason song.

6. If available, include a website address and e-mail address. The Reason users who open the song will see an option to open their browser or their e-mail program.

Figure 10.30 shows a completely filled-in Song Information dialog.

When the Reason song is opened, the splash window will appear (Figure 10.31).

The Reason user can then click OK to proceed to the song or Show Info to view anything you've included in the More Information box, along with your website and e-mail address (Figure 10.32).

Song information can be included with both Reason song files (.rsn) and published song files (.rps). Remember that with .rsn files the song information can be changed by any user who wants to resave the file. If you are sharing original work that you don't want appropriated or altered in any way, be sure to save your song by choosing File → Publish Song to save your song in the Reason .rps format.

Figure 10.30

A filled-in Song Information dialog

Figure 10.31

The splash window

Figure 10.32

The included song information

Summary

The lessons in this chapter have solidified your ability to create music with Reason 4 by expanding your recording, editing, arranging, and exporting options. Having a deeper understanding of the features and functions of the sequencer enables you to work with Reason's devices to create music "traditionally" by playing a MIDI keyboard but also allows you to create and to edit music using the Arrange and Edit views and Reason's included tools. Contained within these options are many options for both precision and creativity.

You've also learned how to incorporate Reason's tools functionality with the sequencer's track lanes and clips to create and edit automation. Because of the similarities involved in working with Note, Pattern, and Automation clips, much of what you've learned about each clip type can be applied when working with the others.

Combining the things you've learned in previous chapters with this chapter's information about mixing songs, using the ReWire protocol and your advanced options for saving and exporting from Reason you now have all of the knowledge you need to create music with Reason 4 from the beginning of a project to the end.

About the Companion CD

In this appendix:

- What you'll find on the CD

- System requirements

- Using the CD

- Troubleshooting

What You'll Find on the CD

The following sections are arranged by category and provide a summary of the content you'll find on the CD. If you need help with installing the items provided on the CD, refer to the installation instructions in the "Using the CD" section of this appendix.

Chapter Files

In the Chapter Files directory you will find all the files for completing the tutorials and understanding concepts in this book. This includes samples, loops, and patches for Reason's instruments and other devices, as well as complete Reason songs that demonstrate the results of specific exercises.

BeatHive

In the BeatHive folder you'll find an exclusive Reason ReFill featuring REX loops from `www.BeatHive.com`.

BeatHive.com is an online marketplace where musicians buy and sell loops. Producers from around the world open a loop shop, upload their content, and sell through the Beat-Hive database. Musicians audition, rate, and buy 100 percent royalty-free loops on an individual basis, or in "packs" at a discount.

Fully launched in October, 2006, BeatHive.com currently has more than 10,000 loops for sale, uploaded by top-notch producers from around the world. The site is a developing web application with features and tools continuously added to meet the needs of the online musician community. BeatHive strives to become the greatest loop content resource on the web, providing high quality loops for musicians to purchase and an economic opportunity for talented producers.

System Requirements

Make sure that your computer meets the minimum system requirements shown in the following list. If your computer doesn't match up to most of these requirements, you may have problems using the software and files on the companion CD. For the latest and greatest information, please refer to the ReadMe file located at the root of the CD-ROM.

- A PC running Microsoft Windows 2000, Windows NT4 (with SP4 or later), Windows Me, Windows XP, or Windows Vista.
- A Macintosh running Apple OS X or later.
- An Internet connection
- A CD-ROM drive

Using the CD

To install the items from the CD to your hard drive, follow these steps.

1. Insert the CD into your computer's CD-ROM drive. The license agreement appears.

> Windows users: The interface won't launch if you have autorun disabled. In that case, click Start → Run (for Windows Vista, Start → All Programs → Accessories → Run). In the dialog box that appears, type `D:\Start.exe`. (Replace `D` with the proper letter if your CD drive uses a different letter. If you don't know the letter, see how your CD drive is listed under My Computer.) Click OK.

> Mac users: The CD icon will appear on your desktop, double-click the icon to open the CD and double-click the Start icon.

2. Read through the license agreement, and then click the Accept button if you want to use the CD.

The CD interface appears. The interface allows you to access the content with just one or two clicks.

Troubleshooting

Wiley has attempted to provide programs that work on most computers with the minimum system requirements. Alas, your computer may differ, and some programs may not work properly for some reason.

The two likeliest problems are that you don't have enough memory (RAM) for the programs you want to use, or you have other programs running that are affecting installation or running of a program. If you get an error message such as "Not enough memory" or "Setup cannot continue," try one or more of the following suggestions and then try using the software again:

Turn off any antivirus software running on your computer. Installation programs sometimes mimic virus activity and may make your computer incorrectly believe that it's being infected by a virus.

Close all running programs. The more programs you have running, the less memory is available to other programs. Installation programs typically update files and programs; so if you keep other programs running, installation may not work properly.

Have your local computer store add more RAM to your computer. This is, admittedly, a drastic and somewhat expensive step. However, adding more memory can really help the speed of your computer and allow more programs to run at the same time.

Customer Care

If you have trouble with the book's companion CD-ROM, please call the Wiley Product Technical Support phone number at (800) 762-2974. Outside the United States, call +1(317) 572-3994. You can also contact Wiley Product Technical Support at `http://sybex.custhelp.com`. John Wiley & Sons will provide technical support only for installation and other general quality control items. For technical support on the applications themselves, consult the program's vendor or author.

To place additional orders or to request information about other Wiley products, please call (877) 762-2974.

Index

Note to the reader: Throughout this index **boldfaced** page numbers indicate primary discussions of a topic. *Italicized* page numbers indicate illustrations.

Wavetable oscillator, in Thor, *189*, 189
wavetable synthesis, **151**
Web resources
    on audio hardware interfaces, 8
    audio magazines, 8
    for free samples, **210**
    for ReFills, 24
website, for Propellerhead, 23
White, Paul, *Basic Mixing Techniques*, 393
Width knob, for PH-90 Phaser, 271
Window menu
    >> Attach Sequencer, 32
    >> Detach Sequencer Window, 32
    >> Show Tool Window, 31

Windows (Microsoft)
    audio output, 19
    Reason requirements, 6

Y

Yamaha CS-80, 150
Yamaha's DX7 synthesizer, 150

Z

Zero-G, 85, 209
zoom, with sequencer Magnify tool, 70, **363**